SAT®

TOTAL

PREP

MARKS PREP

SAT® is a registered trademark of College Board, which neither sponsors nor endorses this product.

Senior Editors: Dan Hertz, Anthony Celino, and Shaun Stiemsma

Preface

Dear Student and Parent,

Thank you for purchasing this book, which puts together the content of our two other SAT prep books: *The Comprehensive Guide to the SAT* and *Four Realistic SAT Practice Tests*.

Please take a few minutes to read this Preface and the Introduction that follows the Table of Contents. They contain helpful background information and practical advice on how to best use this book in conjunction with the free resources provided by the College Board.

Nitin Sawhney
Managing Director, Marks Prep

What Makes This Book Different?

Since the SAT was redesigned in 2015, there has been a dearth of accurate and helpful preparation materials. As of the date of our publication, the College Board has only released eight official SATs, which can be found on the Khan Academy website (www.khanacademy.org) along with other SAT preparation material.

Larger test preparation companies have prepared additional practice SAT tests, but, based on our review of many such tests, we believe they have been hurriedly produced. We have found errors on the tests, and we have identified Reading and Writing questions where strong test takers will disagree with the "correct" answers. It's questionable whether students taking these practice tests can rely on their results as an indicator of potential scores on actual tests.

The materials published by the College Board and Khan Academy website are helpful but insufficient for the most challenging material on the SAT: the most difficult reading comprehension passages and questions, the trickier questions on the Writing section, and the algebra and statistics content that are not covered by most high school math courses. This very challenging material is still unfamiliar to many teachers, and consequently, for many students and teachers, the new SAT is more resistant to improvement than the ACT.

With carefully constructed strategies for each question type on the new test, Marks Prep's full-time tutors have simplified the test. Using these strategies, our students taking the new SAT have achieved similar percentile improvements in average scores as our students who have taken the old SAT and ACT. In this book, written after months of careful preparation, we clearly lay out our methods so others who cannot access our tutoring services may benefit similarly.

Why Not Simply Take the ACT?

Many students can do very well on the ACT and should consider that test. However, the ACT, which requires students to work very quickly, particularly on the Math, Reading, and Science sections, is not the best test for every test taker. The SAT, in contrast to the ACT, has more involved questions, but also allows more time per question. Thus, it can be the better test for those who like to work carefully and not be rushed.

What Is Marks Prep?

Marks Prep is the test preparation and tutoring division of Marks Education, which provides tutoring, test preparation, and admissions counseling to students all over the world.

Each Marks Prep tutor is an experienced full-time educator and a top 1% test taker who sits for the SAT and other tests every year, in real test centers, along with our students. We use the knowledge gained from taking these tests and working with our students to write efficient strategies and materials for all the tests we tutor—from the SSAT and ISEE to the SAT, ACT, GRE, GMAT, MCAT, and LSAT.

The full-time tutors at Marks Prep have, for the past ten years, tutored hundreds of students each year across the United States and the world, via Skype and other platforms. Students who have worked with us for at least six sessions have, on average, improved their scores by 340 points on the (pre-2016) SAT, 220 points on the new SAT (from baseline 10th grade PSATs) and almost 7 points on the ACT. In contrast to many other firms, we use only actual College Board PSATs and real past ACTs for baseline tests. More specific score improvement data for all tests (including graduate school tests) are available on our website, www.markprep.com.

We also work with several schools and non-profits to help them improve their students' standardized test scores, change college outcomes, and markedly change their School Profile.

Table of Contents

Mathematics Test Manual

How to Use this Book

In order to make best use of this book, you should either a) have scores from a recent actual SAT or b) first take a full-length timed diagnostic SAT either from the College Board website or from the second half of this book. Please take the scores on each part of the test and write them on the first row of the table on page 8 of this book.

Then carefully review the errors from your test. This process should give you a good idea of your strengths and weaknesses and the areas you most urgently need to review. Next, use the table below to cover the areas that were weakest on your test.

Areas of Weakness	Focus on
Math	
• If you need improvement on Section 3 (the non-calculator section)	Pages 133–136 and 140–198
• If you did relatively well on Section 3, but would like to improve on Section 4	Pages 199–240
Reading	
• If your score was low	The entire Reading section of the book, pages 9–36
• If your score was low because you ran out of time	Page 12
• If you struggled with Command of Evidence questions	Pages 15–17
• If you struggled with Words in Context questions	Pages 18–21
Writing	
• If you could improve on Expression of Ideas (or the questions about meaning of the passage)	Pages 41–68
• If you could improve on Standard English Conventions (grammar and punctuation questions)	Pages 69–114

After each layer of review, take another full-length timed practice test from this book or from the College Board website. If using the website, please be sure to print the test out, so you can write on the test book. Writing your work, on all sections of the test, is an important strategy. Then note your score on page 8 of this book, review errors on the practice test, and cover relevant parts of this book.

NOTE: Explanations for all four of the tests in this book can now be found on our website: marksprep.com.

SAT Score Tracker

Date	Raw Scores				Scaled Scores				
	Reading	Writing	Math—No Calc	Math—Calc	Reading	Writing	R/W Total	Math Total	Total Score

Reading Test Manual

The Reading Test of the SAT is composed of five passages and at least two tables/graphs. One literary passage, two science passages, and two social science passages combine for a total of 52 questions to answer in 65 minutes.

Most reading passages are challenging, *so you have to read the passage carefully*. Also, because the answer choices are meant to confuse you, we strongly believe that for the best chance at a top score, you should follow an R–W approach: **Read** *and then* **Write** *about the passage and each of the questions*. This strategy has allowed thousands of our students to avoid the traps in the answer choices by basing their responses on their own understanding of the passage.

In the following pages, we will explain the R–W strategy, as well as special adaptations of this strategy to prepare you for three special question types.

Overview and Strategy

Passage Strategy

While the difficulty of these passages varies, all are rhetorically sophisticated. Each tests your ability to understand not only the ideas and facts presented in the passage but also the author's intention and rhetorical strategies. Thus, it is essential to read well and to answer each question carefully. The following three steps will help you to navigate both the complexity of the passages and the trickiness of the questions.

1. R–W 1: **Read** and **Write** about the **whole passage**!

    Read the entire passage carefully and actively.

    - It is important to read the passage carefully before you answer any questions. Start by reading the introductory note above the passage, which will often contain essential information about the date, author, genre and purpose of the passage. As you read, mark up the passage by underlining key ideas, circling names, dates, and figures, and noting confusing passages or unfamiliar terms. Actively reading the passage in this way will help to assure deep comprehension of the main ideas of the passage.

    Write down the main point of the passage *before* you move on to the questions.

    - Most passages have a main point, and writing it down in 5–10 words is a good way to check that you have understood the passage. One way to do this quickly and accurately is to ask write a topic in 3 or 4 words, and then write an action or description of what the author says about the topic in another 5 words or so. This strategy helps most students come up with a main idea that's neither too broad nor so specific or lengthy that it is not helpful.

    - For the literature passage, which is first on the test, write down, in a total of about ten words, the names of the key characters and what is revealed about their personalities or relationships. What you write down for the main point of the passage will almost always be directly useful on at least one of the questions, and knowing it well can help you rule out wrong answers on most questions, even when the question is about a specific detail.

2. R–W 2: **Re-read** and **Write** to **answer each question**!

    Read the question and **find** the answer in the passage by **reading** the relevant lines once more.

    - When you get to the questions, cover up the answer choices and find the answer to each question in the passage for yourself. Then, before you look at the answer choices, *always* **write down** the correct answer you have found. Remember to be literal: just copy over the language of the passage because the correct answer choice is often just a paraphrase of information in the passage.

    - Quite often the question will direct you to a misleading line number. In these lines, you will find the word or phrase that the question refers to, but, in most cases, the answer to the question is *not* in those lines. Read at least one or two sentences before and after the line(s) to which you're directed. In most cases, you'll find the answer to the question. If you can't find the answer, skip the question, bubbling in a placeholder answer and circling the question number so that you can come back to it later.

    - Many questions are based on understanding the intention, tone, etc. of the author. On those questions, you will need to **write** your own *inference* about the answer. Avoid making large inferential leaps: just write down your own explanation of the purpose, tone, etc. in a few basic words. If you cannot determine the answer to the question based on your own reading, just skip it, again circling the question and bubbling a temporary answer.

    - Remember, the answer-choices are there to confuse you. Avoid the temptation to look at the answer choices before you *write down* your own answer.

3 Compare the answer choices to the response you wrote down and choose the answer that best matches the idea you wrote down before looking at the answer choices.

- If you have gone through the first two steps, in many cases the correct answer will jump out at you when you look at the answer choices. If it doesn't, start by crossing out the answers you know are wrong, using both the main point of the passage and your own written answer to the question. If you're down to two answer choices, try to find the *incorrect* one, which will always have at least one or two words that are not indicated by the passage. Once you find the words that make the wrong answer wrong, you can confidently choose the one that's left!

- Remember also that in most cases, the correct answer is the less extreme of the two answer choices, and language of the answer choices is often very general, so don't fixate on how well the specific words of the answers match the answer you wrote at first, but on how the idea of the answer fits with the answer you found.

Time Saving Strategies

Section Management

The five passages on the SAT Reading Test vary greatly in their level of difficulty: many test-takers find one or two of the passages fairly easy, but often one or two passages will be almost prohibitively difficult, and it will take much more time to read these. In order to maximize your score, **focus on passages that you will be able to read quickly and understand thoroughly**. This ensures that you spend your time on the passages that will get you the most points.

Dates of Passages

Every passage on the SAT includes a brief introduction that gives some background information about the passage, its author, and its context. This information *always* includes the date of publication.

Thus far, every SAT released has at least *one* passage that was not written in the last century, and almost all test takers find such passages more difficult and time consuming. Always read the background information, and **simply skip any passage that is from the 1800s or earlier**. Do this passage last.

If you read quickly through the other passages, you will have extra time to read the older passages. And even if you use up most or all of the time reading the other passages, you will have skipped the passage that would have taken longest and would have most likely led to the most errors. So either way, by skipping the hardest passage, you maximize the number of questions you can answer correctly.

Types of Passages

Since every SAT Reading Test is made up of the same types of passages, you can also maximize your score by starting with passage types that are your greatest strengths. If you struggle with fiction, as many students do, don't start with the first passage. Even if it is fairly recent and you enjoy reading literary texts, it still often takes more time, and thus it can be a good passage to save for later or just to skip. The remaining passages are divided between science and history/social science, so you can also play to your strengths in completing these passages. For example, if you find science passages with unfamiliar terms and concepts difficult, you can complete the history/social science passages first. However, if you find political philosophy hard to follow or historical debates somewhat dry, you can start with science passages.

Question Management

Just as you need to choose which passages to focus on in order to maximize your score, so you must effectively manage how you handle specific questions on each passage in order to maximize your reading score.

Skipping

Every question on the SAT reading is worth the same amount; thus, if you cannot find the answer, **skip the question**! Circle the question number and grid in a random placeholder on your answer sheet. After you have answered the rest of the questions on the passage, come back and try the question you skipped once more. You may now know the passage better and be able to answer the question correctly, because the questions create a cohesive "story" of the passage as a whole.

REMEMBER: If you skip quickly, you give yourself time to attempt easier questions that come later in the test. The test tries to trick students into spending the most time on questions that they have the least likelihood of getting correct, so don't fall into that trap! Since each question is worth the same, there is no reason to agonize over a hard question if you have more easy questions yet to answer on the test.

Prioritizing Questions

Many students find it difficult to complete the full section in the allotted time. If you realize that you do not have enough time to read a full passage and answer all the questions, **find these specific question types that are easier to answer** without reading the passage. Here's what to look for:

- If the passage has supplementary materials like a graph or a table, answer questions on these first, as often several can be answered without reference to the passage (see pages 22–23 for more on how to answer this type of question).
- Most passages have 2 words-in-context questions (see pages 18–21 for more on these questions), and these can almost always be answered by reading only one sentence. Further, they always point you directly to the specific line the word appears in, so you don't have to search the whole passage to find the answer!

Most passages have at least a few other questions that refer to specific lines, and so you can also usually answer these fairly quickly. Be sure to read a few lines before and after the specified lines in order to answer the question, because line number references are often misleading if the information is taken out of context.

Final Note: Rereading

If you have daydreamed your way through the passage and get to the end and realize that you have no idea what it was all about, don't worry. This happens often, even to the best of us. However, DON'T give in to the temptation to go on to the questions anyway. The SAT reading requires that you really understand the passage, and so you will be setting yourself up for failure if you try to answer the questions.

Instead, go back and carefully read the first paragraph or two, until you are confident that you can write down the main point of the passage. Then go on to the questions.

Furthermore, the test provides enough time for most test-takers to reread portions of the passage in order to answer the questions. For example, if the question asks about the purpose of the fourth paragraph and you cannot remember it clearly enough just by looking back at it, then take the time to re-familiarize yourself with the material. Focus on the first sentence or two to understand how it relates to the rest of the passage, and then read the rest of the paragraph quickly and **write down** your answer.

Special SAT Reading Strategies

The general strategy outlined in the previous pages is useful for all passages on the SAT Reading Test, but there are three special question types that can be easier to solve if you use the specific strategies outlined on the following pages. Together, these questions account for about half the total questions on the test, and many students struggle more with these questions than any others. Thus, you will want to take the time to recognize these questions and master the strategies that will allow you to answer them correctly.

Command of Evidence Questions

These questions are the hallmark of the SAT, and most passages will have two *pairs* of evidence-based questions. These are recognizable by being in pairs, with the first question asking a difficult detail or interpretive question and the second giving four choices with line numbers referring to different parts of the passage, one of which is the "evidence" needed to solve the initial question.

Words in Context Questions

The SAT does not directly test vocabulary knowledge as it has in the past, so there is less need to spend a lot of time memorizing vocabulary words to prepare for the test. However, the test continues to test vocabulary by asking for the meaning of specific words and phrases—sometimes "hard" words and sometimes abnormal uses of common words—in the context of the passage.

Figure-Based Questions

Another feature of the SAT Reading Test is the inclusion of tables, graphs, and other figures that relate to the content of some of the reading passages. Usually, two of the five passages will include "supplemental materials" like these, and there will be several questions based on either the figure itself or the figure considered in conjunction with the passage.

Command of Evidence Questions

Most reading passages on the SAT will have two sets of paired evidence-based questions. On these pairs of questions, the first asks about the passage in some way—often a very difficult question—and the second asks where the best evidence for the answer to the preceding question appears within the passage.

For example:

1

Picard indicates that the process he describes in the passage

A) protects the traditional and ceremonial usages of threatened landmasses.

B) is rendered obsolete through the use of faster than light travel.

C) violates central tenets of the Federation.

D) dramatizes an insignificant but inevitable outcome of the described events.

2

Which choice provides the best evidence for the answer to the previous question?

A) Lines 12–17 ("Worf ... honor.")

B) Lines 17–19 ("It ... Vulcans.")

C) Lines 23–24 ("For ... ourselves.")

D) Lines 30–34 ("We ... travel.")

Note that these questions, although sequential, will not necessarily appear on the same page. Thus, it can be a good idea to mark these questions when you start answering questions on a passage, because many of them are *much* easier to answer if you look at the "evidence" in the second question before answering the first question.

The primary strategy for answering these questions is as follows:

1. Read the first of the two paired questions, and underline the key words in the question.

2. Then, *without looking at the answer choices to the first question*, go to the second question of the pair. Look for the answer to the first question by re-reading the lines indicated in the answer choices from the second question. Choose the lines that most clearly and directly answer the first question.

3. Then go back to the first question and find which answer paraphrases or best fits the information in your chosen lines, and then select that answer choice.

   NOTE: Sometimes, you may find that two or more of the options for the second question in the pair seem to answer the first question, especially if the first question is fairly open-ended or central to the passage as a whole. In order to handle this situation, work carefully to "pair" the answers for the first question with the line references in the second. Only one of the line references from the second question will "fit" with an answer from the first question, so you then can choose both answers together.

Command-of-Evidence Practice Passage

Questions 1–7 are based on the following passage.

The following excerpt is adapted from a speech given by the Fourteenth Dalai Lama upon receiving the Congressional Gold Medal in 2007.

Today we watch China as it rapidly moves forward. Economic liberalization has led to wealth, modernization and great power. I believe that today's economic success of both India and China,
5 the two most populated nations with long histories of rich culture, is most deserving. With their newfound status, both of these two countries are poised to play an important leading role on the world stage. In order to fulfill this role, I believe it
10 is vital for China to have transparency, rule of law and freedom of information. Much of the world is waiting to see how China's concepts of "harmonious society" and "peaceful rise" would unfold. In today's China, a state of many
15 nationalities, a key factor is how it ensures the harmony and unity of its various peoples. For this, the equality and the rights of these nationalities to maintain their distinct identities are crucial.

With respect to my own homeland Tibet, today
20 many people, both from inside and outside, feel deeply concerned about the consequences of the rapid changes taking place. Every year, the Chinese population inside Tibet is increasing at an alarming rate. And, if we are to judge by the example of the
25 population of Lhasa, there is a real danger that the Tibetans will be reduced to an insignificant minority in their own homeland. This rapid increase in population is also posing serious threat to Tibet's fragile environment. Since Tibet is the
30 source of many of Asia's great rivers, any substantial disturbance in Tibet's ecology will impact the lives of hundreds of millions. Furthermore, with Tibet situated between India and China, the peaceful resolution of the Tibet
35 problem also has important implications for lasting peace and friendly relation between these two great neighbors.

1

According to the Dalai Lama, what does China need to do to maintain unity in its heterogeneous population?

A) Liberalize its economic systems to ensure equal distribution of wealth.

B) Develop greater transparency, maintain the order by fair statutes, and grant freedom of speech and unrestricted access to information.

C) Ensure that all people groups are treated equally and permitted to maintain their individual characteristics.

D) Maintain and promote an understanding of its long history and rich culture.

2

Which choice provides the best evidence for the answer to the previous question?

A) Lines 2–3 ("Economic … power")

B) Lines 3–6 ("I believe … deserving")

C) Lines 9–11 ("I believe … information")

D) Lines 16–18 ("For this … crucial")

3

The primary environmental concern regarding Tibet that the author addresses is

A) the possibility that the Chinese population in Tibet may overtake its Tibetan population.

B) the probable effect upon all of Asia if a growing population in Tibet pollutes its freshwater sources.

C) the likelihood that China will threaten the natural beauty of his peaceful homeland.

D) the scale of possible pollution because Tibet lies between the two most populous nations on the planet.

4

Which choice provides the best evidence for the answer to the previous question?

A) Lines 22–27 ("Every … homeland")

B) Lines 27–29 ("This … environment")

C) Lines 29–32 ("Since … millions")

D) Lines 33–37 ("Furthermore … neighbors")

5

Although the Chinese government protested the presentation of the Congressional Gold Medal to the Dalai Lama, some political analysts found the speech to be more conciliatory than confrontational towards China. Does the passage support this claim?

A) Yes, lines 3–6 ("I believe … deserving") suggest that China has earned its prosperity.

B) Yes, lines 22–24 ("Every … rate") show approval of China's expanding population.

C) No, lines 11–14 ("Much … unfold") use quotation marks to show ironic indignation at Chinese policies the Dalai Lama sees as oppressive.

D) No, lines 33–37 ("Furthermore … neighbors") indicate that the speaker considers Tibet more important than China and India.

6

According to the author, the resolution of Tibet's concerns impacts other nations because

A) it can serve as a model for nations with similar issues, so that others can learn from its success.

B) Tibet's location means that its peace will promote amiable relations between China and India.

C) it will bring economic benefits to nations throughout the world once its internal affairs are set in order.

D) the freedom and equality of all people anywhere impact the well being of free and equal people everywhere.

7

Which choice provides the best evidence for the answer to the previous question?

A) Lines 1–3 ("Today … power")

B) Lines 19–22 ("With respect … place")

C) Lines 24–27 ("And, if … homeland")

D) Lines 33–37 ("Furthermore … neighbors")

Words In Context Questions

Most reading passages on the SAT will have two questions on the meaning of individual words or phrases in context. These questions will ask about hard or obscure vocabulary words, words and phrases with odd or archaic meanings, and words with several possible meanings. To answer them, you must choose the word or phrase that best matches the meaning of the word or phrase as it is used in the passage. The answer will rarely be the most common meaning of the word, especially if it is an everyday word or phrase.

For example, consider the following text passage:

25   No humane being, past the thoughtless age of boyhood, will needlessly murder any creature which holds its life by the same tenure that he does. The hare in its extremity cries like a child.

In line 27, the phrase "by the same tenure" most nearly means

A) in the same occupation.

B) with the same permanence.

C) under the same conditions.

D) for the same length of time.

Here is the strategy to use on these questions:

1. Read the question, but do not read through the answer choices, as recommended in the "R–W" strategy.

2. Go back to the passage and read the entire sentence in which the word appears. You may need to reread a sentence before and/or after the one in which the word appears for additional context. Use this context to determine what the word or phrase means in the context of the sentence.

3. Write down, next to the question, your own synonym for the word or phrase as it is used in the sentence. Don't worry about picking a perfect word or making sure that the part of speech matches, just make sure that you get the meaning of the word from the sentence itself. You should not look at the answer choices until after you have written down an answer.

4. After you have written in your own synonym, look at the answer choices and pick the word that most closely mirrors the word that you wrote. Be sure to cross out incorrect answers as you reject them, but **do not** reject answers simply because you do not know the meaning of the answer choice. Instead, if you eliminate all the answers you know are wrong, you may end up with only one left, or at least you will be able to make a more educated guess.

- If you are left with two possible answers that might fit, read each in place of the word or phrase in the sentence and choose the one that keeps the same meaning and tone for the sentence as a whole.

- If you cannot write in a synonym for the word or phrase because you don't know its meaning and the context does not seem clear enough to you, try to read each answer into the sentence and choose the one that makes the best sense in the context of the passage. However, *only* use this technique if you *cannot* write in your own word, because often an answer choice will make the sentence as a whole make sense but is not a good synonym for the specified word.

Words In Context Practice Passage

Questions 1–19 are based on the following passage.

The following passage is adapted from P.G. Wodehouse's *My Man Jeeves*, published in 1919.

I'm not absolutely certain of my facts, but I rather fancy it's Shakespeare—or, if not, it's some equally brainy lad—who says that it's always just when a chappie is feeling particularly top-hole, and
5 more than usually braced with things in general that Fate sneaks up behind him with a bit of lead piping. There's no doubt the man's right. It's absolutely that way with me. Take, for instance, the fairly rummy matter of Lady Malvern and her son
10 Wilmot. A moment before they turned up, I was just thinking how thoroughly all right everything was.

It was one of those topping mornings, and I had just climbed out from under the cold shower,
15 feeling like a two-year-old. As a matter of fact, I was especially bucked just then because the day before I had asserted myself with Jeeves— absolutely asserted myself, don't you know. You see, the way things had been going on I was rapidly
20 becoming a dashed serf. The man had jolly well oppressed me. I didn't so much mind when he made me give up one of my new suits, because Jeeves's judgment about suits is sound. But I as near as a toucher rebelled when he wouldn't let me
25 wear a pair of cloth-topped boots which I loved like a couple of brothers. And when he tried to tread on me like a worm in the matter of a hat, I jolly well put my foot down and showed him who was who. It's a long story, and I haven't time to tell you now,
30 but the point is that he wanted me to wear the Longacre—as worn by John Drew—when I had set my heart on the Country Gentleman—as worn by another famous actor chappie—and the end of the matter was that, after a rather painful scene, I
35 bought the Country Gentleman. So that's how things stood on this particular morning, and I was feeling kind of manly and independent.

Well, I was in the bathroom, wondering what there was going to be for breakfast while I
40 massaged the good old spine with a rough towel and sang slightly, when there was a tap at the door. I stopped singing and opened the door an inch.

"What ho without there!"

"Lady Malvern wishes to see you, sir," said
45 Jeeves.

"Eh?"

"Lady Malvern, sir. She is waiting in the sitting-room."

"Pull yourself together, Jeeves, my man," I said,
50 rather severely, for I bar practical jokes before breakfast. "You know perfectly well there's no one waiting for me in the sitting-room. How could there be when it's barely ten o'clock yet?"

"I gathered from her ladyship, sir, that she had
55 landed from an ocean liner at an early hour this morning."

This made the thing a bit more plausible. I remembered that when I had arrived in America about a year before, the proceedings had begun at
60 some ghastly hour like six, and that I had been shot out on to a foreign shore considerably before eight.

"Who the deuce is Lady Malvern, Jeeves?"

"Her ladyship did not confide in me, sir."

"Is she alone?"

65 "Her ladyship is accompanied by a Lord Pershore, sir. I fancy that his lordship would be her ladyship's son."

"Oh, well, put out rich raiment of sorts, and I'll be dressing."

70 "Our heather-mixture lounge is in readiness, sir."

"Then lead me to it."

1

In line 2, the word "fancy" most nearly means

A) decorated.

B) special.

C) imagine.

D) pretend.

2

In line 4, the term "top-hole" most nearly means

A) excellent.

B) overcome.

C) closed.

D) empty.

3

In lines 6–7 the author says "Fate sneaks up behind him with a bit of lead piping" to suggest

A) that one can be murdered at any moment.

B) Fate is a tricky plumber.

C) something bad and unexpected can happen any time.

D) no one can escape the final end of death.

4

In line 13, "topping" is closest in meaning to

A) being immature.

B) very good.

C) uncertain.

D) putting above.

5

In line 16, "bucked" most nearly means

A) blithe.

B) thrown off.

C) tied up.

D) tired.

6

In lines 17 and 18, the word "asserted" is closest in meaning to

A) affirmed the truth about.

B) claimed superiority over.

C) spoken up for.

D) served.

7

In line 27, the word "matter" most nearly means

A) issue.

B) materiality.

C) substance.

D) importance.

8

In lines 31–32, the author uses the phrase "set my heart on" to suggest

A) his romantic feelings.

B) his complete dependence upon a certain outcome.

C) his passion for mundane concerns.

D) his mind was made up.

9

In line 34, the word "painful" most nearly means

A) difficult.

B) damaging.

C) gratuitous.

D) aching.

10

In line 43, the word "without" means

A) lacking.

B) bereft.

C) outside.

D) alone.

11

In line 50, the word "bar" most nearly means

A) clog.

B) fasten.

C) segregate.

D) disallow.

12

In line 54, the term "gathered" most nearly means

A) amassed.
B) grabbed.
C) united.
D) surmised.

13

In line 55, the word "landed" most nearly means

A) arrived.
B) struck.
C) fell.
D) birthed.

14

In line 57, the word "plausible" most nearly means

A) appreciable.
B) believable.
C) able to be molded.
D) clear.

15

In line 60, the word "ghastly" is closest in meaning to

A) like an apparition.
B) frightening.
C) loose.
D) appalling.

16

In context, the phrase "shot out" as it is used in line 60–61 is intended to convey that the narrator was

A) literally fired forth.
B) symbolically darkened.
C) ironically withstood.
D) unceremoniously dropped off.

17

In line 63, the phrase "confide in" most nearly means

A) trust in.
B) reveal to.
C) depend upon.
D) suspect about.

18

In line 68, the word "raiment" means

A) clothing.
B) food.
C) disguise.
D) drizzle.

19

In line 70, the phrase "in readiness" most nearly means

A) located conveniently.
B) dependably constructed.
C) set for use.
D) able to be understood.

Figure-Based Questions

The reading section of the SAT will ordinarily have two passages with "supplemental materials," including graphs, charts and tables. Usually, about five questions are based partly or entirely on those figures. When working with graphs, charts, and tables on the SAT Reading Test, complete the following steps:

1. Focus on the variables listed and the types of data being recorded. Circle or underline the title as well as the axes if the source is a graph or the column headings if it is a table. Pay attention to the scaling on graphs— look out for notes like "in billions" or indications that a graph is drawn not to scale.

2. When reading a question that asks about material on a chart, graph, or table, underline key terms in the question, and find where these terms are represented on the figure. Often, questions will contain multiple **true** answers, only one of which answers the actual question. Underlining key information in the question will help you focus on the details needed to answer the question correctly.

3. After you have read and underlined words in the question, go back to the graph to find the relevant data and circle it.

4. Use the answer choices to eliminate wrong answers. You may need to refer to the text of the passage as well as the figure itself to answer some of these questions, so reread relevant portions of the passage, if needed.

   • Be careful about language involving percentages. A larger percent does not necessarily mean a larger number if they are not drawn from the same total!

Try It!

Table 1

Nebula Class	% Deuterium atoms	% Helium atoms
1	1.7	4.8
2	2.8	3.9
3	3.2	3.3
4	4.0	3.2

1

Based on the data in Table 1, which choice best represents the difference in the percentage of deuterium atoms and helium atoms in a Class 2 Nebula?

A) 0.1%

B) 1.1%

C) 1.2%

D) 3.1%

Figure-Based Questions Practice Set

Answer questions 1–3 based on the table and passage excerpt below.

Tibetan regions population in China in 2000	Total Population (in millions)	Chinese Population (in thousands)	Tibetan Population (in thousands)
Tibet Autonomous Region (TAR)	2.62	157	2,427
All Tibetan Regions	13.5	7,500	6,000

The following excerpt is adapted from a speech given by the Fourteenth Dalai Lama upon receiving the Congressional Gold Medal in 2007.

With respect to my own homeland Tibet, today
20 many people, both from inside and outside, feel
deeply concerned about the consequences of the
rapid changes taking place. Every year, the Chinese
population inside Tibet is increasing at an alarming
rate. And, if we are to judge by the example of the
25 population of Lhasa, there is a real danger that the
Tibetans will be reduced to an insignificant
minority in their own homeland. This rapid
increase in population is also posing serious threat
to Tibet's fragile environment. Since Tibet is the
30 source of many of Asia's great rivers, any
substantial disturbance in Tibet's ecology will
impact the lives of hundreds of millions.
Furthermore, with Tibet situated between India
and China, the peaceful resolution of the Tibet
35 problem also has important implications for lasting
peace and friendly relation between these two great
neighbors.

1

In lines 23-24, the speaker claims that by 2007 the population of Chinese settlers within the TAR is increasing "at an alarming rate." Based on the data above, what must be true about the population of the TAR at the time of the speech?

A) The Chinese population in the region was over 157,000,000.

B) The Tibetan population was less than 2,000,000 in the TAR.

C) There were more than 157,000 Chinese people in the TAR.

D) The Chinese population was more than 7.5 million in all Tibetan regions.

2

According to the data in the table, approximately what percent of the total Tibetan population is in the TAR?

A) 20%

B) 30%

C) 40%

D) 60%

3

Based on the passage and the data in the table, which of the following must be true?

A) In 2000, there were more than 157,000 Chinese people living in the TAR.

B) The total population in all Tibetan regions was less than 13.5 million by 2007.

C) The Chinese population in all Tibetan regions accounted for more than half of the total population in 2007.

D) The Tibetan population in the TAR was less than 2 million in 2007.

Sample Reading Passages

Social Science

Questions 1–11 are based on the following passage.

This passage is adapted from a speech delivered by First Lady Hillary Rodham Clinton on September 5, 1995, to the United Nations 4th World Conference on Women, held in Beijing, China.

If there is one message that echoes forth from this conference, let it be that human rights are women's rights and women's rights are human rights once and for all. Let us not forget that among
5 those rights are the right to speak freely and the right to be heard.

Women must enjoy the rights to participate fully in the social and political lives of their countries, if we want freedom and democracy to thrive and
10 endure. It is indefensible that many women in nongovernmental organizations who wished to participate in this conference have not been able to attend or have been prohibited from fully taking part.

15 Let me be clear. Freedom means the right of people to assemble, organize, and debate openly. It means respecting the views of those who may disagree with the views of their governments. It means not taking citizens away from their loved
20 ones and jailing them, mistreating them, or denying them their freedom or dignity because of the peaceful expression of their ideas and opinions.

In my country, we recently celebrated the 75th anniversary of Women's Suffrage. It took 150 years
25 after the signing of our Declaration of Independence for women to win the right to vote. It took 72 years of organized struggle, before that happened, on the part of many courageous women and men. It was one of America's most divisive
30 philosophical wars. But it was a bloodless war. Suffrage was achieved without a shot being fired.

But we have also been reminded, in V-J Day[1] observances last weekend, of the good that comes when men and women join together to combat the
35 forces of tyranny and to build a better world. We
have seen peace prevail in most places for a half century. We have avoided another world war. But we have not solved older, deeply-rooted problems that continue to diminish the potential of half the
40 world's population.

Now it is the time to act on behalf of women everywhere. If we take bold steps to better the lives of women, we will be taking bold steps to better the lives of children and families too. Families rely on
45 mothers and wives for emotional support and care. Families rely on women for labor in the home. And increasingly, everywhere, families rely on women for income needed to raise healthy children and care for other relatives.

50 As long as discrimination and inequities remain so commonplace everywhere in the world, as long as girls and women are valued less, fed less, fed last, overworked, underpaid, not schooled, [and] subjected to violence in and outside their homes,
55 the potential of the human family to create a peaceful, prosperous world will not be realized.

Let this conference be our and the world's call to action. Let us heed that call so we can create a world in which every woman is treated with respect
60 and dignity, every boy and girl is loved and cared for equally, and every family has the hope of a strong and stable future. That is the work before you. That is the work before all of us who have a vision of the world we want to see for our children
65 and our grandchildren.

The time is now. We must move beyond rhetoric. We must move beyond recognition of problems to working together, to have the common efforts to build that common ground we hope to
70 see.

---

[1] V-J day refers to "Victory over Japan Day," the anniversary of the day in which Japan surrendered, in effect ending World War II.

1

It can reasonably be inferred from the passage that at the time it was written, the problem of women's inequality

A) had been and continued to be a significant issue in the United States and the world due to denial of equal rights and discrimination.

B) was of significant importance only from a historical perspective, because women had achieved suffrage, so that inequality was no longer a pressing concern.

C) was on the rise due to complex social and genetic factors that were not then fully understood, but had led to systematic prejudice.

D) would likely be solved through the specific steps delineated in the passage, which would be enacted gradually to create meaningful change.

2

The author most likely repeats the phrase "it means" in the third paragraph in order to

A) clarify the limits of the scope of her definition of the term "freedom."

B) convey with increasing intensity the importance of maintaining a free society.

C) provide a list of rights included in freedom as well as behaviors that are prohibited where freedom thrives and endures.

D) reference violations of freedom committed on specific occasions by other countries.

3

In line 36, the term "prevail" most nearly means

A) influence.

B) persuade.

C) defeat.

D) persist.

4

Which of the following would be most in conflict with the author's description of the concept of freedom (lines 15–22)?

A) Sentencing convicted criminals to the death penalty

B) Jailing citizens based on their violent expression of ideas and opinions

C) Penalizing citizens for holding certain dangerous and antisocial viewpoints

D) Allowing people to organize and assemble for open debates

5

The author references "Women's Suffrage" (line 24) in the United States in order to

A) compare an event in American history with the current situation in another country to show how that country's women can succeed.

B) provide a concrete example of one result of the fight for women's equality and emphasize the significance of this right for women.

C) demonstrate that women are capable of fighting bloodless battles because of their more emotional and compassionate demeanors.

D) illustrate one specific technique that can be used to nurture equality in both authoritarian and democratic nations.

6

In this passage, the author advocates most directly for

A) bold, collaborative reform.

B) courageous decisions on an individual level.

C) consistent but gradual policy changes.

D) working to change men's view of gender.

7

Which choice provides the best evidence for the answer to the previous question?

A) Lines 1–4 ("If there … for all") and lines 37–40 ("But we … world's population")

B) Lines 7–10 ("Women must … and endure") and lines 30–31 ("But it … being fired")

C) Lines 46–49 ("And increasingly … other relatives") and lines 50–56 ("As long … be realized")

D) Lines 42–44 ("If we … families too") and lines 66–70 ("The time … to see")

8

The primary rhetorical effect of the list provided in lines 52–54 ("valued less … their homes") is to

A) exemplify the consequences of inequality on women from least significant to most significant in determining quality of life.

B) explain the nuances of gender inequality and encourage careful and deliberate debate on the status of impoverished men and women.

C) illustrate a multitude of effects of inequality on women to demonstrate the importance of solving such inequality.

D) compare and contrast these conditions to those of women in the United States prior to Women's Suffrage and implicitly support suffrage.

9

Based on the passage, which choice best reflects the relationship between women's equality and the cause of liberty throughout the world?

A) The first is substantially more important than the second.

B) Advancements in the first may negatively impact the second but still must be attained.

C) Advancements in the first are necessary to ensure attainment of the second.

D) Neither is likely to be achieved in the near future.

10

Which choice provides the best evidence for the answer to the previous question?

A) lines 7–10 ("Women must … endure")

B) lines 24–31 ("It took … fired")

C) lines 32–37 ("But we … world war")

D) lines 57–62 ("Let us … future")

11

The author's use of the word "rhetoric" in line 67 most nearly means

A) persuasive language.

B) making a point without expecting or desiring a response.

C) words without action.

D) working together.

Science Passage

Questions 12–22 are based on the following passage and supplemental material.

This passage is adapted from Brittany Linkous' "Misconceptions and the Spread of Infectious Disease," published by the Federation of American Scientists Public Interest Reports in 2014.

New and improved medical treatments for infectious diseases are vital to improving global health security; however, public education is equally important. Myths and misperceptions
5 regarding infectious diseases have detrimental effects on global health when a disease outbreak occurs. While it may seem that this problem is isolated to remote regions of the developing world, neither infectious diseases nor misconceptions
10 regarding them are explicitly confined to certain areas.

Outbreaks can be highly disruptive to the movement of people and goods, often leading to increased regulations and restrictions on travel and
15 trade to reduce the potential for further spread of disease. The Severe Acute Respiratory Syndrome (SARS) epidemic in 2003 was but one of the numerous examples in which international travel was disrupted. The disease quickly infected
20 thousands of people around the world and disrupted national economies. Due to the rapid transmissibility of SARS, the World Health Organization (WHO) issued a travel advisory in effort to reduce the international public threat. In
25 2001, the United Kingdom experienced a detrimental hit to the agricultural sector as foot-and-mouth disease spread throughout livestock. Because of the highly transmissible nature of the disease (which affected cattle, pigs,
30 sheep, and goats), the government banned all exports of live animals, meat, and dairy products. Later that same year, the tourist industry estimated that businesses lost nearly $421 million U.S. dollars.

35 In the developing world, pneumonia, diarrhea, malaria, measles, and HIV/AIDS are some of the primary causes of death, especially among children. This is in part attributable to socioeconomic factors that prevent people from
40 having access to routine health services and immunizations. Poor nutrition and unsanitary living conditions also place people at risk. Among children in Africa, the death rate from measles, a viral respiratory disease, has reached an average
45 rate of one per minute. Yet, in the developed regions of the world, measles is commonly treated through immunizations.

Tetanus, an infection caused by the bacteria *Clostridium tetani* (which is ubiquitous in the
50 soil), is common in developing areas where unsanitary medical techniques such as use of contaminated medical bandages continue. Although proper sanitary resources are often scarce in these regions, lack of supplies is not
55 the only cause of disease transmission as proper sanitation techniques could have mitigated transmission. Due to the lack of education about public health, sanitation, and the mechanisms of disease transmission, the spread of infectious
60 diseases like tetanus continues.

Despite modern medical advances and technology, developed countries are also susceptible to infectious disease outbreaks. These outbreaks have been due in part to the
65 misconceptions about vaccines and anti-bacterial drugs that have been used to deter the spread of infectious diseases. Some individuals have the perception that antibiotics are a "cure-all," but this view has led to people taking antibiotics when they
70 are not needed. This overuse has allowed the emergence of antibiotic-resistant strains of bacteria. Vaccines are also misunderstood: this was evident in the recent reemergence of pertussis, also known as "Whooping Cough," in the mid-1970s
75 when Great Britain, Sweden and Japan reduced their usage of the pertussis vaccine due to a common fear of vaccinations. The effect was immediate and drastic—there were over 100,000 cases in Great Britain, 13,000 cases in Japan, and
80 3,200 cases in Sweden. The United States witnessed a similar outbreak in the northwest region of the country in 2012, when over 17,000 cases emerged shortly after an increased rate of vaccine refusals for pertussis. While no vaccine is
85 100% effective, it is evident that popular misconceptions regarding infectious diseases and their spread can have detrimental repercussions on the populace and need to be addressed head-on.

Education, early detection, and access to
90 vaccines are all essential in containing and

preventing the spread of disease in a globalized society. Although myths and misconceptions have hindered their effectiveness, vaccinations can drastically reduce the chances of contracting many
95 diseases. Additionally, developing and utilizing programs that educate the public regarding the implications of infectious diseases and treatments

pertaining to them will significantly reduce the spread of disease. While making better medical
100 practices and medicines available will help to combat the transmission of infectious diseases, there is no substitute for better public health education.

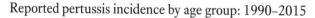

Reported pertussis incidence by age group: 1990–2015

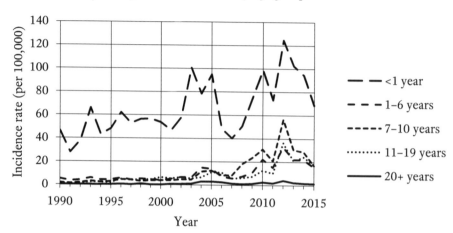

Adapted from the Centers for Disease Control and Prevention Website

12

The main purpose of the article is to

A) offer a comprehensive survey of infectious diseases through history and across the world.

B) inform readers of the importance of understanding the nature of infectious diseases and how to treat them.

C) persuade readers that vaccines and antibiotics are the best solution to all global public health issues.

D) dissuade readers from believing that infectious diseases are only a problem in developed countries.

13

As it is used in line 26, "detrimental" most nearly means

A) fiduciary.

B) complementary.

C) fatal.

D) harmful.

14

The author mentions the 2001 outbreak of foot-and-mouth disease in the UK as an example of

A) the kinds of problems created by people misunderstanding infectious diseases.

B) the ways in which economic factors can affect the spread of infectious diseases.

C) the impact that infectious diseases can have on global economies and trade.

D) mistaken ideas about responding to outbreaks of infections.

15

Which choice offers the best evidence for the answer to the preceding question?

A) Lines 4–7 ("Myths … occurs")

B) Lines 7–11 ("While … areas")

C) Lines 12–16 ("Outbreaks … disease")

D) Lines 21–24 ("Due … threat")

16

As it is used in line 49, the word "ubiquitous" most nearly means

A) pervasive.

B) constant.

C) located.

D) global.

17

The author claims that one side effect of the overuse of anti-bacterial drugs is that

A) outbreaks of pertussis have become more widespread.

B) more developed countries are now more susceptible to diseases than in the past.

C) some bacteria have begun to develop resistance to antibiotics.

D) children's natural resistance to strains of bacteria has weakened.

18

Which choice offers the best evidence for the answer to the preceding question?

A) Lines 53–60 ("Although … continues")

B) Lines 63–67 ("These outbreaks … diseases")

C) Lines 67–70 ("Some … needed")

D) Lines 70–72 ("This overuse … bacteria")

19

The author mentions that "no vaccine is 100% effective" (lines 84–85) primarily to

A) warn parents against using vaccines to prevent disease in their children.

B) clarify the risks associated with over-vaccinated populations.

C) qualify the strength of a recommended solution to the spread of infectious diseases.

D) question the wisdom of the widespread acceptance of vaccination as an aspect of public health policy.

20

The graph reveals that pertussis cases in the United States

A) are almost all in those less than 1 year old.

B) were nearly eliminated in 1990 but have gradually grown to the level of an epidemic.

C) are more common among infants than adults.

D) are due to the failure of vaccines to protect public health.

21

The graph offers support for the information in the passage in that

A) the incidence of cases of whooping cough spikes in 2012.

B) both reveal an inverse relationship between the number of people vaccinated and the number of pertussis cases.

C) 2007 marks a 10-year low for the incidence of pertussis among those younger than 1.

D) the outbreak of SARS in 2003 is clear in an increased incidence for all age groups.

22

Based on the argument in the passage and the information in the graph, the author would be most likely to investigate which of the following hypotheses about pertussis?

A) Was there a decrease in pertussis vaccinations between 2002 and 2005?

B) Were anti-bacterial drugs overused to treat pertussis in 1993?

C) Are adults less likely to develop pertussis than infants?

D) Are people from different parts of the United States more or less likely to develop pertussis based on their local climate?

Literature

Questions 23–32 are based on the following passage.

The following is from the novel *The Beautiful and the Damned* by F. Scott Fitzgerald, published in 1922.

Fifth and Sixth Avenues, it seemed to Anthony, were the uprights of a gigantic ladder stretching from Washington Square to Central Park. Coming up-town on top of a bus toward Fifty-second Street
5 invariably gave him the sensation of hoisting himself hand by hand on a series of treacherous rungs, and when the bus jolted to a stop at his own rung he found something akin to relief as he descended the reckless metal steps to the sidewalk.
10 After that, he had but to walk down Fifty-second Street half a block, pass a stodgy family of brownstone houses—and then in a jiffy he was under the high ceilings of his great front room. This was entirely satisfactory. Here, after all, life
15 began. Here he slept, breakfasted, read, and entertained.

The house itself was of murky material, built in the late nineties; in response to the steadily growing need of small apartments each floor had
20 been thoroughly remodeled and rented individually. Of the four apartments Anthony's, on the second floor, was the most desirable.

The front room had fine high ceilings and three large windows that loomed down pleasantly upon
25 Fifty-second Street. In its appointments it escaped by a safe margin being of any particular period; it escaped stiffness, stuffiness, bareness, and decadence. It smelt neither of smoke nor of incense—it was tall and faintly blue. There was a
30 deep lounge of the softest brown leather with somnolence drifting about it like a haze. There was a high screen of Chinese lacquer chiefly concerned with geometrical fishermen and huntsmen in black and gold; this made a corner alcove for a
35 voluminous chair guarded by an orange-colored standing lamp. Deep in the fireplace a quartered shield was burned to a murky black.

Passing through the dining-room, which, as Anthony took only breakfast at home, was merely a
40 magnificent potentiality, and down a comparatively long hall, one came to the heart and core of the apartment—Anthony's bedroom and bath.

Both of them were immense. Under the ceilings of the former even the great canopied bed seemed
45 of only average size. On the floor an exotic rug of crimson velvet was soft as fleece on his bare feet. His bathroom, in contrast to the rather portentous character of his bedroom, was gay, bright, extremely habitable and even faintly facetious.
50 Framed around the walls were photographs of four celebrated thespian beauties of the day: Julia Sanderson as "The Sunshine Girl," Ina Claire as "The Quaker Girl," Billie Burke as "The Mind-the-Paint Girl," and Hazel Dawn as "The Pink
55 Lady." Between Billie Burke and Hazel Dawn hung a print representing a great stretch of snow presided over by a cold and formidable sun—this, claimed Anthony, symbolized the cold shower.

The bathtub, equipped with an ingenious
60 bookholder, was low and large. Beside it a wall wardrobe bulged with sufficient linen for three men and with a generation of neckties. There was no skimpy glorified towel of a carpet—instead, a rich rug, like the one in his bedroom a miracle of
65 softness, that seemed almost to massage the wet foot emerging from the tub....

All in all a room to conjure with—it was easy to see that Anthony dressed there, arranged his immaculate hair there, in fact did everything but
70 sleep and eat there. It was his pride, this bathroom.

23

Throughout the passage, the author's style is best described as

A) psychologically complex.

B) curtly pragmatic.

C) blissfully oblivious.

D) lavishly descriptive.

24

The author refers to "his own rung" in lines 7–8 to indicate

A) the means by which Anthony climbs down from the bus.

B) the stop closest to Anthony's apartment.

C) Anthony's sense of possession of the bus route.

D) the feeling that resonates within Anthony as he rides the bus.

25

As it is used in line 25, the word "escaped" most nearly means

A) absconded.

B) avoided.

C) departed.

D) emerged.

26

As it is used in line 31, the word "somnolence" most nearly means

A) bewilderment.

B) tiresomeness.

C) seriousness.

D) leisure.

27

The passage's description of his apartment suggests that Anthony is

A) fastidious about his appearance and refined in his tastes.

B) defined entirely by his love of possessions.

C) shrewd in buying only the very best furnishings.

D) lonely, feeling incomplete because he has no one to love.

28

The narrator says Anthony's apartment is where his "life began" (lines 14–15) because

A) he always desired to stay there, uncomfortable leaving the safe and cozy space it provided.

B) it was where he took his morning meal, hosted guests, slept at nights, and more.

C) it sustains him and provides him with all he needs, acting as a surrogate parent.

D) it is an allegory for his life, with each room presenting a different aspect of his existence.

29

Which choice provides the best evidence for the answer to the previous question?

A) Lines 15–16 ("Here … entertained")

B) Lines 18–22 ("in response … desirable")

C) Lines 55–58 ("Between … shower")

D) Lines 67–70 ("All in … there")

30

The description of the pictures on the wall of Anthony's bathroom (lines 50–58) serve primarily to

A) exemplify the lighter atmosphere of the bathroom relative to the bedroom.

B) mock the pedestrian tastes of the day.

C) clarify the attributes Anthony finds attractive in women.

D) contradict Anthony's view of himself.

31

Based on the passage as a whole, the most important part of the apartment to Anthony is

A) the bathtub, because he loves to read his favorite books while soaking in the tub.

B) the front room, which allows him to impress guests with his Chinese art and decadent furniture.

C) the bathroom, which he sees as almost magical in nature.

D) the bedroom, due to both its size and its comfortable bed.

32

Which choice provides the best evidence for the answer to the previous question?

A) Lines 29–36 ("There ... lamp")

B) Lines 43–45 ("Both ... size")

C) Lines 59–62 ("The bathtub ... neckties")

D) Lines 67–70 ("All ... bathroom")

Challenge Passage

Questions 33–44 are based on the following passage.

This passage is adapted from a speech regarding the United States Constitution given by Benjamin Franklin at the 1787 Constitutional Convention.

Mr. President:

I confess that there are several parts of this constitution which I do not at present approve, but I am not sure I shall ever approve them; for having
5 lived long, I have experienced many instances of being obliged by better information, or fuller consideration, to change opinions even on important subjects, which I once thought right, but found to be otherwise. It is therefore that the older
10 I grow, the more apt I am to doubt my own judgment, and to pay more respect to the judgment of others.

Most men indeed as well as most sects in religion, think themselves in possession of all truth,
15 and that wherever others differ from them it is so far error. Steele, a Protestant, in a Dedication, tells the Pope, that the only difference between our Churches in their opinions of the certainty of their doctrines is, the Church of Rome is infallible and
20 the Church of England is *never in the wrong*. But though many private persons think almost as highly of their own infallibility as of that of their sect, few express it so naturally as a certain French lady, who in a dispute with her sister, said "I don't know how
25 it happens, Sister, but I meet with nobody but myself, that's always in the right." "Je ne trouve que moi qui aie toujours raison."

In these sentiments, Sir, I agree to this Constitution with all its faults, if they are such;
30 because I think a general Government necessary for us, and there is no form of Government but what may be a blessing to the people if well administered, and believe farther that this is likely to be well administered for a course of years, and
35 can only end in Despotism, as other forms have done before it, when the people shall become so corrupted as to need despotic Government, being incapable of any other.

I doubt too whether any other Convention we
40 can obtain may be able to make a better Constitution. For when you assemble a number of men to have the advantage of their joint wisdom, you inevitably assemble with those men, all their prejudices, their passions, their errors of opinion,
45 their local interests, and their selfish views. From such an assembly can a *perfect* production be expected? It therefore astonishes me, Sir, to find this system approaching so near to perfection as it does; and I think it will astonish our enemies, who
50 are waiting with confidence to hear that our councils are confounded like those of the Builders of Babel;[2] and that our States are on the point of separation, only to meet hereafter for the purpose of cutting one another's throats.
55 Thus I consent, Sir, to this Constitution because I expect no better, and because I am not sure that it is not the best. The opinions I have had of its *errors*, I sacrifice to the public good. I have never whispered a syllable of them abroad. Within these
60 walls they were born, and here they shall die. If every one of us in returning to our Constituents were to report the objections he has had to it, and endeavor to gain partisans in support of them, we might prevent its being generally received, and
65 thereby lose all the salutary effects and great advantages resulting naturally in our favor among foreign Nations as well as among ourselves, from our real or apparent unanimity.

Much of the strength and efficiency of any
70 Government in procuring and securing happiness to the people depends on *opinion*, on the general opinion of the goodness of the Government, as well as of the wisdom and integrity of its Governors. I hope therefore that for our own sakes as a part of
75 the people, and for the sake of posterity, we shall act heartily and unanimously in recommending this Constitution (if approved by Congress and confirmed by the Conventions) wherever our influence may extend, and turn our future thoughts
80 and endeavors to the means of having it *well* administered.

On the whole, Sir, I can not help expressing a wish that every member of the Convention who may still have objections to it would, with me, on
85 this occasion doubt a little of his own infallibility and, to make *manifest our unanimity*, put his name to this instrument.

---

[2] This refers to the biblical story of the failed attempt to build a tower to reach heaven.

33

Based on the passage, how does the author most nearly view the Constitution?

A) It must be revised before it is to take effect so that it will adequately provide the necessary tools for governing the state.

B) Although it would not likely gain approval from the King, it has garnered unanimous support among members of the Constitutional Convention.

C) While perhaps flawed in some ways, its ratification remains a necessary step in providing for the establishment of a unified government.

D) Its remaining flaws are insignificant in themselves, but its passage is undesirable because it will inevitably lead to despotism.

34

Which choice provides the best evidence for the answer to the previous question?

A) Lines 28–38 ("In these … any other")

B) Lines 41–45 ("For when … selfish views")

C) Lines 60–68 ("If every one … unanimity")

D) Lines 82–87 ("On the whole … this instrument")

35

The overall tone of this passage is best described as

A) persuasive.

B) scholarly.

C) zealous.

D) disappointed.

36

In lines 4–12 ("for having … of others"), the author suggests that aging

A) is an unfortunate but necessary and inevitable aspect of life for himself and others.

B) has made him willing to change his opinions over time due to the increased access to new and different information.

C) provides him with a wealth of knowledge and experience that cannot be accumulated in any other way.

D) leads to individuals strengthening their opinions over time except when they are presented with new information.

37

According to the author, the Church of Rome and the Church of England are

A) essentially identical in theology.

B) highly differentiated in their treatment of certainty.

C) both bureaucratic and hierarchical.

D) ironically similar in their notions of infallibility.

38

The primary rhetorical effect of the French lady's quote in lines 24–27 ("I don't know … raison") is

A) to contradict the idea that the doctrines of infallibility held by the listed churches are fundamentally the same.

B) to emphasize the importance of the issue of infallibility in sects both religious and secular.

C) to highlight Benjamin Franklin's skills and expertise developed through his involvement in international affairs.

D) to extend the issue of infallibility beyond churches and other organized groups to private individuals.

39

In line 35, "Despotism" most nearly means

A) monarchy.

B) chaos.

C) tyranny.

D) leadership.

40

The intended effect of the question in lines 45–47 ("From such … expected?") is

A) rhetorical, in order to suggest a clearly negative answer.

B) dramatic, in order to reveal the author's unexpected answer.

C) inquisitive, in order to open the audience to new line of consideration.

D) uncertainty, to show the author's genuine pursuit of the unknown.

41

Which of the following would be most in conflict with the author's views based on lines 47-60 ("It therefore … they shall die")?

A) Because the constitution provides for a new and different form of government, other countries anticipate its failure.

B) The Constitution's flaws should be debated locally and globally so that the best possible version can be passed.

C) Different states hold various and contradictory interests, causing tension in the Convention.

D) While not flawless, the Constitution is the best possible governing document in the current situation.

42

In line 63, "partisans" most nearly means

A) divisive government leaders.

B) anarchists against the unity of the state.

C) zealots for personal ideals.

D) followers of a particular view or faction.

43

In lines 60-87 ("If every one … this instrument") the author focuses on unanimity primarily because

A) individual doubts are irrelevant in any collective decision.

B) the members need to be united in accepting the constitution in order to begin the task of successfully governing.

C) allowing multiple opinions undermines unity and eliminates the possibility of successful rule.

D) it will extend America's influence and improve reputation throughout Europe and the world at large.

44

Which choice provides the best evidence for the answer to the previous question?

A) Lines 60-63 ("If every one … of them")

B) Lines 69-73 ("Much of the … Governors")

C) Lines 73-81 ("I hope … administered")

D) Lines 83-85 ("every member … own infallibility")

Writing and Language Test Manual

The SAT Writing and Language Test is composed of four passages with 44 questions of two types:

Expression of Ideas questions test your understanding of basic rhetorical and compositional elements based on your comprehension of the reading material.

Standard English Conventions questions test your knowledge of specific grammar and usage rules.

Overview and Strategy

Each passage on the SAT has 11 questions of two different types: Expression of Ideas (6) and Standard English Conventions (5). The two types require different approaches, so it is important to recognize them.

Expression of Ideas (EOI)

These questions assess your **rhetorical, compositional,** and **organizational skills**. These questions can be answered by using contextual clues within the passage, and the correct answer must be chosen based on either the **meaning** of the words or **principles** of effective composition: they are *not* based on grammar rules.

Standard English Conventions (SEC)

These questions test your knowledge of **standard grammatical conventions**, such as the accepted rules for punctuation, sentence structure, word usage, idioms, subject-verb agreement and more. Most questions feature an underlined portion of a passage that can range from one word to an entire sentence. You must decide whether to keep the underlined part as it is or to choose one of three possible revisions, based on which best conforms to the academic standards for written English.

Strategy

1. READ!
   1.1. READ the entire passage as you answer questions rather than skipping from one underlined section to the next. Especially for EOI questions, having the entire context of the passage is **essential**.
   1.2. READ at least to the end of the sentence of the underlined section before answering any question. Often, even on grammar questions, an answer can seem to be correct when you first read it, but something *after* the underlined portion makes it an error.
2. IDENTIFY what is being tested on each question.
   2.1. Identify the question as EOI or SEC: if there is a specific question before the answer choices, it is an EOI question, and you need to follow the directions in the question, using the strategies in the following pages. If there is no question, go to 2.2.
   2.2. Specify the exact rule or principle, such as comma usage or redundancy.
   2.3. For every question on which you are not sure what is being tested, circle the question in the test booklet and return to it when you have finished the rest of the passage.
3. MARK directly on the test booklet to ELIMINATE answer choices.
   3.1. Cross out what makes each wrong answer incorrect, so that you are specifically attending to the small differences between answers.
   3.2. If there are two elements being tested on a question—such as apostrophe use and verb form—deal with each error one at a time, starting with the one you know better.
4. When in doubt, READ IT OUT.
   4.1. If you are stuck between two answer choices, read the entire sentence in your head and choose the one that "sounds" better.
   4.2. Many students use this method as their primary approach to this section, but it will lead to many errors on questions you could otherwise get correct, so *only* use this strategy if you are stuck!

Writing and Language Strategy Flow Chart

Refer to this flow chart to help you navigate the questions on the SAT Writing and Language Test

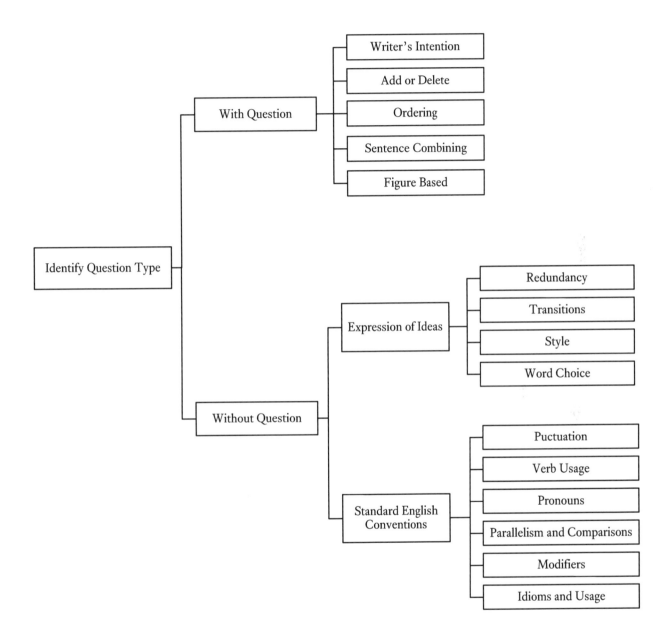

Expression of Ideas

The SAT Writing and Language Test offers more contextual, reading-based questions—called "Expression of Ideas" on the test—than rule-based grammar questions. Thus, it is essential to read the whole passage carefully in order to have a clear sense of the content, style, and purpose of the passage as you read it. There are a few types of Expression of Ideas questions that you will want to familiarize yourself with, all of which will be covered in depth in the following pages:

"Questions" Without Questions   These questions look just like grammar-based questions, so the trick is to recognize them!

Writer's Intention Questions   These questions ask which choice best accomplishes some specific purpose that the writer wants to accomplish.

Add/Delete Questions   These questions ask whether to take out an underlined section or add a phrase or sentence, usually with two "yes" options and two "no" options, each with different reasons.

Ordering Questions   These questions require you to put a sentence in the correct place in a paragraph or to put a paragraph in the correct place in the passage as a whole.

Sentence Combining Questions   These questions ask you to combine two separate sentences into one clearer and more concise sentence.

Figure-Based Questions   These questions ask about figures included with the passage, usually in connection with what is written in the passage.

"Questions" Without Questions

The standard format for questions on the SAT Writing and Language Test actually has no question: it simply lists four options for an underlined part of the passage. Nearly all Standard English Conventions—grammar-based—questions are in this format; however, some Expression of Ideas questions also use the same format.

Here is a strategy for these questions:

1. When you come across a question without a specific question, you *must* first determine whether it is a Standard English Conventions (grammar) or Expression of Ideas (context) question. One key to differentiate between the two question types is that *all the answer options for Expression of Ideas questions will be grammatically correct.* These questions only test your rhetorical skills and contextual understanding of the passage and do not ask you to correct grammatical errors.

2. Once you have identified the question as an Expression of Ideas question, identify the exact principle being tested by the question. There are four main concepts tested by questions without questions: style, redundancy, transitions, and word choice. Knowing these types can help you to recognize them!

Style

Style questions ask you to evaluate the style of a certain phrase in the context of the passage. Is the phrasing too technical? Colloquial? Awkwardly worded? Too wordy? Try to understand the tone of the passage and then determine which of the choices provided best fits with the tone of the rest of the passage. Don't be tempted by answers merely due to difficult words—if the style is less formal, then long, difficult words are not in keeping with the style of the passage!

Style—Try It!

Though many may disagree, the movement toward greater transparency in the war on terror **1** is gathering momentum.

1

A) NO CHANGE
B) is really picking up speed as it heads into the last turn.
C) seems unequivocally to be resistant to gravitational and frictional forces limiting its acceleration.
D) is running wild and kicking it into high gear.

Redundancy

Redundancy questions ask you to consider what details are repetitive in an underlined section. You can often recognize these questions by noticing that some answer choices include content that others cut out. Eliminate answer choices that are internally redundant or include information contained elsewhere in the sentence or the paragraph. *Sometimes, the information that makes what is underlined redundant comes **after** the underlined portion, so be sure to read at least to the end of the sentence before choosing.* The right answer will be the most concise answer that still contains all relevant information.

Redundancy—Try It!

Without a doubt, the meat industry of the future will undoubtedly be unable to maintain its current practices in the coming years.

2

A) NO CHANGE
B) of the next generation will not certainly be able
C) will not be able
D) will not be able, in the future,

Transitions

Transition questions require you to choose a single word or phrase that most effectively connects two parts of a single sentence, clarifies the movement from the end of one sentence to the beginning of the next, or leads the reader from the close of an earlier paragraph to the start of a new one. Be careful to differentiate these questions from those testing sentence structure: if all the answer choices are grammatically the same, you need to consider the meaning of the words to choose the correct answer. These transitions signal the trajectory of the paragraph or sentence, so consider the relationship between the sentences or paragraphs they connect in order to answer these questions correctly. Ask yourself:

- Do the two parts create a contrast?
- Does the second offer more evidence for the same idea as the first?
- Does the second part offer the next step in a process?

Once you know the relationship, choosing the best word is usually quite simple!

Transitions—Try It!

According to Hans Gruber writing in *Rocking Roll*, if Ian Anderson, a singularly talented flutist and vocalist, had not lost his range and tone, he would have continued his meteoric rise to the heavens of rock and roll. **3** Indeed, many fans believe that his unique combination of raw musical talent and showmanship would have led to stardom greater than that achieved by any other human being.

3

A) NO CHANGE
B) Surprisingly,
C) Therefore,
D) However,

Word Choice

Word choice questions can be based on grammar or context, so distinguishing between the two is crucial. Standard English Conventions word choice questions test your knowledge of the correct usage of a word pair such as **affect** vs. **effect** (See "Idioms and Usage" on page 108 under SEC). In contrast, Expression of Ideas word choice questions are all grammatically correct and test your knowledge of the contextual appropriateness of a word. In order to solve these questions, read the whole sentence and choose the answer that is most logical and suited to the point being made in the sentence. If you are not sure of the exact meaning of some of the word choices, start with those you know, and eliminate all those that don't work. If one of the words you *do* know works in the sentence, choose it rather than an unknown word; if none of the words you know suit the sentence well, choose the unknown word (or one of them) and move on.

Word Choice—Try It!

Of the bombardment of big-budget blockbusters released in the wake of the *Star Wars* franchise, many of the films are, in themselves, well-made and thoughtful films, but they have had a cumulative effect of silencing many kinds of voices.

4

A) NO CHANGE
B) extremity
C) superfluousness
D) abundance

Questions Without Questions Practice Set

Jethro Tull: The Best Band You're Not Listening To!

Although many critics argue that other groups, such as the Rolling Stones and the Beatles, are more influential than "the Tull," 1 however, there can be no debate that the band's lyrics are 2 superior to those of all others, even those of the Stones and the Beatles. 3 The poetry of songwriter and lyricist Ian Anderson is in an entirely different realm of literary merit than the 4 mean verse composed as accompaniment to the repetitive and catchy tunes of most bands.

5 Thus, instead of relying on a repeated chorus and fragmentary expressions of sentiment, Anderson's lyrics are always full of allusions, layered ironies, and complex themes, all of which 6 challenge listeners as much as the finest lyrical poetry that has ever been written in English.

1
A) NO CHANGE
B) furthermore,
C) consequently,
D) DELETE the underlined portion

2
A) NO CHANGE
B) better even than those other, more influential bands, the Stones and the Beatles.
C) better than any other band's, even bands more popular than they are.
D) the best.

3
A) NO CHANGE
B) Therefore, the
C) Inevitably, the
D) Actually, the

4
A) NO CHANGE
B) sinister
C) simple
D) base

5
A) NO CHANGE
B) Rather than
C) Indeed, just
D) Theretofore, not

6
A) NO CHANGE
B) multivalently engage every auditor
C) mess with audiences
D) bug people

7 Nonetheless, any song the band wrote could be cited as **8** a useful illustration of the poetic power of the band's **9** lyrics, for a popular song like the classic "Thick as a Brick" will suffice. It criticizes **10** the insipid ignorance and thoughtlessness of the mass of modern people for being neither thoughtful about their own lives nor knowledgeable about the world around them. Creating a timeless **11** image, Anderson alludes to classical mythology: "Believe in the day! / The Dawn Creation of the Kings has begun / Soft Venus (lonely maiden) brings the ageless one."

7
A) NO CHANGE
B) However, every
C) Any
D) In any case, a

8
A) NO CHANGE
B) an adept picture
C) an illustrious incident
D) a pictorial instance

9
A) NO CHANGE
B) lyrics; thus,
C) lyrics, yet
D) lyrics; moreover,

10
A) NO CHANGE
B) the oblivious foolery of
C) the silly and obnoxious stupidity of
D) DELETE the underlined portion

11
A) NO CHANGE
B) illusion,
C) morality,
D) mirage,

[12] Therefore, turning to the mundane reality of contemporary existence, Anderson finds that "Cats are on the upgrade / Upgrade? Hipgrave. Oh, Mac." No sensitive listener can fail to recognize his or her own culpability in the contrast, confirming Anderson's contention that his listeners are "Thick as a Brick" even as they are woken from their [13] tripping foolhardiness by the song's call to "rise up from the pages of … comic-books."

[14] Additionally, with the band's combination of instrumental virtuosity and lyrical brilliance, few rock groups in history can approach the genius of Jethro Tull in either one of these [15] spaces. Their star burned too brightly to burn long, but no star before or since has burned brighter.

12
A) NO CHANGE
B) In contrast,
C) For example,
D) Still

13
A) NO CHANGE
B) somnolent obviousness
C) worn-out dumbness
D) sleep of ignorance

14
A) NO CHANGE
B) Nonetheless,
C) In conclusion,
D) However,

15
A) NO CHANGE
B) areas.
C) regions.
D) ranges.

Writer's Intention Questions

These questions have text prompts that ask you to accomplish a specific objective with the underlined text. For example, you may be asked to make things more concise, or you may be asked to make the phrase more vivid and detailed, or you may be asked to reiterate the main point of the passage. There is a wide range of questions you may be asked, but you always need to pay close attention to exactly what the question asks for.

Read over the question carefully and underline the key words that will allow you to choose the correct answer. Remember: *All of the answers will be grammatically correct, and many of them could be considered "good writing" based on the overall context, but only one choice will accomplish the question's objective.*

For example:

1. Which choice provides the most relevant detail?

    You want to underline the words "relevant detail" and then look over the answers and evaluate each *only* in terms of whether it provides a relevant detail. Only one answer will, and that is the correct answer!

2. Which choice best concludes the paragraph by re-stating the author's thesis?

    You might be tempted to underline "concludes the paragraph" as well, which would be fine, but the key to the question is to understand that the conclusion of the paragraph must re-state the author's thesis. In order to answer this question correctly, you must read the entire passage carefully so that you know what the thesis of the passage is.

Writer's Intention Questions — Try It!

However, once the door to paying athletes is opened, it is difficult to predict how the business and competitive aspects of college sports will be affected. Coaches will probably have to be paid less, players will become essentially employees rather than students, and **1** professional teams will continue recruiting from the top programs in the country. But from there, the changes could be even more dramatic.

1

Which choice best emphasizes the writer's position that there will be specific changes to college sports?

A) NO CHANGE

B) some teams will be forced to drop out of their leagues.

C) college education will be even more useful for future employment opportunities.

D) many other changes will certainly occur for many schools.

Writer's Intention Practice Set

Home or Office? Home AND Office!

[1] To many people, working from home seems ideal. You don't have to fight traffic to get to the office, you can work in the same clothes you exercise in, and [2] you can make the same amount of money. Although many people find that these benefits do dramatically improve their work life, [3] there are still questions about whether working from home rather than commuting to an office is really better.

1

Which choice provides the best introduction for the tone and content of the essay as a whole?

A) NO CHANGE

B) Everyone loves working from home, because a home office is a worker's paradise.

C) Working from home is a great way to avoid work and still make money.

D) You should try working from home: you'll love it!

2

The writer wants to provide a third apparent benefit of working from home that is similar to those discussed earlier in the sentence. Which choice best accomplishes this?

A) NO CHANGE

B) one can accomplish more in less time.

C) you don't have to follow an office schedule for your work time.

D) workers can still manage their time effectively.

3

The writer wants to end this paragraph by offering a specific outline of the rest of the essay. Which choice best accomplishes this?

A) NO CHANGE

B) other people have found drawbacks.

C) lots of employers don't like having employees work from home.

D) there are issues to resolve in terms of managing employees, collaborating on projects, and maintaining a work–life balance.

4 One perspective that must be considered is the management angle. Technology helps managers to keep track of time for employees working remotely: **5** many managers require employees either to log into a shared "virtual space" when working or to track their own time with online tools. However, some managers have a difficult time effectively assessing the quality of the work-time logged by employees who work from home, because they cannot directly observe workers who are not in the same physical space. Further, the freedom from a 9–5 schedule for many work-from-home employees means that managers may not be available when they are working, and vice versa. **6** Since none of these problems are insurmountable, many offices that allow employees to work from home find that it is still helpful to require employees to come together for at least part of the work week.

Many companies have found ways to work around these common management issues, but collaborative work is another difficulty for a business in which employees work remotely. **7** Again, technological advancements can ease the cumbersome burden of collaborative efforts for employees who need to labor closely together on significant endeavors. Shared drives often allow

4

Which choice provides the most appropriate introduction to the main idea of this paragraph?

A) NO CHANGE

B) Managing remote employees is one of the unique challenges for offices with work-from-home employees.

C) Let us address the first challenging aspect of working from home: technology.

D) Managers hate having employees who work from home.

5

Which choice most logically completes the sentence with supporting details?

A) NO CHANGE

B) employees sometimes have to track their own time, which makes managers' jobs easier.

C) technology is a distraction for some workers, however, and so is also risky for companies.

D) some employees do not use technology in their work.

6

Which choice most effectively sets up the information that follows?

A) NO CHANGE

B) In order to try to address these kinds of issues,

C) Thus, requiring employees to work from a shared office space for some time is common, so

D) Nonetheless, if employees are able to,

7

Which choice best maintains the tone and style of the rest of the passage?

A) NO CHANGE

B) However, technology can connect remote workers who need to work collaboratively.

C) Tech to the rescue again!

D) For workers who insist on working from home, technology can help approximate, but never replace, working in the same office.

workers to access and edit documents simultaneously and [8] live video chatting allows employees miles—even thousands of miles—apart to work closely together. However, John McClane, an editor at a political magazine that creates articles and features [9] often authored by teams of 10-15 people, claims, "There is simply no replacement for having my colleagues across the hall from me. Not only is there palpable excitement in our office space as we work together, but there are also constant exchanges of creative thoughts and challenging ideas that make every project we do better than it could be if we were not working so closely together." Nonetheless, some companies have found ways to make remote office workers effective parts of team projects, [10] but others have employees work separately on their own major projects.

[8]

Which choice provides a second relevant example of collaborative technology?

A) NO CHANGE

B) workers can still work together at other locations that might be more convenient than their shared office space.

C) employees can plan to meet at regular intervals to compare and combine their work.

D) employees can often use their home computers to access programs needed to complete tasks.

[9]

Which choice provides the most relevant detail?

A) NO CHANGE

B) that present both sides of political issues,

C) commonly involving graphic representation of data,

D) that require great skill to craft,

[10]

The writer wants to close the paragraph by suggesting that face-to-face meetings are still valuable for collaborative work. Which choice best accomplishes this?

A) NO CHANGE

B) so face-face meetings are eliminated and time is saved for all employees.

C) and others do not need to have employees work together in person.

D) but many require employees to come together for critical parts of major projects.

Although these kinds of issues are commonly acknowledged as problems of working from home, many home-office workers are finding that, along with personal benefits, there are serious drawbacks. [11] Many employees find that their work is not as effective or efficient when they work from home. Though managers might fear that people working from home may not really be working, most employees find that they actually work more hours than they used to, because it is so "convenient" to work. For example, architect Richard Thornburg, who has worked remotely for four years after working from an office space for over a decade, found that he missed the feeling of leaving the office for the day, [12] so that every day seemed the same. To try to create a clear boundary between work and his own life, Thornburg explains that he has taken to [13] frequenting local coffee shops and libraries that offer private work spaces. Thornburg affirms that he feels "pretty zen" about finding a definite work space and time without "going bananas every day during rush hour."

As new technologies create new possibilities for work arrangements, both employers and employees will have to continue [14] to balance efficiency, teamwork, and productivity with convenience and personal priorities.

11

Which choice best sets up the examples that follow?

A) NO CHANGE

B) The same technologies that enable remote work also mean that employees never leave the office, because they are always connected through their computers and phones, so many feel they are never "done for the day."

C) One major concern for managers is the fact that they cannot directly observe their employees working, so many employees "pad" their work time.

D) These drawbacks are sometimes even more serious than employees realize when they first work from home instead of a shared office space.

12

Which choice best completes the sentence with an explanation that supports the main idea of the paragraph?

A) NO CHANGE

B) and the relaxing hour of time spent riding public transportation home.

C) which gave him a clear division between work time and personal time.

D) a feeling he missed when working from home.

13

Which choice best completes the sentence with a specific supporting detail?

A) NO CHANGE

B) waking up early to jog before work starts.

C) doing whatever he can to improve his work.

D) meeting with friends at bakeries and cafes.

14

Which choice best concludes the essay by summarizing the ideas about working from home?

A) NO CHANGE

B) to work from a shared office space.

C) to make special exceptions and arrangements in order for remote working to succeed.

D) to try harder if they want to work from home.

Add/Delete Questions

On the SAT Writing and Language test, you will also encounter questions that ask you if you should add or delete a clause or sentence from the passage. The four answer choices will provide you with "yes" or "no" answers followed by reasons for adding or deleting that portion.

Add

When faced with questions asking about adding a sentence or phrase, your primary question should be: "Is the part that we're adding relevant?" If it's irrelevant, adding something off-topic or redundant, you should not choose to add it and immediately cross off the "yes" answer choices. On the other hand, if it adds clarification of something that would otherwise be confusing or adds a new detail to support the main purpose of the paragraph, it should be added, and you can cross out both "no" answer choices. Usually, if you can make the decision about whether the element should be added to the passage or not, the justification for that answer is easy to choose, because often only one is even true or relevant to the sentence in question.

Add—Try It!

When the fresh sound of the Beatles took the world by storm, Jethro Tull began as just one among many of the British bands to rise to prominence. [1] The band released its first LP in 1968, but the record, influenced primarily by the blues roots of guitarist Mick Abrahams, would be almost unrecognizable to the band's later flocks of frenzied fans who came to love the flute-centered progressive rock of their monstrous hits "Aqualung" and "Thick As a Brick."

[1]

At this point, the writer is considering adding the following sentence:

> Other groups that became popular at the same time were the Rolling Stones, the Who, and the Kinks, while Herman's Hermits fell from favor, sounding old-fashioned and boring compared to the new sound produced by the Beatles and other new bands.

Should the writer make that addition here?

A) Yes, because it shows that the writer has a broad knowledge of the music of the period being discussed.

B) Yes, because it effectively introduces the ideas the reader needs to understand the importance of the following sentence.

C) No, because it shifts the focus from Jethro Tull to other bands who are less important to the passage.

D) No, because the information is implied in the previous sentence.

Delete

Similarly, when faced with questions asking whether to keep or delete a sentence or phrase, you want to consider relevance and redundancy as the keys to choosing the correct answer. Again, if the material is off-topic or redundant, cross out the "Kept" options, and choose the best explanation of the reason to delete. Be careful—often the information that makes the added element redundant comes after the underlined portion. On the other hand, if the passage would be unclear or confusing without the underlined portion or if it adds relevant support to the main point of the paragraph, cross out the "Delete" options and choose the answer with an accurate explanation of why the underlined part should be kept.

Delete—Try It!

The band released its first LP in 1968, but the record, influenced primarily by the blues roots of guitarist Mick Abrahams, would be almost unrecognizable to the band's later flocks of frenzied fans [2] who came to love the flute-centered progressive rock of their monstrous hits "Aqualung" and "Thick as a Brick." Though the record was successful enough and critically well-received, it wasn't until Abrahams left the band that flautist and vocalist extraordinaire Ian Anderson was able to fully assert himself as a songwriter, a jazz flute virtuoso, and a singer of remarkable range and inventiveness: once Anderson did so, the band became the monolith of rock history it is known as today, producing unforgettable anthems like "Aqualung" and "Thick as a Brick," which are today so much a part of the soundtrack of our lives.

2

The writer is considering deleting the underlined portion (ending the sentence with a period). Should the writer make this change?

A) Yes, because the information in the underlined portion detracts from the paragraph's focus on the change the band went through from its humble origins to its titanic later success.

B) Yes, because the information in the underlined portion is provided elsewhere in the paragraph.

C) No, because the underlined portion provides information necessary to make sense of the following sentence.

D) No, because the underlined portion gives examples that provide context to explain the claim made earlier in the sentence.

Add/Delete Practice Set

The Billy Goat Gives Up the Ghost

In the history of sports, there has been no "curse" on any professional team quite like the championship drought that haunted the Chicago Cubs for over a century. [1] The Boston Red Sox, for instance, had a considerable drought, usually called the "curse of the Bambino," a nickname for Babe Ruth, when they didn't win the World Series for 86 years after trading Babe Ruth to the Yankees. The Cubs won back-to-back World Series championships in 1907 and 1908, and then went on the longest championship drought in the history of professional sports. [2] After these championships in 1907 and 1908, the team went to the World Series several more times in the first half of the twentieth

---

1

The writer is considering deleting the underlined sentence. Should the sentence be kept or deleted?

A) Kept, because it provides necessary context to understand the severity of the Cubs' championship drought.

B) Kept, because it gives a generalization that proves the claim made in the preceding sentence.

C) Deleted, because the information is easily inferred from the rest of the passage.

D) Deleted, because it takes away from the primary focus of the passage.

2

The writer is considering deleting the underlined phrase, adjusting punctuation and capitalization as needed. Should the writer delete this phrase?

A) Yes, because the information is already clear from the preceding sentence.

B) Yes, because it is too positive in its tone to fit with the rest of the sentence.

C) No, because the timeline of events in the paragraph would be unclear without this information.

D) No, because the information is essential to understand the scope of the "curse."

century, but they never won the series. [3] The Cubs were in the World Series and up 2 games to 1 over the Detroit Tigers. Game 4 was held at the Cubs' home stadium, Wrigley Field, and partway through the game, [4] William Sianis, owner of the Billy Goat Tavern, was supposedly asked to leave due to the smell of the goat he took with him to the game. Sianis allegedly responded angrily, declaring, "Them Cubs, dey ain't gonna win no more." The Cubs went on to lose the game. Emboldened by the success of his initial curse, Sianis, [5] his family claims, went on to send the following telegram to the team's owner: "You are going to lose this World Series and you are never going to win another World Series again. You are never going to win a World Series again because you insulted my goat."

Although the veracity of these

3

The writer is considering adding the following sentence here:

The team's luck became even worse in 1945, after an alleged incident that led to what became known as the "curse of the billy goat."

Should the writer add this sentence?

A) Yes, because it explains why the Cubs' curse became known as "the curse of the goat."

B) Yes, because it effectively sets up the information that follows.

C) No, because it contradicts the main idea of the passage.

D) No, because it repeats information provided earlier in the passage.

4

The writer is considering adding the following phrase here:

as the supposed story goes,

Should the writer add this phrase?

A) Yes, because it clarifies that the event is not known for certain.

B) Yes, because otherwise the reader would not know what the story is about.

C) No, because the lack of certainty regarding the event is clear from other parts of the passage.

D) No, because it contradicts information presented elsewhere in the passage.

5

The writer is considering deleting the underlined portion, adjusting the punctuation as needed. Should this clause be kept or deleted?

A) Kept, because it suggests that there is no physical evidence to support the existence of the telegram.

B) Kept, because the telegram's significance to the story would otherwise be unclear.

C) Deleted, because it introduces aspects not relevant to the story as told.

D) Deleted, because it contradicts information presented elsewhere in the passage.

events cannot be confirmed, the "curse of the billy goat" has certainly felt real to many Cubs fans for years. [6] However, the team finally went to the World Series again in 2016 and edged out the Cleveland Indians, [7] who also have been under a curse since their World Series victory in 1948, with the deciding game requiring extra innings to complete. Now, fans can celebrate the end of the longest curse in professional sports—and no goat can stand in their way!

6

The writer is considering adding the following sentence at this point:

> The Cubs were in the playoffs several times since 1945, often even within 1 game of making the World Series, but the team was unable even to get to the World Series for 71 years.

Should the writer make this addition?

A) Yes, because it provides context to explain why fans felt the curse was real.

B) Yes, because it provides a transition needed to understand the following sentence.

C) No, because the information is already clear from the previous sentence.

D) No, because this example contradicts the idea of the team being under a "curse."

7

The writer is considering deleting the underlined phrase. Should the phrase be kept or deleted?

A) Kept, because the phrase provides a relevant example to illustrate the significance of the victory.

B) Kept, because the irony of both teams being cursed is needed to understand the following sentence.

C) Deleted, because it contradicts the central claim of the passage.

D) Deleted, because it introduces unnecessary information.

Ordering Questions

Some questions ask you to reorder words or sentences in order to make the passage more logical and cohesive. When you reorder sentences you should try to think about both logical sequence and flow. Consider where the sentence fits into the greater narrative of the paragraph—is it introducing an idea? Concluding? Providing evidence? Transitioning? Also, consider how the sentence relates to specific parts of the other sentences in the paragraph.

For example, if the sentence in question has a pronoun (**he**, **she**, **you**, **it**...) or demonstrative adjectives (**this**, **that**, **these**, **those**) for which the previous sentence does not provide context, then the sentence in question is probably in the wrong place.

Sometimes it helps to read the paragraph with the sentence in each potential placement to determine what sounds the most natural.

NOTE: Two elements on these questions are often confusing to students—

- First, do not be fooled by the placement of the question—ordering questions within a paragraph are *always* at the end of the paragraph, but can refer to *any* sentence in the paragraph. To make sure you are dealing with the correct sentence, underline the sentence number in the question.
- Second, notice that sentence numbers appear *before* the sentence they identify, so that placing a sentence *after* sentence [2] does *not* mean adding it right after the number [2], but rather adding it after the end of the sentence labeled [2].

Ordering Questions—Try It!

[1] The impact of *Star Wars* on the landscape of the motion picture industry goes far beyond the financial success or critical reception of any one of the films. [2] Before the first *Star Wars* in 1977, the studio system was one in which executives worked primarily with specific directors who had a vision for making a particular kind of film or telling a particular kind of story. [3] Since *Star Wars*, movies have become an increasingly producer-centered medium, with franchise properties featuring reusable actors and replaceable directors making the most money and receiving the most attention from studios. [4] Ironically, the original *Star Wars* film was a typical representative of this system: it was a long shot for 20th Century Fox, the studio that produced it, because it was a film with no big-name stars in an unpopular genre by an unproven director, but Fox's president Alan Ladd was willing to bet on George Lucas' idiosyncratic vision. [5] In the last decades, studios have depended more and more on "tent-pole" movies, so called because they "hold up" the other films financed by the studio; in fact, in 2014, seven of the top ten movies in box office receipts were sequels, prequels, or spin-offs from existing franchises, and two of those "original" film series currently have sequels in production.

1

To make this paragraph most logical, sentence 4 should be placed

A) where it is now.
B) before sentence 1.
C) after sentence 2.
D) after sentence 5.

There are two other basic types of ordering questions:

1   Best place to add new sentence

These questions will provide a new element, usually a complete sentence, and ask where that element would be best added to the passage, usually within a single paragraph. These questions can also come at the end of the passage and provide possible locations throughout the entire passage to place the new sentence. The same strategies that will help you know where to move an existing sentence within a paragraph should be used to determine where to add the new sentence.

2   Best order for paragraphs

These questions will always come at the end of the entire passage, and they will ask about the arrangement of the paragraphs as a whole, rather than that of sentences within a paragraph. You can know that a question of this kind is coming when you see that all the paragraphs are numbered in the passage. Also, if the paragraph is in the wrong place, you will often recognize it as being out of place from the start, which can allow you to eliminate Choice (A) immediately.

To answer these questions, think about the arrangement of the passage as a whole: Is it ordered chronologically? Then place the paragraph in the proper order based on dates referenced in it. Is it ordered by cause and effect? Place the effect paragraph directly after the cause paragraph. Additionally, transition words can provide important contextual clues: If the paragraph begins with **However**, see which paragraph it is providing contrast to. If it begins with **Second**, put it between the paragraph offering the first reason/evidence and that offering the third (or last) reason/evidence.

Ordering Practice Set

Paragraph 1

[1] The scientific and technological developments of the Second Industrial Revolution helped Europeans conquer much of Africa during the 19th and early 20th centuries. [2] Superior weaponry, for example, gave imperial countries a distinct military advantage over native peoples who found it hard to resist in the face of modern rifles, machine guns and long-range artillery. [3] Advances in science and medicine also contributed to European domination. [4] Finally, improvements in transportation technologies facilitated the conquest of inland continental areas. [5] Steamboats allowed Europeans to travel up rivers in the interior of the African continent where once explorers and traders had been confined to coastal areas. [6] The development of quinine, for example, made it possible to penetrate tropical regions without succumbing to malaria and yellow fever. ▨1

1

To make this paragraph most logical, sentence 6 should be placed

A) where it is now.
B) after sentence 2.
C) after sentence 3.
D) after sentence 4.

Paragraph 2

[1] Famine was a major killer in the primarily agricultural countries of Europe during the long 18th century (1670-1820). [2] In Sweden, for example, the death rate doubled from the epidemics and famine following the harvest failures of 1771 and 1772. [3] Poor harvests usually resulted from bad weather—too much rain or a very cold spring—which afflicted all regions at some time. [4] However, the consequences of a bad harvest and whether a poor harvest led to famine varied greatly across the continent. [5] Similarly, Finland lost one third of its population as a result of the famine in 1696-7. [6] In England, by contrast, although agricultural output fell behind population growth for most of the period between 1755-1820, no serious mortality crises occurred after 1729. ▨2

2

To make this paragraph most logical, sentence 2 should be placed

A) where it is now.
B) after sentence 3.
C) after sentence 4.
D) after sentence 5.

Paragraph 3

[1] After herbicide resistance, the second most common application of genetic engineering in agriculture has been to create "insect resistant" crops. [2] To produce these crops, scientists have inserted into corn, canola, and potatoes genes that make the plants poisonous to insects. [3] These "toxic" genes are found in soil bacteria called *Bacillus thuringiensis*. [4] Proponents of genetic engineering argue that *B. thuringiensis* crops will reduce the need for insecticide and, therefore, protect the environment. [5] In addition to killing pests, genetically engineered *B. thuringiensis* crops are lethal to beneficial insects, including ladybugs, butterflies, and honeybees that pollinate crops. [6] However, environmentalists point out that there are negative implications for the environment of these crops. [7] Further, pest insects are also more likely to evolve resistance to the toxin *B. thuringiensis* if they are free to graze on hundreds of acres of crops exuding the toxin. **3**

3

To make this paragraph most logical, sentence 5 should be placed

A) where it is now.
B) after sentence 1.
C) after sentence 6.
D) after sentence 7.

Paragraph 4

[1] Although they have grown significantly in recent years, many cities in Latin America and Asia such as Sao Paulo, Singapore, Bombay, Manila and Jakarta have historical roots. [2] The growth of such centers was not a natural development reflecting modernization in the country but was rather a forced development intended to maximize the profits of imperialist concerns. [3] The colonial city was a hub to which resources from the rest of the country were channeled and in which the colonial administration was concentrated. [4] The consequence of this pattern was extremely uneven growth within the colony as resources and infrastructure were directed to one center, neglecting a large part of the country. **4**

4

The writer wishes to add the following sentence to this paragraph:

> These cities have evolved from colonial outposts that served as way stations for exporting commodities to imperial nations such as Portugal and England.

This sentence should be placed

A) after sentence 1.
B) after sentence 2.
C) after sentence 3.
D) after sentence 4.

Paragraph 5

[1] Wildlife Services is a federal program operated by the U.S. Department of Agriculture. [2] The program undertakes a diverse range of activities including the protection of aircraft and airports from birds and geese, the protection of crops from blackbirds and the protection of dikes from beavers. [3] Many of these activities are uncontroversial and reflect the mission of the program to provide "federal leadership and expertise to resolve wildlife conflicts to allow people and wildlife to coexist." [4] However, a large portion of Wildlife Services' budget goes towards its "livestock protection" program—a program that kills "predators" or animals such as coyotes, wolves, foxes, bears and bobcats that can prey on domestic sheep, goats or cattle. [5] The methods used to kill the animals include setting M-44 traps that eject sodium cyanide into animals' mouths and catching animals in steel leg holds. [6] Critics of the livestock protection program argue that it is not only inhumane but also ineffective. [7] Despite millions of coyotes killed by Wildlife Services over 90 years, the coyote population—the principal target of the program—is not only stable but has spread geographically from a dozen western states in 1913 into every state in the Union except Hawaii.

5

The writer wishes to add the following sentence to this paragraph:

> Independent studies suggest that coyote populations subject to culling produce larger litters, have higher pup survival rates, and breed more resilient and nocturnal individuals.

This sentence should be placed

A) after sentence 3.

B) after sentence 4.

C) after sentence 5.

D) after sentence 6.

Sentence Combining Questions

Some "Writer's Intention" questions will ask you to combine two underlined sentences into one coherent sentence. When encountering these questions you should think about not only how to convey the underlined information most concisely, but also how to best illustrate the relationships between the ideas. As you choose an answer choice consider:

1   Which choice is stated most clearly, directly and briefly? Choose it!
    The shortest answer is almost always correct!

2   What punctuation and transition words help combine the ideas? Remember that all the answers will be correctly combined, so think about the meaning of the choices, not the grammatical correctness!

3   Is all the information included necessary? Don't choose a sentence that is redundant or wordy!

4   Are the verbs active or passive? Active verbs are usually preferred!

Sentence Combining Questions — Try It!

Most voters see voting as a fairly private activity, something they do as a public duty, but not as a public declaration of their values. People are free to make their voting choices based on whatever criteria they choose. Too many voters don't even know what criteria they are using when they vote.

1

Which choice best combines the two underlined sentences?

A) People are free to make their voting choices based on whatever voting criteria they choose; indeed, too many voters don't even know what voting criteria they are using when they vote.

B) Though free to vote based on any criteria, too many voters don't even know what criteria they are using when they vote.

C) Voting choices can be made by people based on any criteria they choose, and too many voters don't even know what criteria they are using when they vote.

D) People who are allowed to be free to make their voting choices based on whatever criteria they choose sometimes don't even know what criteria they are using when they vote.

Sentence Combining Practice Set

[1] Jeremy decided to cut back on French fries and hamburgers. This followed his coronary bypass surgery.

Which choice most effectively combines the underlined sentences?

A) Jeremy decided to cut back on French fries and hamburgers, a decision he made that followed his coronary bypass surgery.

B) Following his coronary bypass surgery, Jeremy decided to cut back on French fries and hamburgers.

C) Jeremy decided to cut back on French fries and hamburgers, and this decision followed his coronary bypass surgery.

D) Jeremy decided to cut back on French fries and hamburgers, which followed his coronary bypass surgery.

[2] Bilingual children are more adept at solving mental puzzles than monolingual children. This finding was documented in a 2004 study by Ellen Bialystok and Michelle Martin-Rhee.

Which choice most effectively combines the sentences at the underlined portion?

A) monolingual children as documented

B) monolingual children, and this finding was documented

C) monolingual children, a finding that was documented

D) monolingual children, findings documented

[3] Evidence suggests that in a bilingual child's brain, both language systems are active even when the child is using only one language. In some instances, one language system may obstruct the other. This interference is not so much a handicap as a blessing, providing the child with a powerful cognitive workout.

Which choice most effectively combines the sentences at the underlined portion?

A) the other, so this interference

B) the other: this interference

C) the other, but this interference

D) the other; moreover, this interference

[4] Researchers have also discovered that bilingualism protects individuals against certain diseases of old age. These diseases include Alzheimer's and dementia.

Which choice most effectively combines the underlined sentences?

A) Researchers have also discovered that bilingualism protects individuals against certain diseases of old age, these diseases being Alzheimer's and dementia.

B) Protection against certain diseases of old age, including Alzheimer's and dementia may also be provided by bilingualism it has been discovered by researchers.

C) Researchers have also discovered that bilingualism protects individuals against certain diseases of old age, including Alzheimer's and dementia.

D) Bilingualism protecting individuals against certain diseases of old age, including Alzheimer's and dementia, was found by researchers.

5 | In 1962, labor activist Cesar Chavez organized the United Farmworkers Association. This union was dedicated to increasing the hourly wages and improving the living conditions of farm laborers across the United States.

Which choice most effectively combines the underlined sentences?

A) In 1962, labor activist Cesar Chavez organized the United Farmworkers Association, a union dedicated to increasing the hourly wages and improving the living conditions of farm laborers across the United States.

B) Dedicated to increasing the hourly wages and improving the living conditions of farm laborers across the United States, the United Farmworkers Association was organized by labor activist Cesar Chavez in 1962 to advocate for the rights of farm workers.

C) In 1962, labor activist Cesar Chavez organized the United Farmworkers Association, a union created by Chavez that was dedicated to increasing the hourly wages of farm laborers as well as improving the living conditions of farm laborers across the United States.

D) Increasing the hourly wages and improving the living conditions of farm laborers across the United States was the dedicated task of the United Farmworkers Association, which was organized by labor activist Cesar Chavez in 1962.

6 | In addition to increasing the risk of wildfires in the American West, rising global temperatures are expected to raise sea levels. Raised sea levels will cause coastal flooding on the Eastern seaboard, especially in Florida.

Which choice most effectively combines the underlined sentences?

A) In addition to increasing the risk of wildfires in the American West, rising global temperatures are expected to raise sea levels: the result being an increase in coastal flooding on the Eastern seaboard, especially in Florida.

B) In addition to increasing the risk of wildfires in the American West, rising global temperatures are expected to raise sea levels, which will lead to coastal flooding on the Eastern seaboard, especially in Florida.

C) In addition to increasing the risk of wildfires in the American West, rising global temperatures are expected to raise sea levels, and raised sea levels caused by high global temperatures will lead to coastal flooding on the Eastern seaboard, especially in Florida.

D) In addition to increasing the risk of wildfires in the American West, rising global temperatures are expected to raise sea levels; the raised sea levels caused by high global temperatures will lead to coastal flooding on the Eastern seaboard, especially in Florida.

7 | After much deliberation, Henry made his decision. He would ask Julia to marry him.

Which choice most effectively combines the underlined sentences?

A) After much deliberation, Henry made his decision: he decided that he would ask Julia to marry him.

B) After much deliberation, Henry made his decision, and he decided that he would ask Julia to marry him.

C) After much deliberation, Henry made his decision, his decision being that he would ask Julia to marry him.

D) After much deliberation, Henry made his decision: he would ask Julia to marry him.

[8] Following the Second World War, the United States and the Soviet Union entered into a "Cold War." <u>By 1946, the Soviets had occupied much of Central and Eastern Europe. Establishing a sphere of influence in Central and Eastern Europe which they had no intention of relinquishing.</u>

Which choice most effectively combines the underlined sentences?

A) By 1946, the Soviets had occupied much of Central and Eastern Europe, and they established a sphere of influence in this territory which they had no intention of relinquishing.

B) By 1946, the Soviets had occupied much of Central and Eastern Europe, establishing a sphere of influence which they had no intention of relinquishing.

C) By 1946, the Soviet Union had established a sphere of influence in Central and Eastern Europe which territory they had occupied and had no intention of relinquishing.

D) Establishing a sphere of influence, the Soviet Union had occupied much of Central and Eastern Europe by 1946 and had no intention of relinquishing their sphere of influence.

[9] <u>The United States was eager to stem the tide of communism. It bolstered the economies of Western Europe through the Marshall Plan and provided financial and military aid to both Greece and Turkey in 1947.</u>

Which choice most effectively combines the underlined sentences?

A) The United States bolstered the economies of Western Europe through the Marshall Plan and was eager to stem the tide of communism and provided financial and military aid to both Greece and Turkey in 1947.

B) Eager to stem the tide of communism, the United States bolstered the economies of Western Europe through the Marshall Plan and provided financial and military aid to both Greece and Turkey in 1947.

C) Bolstering the economies of Western Europe through the Marshall Plan, the United States was eager to stem the tide of communism and provided financial and military aid to both Greece and Turkey in 1947.

D) The United States was eager to stem the tide of communism, which bolstered the economies of Western Europe through the Marshall Plan and provided financial and military aid to both Greece and Turkey in 1947.

Figure-Based Questions

You will also encounter questions that ask you to extrapolate or identify basic information from graphs, charts, or other types of figures in relation to the passage. These questions will usually ask you to use the data in the figure to revise an underlined portion of the text. For these questions, try to understand the general trends in the figure and the relationship between the points being made in the passage and the information in the figure. Oftentimes, some of the answer choices are inaccurate based on what is in the figure; however, some answers may be accurate but not relevant to the point being made, so be sure to consider the context of the passage in answering.

Figure-Based Questions—Try It!

Studios continue to push to make more and more big-budget "event" movies. While it may certainly be true that these franchise movies make money for studios and enable them to produce small-budget films, the overall attendance at the movies **1** has decreased significantly each year since 1980. Thus, studios should reconsider their heavy investment in franchise properties.

1

Which choice best illustrates the information in the figure and makes the point of the sentence clear?

A) NO CHANGE
B) has steadily declined since 2000.
C) has gone up nearly 300 million since 1980.
D) has fluctuated wildly over the past 35 years.

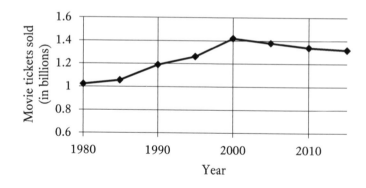

Figure-Based Questions Practice Set

Montgomery County Population Density Zones				
Zone	Definition	Est. Pop.	Pop. %	Sq. Mileage
Rural	<1000/sq. mi.	121,392	11.38	302.2
Suburban	1000-2000/sq. mi.	90,547	8.49	45.2
Urban	2000-3000/sq. mi.	87,251	8.18	32.49
Metropolitan	3000+/sq. mi.	767,627	71.95	127.68

Because of the close proximity of very different types of geographical locations, from vast stretches of undevelopable land to super-densely populated regions, population data are frequently misleading, as is illustrated by population data for Maryland's Montgomery County. For the entire county, the population density is just over 2,000 people per square mile, **1** which classifies the county as a whole as "urban." However, **2** almost a third of the area of the county is actually classified as "rural," but this land accounts for only about one ninth of the total population. Thus, the county is both more rural and more metropolitan than the density of the county as a whole suggests.

1

Based on the table, which of the following accurately characterizes the density of the county as a whole?

A) NO CHANGE

B) which makes the county predominantly a "rural" region.

C) indicating that the county is a "metropolitan" area.

D) which makes all of the county seem to be a "suburban" region.

2

Which choice best supports the point of the paragraph and accurately reflects the data in the table?

A) NO CHANGE

B) over half of the county's total square mileage is classified as "suburban,"

C) the vast majority of the county is considered "urban,"

D) more than half of the county's area is classified as "rural,"

TRAINING PROCESS

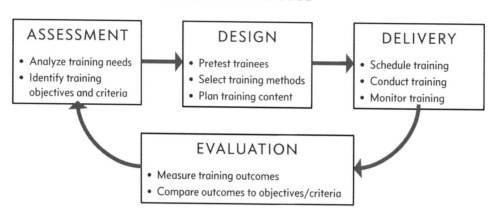

According to Jimenez and Alexander, businesses should develop a training process that is recursive, [3] starting by designing training and then checking how well it works. [4]

3

Which choice most accurately reflects the information in the figure and completes the idea of the sentence?

A) NO CHANGE

B) moving through a rigid procedure that starts with assessment, moves to design and delivery, then concludes with evaluation.

C) starting by assessing their needs, then designing and delivering training, and then evaluating the entire process in order to repeat it with additional training.

D) starting by evaluating the effectiveness of a training, then designing and delivering the training, and finally assessing the needs met by the training before beginning the process over again.

4

Which of the following is most accurate about the process described in the figure?

A) It can begin and end anywhere.

B) It can go forward or backward.

C) It is a process that is intended to be started and finished at the same point.

D) It is a process that is intended to be repeated indefinitely.

Standard English Conventions

Glossary of Grammatical Terms

In order to succeed on the SAT Writing and Language Test, you may need to refresh your memory (or learn for the first time!) about some basic terms and definitions for English grammar. While these terms are not directly tested on the test, knowing them can help you to understand the rules that follow.

Parts of Speech

Noun   a person, place, or thing

Stephen took his sisters to the library to check out a set of books.

Singular noun   refers to just one: **book, building, child, Stephen, library**

Plural noun   refers to more than one: **books, sisters, buildings, children**

Collective noun   a singular word that refers to a group: **flock, family, set, team, organization, class**

Pronoun   a word that replaces a noun, called the pronoun's antecedent

Sally woke up early so she would not be late for the interview.

Subject (nominative) pronoun   replaces the subject of a sentence, the noun doing the action

She is on the varsity team.

Object (objective) pronoun   replaces the object of a sentence, the noun receiving the action

Siobhan passed the ball to him.

Verb   a word indicating an action or suggesting a state of being, paired with a subject or subjects in a sentence

Before Sahim runs outside each morning, he is barely awake.

Adjective   a word that modifies a noun

The mangy, scrappy dog likes to run around the tall, stately oak tree.

Adverb   a word that modifies a verb, adjective, or other adverb

Though he had performed extremely well on the test, Ian sheepishly raised his hand.

Preposition   a word that precedes a noun or pronoun, called its object, and relates it to the rest of the sentence

In the summer, Lisa and Gisi hike along a piece of the Appalachian trail with their friends, Lou and Aditya.

Conjunction   a connecting word that joins two parts of a sentence

After you and Pooja join, our team will have five players, but we are still looking for more people.

Coordinating conjunction   used to join together two grammatically equal elements in a sentence, such as two nouns, two phrases, or two independent clauses. There are seven coordinating conjunctions: **for, and, nor, but, or, yet**, and **so** (a.k.a. FANBOYS). These are the *only* coordinating conjunctions!

I grew up in Denmark, and I still have many friends and relatives there.

Subordinating conjunction   used to join an independent and dependent clause. These include **after, although, as, because, before, if, since, so that, though, unless, until, when, whenever** and many more.

I will speak with my friend when I get back from my vacation so that we can spend time together.

Parts of a Sentence

Subject   the noun or pronoun that is doing the action of the sentence, the noun the sentence is about.

<u>Jane</u> recently decided <u>she</u> would spend her junior year studying in Paris.

Verb   the word or group of words that expresses the action of the sentence. Always paired with a subject, the verb indicates what the subject is doing or what is being done to the subject. Not all "action words" are the **verb** of a clause!

The barking dog <u>runs</u> around the park.

The scurrying mouse <u>was chased</u> by the cat.

Clause   a group of words that contains a subject and a verb. Every sentence must contain at least one independent clause, but many sentences in the passages that make up the Writing and Language Test have multiple clauses.

Independent clause   a clause that can be a sentence on its own. Independent clauses can be joined to a dependent clause or another independent clause.

Though Nick was running late for his flight, <u>he stopped for breakfast anyway</u>.

<u>I often relax after dinner and consider the importance of proper use of em-dashes</u>.

Subordinate/dependent clause   part of a sentence that contains a subject and verb but is not capable of being a sentence in its own right. These can come before or after an independent clause, or they even can be inserted into the middle of another clause, enclosed by paired **commas** or **dashes**.

<u>Because it's nice out</u>, my roommate and I are having dinner on the roof.

Mondays, <u>which are the days I usually have physics tests</u>, are my least favorite.

Phrase   a group of words without a subject or a verb. There are many different types of phrases in the English grammatical system, but there are two types that are essential to know for the purpose of the SAT.

Prepositional phrase   a group of words that begins with a preposition and ends with a noun.

<u>In my opinion</u>, summer vacation is best spent relaxing <u>on the beach</u> or hiking <u>in the mountains</u>.

Appositive phrase   a noun phrase that does not contain a verb and renames or explains another noun. Like some dependent clauses, a nonessential appositive can be inserted into an independent clause by placing a pair of commas or dashes around it.

Wednesdays—<u>often the busiest day of the week</u>—have been very quiet lately.

Henry, <u>my older brother's oldest child</u>, is an exceptionally precocious boy.

Sentence Structure and Punctuation

The SAT Writing and Language Test has more questions about sentence structure than any other aspect of grammar. Often, these questions appear to be about punctuation, but the best way to get them correct consistently is not to memorize a list of rules about punctuation, but to understand the structure of the sentence. There are two essential errors regarding sentence structure tested on the SAT:

1 **Fragment**   any group of words that does not contain an independent clause but is punctuated as a complete sentence. Questions dealing with fragments on the SAT often do not involve punctuation, so they can be tricky to recognize. Consider the following example:

Example 1   The people <u>not minding much because</u> they were anxious to leave before the storm started anyway.

  A) NO CHANGE

  B) didn't mind much because

  C) not minding as much since

  D) not minding too much as

This question is tricky, because most of the changes in the answer choices are irrelevant distractions. Only (B) is correct, because only (B) makes the first part of the sentence an independent clause, and thus makes the sentence *not* a fragment. To catch this error on the test, *always* read at least to the end of the sentence: you will almost always be able to "hear" that it is not a complete sentence.

2 **Run-on sentence (comma splice)**   a sentence with more than one **independent clause** combined with only a comma. This error can be corrected in several different ways, and the SAT will often make you recognize each of these in the course of a test, though you will never have to choose between them, because they are all correct! Consider these examples of comma splices:

Incorrect   We know how good we <u>are, we are</u> sure to win.

   There are many surprising people in the <u>world, some of them live</u> right under our noses.

These comma splices can be corrected any of the following ways:

2.1 IC [, FANBOYS] IC.

This is probably the most commonly used way to combine independent clauses. Coordinating conjunctions are *only* the words **for**, **and**, **nor**, **but**, **or**, **yet**, and **so**, and so you can memorize them as FANBOYS. Note that a **comma** is the *only* punctuation mark to use with a **coordinating conjunction**, and that the part both before and after the conjunction *must* both be independent clauses.

Correct   We know how good we <u>are, so we are</u> sure to win.

   There are many surprising people in the <u>world, and some of them live</u> right under our noses.

Incorrect   We know how good we <u>are, thus we are</u> sure to win.

   There are many surprising people in the <u>world; so some of them live</u> right under our noses.

2.2 IC [;] IC. Often in the form IC [; *conjunctive adverb,*] IC.

A semicolon functions just like a period and a capital letter between clauses, so if you can read what is before and after the semicolon as a sensible complete sentence, then the semicolon is correct. Often, semicolons are used with **conjunctive adverbs**, such as **thus**, **therefore**, **however**, and many more, which come directly after the semicolon and are followed by a comma.

Correct   We know how good we <u>are; thus, we are</u> sure to win.

There are many surprising people in the <u>world; some of them live</u> right under our noses.

NOTE: Conjunctive adverbs do *not* necessarily have to be preceded by a semi-colon; therefore, if the conjunctive adverb is *not* between two independent clauses, simply punctuate with a comma both before and after.

Correct   We <u>know, however,</u> how good we are, and we <u>are, thus,</u> sure to win.

Incorrect   We <u>know; however,</u> how good we are, and we <u>are; thus,</u> sure to win.

2.3 IC [:] IC.

The use of a colon between two independent clauses is not very common, but it comes up often on the SAT, so be sure to know it. Usually, the colon can only be used when the two clauses are very closely related, such as the second explaining or providing an example of the first.

However, you will *not* be asked to judge whether the colon is appropriate based on the relationship between the two clauses, because that decision is somewhat subjective.

Correct   We know how good we <u>are: we are</u> sure to win.

2.4 IC [—] IC.

The dash can be used between independent clauses when there is a strong break between the ideas of the two clauses or whenever a colon could be used. Again, you will never be asked to judge whether the dash is appropriate based on the relationship between the two clauses.

Correct   There are many surprising people in the <u>world—some of them live</u> right under our noses.

2.5 IC [.] IC.

Any two independent clauses can also be split into two complete sentences.

Correct   We know how good we <u>are. We are</u> sure to win.

2.6 IC.

Another way the SAT will frequently correct a comma splice is to turn the original two independent clauses into a single clause by combining the verbs. When combining two verbs or two subjects, rather than two clauses, with the word **and**, no comma is needed.

Correct   We know how good we <u>are and are</u> sure to win.

Incorrect   We know how good we <u>are, and are</u> sure to win.

2.7 IC, DC.

The SAT also often corrects comma splices by turning the second clause into a dependent clause, which makes the comma correct.

Correct   We know how good we <u>are, which makes us</u> sure to win.

There are many surprising people in the <u>world, some of whom live</u> right under our noses.

3   **Complex sentences** are those that contain at least one independent clause and one dependent clause. A sentence that starts with a dependent clause and ends with an independent clause always has a **comma** (and no other punctuation) between the two clauses. Some questions on the SAT will make you choose the correct punctuation in this instance, while others will make you change part of the sentence to make existing punctuation correct; therefore, always be sure to read all the way through the sentence!

     Correct   As I grow <u>older, I</u> begin to see things rather differently.

                        <u>Because he was</u> the best goalie we had, Stephen was chosen to start that fateful day.

     Incorrect   As I grow <u>older: I</u> begin to see things rather differently.

                        <u>He was</u> the best goalie we had, Stephen was chosen to start that fateful day.

Sentence Structure and Punctuation — Try It!

Correct all errors in the underlined portions of the following sentences:

1.   Although he was not previously known to be a great <u>speaker; Jonathan</u> impressed the audience with his witty stories.

2.   Jonah ran a mile in six minutes <u>and then he</u> swam a mile in ten minutes.

3.   <u>However, out</u> of control her personal life may <u>be — Crighton</u> never lets it interfere with her professional life.

4.   Dalby is gifted at <u>Math, however,</u> he has a hard time learning vocabulary.

5.   In their desire to win the contract, the firms bid the price too low, thereby <u>they made</u> the project unviable.

6.   Roger won the <u>match, hence,</u> he gets the <u>trophy, it</u> matters little that his opponent was injured.

7.   <u>Because I grew</u> up watching my brothers play basketball; thus, I decided to try out for the high school team.

8.   That I understood the <u>game, did</u> not mean I could <u>play, I</u> spent most of the season on the bench.

9.   Both the <u>people and</u> their dogs were severely <u>traumatized; because</u> the fire at the dog show started so <u>unexpectedly, and</u> spread so quickly.

10.   People have a few different complaints about the use of wind power, the most common <u>of them</u> is that wind turbines are unsightly.

Sentence Structure Practice Set

Choose the best answer for each of the following sentences.

1. Runners can decrease their likelihood of injury by stretching their legs, they can improve their times by controlling their pace and breathing.

   A) NO CHANGE
   B) legs and
   C) legs; and they
   D) legs, and also

2. Though Jethro Tull continues to play tours in which the band has never quite been able to re-capture the brilliance of their seminal work in the early 70s.

   A) NO CHANGE
   B) tours, despite which the band have
   C) tours; however, the band has
   D) tours, the band has

3. The invention of the modern printing press in Europe is attributed to Johannes Gutenburg, a fifteenth-century publisher. Developing the technology of moveable type in his workshop.

   A) NO CHANGE
   B) publisher, he developed
   C) publisher developed
   D) publisher who developed

4. Fossil fuel combustion contributes to atmospheric levels of nitrogen oxides, some of them cause smog and acid rain.

   A) NO CHANGE
   B) nitrogen oxides
   C) of which
   D) DELETE the underlined portion

5. That the store is currently having a sale on gardening tools which makes now the best time to purchase.

   A) NO CHANGE
   B) that
   C) and
   D) DELETE the underlined portion

6. Temperate grasslands, which cover huge areas, are found in both temperate and tropical regions, they are characterized by low total annual rainfall.

   A) NO CHANGE
   B) regions and
   C) regions; and
   D) regions they

7. Because I am a fan of Bill Murray I am going to see the special showing of his best movie, *Groundhog Day*, at the independent theater down the street.

   A) NO CHANGE
   B) Murray; I am going to see the special showing of his best movie,
   C) Murray, I am going to see the special showing of his best movie
   D) Murray, I am going to see the special showing of his best movie,

8 Recently, many people seeking a career in business find that their writing skills are essential to their success.

A) NO CHANGE
B) people seek a career in business
C) people sought a career in business
D) people, seeking a career in business

9 Heart rate, blood pressure, and overall physical fitness, not to mention intangible aspects like personal fulfillment, all of which have been shown to be negatively correlated with stress levels.

A) NO CHANGE
B) they all
C) all
D) each of which

10 A government taxation plan that benefits those with the greatest means in order to enable them to grow wealth that will "trickle down" and benefit those with less means; "Trickle-down economics" has been a part of the economic discussion in the United States for almost 100 years.

A) NO CHANGE
B) less means—
C) less means,
D) less means

11 The damage was more extensive than Martinez had imagined: upon receiving the news of the blackouts, she immediately sprang into action.

A) NO CHANGE
B) blackouts and immediately springing into action.
C) blackouts, and immediately sprang into action.
D) blackouts. She immediately sprang into action.

12 It is not hard to understand why many Americans feel the need to drive their own cars rather than use public transit—because many people live a great distance from their places of work, many jobs require people to go to multiple locations during the course of their work day, and some public transit systems in the US are not very dependable.

A) NO CHANGE
B) transit: many people
C) transit, many people
D) transit; since many people

13 Many people did not realize what the impact of the decision would be, but some being more forward thinking and immediately recognized the likely effects and acted accordingly.

A) NO CHANGE
B) some
C) some of them
D) some were

[14] To improve the gas economy of their <u>vehicles;</u> most car companies have turned to hybrid automobiles.

A) NO CHANGE
B) vehicles,
C) vehicles:
D) vehicles—

[15] The Velvet Underground's last record evinces less experimentation than any of their earlier <u>albums, however, it</u> was the most radio-friendly and produced several of Lou Reed's most memorable tunes.

A) NO CHANGE
B) albums, but it
C) albums, nonetheless, it
D) albums; but it

[16] In fact, recent studies <u>indicate that, more</u> people spend more time working now than at any previous time in history.

A) NO CHANGE
B) indicate, that more
C) indicate that more
D) indicate that, "more

[17] Therefore, many studios desire to create not only franchises but also "shared cinematic <u>universes," they allow</u> multiple movies each year to cross over with each other in terms of plot and character, creating a constant flood of marketing for each new film.

A) NO CHANGE
B) universes;" of which they allow
C) universes," these allow
D) universes," which allow

[18] Charlie Chaplin, an impressive all-around <u>entertainer, who</u> found the transition from silent film to "talkies" surprisingly difficult.

A) NO CHANGE
B) entertainer,
C) entertainer, he found
D) entertainer; he found

[19] However, the <u>brothers found that</u> their unique blend of atmosphere and cuisine was not easily mass-produced, a development that they were unprepared for after their initial successes.

A) NO CHANGE
B) brothers, finding that
C) brothers, having found
D) brothers found, and that

[20] Caesar's writing in *The Gallic Wars*, though it may not have been high <u>art; it</u> has been a boon for the study of both Latin and history.

A) NO CHANGE
B) art, it
C) art,
D) art. It

Punctuation: Essential and Nonessential Elements

A second aspect of punctuation tested on the SAT is punctuating essential and nonessential elements. Nonessential elements require punctuation, while essential ones require none. In order to distinguish between essential and nonessential elements of a sentence—whether a single word, a phrase, or an entire clause—ask yourself the following question:

> *"If I leave out the element, does the essential meaning of the sentence change?"*

If yes, the element is essential; if no, it is nonessential!

Sometimes, determining whether an element is essential or nonessential may appear subjective: if it is truly ambiguous whether an element is nonessential, the test will *never* give a correctly punctuated essential and nonessential version in the answer choices. Often, simply recognizing where the element in question begins and ends is enough to rule out *all* incorrect answers.

Here are a few basic rules regarding punctuation of essential and non-essential elements:

1   **Essential elements** should *not* be set off by commas.

    Correct   The movie that makes the most money each year is rarely the year's best movie.

    In this sentence the dependent clause "that makes the most money" is essential. The clause is essential because it is needed for the sentence to be logical. Thus, no punctuation is used to set the clause apart.

2   **Nonessential elements** are surrounded by a pair of commas or dashes if they appear in the middle of a clause. If the nonessential element is at the beginning of the sentence, it will be followed by a single comma, and if it is at the end of the sentence, it will be preceded by a single comma.

    Correct   *Rogue One*, which made the most money last year, was not the year's best movie.

    In contrast to the example in 1, the dependent clause "which made the most money last year" is nonessential, despite being very similar to the previous example. Because the sentence has already identified the specific movie, the clause is not essential to understand the sentence. Thus, the clause must be set apart from the rest of the sentence.

    NOTE: Nonessential phrases and clauses can also be set off by parentheses. When parentheses are used, they are always a pair, and all other punctuation remains as it would be if the parentheses and what is within them were not present.

    Correct   His favorite movie (though not one he recommends to many) is *Dogma*.

    Incorrect   His favorite movie, (though not one he recommends to many), is *Dogma*.

3   **That** introduces an essential clause, which does not need to be set off by commas, whereas **which** usually introduces a clause that is non-essential, which requires commas. The words **who, whom,** and **whose** can also be used to introduce clauses, but these clauses can be essential or non-essential.

    Correct   Jokes <u>that are made at the expense of others</u> are not amusing.

                Those comments, <u>which hurt Jake more than he is willing to say</u>, should never have been made.

                I love someone <u>who is not in love with me</u>, but he loves Jenny, <u>who is in love with him</u>.

4   **Participial** (verb form used as an adjective) **phrases** require commas if they are nonessential. Typically, participles identifying which person or thing is referred to are essential.

    Correct   Middle management, <u>seeking to save money</u>, laid off 10 percent of the workforce.

                The barista <u>making lattes on the machine</u> used to babysit for my kids.

5 **Appositive** phrases require commas if they are nonessential but should not have commas if they are essential. Typically, appositives that follow a specific named person or thing are non-essential.

Correct   My <u>mother, Marian</u>, called my <u>friend Anya</u> to say that she would be late.

Essential and Nonessential Elements Exercises—Try It!

Correct all errors with commas and dashes in the underlined portions of the sentences.

1. The <u>dog, that bit my child should never</u> have been off her leash.

2. Your mother, a genuinely <u>kind woman gave</u> me a beautiful gift.

3. She is a member of Habitat For <u>Humanity—which receives</u> donations from the general public.

4. Beethoven, who <u>was musically gifted composed</u> 32 piano sonatas.

5. Removing <u>her socks she walked</u> into the ocean.

6. Those running for the <u>presidency who must be at least 35 campaign</u> for months on end.

7. <u>Teasing, that turns into bullying, has</u> become a major issue in schools.

8. The famous <u>musician—Michael</u> Jackson put out numerous instant hit songs.

9. <u>Children, interested in helping others, are</u> more likely to become compassionate adults.

10. Carrying heavy <u>packages—the mailman, tripped</u> on the porch stoop.

11. <u>My sister, Lily coaches</u> a basketball team with three <u>players, who are injured</u>.

12. My favorite pencil <u>sharpener, which I bought online broke</u> down earlier this morning.

Essential and Nonessential Elements Practice Set

Choose the best answer for each of the following.

1. Elvis ordered the peanut butter and banana <u>sandwich; an item that is served</u> at his favorite restaurant.

    A) NO CHANGE
    B) sandwich, an item that is served
    C) sandwich; an item served
    D) sandwich, an item served,

2. The Olympic gymnast Lilia Podkopayeva, who trained for up to eight hours a day, won the all-around <u>medal which is given</u> for the highest overall score in the competition.

    A) NO CHANGE
    B) medal
    C) medal; which is given
    D) medal, which is given,

3. Although it has been removed from many banned book lists, *The Catcher in the Rye, Salinger's famous novel,* remains a controversial work for many.

    A) NO CHANGE
    B) *The Catcher in the Rye* Salinger's famous novel
    C) *The Catcher in the Rye*, Salinger's famous novel
    D) *The Catcher in the Rye*, Salinger's famous novel—

4. Consider the *Harry Potter* film <u>series, for example,</u> after completing films of the original seven novels, the studio announced not a new film but a new series set in the same universe.

    A) NO CHANGE
    B) series—for example—
    C) series, for example;
    D) series; for example—

5. The court's published opinions—satirized in a series of political essays <u>by Hans Dertz—</u> became known as "The Petty Papers."

    A) NO CHANGE
    B) by Hans Dertz,
    C) by Hans Dertz:
    D) by Hans Dertz

6. The best choice to lead the team was clearly visionary <u>artist Teddy Earner whose</u> work had inspired the project in the first place.

    A) NO CHANGE
    B) artist, Teddy Earner whose
    C) artist, Teddy Earner, whose
    D) artist Teddy Earner, whose

7. Except for Leonardo himself, none of the crew knew how to <u>update, or even how to maintain any</u> of the highly advanced machinery they worked with every day.

    A) NO CHANGE
    B) update, or even how to maintain, any
    C) update or, even, how to maintain, any
    D) update—or even how to maintain, any

8 Surprisingly, people who were most successful in the original experiment achieved <u>new scores. That were well</u> above those of subjects who participated only in the second experiment.

A) NO CHANGE
B) new scores and they were well
C) new scores, that were well
D) new scores that were well

9 In the <u>1590s Elizabeth I's status as the "Virgin Queen"</u> was both a patriotic ideal and a practical problem.

A) NO CHANGE
B) 1590s Elizabeth I's status, as the "Virgin Queen,"
C) 1590s, Elizabeth I's status as the "Virgin Queen"
D) 1590s, Elizabeth I's status as the "Virgin Queen,"

10 Nonetheless, though undeniably <u>popular, earning nearly 1 billion dollars worldwide,</u> the film was seen as humorless, cluttered, and even difficult to follow.

A) NO CHANGE
B) popular (earning nearly 1 billion dollars worldwide),
C) popular: earning nearly 1 billion dollars worldwide,
D) popular—earning nearly 1 billion dollars worldwide,

11 Surprisingly, the players typically thought of as the best of the <u>80s;</u> Larry Bird, Julius Erving, and Magic Johnson, just to name a few—did not play on the US Olympic team in the 1980s, but Michael Jordan did.

A) NO CHANGE
B) 80s,
C) 80s
D) 80s—

12 Jeff Tweedy's original band, Uncle Tupelo—which was hailed as St. Louis' 4th <u>best country band in 1993,</u> was much less experimental than Wilco.

A) NO CHANGE
B) best country band, in 1993—
C) best country band in 1993—
D) best country band, in 1993,

Punctuation: Other Uses

While many questions deal with punctuation on the SAT, it is concerned with only a relatively small set of rules, focused on commas, semicolons, colons and dashes. The rules for each regarding sentence structure and essential elements are in the preceding pages, but there are also a few rules based on other uses of each punctuation mark, which are covered here.

Commas

The **comma** (,) is used in many different ways. The following guidelines help in understanding when to use commas.

1   Use commas to separate items in a **list** of three or more items.

> **Correct**   My friends had gathered from places as far away as <u>Denmark, England, Singapore,</u> and South Africa.

The comma before the word **and** is called a serial comma (also known as an Oxford comma). Its use is debated, and it will therefore not be tested on the SAT. However, the SAT seems to prefer its use, so it should not be considered an error when it appears.

1.1   Use a comma between adjectives that each describe the same noun and are not joined by **and** (but could be).

> **Correct**   My friends and I followed the <u>narrow, winding path</u> up to the <u>ancient, deserted castle</u>.

If you can put **and** between the adjectives, there should be a comma between them because each of the adjectives modifies the noun separately. NOTE: You should *never* place a comma between the *last adjective* and the *noun* itself, so you can often check for a comma there first and eliminate several answer choices.

1.2   Do *not* use a comma between **cumulative** adjectives, which build on each other. If you cannot place "and" between two adjectives, you should *not* put a comma between them.

> **Correct**   At the party we ate a <u>delicious red velvet layer</u> cake.

There are no commas in the list of adjectives above because **layer** describes **cake**, **red velvet** describes the **layer cake**, and **delicious** describes the **red velvet layer cake**. You cannot insert **and** between any of the adjectives and have the phrase make sense, so there should be no commas.

2   Do *not* over-punctuate. The SAT sometimes adds extraneous commas—often where you can "hear" a pause—to sentences in order to confuse you. More commas are not always better, so ask yourself: "Why would I *need* a comma here?"

Consider the following sample question.

Example 2   The best thing to do in many <u>situations, is often the difficult, but</u> still correct thing to do.

A)   NO CHANGE
B)   situations is often the difficult, but
C)   situations, is often the difficult but
D)   situations is often the difficult but

This sentence should not have any commas in it, so while we may be tempted by the apparent pauses in answer choices (A), (B), and (C), the correct answer is (D).

Commas—Try It!

Correct any errors in comma use in the underlined portions of each sentence.

1. Bilbao is a <u>fascinating, Spanish town, but</u> we were too tired to enjoy it.

2. <u>Intense, daily, aerobic</u> exercise helps in <u>blood circulation, heart-health and,</u> blood pressure control.

3. Shaun laughed all the <u>way, to the friendly, neighborhood,</u> Capital Plaza Bank.

4. Dan climbed into his <u>dark, blue Corvette, and</u> sank into the <u>new, black, leather</u> seats.

5. Most of us can cook <u>well, but</u> the problem is we don't have the time to cook healthy, <u>unique appetizing, dishes,</u> that would sustain <u>us, and</u> appeal to our sophisticated palates.

Semicolons, Colons, and Dashes

1. The **semicolon** (;) is used to separate major sentence elements that hold equal grammatical rank. For the purposes of the test, the only rule you need to know about the semi-colon is covered in the sentence structure section. When choosing answers, remember that a semicolon is exactly the same as a period and a capital letter: if you see both options in answer choices and nothing else is different, BOTH are WRONG!

2. The **colon** (:) is used to call attention to the words following it. In addition to its use between two independent clauses, you can use a colon after an independent clause to set off a **list**, **definition**, **example**, or a **quotation**. Remember: you cannot use a colon if there is not a complete independent clause to introduce the element that follows the colon.

   Correct   As I approached the farm stand, I noticed the delicious smells wafting <u>my way:</u> peaches, apples, pears, to name but a few.

                  He was almost ready to do what he had always <u>wanted:</u> marry the girl of his dreams.

   Incorrect My friends sat around discussing our favorite opera, which is: *The Marriage of Figaro*.

                  In order to bake my grandmother's favorite cookies tonight, I need to buy items such as: flour, baking soda, eggs, and chocolate chips.

3. The **dash** (—), also known as the **em-dash**, can be used in the place of a **colon**. As noted in punctuating nonessential elements, a pair of dashes can be used to set of a nonessential word, phrase, or clause, but dashes *cannot* be used in place of a comma for any other use.

   Correct   I invited all my friends to the <u>party—</u>Jack, Jill, Hansel, and Gretel.

                  That traitorous <u>rat—Stephen Bartleby—</u>is now afraid to show his face in Chicago.

   Incorrect When people realize that there is nothing <u>wrong—</u>they will change their minds.

                  Many people choose cars as a reflection of their <u>personality—</u>a proof of their status, and an indication of their values.

Semicolons, Colons, and Dashes—Try It!

Correct any errors in semicolon, colon, or dash use in the underlined portions of each sentence.

1. Anthony played the teak wood <u>guitar—as if</u> his life depended upon it.

2. Tinit descended the wooden <u>steps; opened the creaky old door;</u> and stepped into a musty hallway.

3. Katie plans to stay in Chicago because she loves so much about <u>the city; the beach—the architecture—</u>the parks, and the people.

4. There are many reasons teens drink too much <u>soda, such as:</u> advertising, lack of oversight, <u>peer pressure—</u>and more.

5. Washington, DC, the nation's capital, is well known for its <u>monuments; however,</u> some critics bemoan the lack of originality in its <u>architecture; especially</u> when compared to that of <u>cities like:</u> Paris, <u>Vienna—and</u> even New York City in America.

End Marks and Quotation Marks

On rare occasions, the SAT tests other types of punctuation, such as end marks and quotation marks, so it is useful to know some basic rules regarding each.

1. Most questions that include end marks (periods especially) can be treated as sentence structure questions, as discussed in the section on punctuation and sentence structure. However, occasionally, questions will require you to choose between different end marks, such as a question mark or period. Only use a question mark if a sentence directly asks a specific question.

   Incorrect   Many people wondered whether the advent of computers would eradicate the need for typewriters?

   Correct   Many people wondered: would the advent of computers eradicate the need for typewriters?

2. Quotation marks are a particularly difficult type of punctuation for many students, and the rules regarding punctuating quotes are many and confusing. However, there are only a few rules you need to know in order to get these questions correct on the test:

   2.1 Quotation marks *must* be used in pairs, so if an answer option uses a quotation mark and there is not another quotation mark to open or close the quote, then *no* quotation mark is needed. The test *does not* expect you to know whether something is a quote, so simply use the presence or absence of a pair to decide whether to use quotation marks.

   Incorrect   No one really wanted to question his authority, so he ruled <u>"as an almost uncontested tyrant.</u>

   Correct   No one really wanted to question his authority, so he ruled <u>"as an almost uncontested tyrant."</u>

                  No one really wanted to question his authority, so he ruled <u>as an almost uncontested tyrant.</u>

2.2 Quotes do *not* have to be preceded by punctuation unless the sentence would require punctuation without the presence of quotation marks or the quoted material is a full sentence beginning with a capital letter.

Incorrect   In the end, most students felt <u>that, "grades</u> were less important than learning."

Researchers have found that, perhaps <u>unsurprisingly "more</u> income does not equal more savings."

Correct   In the end, most students felt <u>that "grades</u> were less important than learning."

Researchers have found that, perhaps <u>unsurprisingly, "more</u> income does not equal more savings."

2.3 In certain instances, a full sentence quote can be preceded by a comma, while in others it should be preceded by a colon. The test will *not* make you decide which is correct in a given sentence, so either is acceptable for the purpose of the test.

Correct   *The New York Times* <u>has made such an argument:</u> "Nobody knew the scale of the problem until it was too late."

The New York Times <u>commented,</u> "Nobody knew the scale of the problem until it was too late."

End Marks and Quotations Marks — Try It!

Correct any errors in the underlined

1. Celony didn't realize <u>that, "nobody</u> used dot matrix printers anymore, but how could he have <u>known.</u>

2. Steve's ma <u>declared "The</u> important question is whether you have treated each other <u>with respect?"</u>

Punctuation: Other Uses Practice Set

1 As the films progressed, so did the stylized nature of the action: film critic Blan Doss suggests <u>that, "the</u> fight scenes were as elaborately choreographed as a ballet, and they took on an aspect of musicality."

A) NO CHANGE
B) that "the
C) that: "the
D) that—"the

2 The entire gym was <u>decorated with festive, billowing, colorful, streamers,</u> put up by the homecoming committee.

A) A) NO CHANGE
B) decorated with festive, billowing colorful, streamers
C) decorated, with festive, billowing, colorful streamers,
D) decorated with festive, billowing, colorful streamers

3 Throughout their educational careers, students are required to take notes <u>at classes; lectures; and</u> other academic events.

A) NO CHANGE
B) at: classes, lectures, and
C) at classes, lectures, and
D) at: classes, lectures, and,

4 There are many uses for "junk <u>mail," such as:</u> <u>kindling for a fire,</u> identity theft, and paper airplanes.

A) NO CHANGE
B) mail;" such as, kindling for a fire
C) mail," such as kindling for a fire,
D) mail:" such as: kindling for a fire

5 The group believed they had all the necessary <u>players: a visionary leader, a masterful administrator, an economic guru, an engineering genius, and sixteen hardworking salespeople.</u>

A) NO CHANGE
B) players; a visionary leader, a masterful administrator, an economic guru, an engineering genius, and sixteen hardworking salespeople.
C) players—a visionary leader, a masterful administrator, an economic guru, an engineering genius—and sixteen hardworking salespeople.
D) players: a visionary leader—a masterful administrator—an economic guru—an engineering genius, and sixteen hardworking salespeople.

6 The theoretical physicist and cosmologist George Gamov was a developer of a modern explanation for the origin of the <u>universe; the</u> Big-Bang Theory.

A) NO CHANGE
B) universe; which is
C) universe:
D) universe: being

[7] At least since the time of Robert Malthus, critics have asked if the world can reasonably sustain the growth <u>of humanity's total population, and collective consumption.</u>

A) NO CHANGE
B) of humanity's total population and collective consumption?
C) of humanity's total population and collective consumption.
D) of humanity's total population, and collective consumption?

[8] By working together early in their careers as script supervisors on a soap <u>opera, script doctors on several major motion pictures, and show runners on a popular television show—</u> the two developed a cohesive and seamless style that shows in their later work when they had gained full creative control.

A) NO CHANGE
B) opera; script doctors on several major motion pictures; and show runners on a popular television show;
C) opera, script doctors on several major motion pictures, and show runners on a popular television show;
D) opera, script doctors on several major motion pictures, and show runners on a popular television show,

[9] The aristocracy, the merchant <u>class, and even the poorest</u> members of the social order benefited from the change, but the power of the monarch was clearly in decline.

A) NO CHANGE
B) class, and, even the poorest
C) class, and even the poorest,
D) class—even the poorest,

[10] There was only one problem left to <u>solve: how should the powers gained be exercised without returning to tyranny.</u>

A) NO CHANGE
B) solve—how should the powers gained be exercised—without returning to tyranny?
C) solve: how should the powers gained be exercised without returning to tyranny?
D) solve—how should the powers gained be exercised without returning to tyranny.

[11] When he headed into the woods that night, the contents of his backpack made plain his unpreparedness for the harsh realities of a life lived in the <u>wild; three granola bars, an iPod (with a solar charger),</u> a bottle of water, two magazines, and a Superman sleeping bag.

A) NO CHANGE
B) wild—three granola bars, an iPod—with a solar charger;
C) wild. Three granola bars, an iPod (with a solar charger),
D) wild: three granola bars, an iPod (with a solar charger),

[12] They took only the necessities with them for the long trip on the <u>bus, such as: snacks,</u> drinks, and access to Netflix on their phones.

A) NO CHANGE
B) bus, such as snacks,
C) bus: such as, snacks,
D) bus: snacks;

13 At the school's fall festival, families could compete as a team in multiple events—apple bobbing, pumpkin carving and painting, relay sack racing, and face painting.

A) NO CHANGE
B) apple bobbing, pumpkin carving, and painting, relay sack, racing and face painting.
C) apple, bobbing, pumpkin, carving and painting, relay sack, racing, and face, painting.
D) apple bobbing, pumpkin carving and painting; relay sack racing, and face painting.

14 Those at scene described the smoke as, "billowing from the windows as well as holes that had burned through the roof."

A) NO CHANGE
B) as
C) as:
D) as—

15 Jack Kirby became known for his highly stylized, over-muscled, blocky, figures, surrounded by cluttered geometric shapes, all rendered in primary colors.

A) NO CHANGE
B) highly, stylized, over-muscled, blocky figures surrounded by cluttered geometric shapes; all
C) highly stylized, over-muscled, blocky figures surrounded by cluttered geometric shapes, all
D) highly stylized, over-muscled, blocky, figures surrounded by cluttered, geometric shapes, all

Verb Usage

Verbs that are paired with subjects are called "finite" verbs, or main verbs, because they change their form based on the subject, tense, and mood of the sentence. You can usually recognize a question on verb usage by seeing various forms of a verb in the answer options.

Subject-Verb Agreement

In present tense verbs and all tenses of the verb *to be*, the verb must agree with the subject in *number* (singular or plural). Singular forms of regular verbs end in *–s*, and plurals have no extra ending. To check for subject-verb agreement, follow these steps:

1. In any sentence, first locate the verb.
2. Then find the subject for that verb.
3. Place the subject right before the verb and read it out loud. Does it sound correct?

Subject-Verb Agreement Rules

1   Compound subjects combined with **and** are always plural, and compound subjects combined with **or** or **nor** follow the noun closest to the verb.

    Correct   Danger <u>and adventure await</u> all those who take on the challenge.

                    Either Rogers or his <u>co-stars are</u> responsible for the initial success of the program.

    Incorrect Neither you <u>nor I are</u> able to understand what that must have felt like to people in 1650.

                    Both Yancey <u>and Billips was</u> able to reach the goal.

2   Many indefinite pronouns that logically seem to be plural are actually singular. **Either, neither, everyone, everybody, anyone, any, anybody, no one, not one, someone, somebody, nobody** and **each** are singular. Don't overthink on these—most of them "sound" correct when they are!

    Correct   <u>Every one</u> of the many contestants <u>sees</u> himself as capable of winning.

                    <u>Not one</u> of the players on my baseball team <u>was</u> capable of individual glory, but as a team, we were unbeatable.

                    <u>Each</u> of my friends <u>loves</u> ice cream.

    Incorrect <u>They each brings</u> many things to the table.

                    <u>Everyone</u> in the entire class of 700 students <u>were</u> surprised by the graduation speaker.

3   **None, some** and **all** can be singular or plural depending upon the context implied by the prepositional phrase that accompanies it.

    Correct   <u>Some of the players</u> on the team <u>run</u> fast.

                    <u>None of the food is</u> any good.

                    <u>Some of the cake remains</u> uneaten.

    Incorrect All of the pieces of cake tastes the same.

                    None of our salt are kosher salt.

4   In an **inverted sentence** (a sentence where the verb comes before the subject), place the subject before the verb, and then verify subject-verb agreement. **There** is often used to introduce an inverted sentence, so be sure to find the subject later in the sentence for a sentence that starts "There is/are/was/were…"

Correct   In his desk <u>are</u> a very old, worn <u>dictionary and a box</u> of worms.

There <u>were no clear answers</u> to the problem of its pollutants, however.

Incorrect   Far beyond the farthest pale <u>lives Aimless the wanderer and her sister Blab</u>.

To solve this kind of issue, there <u>is</u> more than two effective, and often equally inexpensive, <u>methods</u>.

5   **Collective** nouns (nouns that describe a group of people or things as one unit—family, team, group, organization, etc.) are always *singular*, unless the name is explicitly plural or the collective noun is made plural to refer to a group of groups.

Correct   The <u>team</u> really <u>pulls</u> together when it needs to.

The <u>Banshees</u> <u>are</u> really an underrated band.

Incorrect   The largest <u>pride of lions, with its numbers dwindling all the time, are</u> rarely seen anymore.

The five <u>families, each more depraved than the last, was</u> gathered for the meeting.

Verb Tense/Mood Rules

1   Verbs vary their form based on *when* an action takes place. Verb tense is indicated by other verbs in the paragraph or by key words such as "within ten years" or "in 1870."

Correct   Some experts <u>are</u> confident that the changes <u>will be</u> widely noticeable in just a few years. Others feel that the effects <u>may never be felt</u> by the average person.

<u>In the 19th century,</u> what we <u>take</u> as commonplace today <u>would have been considered</u> fantasy.

Incorrect   Some experts <u>will be</u> confident that the changes <u>will be</u> widely noticeable in just a few years. Others feel that the effects <u>are never felt</u> by the average person.

<u>In the 19th century,</u> what we <u>took</u> as commonplace today <u>was considered</u> fantasy.

2   **Perfect tenses** (those using forms of **have**) and **modals** (helping verbs, such as **could**, **would**, **may**, etc.) are often used in answer choices to create confusion. Often, you can eliminate answers using subject-verb agreement, as the complexities of when to use perfect tenses and other modals are rarely the only way to choose the correct answer, but here is a quick explanation of when to use them:

2.1   **Perfect tenses** are used to indicate completed actions or actions whose time is relative to another verb in the sentence. They always use forms of **have**, never **of**. Most verbs use the simple past form when the perfect tense is used, but certain verbs have irregular forms, most of which can be recognized by "ear."

   Present Perfect verbs indicate actions that started in the past and are complete in the present. These verbs use **have** for third-person plural subjects and **has** for third-person singular subjects.

   Past Perfect verbs indicate actions that *began* and *were completed* in the past. These verbs use **had** for both plural and singular subjects. The past perfect tense is used to indicate that actions precede other past tense actions or to imply that a past completed action is no longer true.

Correct	After working for 45 years, Michael, together with two other men in his precinct, <u>has finally retired</u> from law enforcement.
	The players <u>had tried</u> to keep up through the first half but by the third quarter were listless.
Incorrect	The years—especially this year in which so much turmoil <u>had erupted</u>—<u>has not been</u> kind to James.
	They <u>had became</u> a larger problem for the community as a whole, and the community <u>haven't sang</u> their praises in response.

2.2   **Modals** are often used to qualify the meaning of a verb. Subjunctive modals (**could**, **would**, **should**) are used to indicate past actions that either did not happen or are unlikely to have happened and future actions that might happen. Modals such as **can**, **may**, and **might** are used to indicate future actions that may happen and either current or past actions that are uncertain. Notice that there is some possible crossover in their use: the SAT will never make you decide based on the subtle differences between the uses of these helping verbs, and often other aspects of the answer choices can be used to eliminate answers.

Correct	Johnson <u>could have</u> left then, but he <u>chose</u> to persevere instead.
	The industry <u>may end up having</u> to be strictly controlled by governments if <u>it cannot self-regulate effectively</u>.
Incorrect	Stevedores <u>can have led</u> a strike, but by that time it <u>would of done</u> little good.
	Nobody <u>should have did</u> it, but everybody <u>does</u>.

Verb Usage—Try It!

Correct any errors with verbs in the underlined portions of each sentence

1. Lacey, unlike her brothers and sisters, <u>write</u> well.

2. Each of the twenty-seven desks <u>has a book</u> on it, and students <u>must chose</u> a desk based on their preferred book.

3. My brother or I <u>rakes</u> the leaves when our parents <u>told</u> us to do so, as they do every fall weekend.

4. Though it is an independent project, they each <u>having</u> to check in with the professor before <u>having started</u> the assignment.

5. Under the banyan tree, there <u>is</u> a tangle of desiccated roots and an ascetic's bowl; within the roots <u>lives</u> a fully grown rat and an albino squirrel, both of whom are territorial.

6. The report issued by the collective offices of the Board of Rectors, the Alumni Commission and the Board of Directors, which <u>should of corrected</u> many school-wide problems, <u>were</u> widely unpopular among the student body.

7. The average English person <u>cannot had any</u> idea how enormous the changes to world history <u>will be</u> when William the Conqueror succeeded in his conquest of England in 1066.

8. Although we won the case, if the judge <u>had find</u> my client guilty, we <u>will appeal</u> to the High Court.

Verb Usage Practice Set

[1] The civilian speaker argued that the most important people in the room were those in the audience who had served in the military.

    A) NO CHANGE
    B) who has served
    C) who was serving
    D) whose serving

[2] In so far as team sports teaching us not a particular skill but the discipline and teamwork required to work hard toward a common goal, they offer long-term tools for academic and professional achievement.

    A) NO CHANGE
    B) team sports has taught us
    C) team sports teach us
    D) team sports taught us

[3] On the quantitative section of the Graduate Management Admissions test (GMAT), a test taken by students applying to graduate school in business and management, students with a strong quantitative curriculum in college has traditionally done very well and still do.

    A) NO CHANGE
    B) colleges have traditionally
    C) colleges had traditionally
    D) college have traditionally

[4] If excess fecal matter is introduced into the ecosystem, it can pollute waterways, depleting the oxygen content of streams and rivers as it decomposes.

    A) NO CHANGE
    B) and depletes the oxygen content
    C) and deplete the oxygen content
    D) which deplete the oxygen content

[5] The now-defunct string trio had been the brainchild of former Irish Studies Professor Sean O'Steamy, wanting to explore further both the musical talents and the Celtic heritage of himself and his colleagues.

    A) NO CHANGE
    B) who wants
    C) who wanted
    D) he wanted

[6] While I await for the doctor's attention, I finished two cups of coffee and read all the magazines in the office.

    A) NO CHANGE
    B) awaiting
    C) waited
    D) awaited

7 As we see in several countries, persistent and severe income inequality <u>are</u> correlated with declines in overall productivity, and, over time, with deep recessions.

A) NO CHANGE
B) is
C) is being
D) has been

8 The Newport Apples, widely considered the first bluegrass players to come to the United States from Australia, <u>was unique for its</u> incorporation of a uniquely Australian aboriginal instrument called the Didgeridoo.

A) NO CHANGE
B) were unique for their
C) was unique for their
D) were unique for its

9 According to the US Environmental Protection Agency, the presence of coal and fossil fuel industry professionals in the scientific bodies meant to regulate those industries <u>have</u> no negative impact upon the environment.

A) NO CHANGE
B) having
C) have had
D) has

10 Proponents of gun safety make the argument that <u>there was</u> numerous reasons for background checks, including keeping guns from violent criminals and people with mental illness.

A) NO CHANGE
B) there is
C) there are
D) there has been

11 For many decades, dogs have guarded the Turner place, protecting it from the angry neighbors who could damage the property, not to mention <u>scared</u> the children of the residence.

A) NO CHANGE
B) scaring
C) scare
D) have scared

12 Some patients do not respond to the new therapy as well as others <u>did</u>, and some even respond adversely.

A) NO CHANGE
B) do,
C) have,
D) will,

13 The centerpiece of the work is dominated by images of cats with various anthropomorphic expressions and <u>including</u> a repeated motif of a large grinning Cheshire on an opulent sofa, an image to symbolize decadence.

A) NO CHANGE
B) included
C) includes
D) had included

14 There <u>were</u> a number of steps you can take to determine whether hunting is the right field for your dog and, if it is, to prepare yourself and your canine for such a career.

A) NO CHANGE
B) has been
C) had been
D) are

15 Not all research into regional varieties of the Arkansas swamp dialect <u>requires</u> such time, effort, and resources, however.

A) NO CHANGE
B) are requiring
C) have required
D) require

Pronouns

You can usually identify questions dealing with pronouns by noticing that the forms of a single pronoun are used in answer choices or by various pronouns being used in the answer choices.

Pronouns and Antecedents

Most pronoun questions on the SAT deal with the relationship between a pronoun and its antecedent, which is the noun that the pronoun refers to. Pronouns must have clear antecedents, and they must agree with their antecedents in number and type.

A pronoun must have a **clear antecedent**.

In some questions, the underlined pronoun may have multiple possible antecedents or the antecedent may be entirely ambiguous. In such cases, choose the version that makes clear the intended meaning of the sentence.

Incorrect   The coach told the quarterbacks to show up early for practice so that <u>they could record some film.</u>

Correct   The coach told the quarterbacks to show up early for practice so that <u>he could record some film of them</u>.

Incorrect   Abe attended all the Redskins games with his <u>roommates; they</u> were always entertaining.

Correct   Abe attended all the Redskins games with his <u>roommates, who</u> were always entertaining.

A pronoun must agree with its **antecedent** in **number** and **type**.

Find the antecedent (the noun that the pronoun is replacing) for each pronoun, and check to see if the antecedent is singular or plural. Remember that a singular antecedent requires a singular pronoun. Also remember that **who** (together with its other forms) refers to people, and **which** refers to things, while **that** can be used for people or things.

Incorrect   The University of North Carolina, <u>who</u> is a top academic school in the state, has one of the most famous basketball teams in the NCAA; as of 2017, <u>they</u> have won six NCAA championships.

Correct   The University of North Carolina, <u>which</u> is a top academic school in the state, has one of the most famous basketball teams in the NCAA; as of 2017, <u>it</u> has won six NCAA championships.

Incorrect   Every <u>student</u> must ensure that <u>they</u> bring <u>their</u> books to class.

Correct   All <u>students</u> must ensure that <u>they</u> bring <u>their</u> books to class.

Pronoun Person

Pronouns must stay *consistent* in **person** throughout each sentence; i.e. if a paragraph uses third person pronouns to refer to an indefinite antecedent, you *cannot* switch to 1st or 2nd person pronouns.

Person	1st (the self)	2nd (person spoken to)	3rd (person spoken about)
Pronouns Used	**I, me, we, us**, etc.	**you, your**, etc.	**she, her, they, them, everyone**, etc.

Incorrect   <u>One</u> must always wash <u>his</u> hands if <u>you</u> do not wish to get sick.

            <u>I</u> love to swim because <u>one</u> feels so weightless in the water.

Correct   <u>You</u> must always wash <u>your</u> hands if <u>you</u> do not wish to get sick.

            <u>I</u> love to swim because <u>I</u> feel so weightless in the water.

Pronoun Case

Pronouns also have different forms based on how they are used in sentences, an attribute called **case**. The two important cases to know for the test are **nominative** (in place of subject nouns) and **objective** (in place of object nouns).

Case	Forms	Uses
Nominative	**I, we, you, he, she, it, they, who**	subjects; comparisons; complements of linking verbs (e.g. forms of "be")
Objective	**me, us, you, him, her, it, them, whom**	direct objects; indirect object; objects of prepositions

Incorrect   Joanna picked her over I.

Correct   Joanna picked her over me.

The most commonly tested case-based pronoun questions deal with choosing **who** or **whom**. As indicated above, **who** is a nominative form and **whom** is an objective form. In order to check which is correct, it is often helpful to replace **who/whom** in the sentence with **he/him** or **they/them**. Consider this sentence:

The leader, who/whom was just elected, didn't know who/whom to trust.

Ask yourself, would you say "he was just elected" or "him was just elected;" "to trust they" or "to trust them"? Since it would be "**he** was just elected" and "to trust **them**," you should choose **who** and **whom**, respectively.

Pronoun Usage

A final note on pronouns: certain forms of pronouns sound the same but are written differently. These are also covered in Usage (see page 108) but here is a summary for pronouns:

it's = it is	you're = you are	they're = they are	who's = who is
its = it possesses	your = you possess	their = they possess	whose = who possesses

Pronouns—Try It!

Correct all errors in the underlined portions of the following sentences.

1. Germany's growth slowed in the late nineteen nineties, the economist argued, because <u>of their problems</u> with high unemployment.

2. I don't know <u>whom the robbers</u> were, but I do know that <u>he or she</u> took all my possessions.

3. The one who is responsible for the theft shall soon be arrested, but <u>they</u> are not sure where <u>they are</u>.

4. I always go to bed early before a big test because <u>you really need sleep</u> to perform well.

5. <u>Who</u> do you fear?

6. When the School Board, <u>who are</u> responsible for the school's reputation, saw that internal assessment grades were rising while standardized test scores were declining, <u>it decided</u> to ask teachers to toughen grading standards.

Pronouns Practice Set

1. Light pollution makes it difficult to see Jupiter and Saturn, obscuring <u>its</u> brightness among the artificial lights of the city.

   A) NO CHANGE
   B) there
   C) their
   D) it's

2. Since the players are expected to master many positions—some of which are unfamiliar— during the course of <u>his</u> four years at the school, studying teammates' strengths is strongly encouraged.

   A) NO CHANGE
   B) his or her
   C) one's
   D) their

3. The memorization of too many formulas can be detrimental to the educational progress of students, <u>which</u> often fail to learn the concepts behind the formulas they are taught.

   A) NO CHANGE
   B) that
   C) who
   D) they

4. People who choose the cheapest package for that truck often find <u>themselves</u> regretting the decision.

   A) NO CHANGE
   B) oneself
   C) their selves
   D) they were

5. Before "Nowhere Man," all Lennon-McCartney compositions that appeared as singles or on an album <u>were known for their</u> basic themes of young love and broken hearts.

   A) NO CHANGE
   B) was known for its
   C) were known for its
   D) was known for their

6. Though controversial in some Wall Street circles, "Fearless Girl" has brought much acclaim to sculptor Kristen Visbal, <u>whom was</u> previously best known for her sculptures of famous football coaches.

   A) NO CHANGE
   B) who is
   C) she was
   D) who was

7. The Nissan Leaf, the Chevy Bolt EV, and the Tesla Model S all made strong statements about the future of the automobile engine, yet none of them dominates the car market in the way that Ford's Model T did in the 1910s and 20s. Still, <u>it</u> might have paved the way for Tesla's Model 3 to become the first cool and affordable fully electric car.

   A) NO CHANGE
   B) those
   C) that one
   D) the Bolt EV

8 One of the side effects of the success that marketers have had in selling processed food is that people have come to believe that monitoring the nutritional value of the food <u>eaten by them</u> is someone else's responsibility.

A) NO CHANGE
B) they eat
C) eaten by him or her
D) you eat

9 Because of last night's 16-inning game, Miami doesn't have three of its eight relievers available for the remainder of today's game, and they've already used four <u>of them</u> in the last two innings.

A) NO CHANGE
B) of those
C) of the other five
D) of the rest of those

10 Nostalgia for comic books contributes to the enthusiasm for superhero movies among those <u>which watch it.</u>

A) NO CHANGE
B) who watch it.
C) whom watch them.
D) who watch them.

Parallelism and Comparisons

Although the answer choices for parallelism questions frequently include slight variations in the forms of words, parallelism and comparison questions can be difficult to recognize. A key way to recognize both issues is to look for lists and comparisons in the sentence as a whole—the form of the items in the list or comparison determine the form of the correct answer for the underlined section.

Lists

When a sentence includes a list, the items listed need to be in the same grammatical form, e.g. all prepositional phrases or all infinitives, rather than a mixture of different grammatical structures.

Incorrect My classmate Alexander has vacationed in Mexico, Italy, and in India.

  Major time wasters on the job include watching sports clips, playing computer games, and to discuss politics.

  Major time wasters on the job include watching sports clips, playing computer games, and political discussions.

Correct My classmate Alexander has vacationed in Mexico, Italy and India.

  My classmate Alexander has vacationed in Mexico, in Italy and in India.

  Major time wasters on the job include watching sports clips, playing computer games, and discussing politics.

Comparisons

When a sentence includes a comparison, the items being compared must be not only grammatically parallel but also logically parallel—you must compare like to like. For example, you cannot compare the cost of one medicine with another medicine, you can only compare the cost of one medicine with *that of* another.

A second element tested on comparison questions is the pronoun used—comparisons of grammatically singular things use "that of" while those of grammatically plural things use "those of."

Incorrect The value one gets from consistent use of a home gym compares favorably with a gym membership.

  The value one gets from consistent use of a home gym compares favorably with those of a gym membership.

Correct The value one gets from consistent use of a home gym compares favorably with that of a gym membership.

A final note on comparisons: adjectives have positive, comparative (using **more** or ending in **–er**) and superlative (using **most** or ending in **–est**) forms.

Positive	Comparative	Superlative
He is a good soccer player.	He has become a better soccer player this year.	He is the best soccer player in the entire school.
You are beautiful.	You are more beautiful than your sisters.	You are the most beautiful person I have ever seen.

Although this aspect is rarely tested, remember that comparative forms of adjectives are used to compare two nouns or to compare one noun to the rest of a group, and that superlative forms are limited to instances when more than two nouns are compared.

Incorrect   Most historians truly believe that he is the <u>better general of those who led the Americans</u>.

Correct   Most historians truly believe that he is the <u>better general of the two</u>.

Most historians truly believe that he is the <u>best general of those who led the Americans</u>.

Idiomatic Constructions for Lists and Comparisons

Watch out for the following idiomatic constructions:

"**Not so much**…" must always be accompanied by "**as**…".

"**Not only**…" must always be accompanied by "**but also**…".

In many constructions "**Just as**…" must be accompanied by "**so**…".

"**Neither … nor**" and "**either … or**" constructions must be followed by the same verb construction.

"**More**…" must always be accompanied by "**than**…"

These structures are always created using exactly these words, and the words/phrases coming *immediately after* them must be grammatically parallel.

Incorrect   After the game, he was not so much <u>tired but rather he was feeling depressed</u>.

Correct   After the game, he was not so much <u>tired as depressed</u>.

Incorrect   The Trailblazers are not only the best defensive team <u>but they are also true humanitarians, as well</u>.

Correct   The Trailblazers are not only the best defensive team <u>but also true humanitarians</u>.

Incorrect   I was not either happy for us nor was I sad for them when the series ended.

Correct   I was <u>neither happy for us nor sad for them</u> when the series ended.

Parallelism and Comparisons—Try It!

Correct any errors in the underlined sections.

1. I like snowboarding <u>better</u> than <u>to skate</u>.

2. Rick is either playing the <u>fool, or he is playing</u> video games.

3. Amanda has trouble with study skills, memory techniques, and <u>managing her time</u>.

4. I neither like football <u>nor do I</u> understand it, but I suppose it is, ironically, my <u>better sport</u>.

5. Most professionals prefer the benefits of working from home <u>to an office</u>.

6. I plan to enjoy the adventure of traveling this summer either in Europe <u>or Central America</u>, but either region seems more exciting than <u>that of travelling in the US</u>.

7. Ashley will <u>write the essay, proofread, and e-mail it</u> before tomorrow.

8. <u>Not only are they paying</u> for our daughter's wedding but also for the honeymoon.

Parallelism and Comparisons Practice Set

1. Appearing with an increase in gang culture, new graffiti popped up throughout the city, mostly on abandoned buildings, unused billboards, and sprayed on highway overpasses.

   A) NO CHANGE
   B) they were sprayed on
   C) on
   D) DELETE the underlined portion

2. Professional athletes must train year round: lift weights, running, and honing their skills.

   A) NO CHANGE
   B) lifting weights,
   C) they lift weights,
   D) to lift weights,

3. The settlers expected the climate of Virginia, with its latitude more southerly than that of Rome, to be fairer than what Rome was like.

   A) NO CHANGE
   B) Rome, to be fairer compared to Rome.
   C) those of Rome, to be fairer than Rome.
   D) that of Rome, to be fairer than the climate of Rome.

4. Despite negative public opinion, the congressman has improved the lives of citizens in his district by implementing free childcare, lower unemployment, and reforming labor laws.

   A) NO CHANGE
   B) low unemployment,
   C) lowering unemployment,
   D) for lower unemployment,

5. For the first time, prints of his works, so long legally prohibited from being mass produced, will be made available to the general public at prices similar to other artists' works.

   A) NO CHANGE
   B) that of prints of other artists' works.
   C) that of other artists' works.
   D) those of prints of other artists' works.

6. Outdated ideas, old practices too, and technologies are looked down upon as relics of the past.

   A) NO CHANGE
   B) also old practices
   C) in addition to old practices
   D) practices,

7 Thanksgiving is my favorite holiday: it is a time to spend with family, an excuse to overindulge in delicious food, and it reminds me to be thankful for all I have.

A) NO CHANGE
B) a reminder
C) I remember
D) remembering

8 The management of a home building project is similar to running to a business—you need to have effective coordination between many different people doing many different tasks.

A) NO CHANGE
B) as the running of a business:
C) to that of a business—
D) with running a business:

9 Not only was I exhausted by the end of the race, but also dehydrated due to the lack of water stations along the course.

A) NO CHANGE
B) but also dehydrating
C) also dehydrated
D) but I was also dehydrated

10 Ever since Mr. Smith became principal, his goal has been to improve school unity by stronger bonds between students, encouraging collaboration among teachers, and hosting school-wide barbeques.

A) NO CHANGE
B) strong bonds
C) strengthening bonds
D) build strong bonds

11 To the first test tube, the scientist added water and magnesium sulfate; to the other, she added water and sodium carbonate was added.

A) NO CHANGE
B) and sodium carbonate.
C) and also adding sodium carbonate.
D) as well as the addition of sodium carbonate.

12 Many people are shocked when they learn the ways in which key skills needed for an office setting are similar to those skills needed for martial arts and acrobatics.

A) NO CHANGE
B) that of the disciplines of
C) people mastering
D) DELETE the underlined portion

Apostrophes

Although questions dealing with apostrophes often cover more than one topic, they are easy to recognize—look for changes in apostrophe use! If you know these well, you can often eliminate answer choices with more complex errors in them.

The **apostrophe** is used to show *possession* (ownership) or indicate a *contraction*.

NOTE: Plural nouns *do not* use apostrophes unless they are also showing possession!

Possession

1   When a **singular** noun *does not* end in **-s**, add **'s** to show possession.

    Incorrect   The <u>girls</u> coat was hidden under the <u>familys'</u> blanket.

    Correct The <u>girl's</u> coat was hidden under the <u>family's</u> blanket.

2   When a **singular** noun *ends* in **-s**, add **'** or **'s** to show possession. You will *not* be tested on which of these two is correct for a given word, as *both* are acceptable for singular nouns ending in **-s**.

    Incorrect   The principal vetoed the senior <u>classes'</u> suggestion for a day off.

                    Many theologians do not understand <u>Jesus teaching's</u>.

    Correct   The principal vetoed the senior <u>class's</u> suggestion for a day off.

                  Many theologians do not understand <u>Jesus' teachings</u>.

3   When a **plural** noun *ends* in **-s**, add **'** to show possession.

    Incorrect   The debate team met for pizza to celebrate the <u>teams'</u> victory.

    Correct   The debate team met for pizza to celebrate the <u>students'</u> victory.

4   When a **plural** noun *does not* end in **-s**, add **'s** to show possession.

    Incorrect   The <u>childrens' toy's</u> were scattered about the playroom.

    Correct   The <u>children's toys</u> were scattered about the playroom.

5   To show **joint** possession, make only the last noun possessive. To show individual possession, make all nouns possessive.

    Incorrect   Are you attending <u>Stephanie's and Sandy's</u> party?

    Correct   Are you attending <u>Stephanie and Sandy's</u> party?

    Incorrect   <u>Stephanie and Sandy's</u> parties were different, but equally fun.

    Correct   <u>Stephanie's and Sandy's</u> parties were different, but equally fun.

Contractions

6   In **contractions**, use an apostrophe in *place of any omitted letters.*

Correct   Suzanne <u>can't</u> believe that her school <u>isn't</u> allowing cell phones on campus anymore.

7   Be sure to know the difference between **possessive pronouns** (*that never take an apostrophe*) and **contracted pronouns** (*that do take an apostrophe*). To check if a contraction is correct, read it as two separate words. For example, *it's = it is, you're = you are, who's = who is,* and *they're = they are.* Remember that **its'** is ***not*** a word.

Incorrect   <u>Their's</u> no doubt <u>you're</u> performance on ChoralSingers.com was incredible! <u>Its</u> evident that <u>your</u> deserving of all <u>you're</u> accolades as <u>you're</u> video is now on <u>it's</u> fifth day as the most watched on <u>they're</u> site.

Correct   <u>There's</u> no doubt <u>your</u> performance on Choral Singers.com was incredible! <u>It's</u> evident that <u>you're</u> deserving of all <u>your</u> accolades as <u>your</u> video is now on <u>its</u> fifth day as the most watched on <u>their</u> site.

Apostrophes—Try It!

Correct any errors in the underlined portions of the following sentences.

1.   <u>Its heart</u> had stopped beating, but the <u>amphibians tail</u> still quivered with life.

2.   Sometimes when the <u>Smiths' friends dog</u> starts to howl, the friend howls in accord.

3.   The <u>grassroots' bring-out-the vote</u> effort rejuvenated the community and increased <u>it's</u> involvement in social welfare.

4.   "<u>Its</u> mid-day," mother exclaimed, "and <u>your</u> still in bed!"

5.   "<u>Your</u> braver than any of them," Scarlet told Rhett, with admiration in <u>her eye's.</u>

6.   These <u>books covers' were</u> torn before <u>they're</u> arrival here.

7.   On <u>Los Angeles'</u> Rodeo Drive, most <u>shop's</u> are too expensive for me to even look at.

8.   <u>Stephen's and Seth's</u> recently finished film is going to be shown at Sundance this year; they hope <u>it's</u> content will challenge <u>there audiences thinking.</u>

9.   Jane <u>Austen's</u> *Emma* is both a love story and a detective novel.

10.   My <u>dogs collar</u> is blue but both of my cousin <u>Joan's dogs collars'</u> are green; when our Chihuahuas play together we can only tell them apart by <u>there collar's.</u>

Apostrophe Practice Set

[1] The Washington Monument is again open to the public after <u>repairs on its</u> elevator.

A) NO CHANGE
B) repairs on it's
C) repair's on its'
D) repairs' on its

[2] Tracking <u>each students' grades</u> throughout high school helps the school board identify any school-wide trends.

A) NO CHANGE
B) student's grades
C) students' grades
D) all student's grades

[3] <u>Kansas' governor</u> addressed the Kansas Legislature in the annual "State of the State," in which he described his new budget proposal.

A) NO CHANGE
B) Kansas governor
C) The governor of Kansas'
D) Kansases governor

[4] Germany's population is declining while the reverse is true for that of most more developed <u>country's,</u> in which populations grow due to longer lives more than compensating for fewer births.

A) NO CHANGE
B) countrys'
C) countries,
D) countries'

[5] Most employers do not even look at a <u>perspective employees' references'</u> until after the interview process.

A) NO CHANGE
B) perspective employee's references
C) prospective employees' references
D) prospective employee's references

[6] Many of <u>Disney's character's origins</u> are more unsettling than those characters' kid-friendly films suggest.

A) NO CHANGE
B) Disneys' character origins
C) Disney character's origins
D) Disney's characters' origins

Modifiers

A **modifier** is a word or phrase that modifies or describes another word or phrase. A modifier *must* be placed immediately next to the word that it is modifying. When the modifier starts the sentence, it must modify the subject of the sentence. If a modifier is placed incorrectly, the meaning of the sentence can become unclear and even inadvertently humorous.

Most commonly, you can recognize a **modifier** question when a sentence has an introductory verbal phrase (called a misplaced or dangling participle) that is not underlined followed by an underlined group of words. These questions are tough to recognize, because they look like the wordiness of the choices is being tested, or perhaps that you are supposed to choose between active and passive forms of the main verb, but you must always choose the subject that is *doing* the **action** of the introductory phrase in order to get these questions correct.

Incorrect	Humming cheerfully, <u>the boat was rowed by the oarsman</u> into the choppy seas.
	Engulfed in flames, <u>the office workers escaped the building</u> just in time.
Correct	Humming cheerfully, <u>the oarsman rowed the boat</u> into the choppy seas.
	Engulfed in flames, <u>the building was evacuated</u> of all the office workers just in time.

In addition to introductory phrases, the SAT occasionally tests other types of modifying phrases and words. For clarity, modifiers must be placed as close as possible to the word that they modify, so choose the placement closest to the word the phrase logically should modify.

Incorrect	By a great stroke of luck, the detective saw the would-be assassin as he was about to pull the trigger <u>with his binoculars</u>.
	By a great stroke of luck, the detective saw the would-be assassin <u>with his binoculars</u> as he was about to pull the trigger.
Correct	By a great stroke of luck, the detective saw <u>with his binoculars</u> the would-be assassin as he was about to pull the trigger.

Note that this sentence sounds "awkward," but is nonetheless the only correct option!

Modifiers—Try It!

Correct any errors in the underlined portions of the following sentences.

1. My cousin sold a house <u>to a nice family with no hard wood floors.</u>

2. On Halloween, we love the people who give <u>brownies to the children </u>wrapped in cellophane.

3. Waking up later than planned, <u>the flight was missed by John.</u>

4. Whistling as they worked, <u>the job was found more manageable by the seven dwarves.</u>

5. Having been abandoned decades before, <u>the scientists were amazed to find the research center still had</u> functioning punch card computers.

6. Never one to minimize the embarrassing aspects of a story, <u>the description Steve gave of the projectile vomit striking his eyeball was both disgusting and hilarious.</u>

Modifiers Practice Set

1.   Running out of new ideas, <u>the blank computer screen stared at me.</u>

  A)   NO CHANGE
  B)   the computer screen was blank.
  C)   I stared at the blank computer screen.
  D)   staring at me was the blank computer screen.

2.   Covered with rainbow sprinkles, <u>his mother admired Jonah's creativity in decorating the sugar cookies.</u>

  A)   NO CHANGE
  B)   Jonah's creativity was admired by his mother in decorating the sugar cookies.
  C)   the sugar cookies Jonah decorated led his mother to admire his creativity.
  D)   Jonah's creativity in decorating the sugar cookies was admired by his mother.

3.   <u>The tourists on Segways blocked the path of the congressional staffers trying to get to work.</u>

  A)   NO CHANGE
  B)   The tourists blocked the path on Segways of the congressional staffers trying to get to work.
  C)   The tourists on Segways blocked the path, trying to get to work, of the congressional staffers.
  D)   Trying the get to work, the tourists on Segways blocked the path of the congressional staffers.

4.   <u>She adopted a kitten for her brother named Princess Kitty.</u>

  A)   NO CHANGE
  B)   Named Princess Kitty, she adopted a kitten for her brother.
  C)   She adopted a kitten named Princess Kitty for her brother.
  D)   She adopted, named Princess Kitty, a kitten for her brother.

5.   Tired of sleeping on her friend's couch, <u>Michelle's excitement rose when she found her own apartment.</u>

  A)   NO CHANGE
  B)   Michelle was excited to find her own apartment.
  C)   after finding her own apartment, Michelle's excitement rose.
  D)   finding her own apartment was exciting for Michelle.

6.   Concerned citizens have questioned the plan, wondering whether the increase in spending <u>sufficiently and permanently will address</u> the housing needs of the neighborhood's poorest tenants.

  A)   NO CHANGE
  B)   will sufficiently and permanently address
  C)   sufficiently will permanently address
  D)   will address sufficiently permanently

7.   Cleopatra <u>dies, bitten by venomous snakes wearing her royal gowns that symbolize Egyptian elegance.</u>

  A)   NO CHANGE
  B)   dies, wearing her royal gowns from venomous snakes that symbolize Egyptian elegance.
  C)   dies, bitten by venomous snakes while wearing her royal gowns that symbolize Egyptian elegance.
  D)   dies wearing her royal gowns that symbolize Egyptian elegance bitten by venomous snakes.

Idioms and Usage

Some of the most difficult questions to recognize what is being tested on the SAT are those that deal with usage and idioms. Often the changes between answer choices will be very small (such as a different preposition or even just a different letter in a word). Both of these topics can also be difficult because there are no rules to memorize in order to get the correct answer.

Idioms

Idioms are expressions that are determined by customary usage rather than any rule. For example, in English we say that we are "capable of using idioms properly" but not "capable to use idioms properly." Because there is no rule for idiom questions (*idiom* comes from Greek and Latin words meaning "peculiar, particular to oneself"), there is no principle or logic to which word or expression should be chosen in a given sentence, and no list could be memorized that would guarantee that you would be prepared for *every* idiom question that could come up on the test. While most idioms questions deal with prepositions, the test has also required students to choose between gerunds (**-ing** verb forms) and infinitives (**to** + verb), and certain idiomatic structures for comparisons and lists (see Parallelism and Comparisons on page 99) are commonly tested as well.

Instead of trying to memorize a list of idioms, be sure to notice when the answer choices vary their prepositions or the structuring of words, and read through the whole sentence and choose the one that sounds most natural. Idiom questions on the test often test other errors at the same time, so if you are not sure which word sounds best, make sure that there is no other error being tested in the answer choices.

> **Incorrect**   He had difficulty staying <u>in topic</u>, but he was <u>capable to keep</u> his audiences engaged <u>about</u> his speeches anyway.
>
> **Correct**   He had difficulty staying <u>on topic</u>, but he was <u>able to keep</u> his audiences engaged <u>in</u> his speeches anyway.

Usage

Usage questions test words that appear or sound very similar but mean different things, sometimes even belonging to different parts of speech. There is no complete list of all such terms, as words from **persecuted** and **prosecuted** and **expect** and **aspect** and many more can and have been tested, but here is a short list of commonly tested words that trip up many test takers.

1   **affect** (v.) and **effect** (n.)

Affect is most commonly a verb meaning to produce an effect. You can replace it in a sentence with verbs like <u>**alter**</u> to make sure that it fits in the sentence.

Effect is a noun that means the result of a cause, or something produced by a cause. You can replace it with nouns like <u>**result**</u> to make sure that it fits the sentence. Remember to link the **e** in result with **effect** and the **a** in **alter** with **affect**!

> **Correct**   The <u>effect</u> of the disease on her lungs <u>affected</u> her ability to run.

2   **fewer** and **less**

Fewer refers to countable items while **less** refers to uncountable amounts.

> **Correct**   I went to <u>fewer</u> practices than he; it is not surprising that I got <u>less</u> playing time in our game.

The distinction between **fewer** and **less** is the same as that between **many** and **much**—the SAT has tested these terms as well, and in "many more people" or "much more of the population."

3 **than** and **then**

Then refers to **time**, whereas **than** is used for **comparisons**. Remember to link the **a** and **e** in each pair to remember which is which. Because the letters that set them apart are buried in the middle of these short words, students will often fail to recognize this change in answer choices that also involve other changes. If you learn to recognize when these words are being tested, you will often be able to easily eliminate two answers on a **than/then** question.

Correct   <u>Then</u>, he knew for certain that he was less <u>than</u> ideally suited to be a lawyer.

First they were less prepared <u>than</u> other teams, but <u>then</u> later they caught up and surpassed all others.

4 **it's** and **its**
they're and **their** and **there**
you're and **your**,
who's and **whose**

A final element of usage commonly tested is the use of related pronoun forms. For more on the distinctions between these forms, see both Pronouns (page 95)and Apostrophes (page 103).

Finally, idioms and usage are often tested on a single question, and so it helps to identify the "parts" of the question and eliminate answers using one element at a time:

Example 3   Although the Russians had an advantage over the American team, <u>the principle affect of</u> their advantage was complacency.

A) NO CHANGE

B) the principal effect about

C) the principle affect about

D) the principal effect of

Many students are not confident about which to choose between **principle** and **principal**, which is the first element changed in the answer choices. However, if you start by isolating the changes and first eliminate based on aspects you are certain of, you can get this question correct without ever having to know the difference between **principle** and **principal**. Instead, start by eliminating all answer choices that have **affect** instead of **effect**, because we can replace the word with **result** but not with **alter**. Then, read the whole sentence with choice (B) and (D) in it, and you will choose (D) as the more "natural" sounding expression.

Idioms and Usage—Try It!

Correct all errors in the underlined portions of the sentences.

1. Even today, a <u>personnel computer</u> is not <u>necessary to learning</u> new things; it is, however, very helpful for research.

2. The headmistress claimed that each of her students has a much stronger work ethic but <u>less advantages of</u> home <u>then students</u> at the larger school nearby have.

3. Your test scores are <u>inconsistent to your performance at</u> school, which is a <u>direct affect from</u> your school's emphases.

4. A study can establish a connection <u>among too</u> variables but it cannot establish cause and <u>effect relationships affectively.</u>

5. The socioeconomic divisions of Washington, DC, are very <u>different to</u> those <u>in Baltimore.</u>

6. Although the police tried to prevent him <u>to leave</u> the country, he <u>alluded</u> pursuit for <u>much more years.</u>

Idioms and Usage Practice Set

[1] Many technology companies are already experimenting with drones as a means <u>from</u> delivering packages.

A) NO CHANGE
B) through
C) of
D) DELETE the underlined portion.

[2] To research the impact of social media on politics, I read a book <u>upon</u> the rise of "fake news."

A) NO CHANGE
B) for
C) with
D) about

[3] Anyone with <u>excess to</u> a protractor, a tape measure, a screw, and some string can calculate the height of any building by constructing an astrolabe and using a little bit of basic trigonometry.

A) NO CHANGE
B) access of
C) access to
D) excess of

[4] The coach pointed to the positive <u>affect of</u> senior leadership as the primary reason the team was undefeated.

A) NO CHANGE
B) affects on
C) effect to
D) effect of

[5] I've travelled through Mexico, Arizona and Texas <u>in order to find</u> the best recipe for guacamole.

A) NO CHANGE
B) in order for finding
C) so to finding
D) so to find

[6] The Governor went <u>so far</u> to blame the sluggish economy on the newspapers that were critical of his proposals.

A) NO CHANGE
B) so far as
C) as far
D) as far in

[7] Aerial photography showed that there had been <u>many less people at the ceremony then</u> at the march.

A) NO CHANGE
B) far fewer people at the ceremony then
C) far fewer people at the ceremony than
D) much less people at the ceremony than

[9] Carbon-14 dating showed that the volcanic <u>explosion proceeded</u> the arrival of large predators to the area.

A) NO CHANGE
B) exposure proceeded
C) exposure preceded
D) explosion preceded

[8] The journalists pointed their microphones <u>toward the actress who was the first to emerge of</u> the limo.

A) NO CHANGE
B) from the actress who was the first to emerge of
C) toward the actress who was the first to emerge from
D) from the actress who was the first to emerge toward

[10] The environmentalist <u>cited the decrease in crop yield near the site</u> of the explosion as evidence for the company's culpability.

A) NO CHANGE
B) sighted the decrease in crop yield near the sight
C) sited the decrease in crop yield near the cite
D) cited the decrease in crop yield near the sight

Table for Identifying SEC Questions

Use this table for quick reference to the information on Standard English Conventions tested on the SAT. Remember to start by noticing the changes in the answer choices to recognize what is being tested, and then ask the right questions to lead you to the correct answer every time.

Error Type	How to recognize it	What to ask	How to solve
Punctuation	Changes in punctuation (type and/or location) and minor word changes are the *only* differences in answer choices.	For all types of punctuation questions, compare answers, crossing out the incorrect punctuation marks in each wrong answer, and choose the one left.	
		Is the punctuation based on	
		… sentence structure?	For sentence structure, be sure to *read* the *whole* sentence and determine its clause structure.
		… nonessential elements?	Look for *pairs* of commas or dashes, and make sure whatever is between them could sensibly be dropped out of the sentence.
		… or lists?	Make sure commas separate any list of 3 or more items, and make sure that there is *no* comma between the last adjective in a list and the word it modifies.
Verbs	Changes in *form* of the verb are the primary differences between the answer choices.	Does the verb need to be conjugated?	Choose the correct conjugation for the subject!
		What is the subject of the underlined verb?	Read the subject and verb together and make sure they "sound" correct.
		What tense should the verb be in?	Choose the tense that matches the context.
Pronouns	Changes in pronoun form are the primary difference between the answer choices.	What is the antecedent of the pronoun? Is it clear?	Make sure that pronoun matches its antecedent in number and gender. Choose a specific noun instead of a pronoun if the antecedent is unclear.
		Is the pronoun a subject or an object?	For **who/whom**, read the sentence with **he** or **they** in place of **who**, and **hi__m** or **the__m** in place of **who__m**.

Error Type	How to recognize it	What to ask	How to solve
Parallelism and Comparisons	Different forms of related words and/or slight rearrangements of words within answer choices are the main difference between answer choices. These can be difficult to recognize due to kinds of differences that are possible in answer choices.	What is the structure of the other elements in the list or comparison?	Choose the answer choice that matches the rest of the list.
		What specific word or words are being compared?	Choose the answer choice that creates a logical and correct comparison.
Idioms and Usage	Changes in the preposition used or very similar-looking words are notable in answers. These are often combined with other error types.	Which preposition or form sounds best in the sentence?	Read the sentence or phrase with each option and choose the one that sounds best.
		Which word is intended?	Identify the meaning of each form, and choose the best for the context.
Apostrophes	Changes in the location and presence of apostrophes are notable in answer choices. These are often combined with other error types.	Is the word with the apostrophe possessive? Is it plural?	Check each answer's use of apostrophes: 's =singular possession, s' =plural possession *Never* choose 's or s' if the noun is *plural* but **not** *possessive*.
		Is the apostrophe intended to convey a contraction?	Read the contraction as the words it is made up of and see if it makes sense.
Modifiers	Usually the underlined section comes after an introductory phrase, and the answer choices vary the subject of the sentence. For most students, these are the toughest to recognize because they look like EOI questions.	What word is the phrase or word intended to modify?	Choose the answer that places the modifier and the word modified as close together as possible. For introductory phrases, make sure to choose the subject that the phrase modifies.

Mathematics Test Manual

There are two SAT Mathematics Tests. They are the third and fourth tests in your SAT sitting:

Math Test—No Calculator has 20 questions over 25 minutes. The first 15 questions have multiple choices, and the last 5 ask for student-produced responses.

Math Test—Calculator has 38 questions over 55 minutes. The first 30 questions have multiple choices, and the last 8 ask for student-produced repsonses.

Overview and Strategies

If there's one good thing about standardized tests, it is that they are predictable. In order for test scores to be consistent, the SAT uses the same *type* of questions from test to test. So, in order to do well, all you need to do is the following:

1. Know each type of question, *and*
2. Learn the strategies (quick ways) to solve each type of question accurately.

We've structured this workbook with the most frequently used strategies first. Next, we tackle the four major categories of questions that come up on the SAT.

- Heart of Algebra, which includes translating, solving, and interpreting linear equations and functions
- Passport to Advanced Math, which includes algebraic changes of form as well as higher level functions
- Problem Solving and Data Analysis, which emphasizes the interpretation of tables and graphs as well as statistical measurements and probability
- Additional Math Topics, which can include topics in geometry, trigonometry, and complex numbers

About 90% of all questions on any SAT come from the first three categories above, and those are split approximately even. It's also useful to note that questions from the Problem Solving and Data Analysis category only appear in the calculator-permitted section and constitute nearly half of that section's questions.

Strategies

A strategy is just a quick way to solve a problem accurately. Often you can come up with your own quick ways. The trick is to pause for a moment before you start solving and think about the easy way to solve the question. If you're like most students, though, during a timed test like the SAT, you won't even think about pausing.

The people who write the SAT Math realize that all of us have certain patterned ways of solving questions—the ways we learn in school. In high-pressure situations, we tend to fall back upon these ways that we know so well. Because test-makers want to reward the ability to think creatively under pressure, they devise questions that can seem difficult if you try to solve them in the most obvious way—the way you've learned in school.

One way you can prepare for these questions is to practice alternative strategies as much as you practice textbook methods in high school. If you become very familiar with the quick way, it's likely that you'll remember it during the SAT.

Back Solving

On the SAT, of the 58 Mathematics questions, 45 provide you with answer choices. Because the answer to the question is right there in front of you, you can often simply *try the various answers* until you see which one works.

There are some questions for which it is easiest to start with simple answer choices: 0 and 1, for example, are very quick to plug in and check, and for this reason they are often the best place to start if they are available.

For other questions, you can use the fact that the answer choices are usually in increasing or decreasing order. This is most helpful in cases like the following:

Example 1   For two consecutive even integers, the result of adding the smaller integer to three times the larger integer is 62. What are the two integers?

   A) 14, 16

   B) 16, 18

   C) 18, 20

   D) 20, 22

It is simplest to begin with a middle answer choice, i.e. 18 and 20. Adding the smaller number to three times the larger yields $18 + 3 \times 20 = 78$. This is clearly greater than the 62 you are looking for, so you know that choice (C) is incorrect. However, choice (D) is *also* incorrect because it will give you something *even larger* than choice (C) did.

You can try choice (B) next, i.e. 16 and 18. Adding the smaller number to three times the larger yields $16 + 3 \times 18 = 70$, which is still too big. You are now actually *done* because you have eliminated *all* answer choices except one, which is (A).

If you wanted to be extra careful, you could test that answer choice (A) does indeed give you the correct answer: Using 14 and 16 gives you $14 + 3 \times 16 = 62$, which is indeed the answer you are looking for.

Extraneous Solutions

Many problems, particularly involving fractions or radicals, can yield extraneous solutions because of the restrictions associated with the domains of such functions. Such a solution is found through the ordinary course of doing correct algebra but does not actually make the equation work. That is, you can do everything correctly and still arrive at an answer, or a solution set, that is not accurate. Of course if you are back solving the choices (whether they be single solutions or solution sets), you don't have to worry about this.

Example 2   The equation $\sqrt{x} + 3 = 1$ can be solved, using correct algebra, by first subtracting 3 and then squaring both sides of the equation. This will generate the solution $x = 4$, and yet if you plug 4 into the original equation, it clearly does not work. If an equation like this is part of a multiple-choice problem, there is no reason to do the algebra and run the risk of selecting an extraneous solution. Just back solve from the beginning.

Back Solving Problem Set

On the following problem set, focus on back solving by using your answer choices.

1. If $(x-3)^2 = (2x-1)(x+3)$, which of the following could equal x?

   A) -2
   B) 0
   C) 1
   D) 2

Note: Figure not drawn to scale

3. If x, x^3, and x^2 lie on a number line in that order (as shown above), which of the following could be a value of x?

   A) 2
   B) $-\dfrac{1}{3}$
   C) $\dfrac{3}{4}$
   D) 1

4. If $\dfrac{x^3}{y}$ is an integer but $\dfrac{x}{y}$ is not an integer, which of the following could be the values of x and y?

   A) $x=2, y=1$
   B) $x=3, y=9$
   C) $x=4, y=2$
   D) $x=3, y=2$

2. When each side of a given square is decreased by 2 inches, the area is decreased by 20 square inches. What is the length, in inches, of a side of the original square?

   A) 3
   B) 4
   C) 5
   D) 6

x	$f(x)$
-2	8
0	4
1	5
3	13
4	20

5   Which of the following functions is represented in the table above?

A) $3x + 4$

B) $2x + 3$

C) $x^3 - 7$

D) $x^2 + 4$

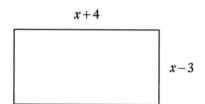

$x + 4$

$x - 3$

6   If the area of the rectangle above is 60, what is the value of x?

A) 5

B) 6

C) 7

D) 8

7   What is the solution set for

$$\frac{x}{x-2} - \frac{8}{x+3} = \frac{10}{x^2 + x - 6}?$$

A) $\{2, 3\}$

B) $\{-3, 2\}$

C) $\{2\}$

D) $\{3\}$

$$4x^2 < (4x)^2$$

8   For what value of x is the statement above <u>false</u>?

A) -4

B)   0

C) $\frac{1}{4}$

D)   1

$$1 \le x^2 \le 9$$

9   Which of the following represents all values of x that satisfy the above inequality?

A)

B)

C)

D)

10   If $5^{k-4} \times 5^k + 16 = 41,$ what is the value of k?

A) 0

B) 1

C) 2

D) 3

11 For which of the following functions is
    $f(-2) = f(2)$ true?

    A) $f(x) = x^2 + x$

    B) $f(x) = x^2 + 1$

    C) $f(x) = x + 2$

    D) $f(x) = x^3 + x$

14 What is the solution set for the equation
    $5 + \sqrt{x+1} = x + 4$?

    A) $\{0\}$

    B) $\{0, 3\}$

    C) $\{-1, 1\}$

    D) $\{3\}$

12 Warren is worth $25.6 billion and Bill is worth
    $23.04 billion. What percent of his net worth
    would Warren have to donate to Bill so that
    each is worth the same amount?

    A) 5%

    B) 8%

    C) 23%

    D) 89%

15 If $\dfrac{1}{5} + \dfrac{1}{6} + \dfrac{1}{7} > \dfrac{1}{5} + \dfrac{1}{6} + \dfrac{1}{x}$, then x could be
    which of the following?

    A) 5

    B) 6

    C) 7

    D) 8

13 What is the solution set for the equation
    $14 + \sqrt{x+2} = 11$?

    A) $\{7\}$

    B) $\{7, -11\}$

    C) $\{1\}$

    D) No solution

Plugging in Numbers

Plugging in Numbers is a useful strategy when a question has variables that maintain a constant relationship. By substituting real numbers for variables, you can solve questions arithmetically instead of algebraically.

There are three main steps to Plugging in Numbers.

1. Choose which number(s) to plug in and write it/them down.

    1.1. If there is an equation, plug in on the side where there is more action.

    1.2. Avoid choosing **0** or **1** as the number you plug in; these will often yield the same result for different choices. For the same reason, try not to use **30°**, **45°**, **60°** or **90°** for angles.

    1.3. Smaller numbers tend to work well in most cases, e.g. **2**, **3**, **4**, or **5**.

    1.4. Plug in different numbers for different variables.

    1.5. For percent problems use **100**.

    1.6. Solve for other variables in equations.

2. Write down and BOX your answer.

3. Plug the number(s) you've chosen into the same variables in the answer choices if necessary. (Note that you *must* try ALL the answer choices)

    3.1. Which one(s) matches your answer?

    3.2. If multiple answer choices work, try different numbers and repeat steps 1 to 3, though any choice you've eliminated is gone for good.

Example 1   If w is the first of three consecutive odd integers, what is the sum of the two even integers between the smallest and greatest odd integer, in terms of w ?

    A) $3w$

    B) $2w + 4$

    C) $w + 10$

    D) $3w + 3$

Notice the complicated wording in the question. Many students will be confused by the time they get to the part about the even integers. So don't let yourself even get to that part without first plugging in a number.

1. Choose a number, specifically an odd integer, to plug in for w like, for example, **3**.

2. If $w = 3$, then the consecutive odd integers are **3**, **5**, and **7**, and the even integers that are between those are 4 and **6**. The sum of 4 and **6** is **10**, so that is the number the correct choice ought to come out to when **3** is plugged in for w.

3. Plugging in **3** for w in all four choices shows that (A) works out to 9, (B) works out to 10, (C) works out to 13, and (D) works out to 12. The answer must be (B). Notice, had you plugged **1** in for w instead of **3**, choices (B) and (D) would have worked. Such a thing can happen with any number but is more common with special numbers like 1 and 0.

Plugging in Numbers Problem Set 1

1. If $y = 3^x + 3^x + 3^x$, then what is y in terms of x?

A) 3^{3x}

B) 9^x

C) 3^{x^3}

D) 3^{x+1}

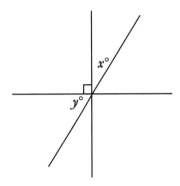

4. In the figure above, which of the following is equal to x?

A) y

B) $90 - x$

C) $90 - y$

D) $180 - y$

2. If r, s, and t are consecutive odd integers, what is the difference between r and t?

A) 1

B) 2

C) 3

D) 4

5. If $\dfrac{1}{x} = \dfrac{x}{y}$, which of the following equals xy?

A) $4x$

B) $3x^2$

C) x^3

D) x

3. If $-1 < x < 0 < y < 1$, which of the following is the greatest?

A) xy

B) $-y$

C) $-(y^2)$

D) x^2

[6] Andrew caught three times as many lobsters as crabs. Half of the lobsters he caught were female. If Andrew randomly chooses a shellfish from his bin, what is the likelihood that he picks a male lobster?

A) $\dfrac{3}{10}$

B) $\dfrac{3}{8}$

C) $\dfrac{5}{12}$

D) $\dfrac{6}{11}$

[7] If x and y are positive consecutive integers, where $y > x$, which of the following is equal to xy?

A) $3x$

B) $4x$

C) $x^2 + y$

D) $x^2 + x$

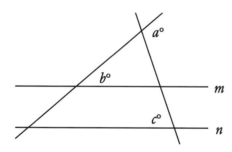

Note: Figure not drawn to scale

[8] In the above figure, lines m and n are parallel. What is the value of c in terms of a and b?

A) $180 - (a + b)$

B) $180 + a - b$

C) $a + b - 180$

D) $a - b$

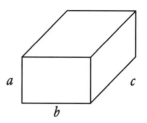

Note: Figure not drawn to scale

[9] In the rectangular prism above, $b = 2a$ and $2c = 3b$. What is the volume of the box?

A) $6a^2$

B) b^3

C) $2b^2 c$

D) $6a^3$

[10] Ricky had d dollars in the bank. He withdrew 3/4 of d to buy a plane ticket to Paris. He then spent 1/3 of what was left on his lodging for the week. What fraction of the original amount remained in his account?

A) $\dfrac{1}{12}$

B) $\dfrac{1}{6}$

C) $\dfrac{1}{4}$

D) $\dfrac{1}{3}$

[11] If J, K, and L are digits in the positive three-digit integer JKL, what is the decimal equivalent of $.JKL \times 10^{-4}$?

A) $0.0JKL$

B) $0.JKL$

C) $JK,L00$

D) $J,KL0,000$

12. 30 percent of x is equal to y percent of 50. What is x in terms of y?

A) $\frac{1}{2}y$

B) $\frac{3}{5}y$

C) $\frac{5}{3}y$

D) $\frac{10}{3}y$

14. If k divided by 7 yields a remainder of 5, which of the following, when divided by 7, yields no remainder?

A) $3k$

B) $k^2 + 3$

C) $k + 3$

D) $k - 3$

13. Yu is taking a test. There are S number of sections, each containing A number of questions. If Yu answers one question, on average, in T minutes, how long will it take her, in hours, to complete the test?

A) $\frac{ST}{60A}$

B) $\frac{SAT}{60}$

C) $\frac{SA}{T}$

D) SAT

15. If $2a = \frac{3b^2}{c}$, what happens to the value of a when b and c are halved?

A) a is halved.

B) a is doubled.

C) a is not changed.

D) a is multiplied by 4.

Plugging in Numbers Problem Set 2

1. Chris, Mark, and Trevor are brothers. The average age of Chris and Mark is x. The average age of Mark and Trevor is y. If Chris is 26 years old, how old is Trevor in terms of x and y?

   A) $\dfrac{x+y}{3}$

   B) $13+y-x$

   C) $26+2y-2x$

   D) $\dfrac{2x+2y}{3}$

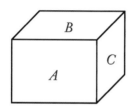

2. If A, B, and C are the areas of the three faces of the rectangular prism (as shown above), in terms of A, B, and C, what is the volume of the prism?

   A) $\sqrt{ABC}$

   B) $A^2B^2C^2$

   C) $\dfrac{A^2B^2}{C^2}$

   D) $\sqrt{\dfrac{AB}{C}}$

3. Jan bought 7 CDs for d dollars each. She gave the cashier t ten dollar bills. How many dollars change should Jan receive in terms of d and t?

   A) $10t-7d$

   B) $t-7d$

   C) $10-d$

   D) $t-7$

4. The sum of two numbers that differ by 2 is s. In terms of s, what is the value of the greater of the two numbers?

   A) $\dfrac{s-2}{2}$

   B) $\dfrac{s+1}{2}$

   C) $\dfrac{2s+2}{2}$

   D) $\dfrac{s+2}{2}$

5. If the average (arithmetic mean) of a, b, and c is z, which of the following is the average $a, b, c,$ and d?

   A) $\dfrac{3z+d}{4}$

   B) $\dfrac{3z+d}{3}$

   C) $\dfrac{z+d}{4}$

   D) $\dfrac{z+d}{3}$

$$a + b = x$$
$$ab = y$$

6 Given that the equations above are true, what is $\frac{1}{a} + \frac{1}{b}$ in terms of x and y?

A) $x + y$

B) $\dfrac{x}{y}$

C) $\dfrac{y}{x}$

D) $\dfrac{1}{xy}$

7 If x and y are positive consecutive even integers where $y > x$, which of the following is equal to $y^2 - x^2$?

A) $4x$

B) $2x + 2$

C) $4x + 2$

D) $4x + 4$

8 If the height of a cylinder is increased by 50% and the radius of its base is decreased by 50%, what is the ratio of the old volume to the new volume?

A) $4 : 9$

B) $8 : 3$

C) $2 : 1$

D) $8 : 1$

9 If the sum of the integers from –6 to an odd integer x, inclusive, is y, where $x > -6$, which of the following shows the relationship between x and y?

A) $y = -5x$

B) $(x + 6) = 2y$

C) $x(x + 1) = 2(y + 21)$

D) $-6 + x = y$

10 If m is $\frac{3}{4}$ of n, and n is $\frac{4}{5}$ of p, what is the value of $\frac{m}{p}$?

A) $\dfrac{2}{3}$

B) $\dfrac{3}{5}$

C) $\dfrac{4}{9}$

D) $\dfrac{7}{9}$

11 The price of a television was first put on sale for 25 percent off and then, after the sale, the new price was increased by 30 percent. The final price was what percent of the initial price?

A) 95

B) 97.5

C) 100

D) 105

12. Before starting school, Jennie, Chrisi, and Kim went shopping. Jennie spent \$35 more than Chrisi and \$15 more than Kim. If Jennie spent j, how much were their total purchases, in dollars, in terms of j ?

A) $j+50$

B) $3j-50$

C) $j+150$

D) $\dfrac{j+150}{3}$

14. If $a=b^4$ for any positive integer b, and $c=a+a^3$, what is c in terms of b ?

A) $b+b^3$

B) $b^{12}+b^4$

C) b^7+b^3

D) b^5+b^3

13. If c percent of $a+b$ is equal to $4b$, what is the value of $\dfrac{a}{b}$ in terms of c ?

A) $\dfrac{c}{25}-1$

B) $\dfrac{400}{c}-1$

C) $\dfrac{100}{c}$

D) $\dfrac{300}{c}$

15. In a high rise apartment building there is one washing machine for every 6 residents, one dryer for every 5 residents, and a parking space for every 4 residents. If there are x total washers, dryers, and parking spaces, then how many residents, in terms of x, live in the high rise building?

A) $\dfrac{37}{60}x$

B) $\dfrac{60}{37}x$

C) $120x$

D) $60x$

Calculators

Since questions in the Heart of Algebra, Passport to Advanced Math, and Additional Math Topics categories can come up both in the Calculator and No Calculator SAT sections, you should be sure to know how to answer all such questions in this manual without a calculator unless you see the icon to the right. Still, knowing how to use your calculator's operations and shortcuts is valuable for many questions.

The following guide references TI-84 calculators that have been upgraded to improve graphics. Many, though not all, of the functions listed below can be found on TI-83 calculators. Other graphing calculators have similar functions. Always check your owner's manual to see what operations your calculator will perform.

The Basics

- The number keys are white. These include both the decimal point $\boxed{.}$ and the negative sign $\boxed{(-)}$. Be sure not to confuse the negative sign with the subtraction symbol.

- Using the up or down arrows, you can select previous answers or entries and insert them into your current line by pressing $\boxed{\text{ENTER}}$. You can use the ENTRY button, $\boxed{\text{2ND}} \rightarrow \boxed{\text{ENTER}}$, to recall previous entries as well.

- Caret ($\boxed{\wedge}$) is used to raise to a power and is found above the four basic operations.

- $\boxed{x^2}$ can be used to both square or, with $\boxed{\text{2ND}}$, square root.

- The comma $\boxed{,}$ is used within other functions discussed later

- Parentheses should be used when operating with negative numbers or fractions, especially when not using n/d fraction mode (discussed later), to assure the order of operations, PEMDAS, is properly applied.

The $\boxed{\text{MATH}}$ button (left column, third from top) $\boxed{\text{MATH}} \rightarrow$ MATH NUM CPX PRB

- Under $\boxed{\text{MATH}} \rightarrow$ MATH you will find the following useful functions:

    - 1:▷Frac: to change a rational decimal to a fraction in lowest terms

    - 4:$\sqrt[3]{}$: to take the cube root of a number

    - 5:$\sqrt[x]{}$: to take any root of a number (put root before symbol)

- Under $\boxed{\text{MATH}} \rightarrow$ NUM you will find these useful functions:

    - 1:abs(: to initiate absolute value

    - 8:lcm(: to find the least common multiple of two numbers separated by a comma

    - 9:gcd(: to find the greatest common divisor (factor) of two numbers separated by a comma

    - D:n/d: to use a horizontal dividing line; you will see $\frac{\square}{\square}$ on the screen and be able to enter calculations on top and bottom

Graphing

- $\boxed{\text{Y=}}$ to input functions where y has been isolated
- $\boxed{\text{WINDOW}}$ to adjust horizontal and vertical minima and maxima of graph screen and set scale for how frequently axes hash marks are shown
- $\boxed{\text{ZOOM}}$ to adjust the view
    - 1: ZBox: to create, with the cursor, a rectangle whose interior will be enlarged
    - 6: ZStandard: to return to basic window from –10 to 10 in each direction
    - 0: ZFit: to adjust window to show as much of inputted graph(s) as possible
    - A: ZQuadrant1: to show only the first quadrant
- $\boxed{\text{TRACE}}$ to have the cursor follow graph(s) in graph screen as the x and y values are reported at the bottom (use up and down arrows to toggle through multiple graphs)
- $\boxed{\text{TABLE}}$ ($\boxed{\text{2ND}}$ → $\boxed{\text{GRAPH}}$) to view a list of x and y coordinates for inputted functions
    - $\boxed{\text{TBLSET}}$ ($\boxed{\text{2ND}}$ → $\boxed{\text{WINDOW}}$)to adjust table information like where x should start and what the x interval should be
- $\boxed{\text{CALC}}$ ($\boxed{\text{2ND}}$ → $\boxed{\text{TRACE}}$) : use the following functions to calculate:
    - 2: zero: an x-intercept (or root); you will need to use the cursor to set left and right boundaries for the root you're looking for
    - 3: minimum and
    - 4: maximum: a turning point (again, between left and right boundaries)
    - 5: intersect: the intersection point between two curves nearest where the cursor selects the curves (toggle using up and down arrows to select the curves)
    - NOTE: It is often easier to graph a polynomial function and calculate its roots, turning points or transformations than to use algebraic methods like factoring or formulas.

Trick for listing factors

- If you want to see a list of factors of a number, divide that number by x in the $\boxed{\text{Y=}}$ screen and then view the table.

Trigonometric Functions

- $\boxed{\text{SIN}}$, $\boxed{\text{COS}}$, and $\boxed{\text{TAN}}$ operate on angles to find trig ratios
- $\boxed{\text{2ND}}$ → $\overset{\text{SIN}^{-1}}{\boxed{\text{SIN}}}$, $\overset{\text{COS}^{-1}}{\boxed{\text{COS}}}$, and $\overset{\text{TAN}^{-1}}{\boxed{\text{TAN}}}$ operate on trig ratios to find angles

Miscellaneous

- CATALOG ($\boxed{\text{2ND}}$ → $\overset{\text{CATALOG}}{\boxed{\text{0}}}$) lists functions alphabetically (jump using green letters)
- F1 ($\boxed{\text{ALPHA}}$ → $\overset{\text{F1}}{\boxed{\text{Y=}}}$) shortcuts to fraction modes
- F2 ($\boxed{\text{ALPHA}}$ → $\overset{\text{F2}}{\boxed{\text{WINDOW}}}$) shortcuts to operations like abs(

Calculator Problem Set

Utilize the functions of the calculator to help you answer the questions in the following set.

1. If $a = \frac{37}{11}b$ and $b = \frac{13}{17}c$, what is a in terms of c?

   A) $\frac{25}{14}c$

   B) $\frac{5}{2}c$

   C) $\frac{481}{187}c$

   D) $\frac{629}{143}c$

2. What is the value of $\frac{3xy^2 - 17}{5\sqrt{z}}$ when $x = -4, y = -3$, and $z = 625$?

   A) $-\frac{1279}{125}$

   B) -1

   C) 1

   D) $\frac{1279}{125}$

3. In the function $y = \left|x^2 - 4\right|$, for how many values of x does $y = 3$?

   A) None

   B) Two

   C) Three

   D) Four

4. What is the value of $\left|-4\right| - \left|20 - 33\right|$?

   A) -17

   B) -9

   C) 17

   D) 57

5. The expression $\dfrac{3 + \frac{3}{5}}{2 + \frac{1}{10}}$ is equal to?

   A) $\frac{12}{7}$

   B) $\frac{9}{5}$

   C) $\frac{22}{7}$

   D) $\frac{22}{5}$

6 Which of the following is an equivalent form of $f(x)=(x-8)(x+4)$ so that the x- and y-coordinates of the vertex appear as constants?

A) $f(x)=x^2+4x-32$

B) $f(x)=(x-2)^2-36$

C) $f(x)=(x-2)^2-32$

D) $f(x)=(x-4)^2-28$

9 In the xy-plane, the graph of which of the following functions has x-intercepts of 2, 4, and 7?

A) $f(x)=(x+2)(x+4)(x+7)$

B) $f(x)=(x-2)(x-4)(x-7)$

C) $f(x)=x^3-56$

D) $f(x)=(x-8)(x-7)$

7 The graphs of $y=-|x|$ and $y=\sqrt[3]{x}$ are *both* in which of the following quadrants?

A) I only

B) I and III

C) III only

D) III and IV

10 If $\cos A=0.16$ and $0°<A<90°$, what is $\sin(90-A)°$?

A) 0.16

B) 0.4

C) 0.8

D) 0.84

8 What are the equations of all the vertical asymptotes for the graph of the function $y=\dfrac{2x-4}{x^2-4}$?

A) $x=2$ and $x=-2$

B) $x=2$ only

C) $x=-2$ only

D) $x=0$, $x=2$ and $x=-2$

No Calculator Section

Section 3 of the SAT has 20 questions, 15 multiple-choice and 5 grid-in, for which you may not use your calculator. Almost all of these 20 questions are Heart of Algebra or Passport to Advanced Math questions. Two or three are from the Additional Math Topics category, and there are no Data Analysis questions in the no-calculator section.

The following suggestions can be used on any math problem but are especially handy when you don't have use of your calculator:

- Identify and <u>underline</u> all math words. Words like **sum**, **multiple** and **parallel**, and even simple math words like **odd** and **even**, can get lost or mistaken for a similar word when tackling a problem with many parts. Underlining them will burn them into your short-term memory and help you check for silly errors once you have your answer.

- Look for possible algebraic form changes. Many times the writers of SAT questions are just trying to see if you recognize that an expression can be written a different way. These form changes are not necessarily simplification steps, and you won't usually be told to apply them, but when something algebraic *can* be done, see what happens when you do it. Form changes include:

  - Applying EXPONENT rules
  - DISTRIBUTING or FOILING (double distributing)
  - FACTORING
  - Writing FRACTIONS in equivalent forms by looking for *common denominators*

- Sketch figures or graphs if none are provided. Often questions involving angle relationships or function types are simple once you have a visual aid. When sketching graphs, you will usually just need a pair of axes and an approximation of specific x and y values, slopes, intercepts, or turning points. Don't waste time making several hash marks or counting out every coordinate.

- Approximate calculations are usually good enough when you don't have a calculator. Non-calculator questions will not include grueling calculations, and when a moderate calculation is expected on a multiple-choice problem, the choices will usually be different enough so that you can use a simpler, approximate calculation. For example, if part of your work includes multiplying 37 by 104, it may be enough to just work out $40 \times 100 = 4000$ because there may only be one choice even in the same ballpark as 4000.

- Be on high alert when in ZONE F! This is a place where numbers don't behave as they should. ZONE F stands for: **Z**ero, **O**ne, **N**egatives, **E**xponents, and **F**ractions. These numbers and number types have properties that will not always follow the normal patterns. For example, there is a natural assumption that when you take numbers to powers, they should get larger, but watch what happens to these ZONE F numbers when they are raised to powers:

$$0^{12} = 0 \qquad\qquad 1^{53} = 1 \qquad\qquad (-2)^5 = -32 \qquad\qquad \left(\frac{1}{3}\right)^2 = \frac{1}{9}$$

In not one of these instances is the answer greater than the base!

Arithmetic Skills Problem Set

Do the following questions without a calculator to practice your basic arithmetic skills. Try to limit the amount of steps necessary to achieve a correct answer, but also pay attention to the order of operations, divisibility rules, fraction rules, and percent shortcuts.

1. Operate: $5 \times 12 - 3$

2. Operate: $18 + 4 \cdot 6 - 1$

3. Operate: $4 + 2^3 - 21 \div 3$

4. Operate: $\dfrac{5 \cdot 3 + 5 \cdot 2^2}{11 - 4}$

5. Operate: $54 \div 9 + 6^2 \div 3$

6. What is the product $\dfrac{3}{5} \times \dfrac{55}{27}$ in lowest terms?

7. What is $\dfrac{2}{3}$ of $\dfrac{12}{13}$ of 26?

8. What is $\dfrac{4}{15} \times \dfrac{5}{7} \times \dfrac{6}{16}$?

9. What is $\dfrac{35}{24} \div \dfrac{21}{40}$?

10. What is $\dfrac{12}{19} \times \dfrac{57}{28} \div \dfrac{15}{7}$?

11. What is the result when 12,000 is divided by 10, multiplied by 3, and then divided by 900?

16. Solve for x: $\dfrac{x}{9} = \dfrac{28}{36}$

12. What is the result when 238 is subtracted from 738 and the difference is divided by 25?

17. Solve for a: $\dfrac{6}{a} = \dfrac{42}{63}$

13. What is the result when 76 is multiplied by $\dfrac{1}{4}$ and the result is subtracted from 20?

18. Solve for n: $\dfrac{33}{110} = \dfrac{6}{n}$

14. What is the result when 300 is divided by the sum of 68 and 7?

19. Solve for c: $\dfrac{c}{c-4} = \dfrac{78}{52}$

15. What is the result when 25 is divided by $\dfrac{1}{5}$ and the result is added to 65?

20. Solve for v: $\dfrac{v}{36} = \dfrac{2v+1}{75}$

21. What is 30% of 45?

22. What is 15% of 120?

23. What is 250% of 40?

24. What is 0.5% of 1400?

25. 16 is 20% of what number?

26. 75% of what number is 66?

27. 90 is 150% of what number?

28. What percent of 40 is 20?

29. 19 is what percent of 95?

30. What percent of 80 is 100?

No Calculator Problem Set

This problem set consists of questions that you will see elsewhere in this book, in both the Heart of Algebra and Passport to Advanced Math chapters. These questions may be easier to do or check using strategies such as Back solving or Plugging in Numbers. Unfortunately you can't use those strategies as easily on the No Calculator section, so it is important to know how to apply the necessary algebraic techniques to answer and check these questions too.

You can try this problem set (without your calculator of course) before working your way through the Heart of Algebra and Passport to Advanced Math chapters, and then try it again once you've strengthened your algebraic skills in those chapters.

1 If $4(x-3)+8x = 3(x+1)+9$, what is the value of x?

A) -3

B) $\dfrac{7}{3}$

C) $\dfrac{8}{3}$

D) $\dfrac{13}{9}$

2 Don weighs 7 pounds less than twice as much as Megan weighs. If Megan weighs m pounds, then which of the following expressions represents Don's weight?

A) $m-7$

B) $2m-7$

C) $2m+7$

D) $7-2m$

$$3x + y = 7$$
$$6x + 2y = 14$$

3 How many solutions are there to the system of equations shown above?

A) None

B) One

C) Infinitely many

D) Two

$$3x + y = 7$$
$$6x + 2y = 10$$

4 How many solutions are there to the system of equations shown above?

A) None

B) One

C) Infinitely many

D) Two

5. $\dfrac{\left(x^2\right)^5 \cdot \left(x^4\right)^3}{x^2} =$

A) x^{12}

B) x^{20}

C) x^{60}

D) x^{118}

8. The formula for the surface area, S, of a rectangular solid is $S = 2lw + 2wh + 2lh$ where l is the length, w is the width, and h is the height. In terms of l, w, and S, what does h equal?

A) $S - 2lw - 2w - 2l$

B) $\dfrac{S - 2lw}{2}$

C) $\dfrac{S - 2lw}{2w + 2l}$

D) $\dfrac{S}{2lw + 2w + 2l}$

6. Which of the following is equal to $25^{\frac{5}{2}}$?

A) 62.5

B) $5^{\frac{5}{4}}$

C) 5^5

D) $\dfrac{1}{25^{\frac{2}{5}}}$

9. What is the range of the function $f(x) = |x| + 2$?

A) All real numbers

B) $f(x) \geq -2$

C) $f(x) \geq 2$

D) $-2 \leq f(x) \leq 2$

7. If $9x^2 - 4y^2 = a(3x + 2y)$, then what is the value of a in terms of x and y?

A) $x - y$

B) $x + 2y$

C) $3x - 2y$

D) $3x + 2y$

10. What are the solutions to $2x^2 + 12x + 8 = 0$?

A) $x = -3 \pm \sqrt{5}$

B) $x = -3 \pm 2\sqrt{10}$

C) $x = -6 \pm 2\sqrt{5}$

D) $x = -6 \pm \sqrt{10}$

11 For the equation $4x^2 + bx + 9 = 0$, which value of b gives the equation two distinct, real solutions?

A) −12
B)   0
C)   12
D)   15

12 If the graph of the function $f(x)$ has x-intercepts at −5, 5, and 7, which of the following could be $f(x)$?

A) $f(x) = (x-5)^2(x-7)$
B) $f(x) = (x-5)^2(x-7)^2$
C) $f(x) = (x+5)(x-5)(x-7)^2$
D) $f(x) = (x+5)^2(x-5)^2(x+7)^2$

13 If x and y are positive numbers and if $\sqrt{x} + \sqrt{y} = 10\sqrt{y}$, what is the value of x in terms of y?

A) $3y$
B) $9y$
C) $10y$
D) $81y$

14 Which of the following functions will have graphs with the same turning point?

   I. $f(x) = -(x+3)^2 - 7$
   II. $f(x) = (x-3)^2 - 7$
   III. $f(x) = |x+3| - 7$

A) I and II only
B) I and III only
C) II and III only
D) I, II, and III

15 A marketer estimates that a website will increase its hits by 50% every 12 days. If the site got 200 hits today, which of the following functions estimates how many hits h the site will have d days from now?

A) $h(d) = 200(.5)^{12d}$
B) $h(d) = 200(.5)^{\frac{d}{12}}$
C) $h(d) = 200(1.5)^{12d}$
D) $h(d) = 200(1.5)^{\frac{d}{12}}$

Heart of Algebra

Algebra uses the language of mathematics to represent, relate, and solve for unknown quantities. It involves translating and organizing numbers, operations, and letters. Solving equations and inequalities that express linear relationships is a central skill upon which much of the remainder of algebra is based.

The College Board recognizes that the following are essential to succeed in a basic Algebra class:

- Translating word problems into algebraic expressions
- Solving linear equations and inequalities
- Understanding function notation
- Interpreting and graphing linear functions
- Solving and graphing systems of linear equations and inequalities

Algebraic Translation and Solving Linear Equations and Inequalities

Terminology

In order to translate word problems, you need to know the following definitions:

Variable   a letter that represents a number or set of numbers

Constant   a number that is unassociated with a variable

Coefficient   a number multiplied by a variable

Term   a constant or a product of a coefficient and variables (also known as a monomial)

Equation   a statement that two expressions have the same value

Inequality   a statement that expressions have a relationship using $<$, $>$, $\leq$, $\geq$, or $\neq$

Words and phrases associated with

Addition   sum, plus, increased by, added to, more than, greater than

Subtraction   difference, minus, decreased by, subtracted from, less than (be careful of the order)

Multiplication   product, times, multiplied by, for every, of (for fractions), twice (two times)

Division   quotient, ratio, divided by, over, rate

Inequalities   is less than, is greater than, no more than, no fewer than, at most, at least, between

Absolute Value

Used to represent the distance that one number is from another, the absolute value of an expression is always non-negative and is represented with vertical bars.

Example 1   To show the distance between the numbers 7 and 13 you can write $|7-13|$ or $|13-7|$, both of which equal the positive quantity 6.

Example 2   In order to express the inequality $10 < x < 20$, you can write $|x-15| < 5$, which translates as "x is always less than five away from 15."

Solving Linear Equations and Inequalities

In order to isolate a variable, you need to undo the operations that are applied to that variable. You must use opposite operations (e.g. subtraction for addition) to do this, and make sure that whatever you do to one side of the equal sign or inequality symbol, you also do to the other side.

Note: When both sides of an inequality are multiplied or divided by a negative number, you must *reverse the inequality symbol*.

Algebraic Translation Problem Set

[1] "27 less than the product of 6 and k is the same as k squared." Which of the following is equivalent to this statement?

A) $27 - 6k = k^2$

B) $6k - 27 = k^2$

C) $27 - 6 + k = k^2$

D) $6k - 27 = 2k$

[2] Which of the following equations is equivalent to the statement "the square root of a number x is equal to fourteen less than three times that number?"

A) $x^2 = 3x - 14$

B) $x^2 = 3x - 14$

C) $\sqrt{x} = 14 - 3x$

D) $\sqrt{x} = 3x - 14$

[3] Which of the following equations is equivalent to the statement "a number x multiplied by four greater than itself is equal to twice the square root of another number y?"

A) $x(x-4) = \sqrt{2y}$

B) $x(x-4) = 2\sqrt{y}$

C) $x(x+4) = 2\sqrt{y}$

D) $x(x+4) = \sqrt{2y}$

$$k^3 - h = 3k$$

[4] The equation above is equivalent to which of the following statements?

A) A number k squared is h greater than the product of three and k.

B) A number k cubed is h greater than the product of three and k.

C) Three times a number k is h greater than the number k squared.

D) Three times a number k is h greater than the number k cubed.

$$f(x) = x(x-2)$$

[5] The equation above describes which of the following situations?

A) A function f of a number x is equal to two less than twice that number.

B) A function f of a number x is equal to a number x multiplied by two less than that number.

C) A function f of a number x is equal to a number x multiplied by two greater than that number.

D) None of the above

$$y = kx^3 - x$$

6 The equation above describes which of the following situations?

A) A number y is equal to the product of a constant k multiplied by the cube root of a number x subtracted from the number x.

B) A number y is equal to a number x subtracted from the product of a constant k multiplied by the cube root of the number x.

C) A number y is equal to the product of a constant k multiplied by the cube of a number x subtracted from the number x.

D) A number y is equal to a number x subtracted from the product of a constant k multiplied by the cube of the number x.

7 Don weighs 7 pounds less than twice as much as Megan weighs. If Megan weighs m pounds, then which of the following expressions represents Don's weight?

A) $m - 7$

B) $2m - 7$

C) $2m + 7$

D) $7 - 2m$

8 Michael and Sylvia are comparing their CD collections, and Michael notices that he has precisely sixteen more than half as many CDs as Sylvia. If Sylvia has s CDs, how many does Michael have?

A) $\frac{1}{2}s + 16$

B) $\frac{1}{2}s - 16$

C) $2s + 16$

D) $16 - \frac{1}{2}s$

9 Eric is four years younger than Margaret and five years older than Lindsey. Which of the following is an expression for Lindsey's age in years in terms of Margaret's age m?

A) $m + 4$

B) $m - 5$

C) $m - 4$

D) $m - 9$

10 A cobbler is paid \$22 for every pair of shoes, s, he repairs and \$18.50 for every pair of boots, b, he repairs. What equation could be used to determine how much money in dollars, m, the cobbler earns?

A) $m = 18.50b + 22s$

B) $m = 22b + 18.50s$

C) $m = (18.50s)(22b)$

D) $m = 40.50bs$

11 George has a large number of quarters (q), dimes (d), and nickels (n). Which of the following equations represents the value, v, of all of the coins, in cents?

A) $0.05n + 0.1d + 0.25q = v$

B) $n + d + q = v$

C) $5n + 10d + 25q = v$

D) $(25 + 10 + 5)ndq = v$

12 Bat can read between 70 and 100 pages of a certain novel per hour. Based on this information, which of the following models how long in hours, h, it could take Bat to read 700 pages of this novel?

A) $7 \le h \le 10$

B) $70 \le h \le 100$

C) $10 \le h \le 17$

D) $h = \dfrac{700}{85}$

13 On Friday, Arian sent at least p e-mail messages each hour for 6 hours and Michael sent q e-mail messages each hour for 4 hours. Which of the following inequalities represents the total number of messages, t, sent by Arian and Michael on Friday?

A) $t \le (4+6)qp$

B) $t \ge 4p + 6q$

C) $t \ge 4q + 6p$

D) $t \ge q + p$

14 In the figure above, what is the value of $|c - d|$?

A) e

B) b

C) c

D) d

15 A soda company advertises that their bottles hold b fluid ounces of soda. Their goal is that every bottle will have a volume within 0.4 fluid ounces of this number. If they've met their goal and an inspector checks a bottle of soda with x fluid ounces in it, which inequality can be used to represent the relationship between b and x.

A) $b + x \le 0.4$

B) $b - x \ge 0.4$

C) $-0.4 \le b - x \le 0.4$

D) $0.4x \le b$

16 Which of the following is a correct interpretation of the equation $|x - 7| = 5$?

A) The value of x is 5 units away from 7.

B) The value of x is 7 units away from 5.

C) The value of x is 7 units less than 5.

D) The value of x is 5 units less than 7.

17 Jeremy can either spend fewer than 4 hours studying for exams and then go to a party, or stay home and study for 8 hours straight. Which of the following most accurately models the number of hours, x, that Jeremy will study?

A) $x < 4$ or $x = 8$

B) $4 < x < 8$

C) $x < 4$ or $x > 8$

D) $x < 8$

18 If $3 < x < 9$, which of the following is true for all possible values of x ?

   A) $|x - 6| > 3$

   B) $|x - 6| < 3$

   C) $|x + 6| < 3$

   D) $|x + 3| < 9$

20 The weight capacity of the elevator at Bryson's Department Store is 2600 pounds. A group of people with a total weight of 1750 pounds gets on the elevator in the lobby and goes up. If, on average, a number of people totaling 328 pounds get on the elevator at each floor (and nobody gets off), which of the following inequalities can be used to determine the set of floors, f, for which the weight of the elevator will be over capacity?

   A) $f \le \dfrac{4350}{328}$

   B) $f \ge \dfrac{4350}{328}$

   C) $1750 + 328f \le 2600$

   D) $1750 + 328f > 2600$

19 If $|3x - 9| < 0$, which of the following is a possible value of x?

   A) 4

   B) 0

   C) –2

   D) No possible value

Solving Linear Equations and Inequalities Problem Set

1. If $3x + 7 = 5 + x$, what is the value of x?

   A) −6

   B) −1

   C) 2

   D) 6

2. If $38,000 = 1,000(3x + 8)$, what is the value of x?

   A) 1

   B) 10

   C) 100

   D) 1,000

3. If $7(x - 11) = -17$, what is the value of x?

   A) $-\dfrac{94}{7}$

   B) $-\dfrac{24}{7}$

   C) $-\dfrac{6}{7}$

   D) $\dfrac{60}{7}$

4. If $\dfrac{5x}{2} + 3 = 13$, what is the value of x?

   A) −2

   B) 3.5

   C) 4

   D) 6.4

5. If $4(x - 3) + 8x = 3(x + 1) + 9$, what is the value of x?

   A) −3

   B) $\dfrac{7}{3}$

   C) $\dfrac{8}{3}$

   D) $\dfrac{13}{9}$

6. What is the value of x if $\dfrac{1}{5}x + \dfrac{1}{3}x = 8$?

   A) 15

   B) 32

   C) 64

   D) 120

7. If $7 + 2x = 31$, then $5x = ?$

   A) 12

   B) 24

   C) 60

   D) 155

8. If $8x - 2 = 4x + 8$, what is the value of $3x$?

   A) 2.5

   B) 6

   C) 7.5

   D) 10

9   If $-5x - 3 = -6x + 9$, what is the value of $\frac{x}{8}$?

A) 3

B) 1.5

C) 1

D) −1.5

10   If $\frac{6}{x+2} = \frac{6}{2x-2}$, what is the value of x ?

A) −4

B) 0

C) 1

D) 4

11   If $a + b < a - b$, which of the following statements <u>must</u> be true?

A) $a > b$

B) $a = b$

C) $a < 0$

D) $b < 0$

12   If $x + 3y < x$, which of the following <u>must</u> be true?

A) $x < 0$

B) $x < y$

C) $y < 0$

D) $y > \frac{1}{3}$

13   For what value of x is $|3x - 5| + 7$ equal to 5?

A) −1

B) 1

C) $\frac{17}{3}$

D) No possible value

14   If $0 < 5x - 3 < 2$, what is one possible value of x ?

15   If $5000 < d + 2000 < 5500$ and d is an integer, what is the least possible value of d ?

Functions

A function consists of a dependent and an independent variable such that for each value for the independent variable (input), there is only one value of the dependent variable (output). Functions are often named $f(x)$ or simply y, in which case y is the dependent variable and x is the independent variable.

Terminology

Domain the set of all numbers that you can plug in to a function for x and produce a real value of y

Range the set of all real y values that result from a function

Composite functions written either as $f(g(x))$ or as $f \circ g(x)$. To get an output for a composite function, you first plug the x-value into the interior function ($g(x)$ above) and then plug the result of that into the outer function ($f(x)$ above).

Functions — Try It!

1. If $f(x) = 2x^3 + x$, then $f(2) = ?$

2. If $f(x) = 3x - 2$, what is the value of $f(6)$?

3. What is the x-value in the previous function for which $f(x) = 13$?

4. If $g(x) = 3x + 2$ and $g(b) = 26$, what is the value of b?

5. If $f(x) = 3x - 2$ and $g(x) = \dfrac{x}{2} + 4$, what value of x does $f(x) = g(x)$?

Questions 6–8 all refer to the following function:

$$f(x) = x^2 + 2$$

6. What is $f(a) = ?$

7. What is $f(2a) = ?$

8. What is $f(2b + 2) = ?$

9. If $f(x) = 6x - 11$ and $g(x) = \dfrac{1}{2}x + 3$, what is $f(g(2))$?

10. If $h(x) = x^3$ and $h(2a) = 64$, what is the value of a?

Functions Problem Set

1 If $f(x) = mx - 13$ and $f(7) = 71$, what is m?

   A) 4

   B) 11

   C) 12

   D) 14

4 If the function $f(x) = x^2 + 3x$, which of the following is equal to $f(f(x))$?

   A) $x^4 + 9x^2$

   B) $x^4 + 6x^3 + 9x^2$

   C) $(x^2 + 3x)^2 + 3(x^2 + 3x)$

   D) $(x + 3)^4 + 3(x + 3)^2$

2 The functions f and g are defined by $f(x) = 3x^3 + x^2 - 4x - 10$ and $g(x) = f(x + 2)$. What is $g(-1)$?

   A) -70

   B) -10

   C) 10

   D) 68

5 If $f(3) = 7$, $f(6) = 5$, $g(5) = 12$, and $g(6) = 10$, what is $g(f(6))$?

   A) 10

   B) 12

   C) 22

   D) 50

3 If $f(t) = \frac{1}{2}t$ and $g(t) = t + 12$, for what value of t is $f(t) = g(t)$?

   A) -24

   B) -18

   C) -12

   D) 24

x	$f(x)$	$h(x)$
0	−5	2
1	−2	10
2	0	3
3	1	9
4	3	4
5	6	8
6	10	5
7	15	7
8	21	6

6. The table above shows some values for functions $f(x)$ and $h(x)$. For which value of x is $h(x) = f(2x)$?

A) 1

B) 2

C) 3

D) 4

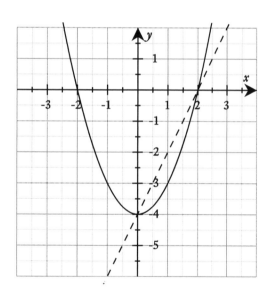

7. For the graphs of the functions $f(x)$ (solid line) and $g(x)$ (dotted line) above, what are all values of x for which $g(x) > f(x)$?

A) $-4 < x < 0$

B) $-2 < x < 0$

C) $0 < x < 2$

D) $x > 2$

8. The equation $g(x) = a \cdot f(x) + 4$ shows how the function g is defined in terms of the function f for all values of x, where a is a constant. If n is a number for which $g(n) = 40$, and $f(n) = 6$, what does a equal?

A) 4

B) 5

C) 6

D) 7

9. If $g(x) = 3x - 4$ and $f(x) = 2x + 3$, , what is the value of $f(3) - g(3)$?

10. The function $f(x)$ is defined by the equation $f(x) = 10x - 2$. If $f(3a) = 88$, then $a = ?$

Linear Functions

Linear functions have the property that as x increases, $f(x)$ (or y) increases or decreases by a constant amount. This constant amount is called the *slope*, and it is represented by m in the two most common forms of a linear function:

- $y = mx + b$, where b represents the y-intercept
- $y - y_1 = m(x - x_1)$, where (x_1, y_1) is a known set of coordinates that satisfy the function

A slope can also be found by dividing the change in y values by the change in x values. This is easily remembered by the formula:

- $\dfrac{\text{rise}}{\text{run}}$ or $\dfrac{y_2 - y_1}{x_2 - x_1}$

Linear functions graph as lines whose steepness is dependent on their slopes. Positive sloped lines run uphill (from left to right), negative sloped lines run downhill, and zero sloped lines are strictly horizontal. Note that a vertical line has no slope since there is no "run."

Parallel lines   lines that have the same slope but different y-intercepts

Perpendicular lines   lines which meet at a 90° angle and whose slopes are negative reciprocals of each other.

Interpreting Linear Formulas

Any formula which attempts to model a real-world scenario using a linear formula has two important components:

- A linear coefficient of the independent variable which represents the change in the dependent variable every time the independent variable increases by 1
- A constant term which represents a starting or ending point

Linear Functions — Try It!

The total cost in dollars, d, of renting a bicycle in Washington, D.C. can be modeled by the equation $d = 10h + 15$, where h is the length of the rental in hours.

Try it 1 What is the meaning of the number 10 in the formula above?

    A) It is the minimum number of hours a bicycle must be rented.

    B) It is the amount charged per hour, after an initial fee, to rent a bicycle.

    C) It is the initial charge to rent the bicycle.

    D) It is the maximum number of bicycles that can be rented per hour.

Try it 2 In the formula above, what is the meaning of the number 15?

    A) It is the minimum number of hours a bicycle must be rented.

    B) It is the amount charged per hour, after an initial fee, to rent a bicycle.

    C) It is the initial charge to rent the bicycle.

    D) It is the maximum number of bicycles that can be rented per hour.

Linear Functions Problem Set

1 If t is a linear function, $t(1) = 7$ and $t(-1) = 9$, what is the slope of t?

A) –2

B) –1

C) 2

D) 3

2 A line in the xy-plane passes through the point $(0, 5)$ and has a slope of $\frac{3}{4}$. Which of the following points lies on the line?

A) $(3,9)$

B) $(9,3)$

C) $(4,8)$

D) $(8,4)$

3 A line in the xy-plane has a positive slope and contains points in the second quadrant. Which quadrant will this line never pass through?

A) Quadrant I

B) Quadrant III

C) Quadrant IV

D) It will pass through all four quadrants

4 The line k in the xy-coordinate plane is given by the equation $5x + 2y = 10$. Line j has a slope that is twice the slope of line k and a y-intercept that is three times the y-intercept of line k. What is the equation of line j?

A) $y = 10x + 30$

B) $y = 5x - 15$

C) $y = 5x + 15$

D) $y = -5x + 15$

5 The line in the xy-plane that represents the graph of the function $y = 3x + 5$ is parallel to line k. If line k goes through the points $(0, -5)$ and $(a, 1)$, what is the value of a?

A) –11

B) 2

C) 8

D) 21

6 In the xy-coordinate plane, line l contains the points $(3,5)$ and $(5,8)$ and line m contains the points $(3,1)$ and $(0, k)$. If lines l and m are perpendicular, what is k?

A) –3

B) –1

C) 3

D) 5

7. In the function $g(x) = 4x + k$, k is a constant. If $g(-3) = 1$, what is the value of $g(1)$?

A) -3

B) 5

C) 13

D) 17

8. A line that passes through the points $(3, n)$ and $(n, 19)$ in the xy-plane also passes through the point $(1, 1)$. What is the value of n?

A) 7

B) 13

C) 15

D) 16

9. The graph of line m in the xy-plane has a slope of 3 and goes through the point $(-1, 2)$. A second line, n, goes through the points $(3, 2)$ and $(4, -1)$. If m and n intersect at the point (a, b), then what is the value of $a + b$?

A) 1

B) 6

C) 8

D) 9

10. In the function $H(t) = 120 + 12t$, H is the altitude of a balloon in feet, and t is the number of minutes after liftoff. Which of the following scenarios is described by the above equation?

A) The balloon starts at an altitude of 12 feet, and travels upwards at a velocity of 120 feet per minute.

B) The balloon starts at an altitude of 120 feet, and travels upwards at a velocity of 12 miles an hour.

C) The balloon starts at an altitude of 0 feet and travels upwards at a velocity of 120 feet per minute.

D) The balloon starts at an altitude of 120 feet, and travels upwards at a velocity of 12 feet per minute.

11. For the function $P(t) = 200 + 100t$, P represents the population size of a colony of bacteria, and t represents the number of hours after the beginning of an experiment. Which of the following is modeled by the aforementioned function?

A) The colony started out with 200 bacteria, and increased by 100 every hour.

B) The colony started out with 200 bacteria, and doubled every hour.

C) The colony started out with no bacteria, and increased by 100 bacteria every hour.

D) The colony started out with 100 bacteria, and increased by 200 every hour.

12 At Jones Auto Rental, it costs \$120 to secure a luxury rental car, and an additional \$40 per day to use the car. The total cost of renting a luxury car can be represented by the equation $c = 40d + 120$. If Ryan decides to rent a car with additional insurance coverage per day, I, which of the following equations could he use to calculate his total cost?

A) $c = 40d + 120 + I$

B) $c = 40Id + 120$

C) $c = 40d + 120I$

D) $c = (40 + I)d + 120$

13 A farmer uses the equation $c = 4x + 15.3$ to estimate the circumference, c, of a cantaloupe, in centimeters, after x weeks. Based on this model, what is the estimated per-week increase, in centimeters, of a cantaloupe's circumference?

A) 4

B) 11.3

C) 15.3

D) 19.3

Questions 14 and 15 refer to the following information.

A moving company is able to estimate the price of a job, p, in dollars, using the equation $p = 80 + 45nh$, where n is the number of movers and h is the number of hours the job will take using n movers.

14 Which of the following best interprets the meaning of 45 in the equation?

A) It is the number of person-hours required to complete a job.

B) It is the amount charged per person-hour of labor.

C) It is the amount charged regardless of the time spent working on the job.

D) It means that the job is billed out in 45-minute intervals.

15 Which of the following best interprets the meaning of 80 in the equation?

A) It is the number of person-hours required to complete a job.

B) It is the amount charged per person-hour of labor.

C) It is the initial amount charged regardless of the time spent working on the job.

D) It means that the job is billed out in 80-minute intervals.

Questions 16 and 17 refer to the following information.

Jacob is a Major League Baseball pitcher who is recovering from surgery. His manager has put a limit on the amount of pitches he can throw in games this year. Throughout the year, the amount of pitches, p, Jacob can still throw can be estimated by the inequality $p \leq 2250 - 15x$, where x represents the number of innings Jacob has already pitched.

16. What is the meaning of the value 2250 in the inequality?

   A) It is the minimum number of pitches Jacob throws in an inning.

   B) It is the amount of pitches Jacob has already thrown.

   C) It is the maximum number of pitches Jacob can throw for the year.

   D) It is the number of games Jacob has played.

17. What is the meaning of the value 15 in the inequality?

   A) It is the average number of pitches Jacob throws each inning.

   B) It is the average number of pitches Jacob throws each game.

   C) It is the number innings Jacob pitches each game.

   D) It is the number of games Jacob pitches each year.

18. Hose A takes 3 hours to fill an 80-gallon pool and Hose B takes 7 hours to fill the same pool. The following equation can be used to figure out how many hours it would take the two hoses, running simultaneously, to fill the pool: $\frac{80}{3}x + \frac{80}{7}x = 80$. Which of the following describes what $\frac{80}{7}x$ represents in the equation?

   A) The time it takes the faster hose to fill the pool

   B) The time it takes the slower hose to fill the pool

   C) The portion of the pool filled by the faster hose

   D) The portion of the pool filled by the slower hose

19. If $m(x) = 30x + c$ where c is a constant and $m(3.5) = 123$, what is the value of c?

20. If $f(x) = mx - 11$ and $f(10) = 19$, what is m?

Systems of Equations and Inequalities

A system of linear equations in two variables consists of two equations and can be written in the following form, where A, B, C, D, E, and F are constants:

$$Ax + By = C$$
$$Dx + Ey = F$$

A **solution** to a linear system like this is an ordered pair (x, y) that satisfies both equations.

Infinite Solutions

When one equation is just a multiple of the other, there will be infinitely many solutions. You can tell that this is the case if $\dfrac{A}{D} = \dfrac{B}{E} = \dfrac{C}{F}$.

No Solutions

When the left side of one equation is a multiple of the left side of the other, but the right sides don't have the same relationship, there are no solutions. This will happen if $\dfrac{A}{D} = \dfrac{B}{E} \neq \dfrac{C}{F}$.

One Solution

If neither of the scenarios above is true, that is if $\dfrac{A}{D} \neq \dfrac{B}{E}$, then there is a single solution (x, y).

Graphing Method

Graph both equations by first isolating y. The point of intersection, if one exists, is the solution.

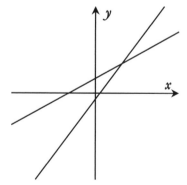 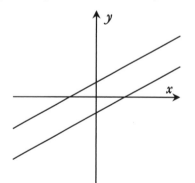 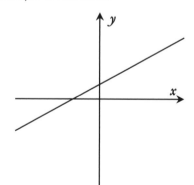

One solution
- Two intersecting lines
- Different slopes

No solutions
- Parallel lines
- Same slope
- Different y-intercept

Infinitely Many Solutions
- Both lines are the same graph
- Same slope
- Same y-intercept

Substitution Method

1. Solve one equation for one of its variables.
2. Substitute the expression from step 1 into the other equation and solve for the other variable.
3. Substitute the value obtained in step 2 into the equation from step 1 and solve.

Example 1   Follow the steps to solve the linear system below.

$$-3x + 2y = 4$$
$$4x + y = -9$$

Step 1	Step 2	Step 3
$4x + y = -9$	$-3x + 2y = 4$	$y = -4x - 9$
$y = -4x - 9$	$-3x + 2(-4x - 9) = 4$	$y = -4(-2) - 9$
	$-3x - 8x - 18 = 4$	$y = 8 - 9 = -1$
	$-11x = 22$	The solution is $(-2, -1)$.
	$x = -2$	

In the second step, if you get an equation that is never true, like $16 = 6$, there is no solution. If you get an equation that is always true, like $12 = 12$, there are infinitely many solutions.

Elimination Method

1. Multiply one or both equations by a constant so the coefficients of one variable are opposites.
2. Add the equations from step 1 to eliminate a variable, and solve for the remaining variable.
3. Substitute the value obtained in step 2 into one of the original equations and solve.

Example 2   Follow the steps to solve the linear system below.

$$2x + 3y = 11$$
$$5x - 2y = -20$$

Step 1	Step 2	Step 3
$2(2x + 3y = 11)$	$4x + 6y = 22$	$2x + 3y = 11$
$3(5x - 2y = -20)$	$15x - 6y = -60$	$2(-2) + 3y = 11$
	$19x = -38$	$3y = 15$
	$x = -2$	$y = 5$
		The solution is $(-2, 5)$.

Word Problems

The SAT often has at least one word problem that can be solved by writing and solving a system of linear equations. For this you have to first define your variables.

Example 3   A test has nineteen questions and is worth fifty points. The test consists of true/false questions worth 2 points each and multiple-choice questions worth 3 points each. How many true/false questions are on the test?

Let x = Number of true/false questions.

Let y = Number of multiple-choice questions.

You can now set up the equations:

$x + y = 19$

$2x + 3y = 50$

This can be solved by any of the three methods (elimination is exemplified below).

$$-2(x + y = 19) \rightarrow -2x - 2y = -38 \qquad x + y = 19$$
$$2x + 3y = 50 \rightarrow \underline{\quad 2x + 3y = 50 \quad} \qquad x + 12 = 19$$
$$y = 12 \qquad\qquad x = 7$$

So there are 7 true/false questions and 12 multiple-choice questions.

Systems of Linear Inequalities

These should be graphed so that you can see the region of solutions in the intersection of the two shaded solution sets. Solid lines are used for $\leq$ or $\geq$, and dashed lines are used for $<$ or $>$. Shade in the direction of any test point that works in the inequality.

Example 4 $y > -x - 1$

$y \leq \dfrac{2}{3}x + 3$

Graphing the system of inequalities above shows that though points like $(2,8)$ and $(0,-4)$ will only satisfy one of the inequalities, points like $(5,3)$ are in the solution set for the entire system.

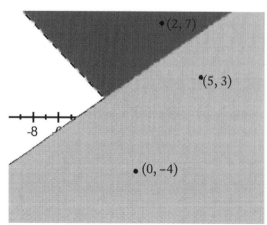

Systems of Equations and Inequalities Problem Set

$$3x + 2y = 7$$
$$2x + 3y = 7$$

1 Which of the following is a solution to the system shown above?

A) $(1,1)$

B) $(2,1)$

C) $\left(\dfrac{8}{5}, \dfrac{8}{5}\right)$

D) $\left(\dfrac{7}{5}, \dfrac{7}{5}\right)$

$$3x + y = 7$$
$$6x + 2y = 14$$

2 How many solutions are there to the system of equations shown above?

A) None

B) One

C) Infinitely many

D) Two

$$3x + y = 7$$
$$6x + 2y = 10$$

3 How many solutions are there to the system of equations shown above?

A) None

B) One

C) Infinitely many

D) Two

$$3x + 2y = 7$$
$$6x + 2y = 10$$

4 How many solutions are there to the system of equations shown above?

A) None

B) One

C) Infinitely many

D) The answer cannot be determined

$$2x + 6y = 18$$
$$5x + 15y = 45$$

5 What is the solution to the system of equations shown above?

A) $(3, 2)$ only

B) $(2, 6)$ only

C) There are infinitely many solutions

D) $(3, 2)$ and $(2, 6)$

6 A school math club is selling boxes of two types of cookies to raise money: chocolate chip for $4 a box and peanut butter for $6 a box. If $856 was raised and 169 boxes were sold, which of the following can be used to find how many boxes of each type were sold?

A) $x + y = 856$
    $4x + 6y = 169$

B) $4x + y = 169$
    $6x + 4y = 856$

C) $x - y = 169$
    $6x + 4y = 856$

D) $x + y = 169$
    $4x + 6y = 856$

$$ax + by = 16$$
$$3x + 6y = 24$$

7 If the system of equations shown above has an infinite number of solutions, what is the value of ab?

A) 2
B) 6
C) 8
D) 9

8 Fred and Bill go to the store. Fred buys 3 chocolate bars and 2 packs of gum for $4.75. Bill buys 3 chocolate bars and 1 pack of gum for $4.25. How much does one chocolate bar cost?

A) $0.75
B) $1.00
C) $1.25
D) $1.50

9 Fred and Bill go back to the store. This time, Fred buys 2 packs of cookies and 1 pack of donuts for $3.25. Bill buys 4 packs of cookies and 2 packs of donuts for $6.50. How much does 1 pack of donuts cost?

A) $0.75
B) $1.25
C) $1.75
D) The answer cannot be determined.

10 Jerry has \$3.06 in pennies, nickels, dimes, and quarters. The number of nickels is the same as the number of dimes, there are 6 pennies, and there are 25 coins in all. How many quarters are there?

A) 5

B) 7

C) 9

D) 11

11 A farmer has cows and chickens. Between all the animals, there are 134 legs. There are 37 animals. Which system below represents this situation?

A) $4x + 2y = 134$
    $x + y = 37$

B) $4x + 2y = 37$
    $x + y = 134$

C) $4x + 4y = 37$
    $x + y = 134$

D) $x + y = 37$
    $2x + y = 134$

12 The Fairfield High School History Club held a car wash to raise funds for a field trip to a museum. They charged \$5 to wash a car and \$7 to wash a truck. If they earned a total of \$275 by washing a total of 43 vehicles, how many cars were washed?

A) 13

B) 17

C) 19

D) 21

13 Ralph is gambling on the throw of a die. For every time he guesses the number on the die correctly, he wins \$7, and for every time he guesses incorrectly, he loses \$3. After 10 throws, Ralph has neither won nor lost any money. How many times did he guess correctly?

A) 3

B) 5

C) 7

D) 9

14 At George's elementary school, the children have bicycles and tricycles. The number of bicycles is 7 less than twice the number tricycles, and altogether there are 70 wheels. How many bicycles are there?

A) 17

B) 20

C) 23

D) 30

$$y + 2x < -1$$
$$y - 3x > 4$$

15 For how many positive values of x is there a solution to the system of inequalities shown above?

A) Infinitely many

B) One

C) Two

D) None

$$y < -20x + 3k$$
$$y > 30x + 4m$$

16 If $(0, 0)$ is a solution to the system of inequalities above, which of the following relationships between k and m must exist?

A) $k > m$

B) $m > k$

C) $m = k$

D) The relationship cannot be determined.

$$\frac{2}{3}x + \frac{3}{4}y = 12$$
$$\frac{10}{12}x + \frac{4}{8}y = 15$$

19 What is the x coordinate of the solution to the system of equations shown above?

$$15x - 6y = 48$$
$$mx - ny = 18$$

17 In the system of equations shown above, m and n are constants. If the system has an infinite number of solutions, what is the value of $\frac{m}{n}$?

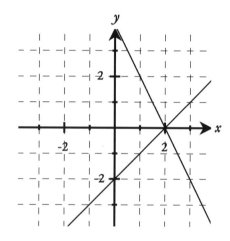

18 Given that $2x + 4y + 6z = 12$ and $x + 3y + 5z = 3$, what is the value of $x + y + z$?

20 What is the x-value for the solution to the system of equations given by the lines shown in the figure above?

Passport to Advanced Math

The College Board emphasizes two key components of what must be mastered to succeed in an Algebra 2 or even a Pre-calculus class: Form Changes and Higher-Level Functions.

Form Changes

Form Changes are the ways in which you can make a quantity or mathematical expression look different in order to operate. A form change does not necessarily imply a simplification. Form changes include:

- Applying exponent rules
- Distributing and FOILing
- Factoring
- Operating with radicals and fractional exponents
- Altering fractions to utilize common denominators
- Using algebra to move expressions around an equal sign (solving literal equations)

Higher-Level Functions

These are functions whose relationships are more complicated than strict linear trends. You should know the characteristics associated with such functions as well as how they can be graphed and how those graphs can be transformed. They include:

- Quadratic functions
- Polynomial functions of degree greater than 2
- Exponential functions
- Absolute value functions
- Rational functions
- Radical functions

Exponents

The following problems highlight the rules of exponents.

$$a^0 = 1 \qquad\qquad\qquad\qquad a^{-x} = \frac{1}{a^x}$$

$$a^x a^y = a^{x+y} \qquad\qquad\qquad\qquad \frac{a^x}{a^y} = a^{x-y}$$

$$\left(a^x\right)^y = a^{xy} \qquad\qquad\qquad\qquad a^x \cdot b^x = (ab)^x$$

Try It!

If you want to test your understanding of the rules above, do not use a calculator:

1. $5^3 \cdot 5^6 = 5^x$ 2. $\dfrac{7^5}{7^3} = 7^x$

3. $2^{-4} = x$ 4. $\left(\left(2^2\right)^2\right)^2 = 2^x$

5. $3^{-2} \cdot 4^{-2} = x^{-2}$ 6. $3 \cdot 3^2 \cdot 3^{-1} = 3^x$

When two different bases are used, see if you can change the base of one expression into the base of the other (usually change to the smaller base). Consider the following example:

Example 1 $\left(8^2\right)^3 = 2^x$

         First use that $8 = 2^3$, so $\left(8^2\right)^3 = \left(\left(2^3\right)^2\right)^3$.

         Then use the rules for exponents to get that $\left(2^6\right)^3 = 2^{18}$, so $2^{18} = 2^x$; thus $x = 18$.

Try It!

1. $\dfrac{9^9}{9^{-9}} = 3^x$ 2. $4 \cdot 8 \cdot 16 = 2^x$

Exponents Problem Set

1. $\dfrac{\left(x^2\right)^5 \cdot \left(x^4\right)^3}{x^2} =$

A) x^{12}

B) x^{20}

C) x^{60}

D) x^{118}

2. $\dfrac{x \cdot 10^6}{y \cdot 10^{-1}} =$

A) $xy \cdot 10^{-6}$

B) $xy^{-1} \cdot 10^7$

C) $xy \cdot 10^7$

D) $xy^{-1} \cdot 10^5$

3. If $3^x = 5$, then $3^{3x} = ?$

A) 5

B) 10

C) 25

D) 125

4. $\dfrac{\left(3^x \cdot 3\right)^3}{9^x} =$

A) 3^{6x}

B) 3^{3-x}

C) 3^{4x}

D) 3^{x+3}

5. $6x^6 12x^6$ is equivalent to:

A) $18x^{12}$

B) $18x^{36}$

C) $72x^{12}$

D) $72x^{36}$

6. If $4^x = 100$, then which of the following must be true?

A) $1 < x < 2$

B) $2 < x < 3$

C) $3 < x < 4$

D) $x = 25$

7. Which of the following is equivalent to $(2x^3)^6$?

A) $2x^9$

B) $2x^{18}$

C) $64x^9$

D) $64x^{18}$

8. Which of the following is equivalent to $(y^5)^{10}(y^{10})^5$?

A) y^{30}

B) $2(y^{50})$

C) y^{100}

D) y^{2500}

9 If $a^x = 2$ and $a^y = 8$, what does a^{x-y} equal?

   A) -6

   B) $\dfrac{1}{4}$

   C) 4

   D) 16

10 If $(w^2 \cdot w^4)^x = w^{72}$ and $(w^y)^y = w^{49}$, where $w > 1$ and $y > 1$, what is the product of x and y?

   A) 19

   B) 63

   C) 84

   D) 124

11 Which of the following values of x satisfies the equation $(4)(2^x) = 8^4$?

   A) 4

   B) 6

   C) 8

   D) 10

12 Which of the following has the greatest value?

   A) 2^{400}

   B) $\left(2 \cdot 2^3\right)^{300}$

   C) 8^{300}

   D) $\left(4 \cdot 2^2\right)^{200}$

13 If $\left(a^2\right)^3 \cdot a^3 = a^x$, what is x ?

14 If g, h and k are positive integers greater than 1 such that $gx^k = x^{k+1}$, what is $g - x$?

15 If $13^9 = 13 \cdot 13^a$, then $a = ?$

Distributing and Factoring

Distributing

Any term that is multiplied by an entire expression involving addition and/or subtraction may also be multiplied by each of the terms within the expression before the calculation is performed.

$$a(b+c-d) = ab + ac - ad.$$

FOIL

This term is an mnemonic device to help us to remember how to *double distribute* when multiplying two binomials:

$$(a+b)(c+d) = \underset{\text{Firsts}}{ac} + \underset{\text{Outers}}{ad} + \underset{\text{Inners}}{bc} + \underset{\text{Lasts}}{bd}$$

Some students learn to double distribute using a 2×2 box structure instead. Either way, and no matter the sizes of the polynomials being multiplied, you must be sure to multiply each term of one of the polynomials by each term of the other polynomial.

Factoring

Factoring means breaking an expression up into its component factors. One way to factor a polynomial is to pull out a common factor, which is like reversing the process of a single distribution.

Example 1 $6x^8 - 9x^3 + 12x^2 = 3x^2(2x^6 - 3x + 4)$

Factoring can also entail reversing the process of FOIL.

Example 2 $x^2 - 5x - 36 = (x-9)(x+4)$

It helps to remember a few formulas for perfect squares of binomials and for the difference of two squares:

$$\left.\begin{array}{l} (x+y)^2 = x^2 + 2xy + y^2 \\ (x-y)^2 = x^2 - 2xy + y^2 \end{array}\right\} \text{The perfect square formulas}$$

$$x^2 - y^2 = (x+y)(x-y)\big\} \text{The difference of two squares}$$

Example 3   Consider the following polynomial: $2x^3 + 8x^2 + 8x$

     The first step is to look for common factors:

     In this case, $2x$ goes into each term, so you can factor that out:

     $2x^3 + 8x^2 + 8x = 2x(x^2 + 4x + 4)$

     The next step is to see if the problem fits a formula or if you can easily reverse FOIL.

     This particular polynomial has a factor that is a perfect square of $(x+2)$ because

     $(x+2)^2 = x^2 + 4x + 4,$

     so the complete factoring of the polynomial can be written as

     $2x^3 + 8x^2 + 8x = 2x(x^2 + 4x + 4) = 2x(x+2)^2$

Distributing Problem Set

1. Which of the following expressions is equivalent to $-7x(2x^3 - 5x + 3)$?

   A) $-14x^3 + 35x - 21$

   B) $-14x^4 - 35x^2 + 21x$

   C) $-14x^4 + 35x^2 - 21x$

   D) $-5x^4 - 12x^2 - 4x$

2. Which of the following expressions is equivalent to $(x-4)(3x+1)$?

   A) $3x^2 - 13x - 4$

   B) $3x^2 - 11x - 4$

   C) $3x^2 - 3x - 4$

   D) $3x^2 + 13x - 4$

3. The expression $(5a - 7b^2)(5a + 7b^2)$ is equivalent to:

   A) $10a$

   B) $10a - 14b^2$

   C) $25a^2 - 49b^4$

   D) $25a^2 + 49b^4$

4. For all x and y, $(3x + y)(x^2 - y) = ?$

   A) $3x^3 - y^2$

   B) $3x^3 - 3xy - y^2$

   C) $3x^3 - 4xy + x^2 y^2$

   D) $3x^3 - 3xy + x^2 y - y^2$

5. The expression $m^4 n^3(m + mn)$ is equivalent to:

   A) $2m^4 n^3$

   B) $m^4 n^3 + m^4 n^4$

   C) $m^5 n^3 + m^5 n^4$

   D) $m^5 + m^5 n^4$

6. Which of the following is equivalent to $(5x - 3)^2$ for all values of x?

   A) $10x - 6$

   B) $25x^2 - 9$

   C) $25x^2 - 15x - 9$

   D) $25x^2 - 30x + 9$

7. Which of the following is equivalent to $3a(2a - b)^2$?

   A) $7a^2 - 7ab + 4ab^2$

   B) $12a^3 - 12a^2 b + 3ab^2$

   C) $18a^3 - 9a^2 b$

   D) $36a^4 - 36a^3 b + 9a^2 b^2$

8. If $x + y = 2$ and $c + d = 5$, what is the value of $xc + yd + xd + yc$?

   A) 7

   B) 10

   C) 14

   D) 20

9. If $(a + b)^2 = 169$ and $(a - b)^2 = 25$, then $ab = ?$

10. If $(4x^3 - 2x + 5) - 3(6x^2 - 5x + 10)$ is written in the form $ax^3 + bx^2 + cx + d$, where a, b, c, and d are constants, what is the value of c?

Factoring Problem Set

[1] Which of the following is a factor of $x^2 - 6x + 5$?

A) $x - 1$

B) $x - 2$

C) $x - 6$

D) $x + 5$

[2] If $a^2 - b^2 = 45$ and $a - b = 5$, then $b = ?$

A) $\dfrac{1}{3}$

B) 2

C) 5

D) 7

[3] Which of the following is equivalent to $25m^2 - 81n^{10}$?

A) $(5m - (3n)^4)(5m + n^6)$

B) $(5m - 9n^5)(5m + 9n^2)$

C) $(5m + 9n^5)(5m - 9n^5)$

D) $(5m - 9n^5)(5m - 9n^5)$

[4] $(7x + 10) - (4x - 8)$ is equivalent to

A) $3(x + 6)$

B) $3x + 2$

C) $3(x + 2)$

D) $3(x + 18)$

[5] For $x^2 \neq 36$, $\dfrac{(x+6)^2}{x^2 - 36} = ?$

A) $-\dfrac{1}{6}$

B) $\dfrac{1}{x - 6}$

C) $\dfrac{1}{x + 6}$

D) $\dfrac{x + 6}{x - 6}$

[6] If $a^2 = b^2 + 80$, which of the following expressions must equal 80?

A) $2(a + b)$

B) $a^2 + b^2$

C) $(a - b)(a - b)$

D) $(a + b)(a - b)$

[7] Where $\dfrac{x + 3}{x^2 - 2x - 15}$ is defined, it is equivalent to which of the following expressions?

A) $-\dfrac{3}{x - 15}$

B) $\dfrac{1}{x - 5}$

C) $\dfrac{3}{x + 5}$

D) $\dfrac{1}{x + 5}$

8   Which of the following is not a factor of $x^5 - x^3$?

A) x^3

B) $x - 1$

C) $x^2 - 1$

D) $x^3 - 1$

12   If $pq = 11$ and $p - q = 3$, what is the value of $p^2 q - pq^2$?

A) 14

B) 22

C) 33

D) 88

9   If $x \neq 0$, $x \neq -1$, $x \neq 1$, $\dfrac{x-1}{x^4 - x^2}$ is equivalent to which of the following?

A) $\dfrac{-1}{x^3 - x}$

B) $\dfrac{1}{x^2(x-1)}$

C) $\dfrac{1}{x^2(x+1)}$

D) $\dfrac{x}{x^3 - 1}$

13   If $x^4 - y^4 = 81$ and $x^2 + y^2 = 9$, then what is $x^2 - y^2$?

10   If $9x^2 - 4y^2 = a(3x + 2y)$, then what is the value of a, in terms of x and y ?

A) $x - y$

B) $x + 2y$

C) $3x - 2y$

D) $3x + 2y$

14   If $\dfrac{m^{x^2}}{m^{y^2}} = m^{10}$ and $x + y = 5$, what is the value of $x - y$?

11   Which of the following is equivalent to $\dfrac{x^2 - 121}{11 - x}$, for $x \neq 11$?

A) $x + 11$

B) $-x + 11$

C) $-x - 11$

D) $x - 11$

15   If $a + b = c$ and $3a + 5c + 3b = 56$, what is the value of c ?

Radicals and Fractional Exponents

A radical, or root, is the opposite of a power. That is, if taking x to the nth power gives you y, then x is the nth root of y. This can be shown with a radical symbol as follows: $x^n = y$ means $x = \sqrt[n]{y}$

Square roots invert squaring, cube roots invert cubing, fourth roots invert taking a number to the fourth power, and so on.

You can also express roots using fractional exponents. For example, $\sqrt{x} = x^{\frac{1}{2}}$ and $\sqrt[3]{x} = x^{\frac{1}{3}}$.

Power-Over-Root Rule

When an exponent is expressed as a fraction, raise the base to the power of the numerator and turn the denominator into a root. You can do this in either order:

$$x^{\frac{a}{b}} = \sqrt[b]{x^a} = \left(\sqrt[b]{x}\right)^a$$

Example 1 $32^{\frac{3}{5}} = \left(\sqrt[5]{32}\right)^3 = 2^3 = 8$

When a radical is in an equation, isolate the radical, and then raise both sides to the appropriate power. If a variable is raised to a fractional exponent, take both sides to the reciprocal power. Always watch out for extraneous solutions, and keep in mind that $\sqrt{\ }$ means only the positive, or principal, square root.

Example 2   Solve for x: $\sqrt{x+14} - 2 = x - 8$

First, add 2 to both sides:

$$\sqrt{x+14} = x - 6$$

Then, square both sides:

$$\left(\sqrt{x+14}\right)^2 = (x-6)^2$$
$$x + 14 = x^2 - 12x + 36$$

Solve the resulting quadratic equation, and then check for extraneous solutions:

$$x^2 - 13x + 22 = 0$$
$$(x-11)(x-2) = 0$$
$$x = 11 \text{ and } x = 2$$

Check the solutions:

$$\sqrt{11+14} = 11 - 6$$
$$\sqrt{25} = 5 \text{ (good)}$$
$$\sqrt{2+14} = 2 - 6$$
$$\sqrt{16} = -4 \text{ (reject)}$$

The solution is therefore only $x = 11$.

Example 3   Solve for x: $2x^{\frac{3}{4}} - 5 = 11$

First add 5 to both sides:

$$2x^{\frac{3}{4}} = 16$$

Divide through by 2:

$$x^{\frac{3}{4}} = 8$$

Take both sides to the reciprocal power:

$$\left(x^{\frac{3}{4}}\right)^{\frac{4}{3}} = 8^{\frac{4}{3}}$$

Finally, apply the power-over-root rule:

$$8^{\frac{4}{3}} = \left(\sqrt[3]{8}\right)^4 = 2^4 = 16$$

The solution is therefore $x = 16$.

Radicals and Fractional Exponents Problem Set

[1] The expression $x^{-3}y^{\frac{1}{3}}$ is equivalent to which of the following?

A) $\dfrac{\sqrt[3]{y}}{x^3}$

B) $\dfrac{1}{xy}$

C) $\dfrac{\sqrt[3]{x}}{y^3}$

D) $\dfrac{y\sqrt{y}}{x^3}$

[2] Which of the following is equal to $25^{\frac{5}{2}}$?

A) 62.5

B) $5^{\frac{5}{4}}$

C) 5^5

D) $\dfrac{1}{25^{\frac{2}{5}}}$

[3] $\left(64m^6n^3p^{12}\right)^{\frac{1}{3}} =$

A) $4m^2np^4$

B) $64m^6np^4$

C) $4m^6n^3p^{12}$

D) $4m^6np^4$

[4] If a and b are both greater than 1, which of the following is equivalent to $\dfrac{a^{\frac{1}{5}}b^{-4}}{a^{-3}b^{\frac{1}{2}}}$?

A) $\dfrac{a^{\frac{3}{5}}}{b^2}$

B) $\dfrac{\sqrt[5]{a^3}}{b^2}$

C) $\dfrac{(a^3)\sqrt[5]{a}}{(b^4)\sqrt{b}}$

D) $\dfrac{\sqrt[5]{a^3}}{(b^4)\sqrt{b}}$

[5] If $a^{\frac{1}{3}} = b^4$ and $b^{-2} = c^3$, what is a in terms of c?

A) c^{-18}

B) c^{27}

C) c^6

D) c^{-2}

[6] $16^{\frac{1}{6}}$ is equivalent to all of the following except one. Which one?

A) $\sqrt[3]{4}$

B) $8^{\frac{2}{9}}$

C) $2^{\frac{2}{3}}$

D) $\sqrt[12]{32}$

7 If x and y are positive numbers and if $\sqrt{x} + \sqrt{y} = 10\sqrt{y},$ what is the value of x in terms of y?

A) $3y$

B) $9y$

C) $10y$

D) $81y$

9 What is the solution set for the equation $\sqrt[3]{x-5} = 2$?

A) $\{-3, 13\}$

B) $\{9\}$

C) $\{13\}$

D) No solution

8 If $b > 0$ and $\left(b^2 + 51\right)^{\frac{1}{2}} = 10,$ what is the value of b?

A) 3

B) 5

C) 7

D) 10

10 If $x = \sqrt{3},$ $y = 2x,$ and $4y = \sqrt{24z},$ what is the value of z?

Fractional Operations and Equations

Fractional expressions often require a change of form in order to operate. You can change the form of a fraction by reducing it or by multiplying the top and bottom by the same expression. Both of these actions constitute a form change, but not a value change, because you are technically multiplying or dividing by 1.

Reducing

Reducing is just dividing the top and bottom of a fraction by the same thing. Polynomials will often need to be factored before you can see what can be divided out.

Example 1 $\dfrac{x^2 - 5x + 6}{x^3 - 2x^2} = \dfrac{(x-2)(x-3)}{x^2(x-2)} = \dfrac{x-3}{x^2}$

Adding and Subtracting

Fractions can be added or subtracted when they have common denominators, so you may have to multiply the top and bottom of one or both fractions by some expression in order to achieve this.

Example 2 $\dfrac{3}{x+2} - \dfrac{2}{x} = \dfrac{3}{x+2}\cdot\left(\dfrac{x}{x}\right) - \dfrac{2}{x}\left(\dfrac{x+2}{x+2}\right) = \dfrac{3x}{x(x+2)} - \dfrac{2(x+2)}{x(x+2)} = \dfrac{3x - 2x - 4}{x(x+2)} = \dfrac{x-4}{x^2+2x}$

Multiplying

Multiply fractions across—top with top and bottom with bottom. You may reduce before or after multiplying.

Example 3 $\dfrac{3}{x+2}\cdot\dfrac{x-2}{x} = \dfrac{3\cdot(x-2)}{(x+2)\cdot x} = \dfrac{3x-6}{x^2+2x}$

Dividing

In order to divide fractions you must first flip the second fraction to its reciprocal and then **multiply** across as usual. Some students use "keep-change-flip" to remember this. It means that you should **keep** the first fraction as it is, **change** the sign from division to multiplication, and then **flip** the second fracton upside down.

Example 4 $\dfrac{2x}{x+4} \div \dfrac{3x-2}{x^2-1} = \dfrac{2x}{x+4}\cdot\dfrac{x^2-1}{3x-2} = \dfrac{(2x)(x^2-1)}{(x+4)(3x-2)} = \dfrac{2x^3-2x}{3x^2-2x+12x-8} = \dfrac{2x^3-2x}{3x^2+10x-8}$

Complex Fractions

Complex fractions are fractions that contain other fractions within them. The most efficient way to simplify a complex fraction is to multiply every term by the Least Common Denominator (LCD) of all terms.

Example 5   Simplify $\dfrac{4-\dfrac{49}{x^2}}{2-\dfrac{7}{x}}$.

This has an LCD of x^2: $\dfrac{4(x^2)-\dfrac{49}{x^2}(x^2)}{2(x^2)-\dfrac{7}{x}(x^2)} \;=\; \dfrac{4x^2-49}{2x^2-7x} \;=\; \dfrac{(2x+7)(2x-7)}{x(2x-7)} \;=\; \dfrac{2x+7}{x}$

Fractional Equations

You can add or subtract on either side of the equation, if applicable, using common denominators and then cross-multiply to solve, or you can multiply the entire equation through by the LCD.

Beware that some fractional equations have extraneous solutions if they make the bottom of one of the original fractions equal zero. In multiple-choice problems, you are better off back solving from the beginning to avoid being trapped by this.

Example 6   Solve for x if $\dfrac{1}{x+2}+\dfrac{2}{x}=\dfrac{-2}{x(x+2)}$.

Multiply through to get a common denominator: $\dfrac{1}{x+2}\left(\dfrac{x}{x}\right)+\dfrac{2}{x}\left(\dfrac{x+2}{x+2}\right)=\dfrac{-2}{x(x+2)}$

$\dfrac{x}{x(x+2)}+\dfrac{2(x+2)}{x(x+2)}=\dfrac{-2}{x(x+2)} \quad\Leftrightarrow\quad \dfrac{x+2x+4}{x(x+2)}=\dfrac{-2}{x(x+2)}$

Set the numerators equal to get $3x+4=-2$, so $3x=-6$ and $x=-2$.

But this is *not* a solution! The domain of our original equation did *not* include $x=-2$, so this equation actually has no solutions.

Fraction Decomposition

A fraction of algebraic expressions can be divided out to produce a quotient and, often, a remainder. Just like with numbers, the remainder must then go over the original denominator to produce a proper fraction.

Example 7 $\dfrac{6x+13}{3x+5} \;=\; \dfrac{6x+10+3}{3x+5} \;=\; \dfrac{6x+10}{3x+5}+\dfrac{3}{3x+5} \;=\; 2+\dfrac{3}{3x+5}$

These questions are usually easier to do by plugging in numbers or back solving the choices when you can.

Fractional Operations and Equations Problem Set

1. Where $x \neq 0$, express the sum $\dfrac{2x+5}{2x} + \dfrac{3x-4}{3x}$ in lowest terms.

   A) $\dfrac{2x+1}{x}$

   B) $12x-7$

   C) $\dfrac{5x+1}{5x}$

   D) $\dfrac{12x+7}{6x}$

2. Which of the following is equivalent to the product $\dfrac{a^2-49}{a^2+4a-21} \times \dfrac{a^2-9}{a-7}$?

   A) $\dfrac{a(a^2-9)}{a^2+4a-21}$

   B) $\dfrac{a+7}{a-3}$

   C) $a-7$

   D) $a+3$

3. When divided and reduced, $\dfrac{x^2+10x+25}{x^2-9} \div \dfrac{x^2-25}{x-3}$ equals

   A) $\dfrac{10x-1}{x-3}$

   B) $\dfrac{x+5}{x+3}$

   C) $\dfrac{(x+3)(x+5)}{x+5}$

   D) $\dfrac{x+5}{(x+3)(x-5)}$

4. If the expression $\dfrac{x^2}{x+5}$ is written in as $\dfrac{25}{x+5} + C$, what is C in terms of x?

   A) $x+5$

   B) $x-5$

   C) x^2

   D) x^2-25

5. For $x \neq 0$ and $y \neq 0$, which of the following is a simplified form of $\dfrac{\dfrac{x}{y} - \dfrac{y}{x}}{1 + \dfrac{x}{y}}$?

   A) $\dfrac{-y}{x}$

   B) $\dfrac{x-y}{x}$

   C) $\dfrac{y-x}{x}$

   D) $-y$

6 For $x \neq 0$, which of the following is a simplified form of $\dfrac{2 - \dfrac{2}{7x}}{x - \dfrac{1}{49x}}$?

A) $\dfrac{2}{x+1}$

B) $\dfrac{7}{x+1}$

C) $\dfrac{14}{7x+1}$

D) $\dfrac{2x-14}{x^2-1}$

7 Which of the following is equivalent to $\dfrac{8x+11}{2x+5}$?

A) 3

B) $\dfrac{4x+11}{5}$

C) $4 - \dfrac{9}{2x+5}$

D) $4 - \dfrac{2}{2x+5}$

8 If $\dfrac{1}{3}a - \dfrac{1}{5}b = 4$, what is the value of $5a - 3b$?

9 If $x + y = 5$ and $xy = 20$ what is the value of $\dfrac{1}{x} + \dfrac{1}{y}$?

10 What is the negative of x in the equation $\dfrac{3x+2}{x} = \dfrac{4x-2}{3x} + \dfrac{1}{3}$?

Literal Equations Problem Set

Using the same rules of algebra you use when there is only one variable, solve for the stated variable in terms of the others.

1. If $ax + b = c$, which of the following expressions gives the value of x in terms of a, b, and c?

   A) $c - b - a$

   B) $\dfrac{c}{a} - b$

   C) $\dfrac{c + b}{a}$

   D) $\dfrac{c - b}{a}$

2. The formula for kinetic energy is $K = \dfrac{1}{2}mv^2$.

   Which of the following expressions gives the value of velocity, v, in terms of m and K?

   A) $\sqrt{\dfrac{2K}{m}}$

   B) $\sqrt{\dfrac{K}{2m}}$

   C) $\sqrt{\dfrac{m}{2K}}$

   D) $\sqrt{2mK}$

3. If $kx = -x^2$ for all values of x, what is the value of k?

   A) -2

   B) -1

   C) $-x$

   D) x

4. If $7a + k = 4a + 2$, what is k in terms of a?

   A) $2 - 3a$

   B) $3a - 2$

   C) $3a + 2$

   D) $11a + 2$

5. If $ar - f = b$ and $a \neq 0$, what does $r = ?$

   A) $\dfrac{b + f}{a}$

   B) $\dfrac{b - f}{a}$

   C) $b + f - a$

   D) $b - f + a$

6. If the equation for the slope, m, of a line that goes through the point (x_1, y_1) is represented as $m = \dfrac{y - y_1}{x - x_1}$, which of the following equations expresses y properly?

   A) $y = m(x - x_1) - y_1$

   B) $y = m(x - x_1) + y_1$

   C) $y = \dfrac{m - y_1}{x - x_1}$

   D) $y = (m + y_1)(x - x_1)$

7 The weight in grams of a certain insect's larva can be modeled by the function $w = \dfrac{1}{12}t + 8$, where t equals time in hours after an initial measurement. Which of the following expresses the time after measurement in terms of the larval weight?

A) $12w - 8$

B) $\dfrac{1}{12}w - 8$

C) $\dfrac{1}{12}w + 8$

D) $12(w - 8)$

8 If $m = n^{-1}p^{-2}q$, which of the following expressions gives the value of n in terms of m, p, and q?

A) mp^2q

B) $\dfrac{mp^2}{q}$

C) $\dfrac{p^2}{mq}$

D) $\dfrac{q}{mp^2}$

9 If $a = b(c + d)$, which of the following expressions gives the value of d in terms of a, b, and c?

A) $c - b - a$

B) $a - b - c$

C) $\dfrac{a - bc}{b}$

D) $\dfrac{a}{bc}$

10 The formula used to convert degrees Celsius to degrees Fahrenheit is $F = \dfrac{9}{5}C + 32$. Which of the following formulas will convert degrees Fahrenheit to degrees Celsius?

A) $C = \dfrac{9}{5}F + 32$

B) $C = \dfrac{9}{5}F - 32$

C) $C = \dfrac{5}{9}F - 32$

D) $C = \dfrac{5}{9}(F - 32)$

11 If $a = \dfrac{b}{b + c}$, what is the value of b in terms of a and c?

A) $\dfrac{ac}{c - a}$

B) $\dfrac{c}{1 - a}$

C) $\dfrac{ac}{a - 1}$

D) $\dfrac{ac}{1 - a}$

12 The standard form of a quadratic function is $y = ax^2 + bx + c$. Which of the following gives b in terms of y, a, c, and x?

A) $y - ax^2 - x - c$

B) $\dfrac{y - ax^2 + c}{x}$

C) $y - c - ax$

D) $\dfrac{y - c}{x} - ax$

13　The formula for the surface area, S, of a rectangular solid is $S = 2lw + 2wh + 2lh$ where l is the length, w is the width, and h is the height. In terms of l, w, and S, what does h equal?

A)　$S - 2lw - 2w - 2l$

B)　$\dfrac{S - 2lw}{2}$

C)　$\dfrac{S - 2lw}{2w + 2l}$

D)　$\dfrac{S}{2lw + 2w + 2l}$

14　The formula for the surface area, S, of a right circular cylinder is $S = 2\pi r^2 + 2\pi rh$, where r is the radius of the base and h is the height. If the radius of the base of a right circular cylinder is x and the surface area is y, what is the height in terms of x and y?

A)　$\dfrac{y - 2\pi x^2}{2\pi x}$

B)　$\dfrac{y - 2\pi x}{2\pi}$

C)　$y - x$

D)　$y - 2\pi x$

$$h = \dfrac{\left(\dfrac{a}{23}\right)\left(\dfrac{b}{c}\right)^x}{35 - \left(\dfrac{12}{a}\right)^{x-1}} I$$

15　The formula shown above can be used to predict the height in inches, h, of a tree with initial height I when a, b, and c ounces of three different fertilizers are used and x months have passed. Which of the following expresses I in terms of h, a, b, c, and x?

A)　$I = \dfrac{35 - \left(\dfrac{12}{a}\right)^{x-1}}{\left(\dfrac{a}{23}\right)\left(\dfrac{b}{c}\right)^x} h$

B)　$I = \dfrac{\left(\dfrac{a}{23}\right)\left(\dfrac{b}{c}\right)^x}{35 - \left(\dfrac{12}{a}\right)^{x-1}} h$

C)　$I = \dfrac{\left(\dfrac{12}{a}\right)}{\left(\dfrac{a}{23}\right)\left(\dfrac{b}{c}\right)^x} h + 35$

D)　$I = \dfrac{\left(\dfrac{12}{a}\right)}{35 + \left(\dfrac{a}{23}\right)\left(\dfrac{b}{c}\right)} h$

Quadratic Functions

Quadratic functions graph as parabolas and can be written in three distinct forms: **standard form**, **vertex form**, and **factored form**. The parabola will have an **axis of symmetry** that goes through its **vertex**, or turning point. The lead coefficient, a, cannot equal 0. The parabola will smile when a is positive, making the vertex a **minimum**, and frown when a is negative, making the vertex a **maximum**. All quadratics have a y-intercept where $x = 0$ and **roots** where $f(x) = 0$. When the roots are real numbers, they are the x-intercepts of the parabola.

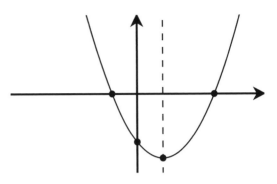

Standard Form

$f(x) = ax^2 + bx + c$

- Axis of symmetry: $x = \dfrac{-b}{2a}$

- y-intercept: $(0, c)$

- Roots: $x = \dfrac{-b \pm \sqrt{b^2 - 4ac}}{2a}$

  - Sum of the Roots: $\dfrac{-b}{a}$

  - Product of the Roots: $\dfrac{c}{a}$

- Discriminant: $D = b^2 - 4ac$

  - Real roots when D is positive

  - One double root when $D = 0$

  - Imaginary roots when D is negative

Vertex Form

$f(x) = a(x - h)^2 + k$

- This form can be constructed from standard form by **completing the square**.
- The vertex is (h, k) and the axis of symmetry is $x = h$.
- The SAT will often describe this form as one where "the coordinates of the vertex can be seen as constants."

Factored Form

$f(x) = a(x - r_1)(x - r_2)$

- This form can be constructed from standard form by factoring (when it is factorable).
- The SAT will often describe this form as one where "the x-intercepts can be seen as constants." Those x-intercepts, or roots, are r_1 and r_2.
- The axis of symmetry goes through the midpoint of the roots, so its equation is $x = \dfrac{r_1 + r_2}{2}$.

Quadratic Functions Problem Set

1. A ball is thrown up from a height of 4 feet. The equation describing the ball's height after t seconds is $h(t) = 4 + 10t - 16t^2$. What is the ball's height after 0.4 seconds?

   A) It will have hit the ground

   B) 1.6 feet

   C) 5.44 feet

   D) 10.56 feet

$$a(x) = x^2 + 1$$
$$b(x) = -x$$

2. Given the functions $a(x)$ and $b(x)$ defined above, for how many values of k is it true that $a(k) = b(k)$?

   A) None

   B) One

   C) Two

   D) Three

3. What are the solutions to $2x^2 + 12x + 8 = 0$?

   A) $x = -3 \pm \sqrt{5}$

   B) $x = -3 \pm 2\sqrt{10}$

   C) $x = -6 \pm 2\sqrt{5}$

   D) $x = -6 \pm \sqrt{10}$

4. What is the sum of the roots of the quadratic function $y = 3x^2 - 15x + 8$?

   A) -15

   B) -5

   C) 5

   D) 15

5. What is the product of the values of a that satisfy $a^2 - 12a + 9 = 0$?

   A) -9

   B) 9

   C) $-18\sqrt{3}$

   D) $18\sqrt{3}$

x	$f(x)$
0	-6
1	-6
2	-4
3	0

6. If $f(x)$ is a quadratic equation represented by the table of values shown above, which of the following could be $f(x)$?

   A) $f(x) = x^2 - 6$

   B) $f(x) = x^2 + 3x + 6$

   C) $f(x) = x^2 - x + 3$

   D) $f(x) = x^2 - x - 6$

7 For a certain quadratic equation
$ax^2 + bx + c = 0$, the 2 solutions are $x = -\dfrac{2}{3}$
and $x = \dfrac{1}{2}$. Which of the following are factors
of $ax^2 + bx + c$?

A) $(3x + 2)$ and $(2x - 1)$

B) $(3x + 1)$ and $(2x - 3)$

C) $(3x - 2)$ and $(2x + 1)$

D) $(3x - 2)$ and $(2x - 1)$

8 For the function $f(x) = ax^2 + bx + c$, where
$a = 3$, $b = 0$, and c is a constant, if
$f(-2) = 12$, what is the value of $f(2)$?

A) –12

B) 4

C) 12

D) 36

9   The function $h(t) = -4.9t^2 + 70t$ can be used
to model the height of a projectile with an
initial velocity of 70 meters per second t
seconds after it is fired. Approximately how
many seconds after being fired will the
projectile hit the ground?

A) 4.9

B) 7.1

C) 14.3

D) 70

10 What is the distance between the two points
where the parabola with equation
$y = x^2 - 20x + 96$ intersects the line given by
the equation $y = 60$?

A) 4

B) 16

C) 18

D) 20

$$y = x^2 - x - 6$$
$$y = x^2 - 3x + 6$$

11 What is the x-value of the solution of the
system of equations shown above?

A) 2

B) 3

C) 6

D) No solution

12 A square-shaped piece of cardboard will have squares of side-length x cut from each corner. The resulting edges will be folded up, forming a box with no top. The side of the original cardboard square is y. What is the volume of this box?

A) $x(y-x)(y-x)$

B) $x(y-2x)(y-2x)$

C) $x^2 y$

D) $(x-y)^3$

15 If m is constant, what are the solutions of $3x^2 = 2mx - m$?

A) $x = \dfrac{m}{3} \pm \dfrac{\sqrt{m^2 - 3m}}{3}$

B) $x = \dfrac{m}{3} \pm \dfrac{\sqrt{m^2 - 12m}}{3}$

C) $x = \dfrac{2m}{3} \pm \dfrac{\sqrt{m^2 - 3m}}{3}$

D) $x = m \pm \sqrt{m^2 - 3m}$

Questions 13 and 14 refer to the following information:

$$y = a(x-5)(x+1)$$

13 What is the x-coordinate of the vertex of the parabola that represents the quadratic equation above (when $a \neq 0$)?

A) 5

B) 2

C) –1

D) –2

16 Which of the following is the vertex form of the quadratic function $y = x^2 + 12x + 32$?

A) $y = (x+8)(x+4)$

B) $y = (x+6)(x-4)$

C) $y = (x+6)^2 - 4$

D) $y = (x-6)^2 - 4$

14 What is the y-coordinate, in terms of a, of the vertex of the parabola that represents the quadratic equation above (when $a \neq 0$)?

A) $-9a$

B) $-5a$

C) $-4a$

D) $4a$

17 If $x^2 + 2ax + a^2 = 16$, what is one possible value of $x + a$?

  A) 2

  B) 4

  C) 8

  D) 16

$$(2x + 3)(x + 2) = (x + 3)(x - 3)$$

19 The above equation has how many real solutions?

18 For the equation $4x^2 + bx + 9 = 0$, which value of b gives the equation two distinct, real solutions?

  A) –12

  B) 0

  C) 12

  D) 15

20 If $x > 0$ and $x^2 - 10x - 24 = 0$, what is the value of x ?

Polynomial Functions

Polynomial functions (ex. $f(x) = x^3 + 2x^2 - 6$) written in standard form $f(x) = ax^n + bx^{n-1} + cx^{n-2}...$ are identified by their degree, n, the highest exponent to which x is raised. *Linear* functions are polynomial functions with degree 1, and *quadratic* functions are polynomial functions with degree 2. Other examples of polynomial functions are *cubic* functions (degree 3) and *quartic* functions (degree 4).

Factored form $f(x) = a(x - r_1)(x - r_2)(x - r_3)...$ where r_k is a root of the polynomial. The relationship between a root, r, and a factor, $(x - r)$, is very important.

Roots   The number of roots of a polynomial is equivalent to its degree. When roots are real numbers, they are the x-intercepts of the polynomial's graph. The **multiplicity** of root r is the number of times $(x - r)$ is a factor of a polynomial. If a root has a multiplicity of 2, it is a double root, and the graph will appear to bounce off of that root on the x-axis. If a root has a multiplicity of 3, it is a triple root, and the graph will show inflection (a brief plateau) as it crosses the x-axis at that spot.

End behavior   Odd-degree polynomials will end in different directions. If a is positive, odd-degree polynomials will go to $-\infty$ as x goes to $-\infty$ and will go to ∞ as x goes to ∞. If a is negative, the reverse happens. Even-degree polynomials go to ∞ in both directions if a is positive and go to $-\infty$ in both directions if a is negative.

Example 1 $f(x) = x^3 - 3x^2 - 6x + 8$ *Example 2* $f(x) = -(x + 1)^2(x - 3)^2$ *Example 3* $f(x) = -(x + 3)^2(x - 1)^3$

$$= (x + 2)(x - 1)(x - 4)$$

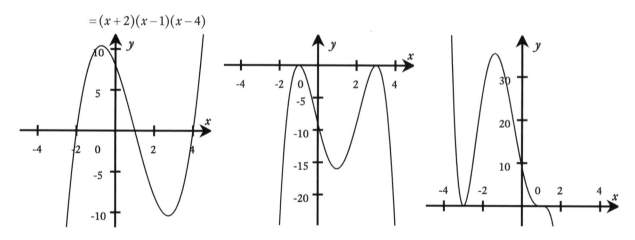

Remainders   When a polynomial function, $P(x)$, is divided by a binomial, $(x - c)$, the remainder will be equal to $P(c)$. If the remainder is 0, then $(x - c)$ is a factor of $P(x)$, and c is one of its roots.

Factoring by grouping   Some cubic and higher-degree functions can be factored by grouping terms two at a time and pulling out factors of each pair to reveal further factoring.

Example 4 $f(x) = x^3 + 3x^2 - 16x - 48 = (x^3 + 3x^2) + (-16x - 48)$

$$= x^2(x + 3) - 16(x + 3) = (x + 3)(x^2 - 16)$$

$$= (x + 3)(x + 4)(x - 4)$$

Polynomial Functions Problem Set

1. Which of the following is <u>not</u> a root of the function $y = 3(x+3)(x-5)(x+5)$?

   A) -5

   B) -3

   C) 3

   D) 5

2. If a polynomial function $p(x)$ has real roots of -6, 1 and 2, which of the following must be a factor of $p(x)$?

   A) $x-12$

   B) $x-6$

   C) $x-2$

   D) $x+2$

3. Which of the following functions has three real distinct roots?

   A) $y = (x-9)^2(x-3)^2(x+1)^2$

   B) $y = (x-9)^3$

   C) $y = (x-9)^2(x-3)$

   D) $y = (x-3)(x-3)(x+1)$

4. If the graph of the function $f(x)$ has x-intercepts at -5, 5, and 7, which of the following <u>could</u> be an expression for $f(x)$?

   A) $f(x) = (x-5)^2(x-7)$

   B) $f(x) = (x-5)^2(x-7)^2$

   C) $f(x) = (x+5)(x-5)(x-7)^2$

   D) $f(x) = (x+5)^2(x-5)^2(x+7)^2$

5. The graph of a polynomial $f(x)$ passes through the following points: $(-2, 3)$, $(0, 1)$, $(2, 0)$, and $(4, -4)$. Which of the following must be a factor of $f(x)$?

   A) $x-4$

   B) $x-2$

   C) $x-1$

   D) $x+2$

6. When the polynomial function $f(x)$ is divided by $x-8$, the remainder is 5. Which of the following <u>must</u> be true?

   A) $x-8$ is a factor of $f(x)$

   B) $x-3$ is a factor of $f(x)$

   C) $f(8) = 5$

   D) $f(5) = 8$

7. What are the roots of the function $y = 3x(4x^2-9) + 5(4x^2-9)$?

   A) -3, 0, and 2

   B) $-\dfrac{5}{3}$, $-\dfrac{3}{2}$, and $\dfrac{3}{2}$

   C) $-\dfrac{5}{3}$, $-\dfrac{3}{2}$, and $\dfrac{5}{3}$

   D) $-\dfrac{5}{3}$, $-\dfrac{2}{3}$, and $\dfrac{2}{3}$

8 When the polynomial function $f(x)$ is divided by $x+6$, the remainder is 0. Which of the following <u>must</u> be true?

    I. $x-6$ is a factor of $f(x)$
    II. $x+6$ is a factor of $f(x)$
    III. $f(6)=0$

A) I only
B) II only
C) I and III only
D) II and III only

9 Which of the following accurately describes the graph of the function $y = a(x+2)(x-3)^2$, where $a>0$?

A) After it crosses the x-axis at -2, all y-values are non-positive.
B) After it crosses the x-axis at -2, all y-values are non-negative.
C) After it crosses the x-axis at -2, all y-values are positive.
D) After it crosses the x-axis at -2, all y-values are negative.

10 Between which of the following x-values <u>must</u> the graph of the function $y = 2x(x+5)(x-4)$ turn?

A) -5 and -4
B) 0 and 2
C) -5 and 0
D) 4 and 5

11 If $a(x) = x^3 - 5x^2 + 6x$ and $b(x) = x^2 - 5x + 6$, which of the following polynomials will be divisible by $x+5$?

A) $a(x) + b(x)$
B) $a(x) + 5b(x)$
C) $5a(x) + b(x)$
D) $5(a(x) + b(x))$

12 If $x > 0$, what is one possible solution to the equation $x^5(x^2 - 13) = -36x^3$?

13 What is the only positive real solution to the equation $(25x^2 - 16)(9x^2 + 4) = 0$?

14 For what real value of x is the equation $x^3 - 3x^2 + 7x - 21 = 0$ true?

15 For what real value of x is the equation $6x^3 - 9x^2 + 2x - 3 = 0$ true?

Exponential Functions

Exponential functions have the form $f(x) = a(b)^x$ where a is the y-intercept and b is the base, or common ratio. The base b should always be greater than zero and not equal to one. Otherwise, exponential functions can be grouped into two categories:

Exponential Growth

This occurs when $b > 1$ and has constantly increasing values as x increases. The graph is asymptotic to the x-axis as x gets smaller, and the rate of increase is dependent on the size of b.

The example to the right is the graph of $y = 3(2)^x$, which, for $x \geq 0,$ models the act of starting at the number 3 and doubling every time x increases by one.

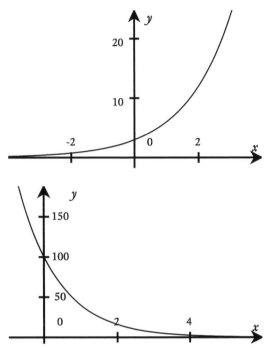

Exponential Decay

This occurs when $0 < b < 1$ and has constantly decreasing values as x increases. Therefore the graph is asymptotic to the x-axis as x gets larger.

The example to the right is the graph of $y = 100(.4)^x$.

Notice how, like in the growth example, the graph crosses the y-axis at $(0, a)$.

Applications

Exponential growth and decay functions are often used to model things that change as a percentage of themselves like populations, bank accounts, and masses of radioactive elements.

The compounding formula $A(t) = P(1 \pm r)^t$ can be used to analyze both exponential growth and exponential decay scenarios. In this formula, P represents the principal (initial) amount, r the rate of change (as a decimal), and t the number of times the rate is compounded.

Example 1   What function can be used to show the amount, $A(t)$, a house is worth after t years if the house was bought for $425,000 and its value increases steadily at 3.5% per year?

Since $P = 425,000$ and $r = 0.035,$ you can use $A(t) = 425,000(1.035)^t$.

Example 5   What is the daily rate of decline of a population of bees if the formula $B(t) = 500(.83)^{7t}$ is used to estimate the bee colony's population t weeks after a certain pollutant was released near its hive?

The formula is already accounting for the daily rate since the exponent $7t$ represents the amount of days in t weeks. Since $1 \pm r = .83$, r must be a decrease of .17, which means a 17% daily decline.

Exponential Functions Problem Set

1. An exponential growth function,
   $A(t) = 5000(1.2)^t$, models the amount of money in a certain brokerage account, with a $5000 principal amount, t years after the principal is paid. If the return is calculated annually, what is the annual return rate on this account?

   A) 1.2%

   B) 2%

   C) 20%

   D) 120%

2. The value of a car depreciates (decreases) at an annual rate of 15 percent. If the initial value of the car is $22,000, which of the following functions models the value of the car, in dollars, after x years?

   A) $f(x) = 22,000(.15)^x$

   B) $f(x) = 22,000(.85)^x$

   C) $f(x) = .15(22,000)^x$

   D) $f(x) = .85(22,000)^x$

3. The population of bacteria on a cookie that has been recently dropped on the ground begins at 30. After that, it can be expressed by the equation $c(t) = 30r^t$, where r is a constant and t is hours. If the population increases 30% each hour, what is the value of r?

   A) 0.3

   B) 0.7

   C) 1

   D) 1.3

4. Nate was 98 cm tall at the start of 2006. He grew steadily by 7% each year for the next several years. Which of the following functions gives his height h, in centimeters, after the next k years?

   A) $h(k) = 98 + 0.07^k$

   B) $h(k) = 98^k(1.07)$

   C) $h(k) = 98(0.07)^k$

   D) $h(k) = 98(1.07)^k$

5. Which of the following describes a function exhibiting exponential decay?

   A) Each year, 10 percent of the initial value of a house is added to the house's total value.

   B) Each year, 10 percent of the initial value of a house is subtracted from the house's total value.

   C) Each year, $10,000 is subtracted from the total value of a house.

   D) Each successive year, 10 percent of the current value of a house is subtracted from the house's total value.

6. A common formula for annually compounded interest is $A = P(1+r)^t$, where P means principal amount, r means rate as a decimal and t means time in years. What is the significance of the number 1 in the formula?

   A) All interest-bearing accounts gain at least 1% interest.

   B) The principal is always at least $1.

   C) The interest is always taken on 100% of the initial value.

   D) The interest is always taken on 100% of the current value.

7. The population of an invasive pest is predicted to double every year. The initial population is 2,000. How many years will it take for the population to increase to where it is at least 30 times its initial size?

A) 3

B) 5

C) 10

D) 15

8. A marketer estimates that a website will increase its hits by 50% every 12 days. If the site got 200 hits today, which of the following functions estimates how many hits h the site will have d days from now?

A) $h(d) = 200(.5)^{12d}$

B) $h(d) = 200(.5)^{\frac{d}{12}}$

C) $h(d) = 200(1.5)^{12d}$

D) $h(d) = 200(1.5)^{\frac{d}{12}}$

9. The number of deer in Morgan Park is decreasing at the rate of 7.5% per year. There are currently 380 deer in Morgan Park. In how many years will there be fewer than 30 deer in Morgan Park?

A) 15

B) 16

C) 32

D) 33

10. Which of the following is the closest to the difference after 5 years in the amount of money in an account that gains 4% interest compounded annually and an account that gains 5% interest compounded annually if both accounts began with $500?

A) $25.00

B) $25.25

C) $29.81

D) $30.00

11. Which of the following might be modeled by the function $f(x) = 3(2)^{\frac{x}{10}}$?

A) A population of initially three elephants, which will double in size every 10 years

B) A population of initially two lions, which will triple in size every 10 years

C) A bank account with continuously compounding interest, which will double every 10 months

D) A bank account with annually compounding interest, with an interest rate of 50 percent

12. An area entomologist predicted that the population of an invasive insect will triple in size every 6 months. The population density at the beginning of 2015 was estimated to be 1000 insects per acre. If D represents the population density (in insects per acre) n years after 2015, then which of the following equations models the population over time?

A) $D = 1000(3)^{\frac{n}{2}}$

B) $D = 1000 + (3)^{2n}$

C) $D = 1000(3)^{2n}$

D) $D = 1000n + (3)^{n}$

13 What are the domain and range of the function
$y = 3^{(x-5)}$?

A) Domain: All real numbers
Range: All real numbers

B) Domain: All real numbers
Range: $y > -5$

C) Domain: All Real Numbers
Range: $y > 0$

D) Domain: $x > 5$
Range: All Real Numbers

14 A financial institution advertises that you can use the following formula to calculate the amount of money you will have in an account after y years if you invest $1000 and interest is compounded annually: $1000(x)^y$. If one of their funds predicts 6% annual growth, what should be the value of x that is used in the formula?

15 Using the formula, principal and interest rate in the previous question, how much *interest* will be gained by the account after seven years (round to the nearest dollar)?

Additional Functions and Transformations

Though linear functions, quadratic functions, higher-level polynomial functions, and exponential functions are the most commonly tested functions on the SAT, you should be aware of some of the characteristics of other types of functions, and you should know basic function transformation rules as well.

Absolute Value Functions

$y = |x|$ is the parent absolute value function. It behaves like the parent linear function $y = x$ except that negative y-values are reflected to their positive counterparts. Though the domain of an absolute value function is all real numbers, the range, like a quadratic, depends on where the vertex is.

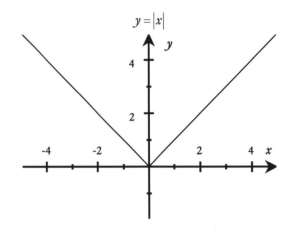

Rational Functions

When a function expresses a fraction of two polynomials, it is called a rational function. These functions can have restricted domains that exclude any x-value that makes the bottom equal zero. Usually, those domain restrictions manifest as vertical *asymptotes*, invisible vertical lines that the graph will bend away from but never cross (though any number that makes both the top *and* bottom of the function equal zero produces a hole in the graph instead of a vertical asymptote). Rational functions, like exponential functions, can also have horizontal asymptotes, which describe the *end behavior* of the graph as x gets very large or small.

Example 1 $y = \dfrac{4x-1}{x^2-x-6} = \dfrac{4x-1}{(x+2)(x-3)}$

Example 2 $y = \dfrac{x^2+1}{x^2+4x-12} = \dfrac{x^2+1}{(x+6)(x-2)}$

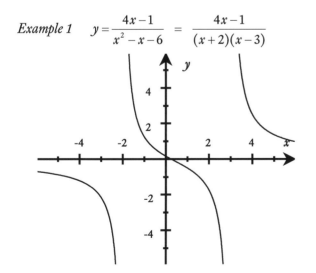

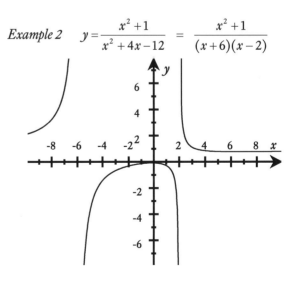

Radical Functions

When a function takes a root of an expression, it is called a radical function. Square root functions are the most common of these. The graph of a square root function looks like half of a rotated parabola. In square root functions, any x-value that makes the expression under the radical negative cannot be in the domain.

Example 6 $y = \sqrt{x+2}$

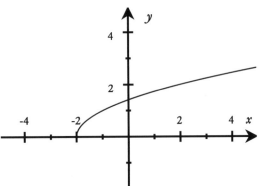

The domain of this function can be found by setting the inside greater than or equal to zero: $x + 2 \geq 0$, so $x \geq -2$.

The range can be expressed as $y \geq 0$ because the $\sqrt{\ }$ symbol only calls for non-negative square roots.

Function Transformations

Graphs of functions are flipped, shifted, stretched, or squeezed by operations on the parent function (its simplest form).

$$y = f(x) \ \rightarrow \ y = a\left[f\left(b(x-h)\right)\right] + k$$

$h = $ horizontal shift

$k = $ vertical shift

$$a \Rightarrow \begin{cases} a > 1 & \rightarrow \text{vertical stretch} \\ 0 < a < 1 & \rightarrow \text{vertical squeeze} \\ a < 0 & \rightarrow \text{reflect over } x\text{-axis} \end{cases}$$

$$b \Rightarrow \begin{cases} b > 1 & \rightarrow \text{horizontal squeeze} \\ 0 < b < 1 & \rightarrow \text{horizontal stretch} \\ b < 0 & \rightarrow \text{reflect over } y\text{-axis} \end{cases}$$

Example 7 $y = x^2$ $\rightarrow$ $y = 2(x-1)^2 - 3$

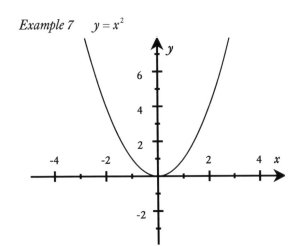

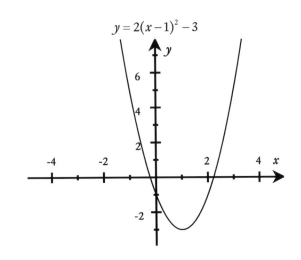

Additional Functions and Transformations Problem Set

1 What is the domain of the function

$$f(x) = \frac{(x-7)(x+4)}{(x-7)(x+1)}?$$

A) All real numbers except -1

B) All real numbers except -1 and 7

C) All real numbers except -4 and 7

D) All real numbers except -1, -4, and 7

4 What is the domain of the function

$$f(x) = \sqrt{2x-5}?$$

A) $x \geq 2.5$

B) $x \geq 5$

C) $x > 2.5$

D) All real numbers

2 Which of the following is not in the domain of

the function $y = \dfrac{x^2 - 16}{x + 16}?$

A) -16

B) -4

C) 4

D) 16

5 If $f(x) = \sqrt{x^2 + 1}$ and $g(x) = x + 2$, what is the x-coordinate of the point of intersection of f and g?

A) -1

B) $-\dfrac{3}{4}$

C) 2

D) No solution

3 What is the equation(s) of any vertical

asymptotes for the function $y = \dfrac{x-6}{x^2 - 2x - 24}?$

A) $x = -4$ only

B) $y = -4$ only

C) $x = -4$ and $x = 6$

D) $y = 0$

6 What is the domain of the function

$$f(x) = \frac{x-5}{\sqrt{x-2}}?$$

A) All real numbers

B) $x \geq 2$

C) $x > 2$

D) $x > 2$ and $x \neq 5$

7　What is the range of the function
　$f(x) = |x| + 2$?

　A)　All real numbers
　B)　$f(x) \geq -2$
　C)　$f(x) \geq 2$
　D)　$-2 \leq f(x) \leq 2$

8　Which of the following functions has two distinct x-intercepts?

　A)　$y = |2x - 7|$
　B)　$y = |2x| - 7$
　C)　$y = |2x + 7|$
　D)　$y = |2x| + 7$

9　Which of the following functions has no positive y-values?

　A)　$y = |x| - 1500$
　B)　$y = \left| \dfrac{x}{15} - 1000 \right|$
　C)　$y = |-150x - 10|$
　D)　$y = -15|x - 100|$

10　Which of the following functions will have a graph that will look like the graph of $y = x^2$ reflected over the x-axis and shifted 4 units to the left?

　A)　$y = (-x - 4)^2$
　B)　$y = -(x - 4)^2$
　C)　$y = (-x + 4)^2$
　D)　$y = -(x + 4)^2$

11　If $f(x) = |3x - 12| - 3$, for what value(s) of x does $f(x) = 0$?

　A)　3 only
　B)　5 only
　C)　-5 and 5
　D)　3 and 5

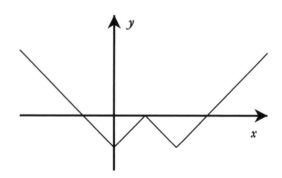

12　For which of the following functions could the figure shown above be the graph?

　A)　$y = |x - 3|$
　B)　$y = |x - 3| - 3$
　C)　$y = ||x - 3| - 3|$
　D)　$y = ||x - 3| - 3| - 3$

13. Which of the following has a graph in the *xy*-plane where the value of y is never larger than -3?

A) $y = |x| - 3$

B) $y = -(x-3)^2$

C) $y = x^3 - 3$

D) $y = -x^2 - 3$

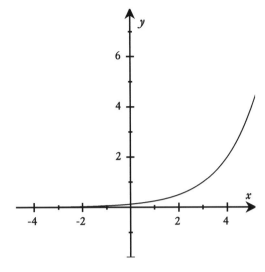

14. The function graphed above is given by the equation $y = x^2 - m$. Which of the following <u>must</u> be true?

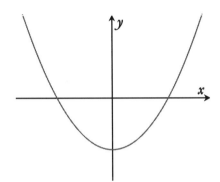

A) $m > 0$

B) $m < 0$

C) m is odd

D) m is even

15. Which function is represented by the figure above?

A) $y = 2^x$

B) $y = 2^{(x+3)}$

C) $y = 2^x + 3$

D) $y = 2^{(x-3)}$

16. Which of the following functions will have a graph with a discontinuity?

A) $y = 1.5^{x-3} - 8$

B) $y = -|x-12|$

C) $y = \dfrac{x-3}{x^2+4}$

D) $y = \dfrac{x+3}{x^2-4}$

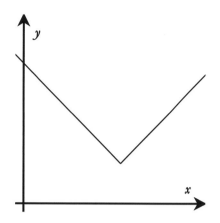

17 Which of the following could be the function represented by the figure above?

A) $y = (x-5)^2 + 2$

B) $y = |x-5| + 2$

C) $y = (x+5)^2 + 2$

D) $y = |x+5| + 2$

18 Which of the following is the equation for an asymptote of the function given by $y = 3^{3x-2} + 2$?

A) $x = 0$

B) $y = 0$

C) $x = 2$

D) $y = 2$

19 Which of the following functions will have graphs with the same turning point?

    I. $f(x) = -(x+3)^2 - 7$

    II. $f(x) = (x-3)^2 - 7$

    III. $f(x) = |x+3| - 7$

A) I and II only

B) I and III only

C) II and III only

D) I, II, and III

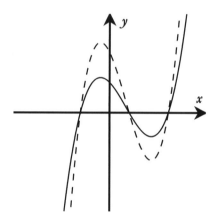

20 The solid curve above is the graph of the function $y = f(x)$. Which of the following could be an expression for the dashed curve in terms of constant a, where $a > 1$, and $f(x)$?

A) $y = f(x+a)$

B) $y = f(x) + a$

C) $y = a(f(x))$

D) $y = \dfrac{f(x)}{a}$

Problem Solving and Data Analysis

Using data to express and predict the complex systems that govern our world is perhaps the most widespread application of mathematics. When you can interpret graphs and tables and synthesize information into statistical measurements or predictive functions, you increase your fluency both in mathematical analysis and scientific and cultural understanding.

The College Board tests these skills in limited ways in the Evidence-Based Reading and Writing sections, and there are no questions in this domain in the No Calculator Mathematics section, but Problem Solving and Data Analysis is the main attraction in Section 4: Math Test—Calculator. Nearly half of all questions in this section will test your ability in the following categories:

- Analysis of tables and graphs
- Probability
- Percent
- Rates and unit conversion
- Statistical measurements of center, correlation, and spread

Keep in mind that because *all* of the questions you'll find in this chapter would be in Section 4 of the SAT, a calculator can be used on every one of these questions.

Data Analysis and Probability

Tables and Graphs

When answering questions that refer to tables or graphs, actively engage the data. Use your pencil to circle data points that are addressed in tables and to draw lines from relevant positions on axes to their corresponding points on graphs. This will have the effect of siphoning the pertinent information away from the noise of all the other information that is presented.

Some basic measurements can be gathered from data sets whether those sets are presented in lists, tables or graphs. They include:

Mean   the average of a set of numbers, found by dividing the sum of the set by the amount of numbers in the set

Median   the middle number when a set of numbers is placed in numeric order
When there is an even amount of numbers in a set, the median is the average of the two in the middle.

Mode   a number that occurs most often in a set of numbers (there can be more than one mode in a set)

Range   the difference between the highest and lowest numbers in a set

Fractional or Decimal Probability

- A probability is determined by the simple fraction $\dfrac{\text{desired outcomes}}{\text{total possible outcomes}}$.

- This can be converted into a decimal or a percent, but it will always be between 0 and 1.

- The sum of all possible probabilities for an event must add to 1.

- Independent events do not affect each other's outcomes. If you get tails on twenty straight flips of a fair coin, you will still have a one-half probability of it coming up tails on the next flip.

- When an event occurs multiple times "without replacement," meaning that a selection cannot be repeated, you must reduce outcomes by one each time.

Conditional Probability

The probability of an event given that another event has occurred

Often conditional probability questions are asked when a table is given. The condition that is referenced is usually represented by a row or column of the table, so the conditional probability can be found by placing a single data point (cell of the table) over the sum of a row or column.

Example 1   According to the table below, what is the probability that if a boy from Laco High School is chosen at random he will have blue eyes?

Students at Laco High School

	Boys	Girls
Brown Eyes	45	38
Blue Eyes	20	31

Because there are a total of 65 boys at Laco High School (the sum of 45 and 20), the probability of selecting a blue-eyed boy once it is known that a boy is selected is $\dfrac{20}{65}$.

Data Analysis Problem Set

Questions 1–3 refer to the following information

A group of students doing research on stream quality collected and analyzed samples from 6 sites along a mountain stream. The students measured water temperature, and concentrations of nitrates, phosphates, and sulfates in parts per million (ppm). Data collected are shown below.

Site	Elevation (ft)	Water Temp (°F)	Nitrates (ppm)	Phosphates (ppm)	Sulfates (ppm)
1	4310	44	0.0012	0.035	5.76
2	4260	44	0.0032	0.030	5.60
3	3710	46	0.0060	0.025	5.21
4	3240	47	0.0011	0.007	1.24
5	3380	48	0.0213	0.182	4.21
6	2700	50	0.0204	0.180	3.95

1. Which site had the highest ratio of phosphate concentration to nitrate concentration in the samples?

A) Site 1

B) Site 3

C) Site 5

D) Site 6

2. Which of the following is closest to the average rate that water temperature, in degrees Fahrenheit, changes with each 100 feet of decrease in elevation?

A) 0.294

B) 0.373

C) 2.68

D) 3.73

3. One of the students is inexperienced, and accidentally left some distilled water in the collection bottle for one of the sites, which diluted that particular sample. According to the table, which site was most likely the one with water in the collection bottle?

A) Site 2

B) Site 3

C) Site 4

D) Site 6

Questions 4–7 refer to the following information

The table below presents information about elements in Group 1 and Group 7 of the periodic table. Group 1 is the alkaline earth metal elements, and Group 7 is the halogen elements (non-metals).

Element	Atomic Number	Electronegativity	First Ionization Energy (kJ/mol)	Atomic Radius (pm)	Ionic Radius (pm)
Group 1 Metals					
Li	3	1.0	520	152	90
Na	11	0.9	496	186	116
K	19	0.8	419	227	152
Rb	37	0.8	403	248	166
Cs	55	0.7	377	265	181
Group 7 Halogens					
F	9	4.0	1681	72	119
Cl	17	3.0	1251	100	167
Br	35	2.8	1140	114	182
I	53	2.5	1008	133	206

NOTE: kJ/mol means kilo-joules per mole, pm means 10^{-12} meters.

4 For the Group 1 metal elements, as atomic number increases, which of the following two properties display alike trending behavior?

A) Electronegativity and First Ionization Energy

B) Electronegativity and Ionic Radius

C) Atomic Radius and First Ionization Energy

D) Ionic Radius and First Ionization Energy

5 If the table included group 7 Halogen element At, with atomic number 85, what would the electronegativity value of At most likely be?

A) 5.0

B) 2.6

C) 2.2

D) 0.6

6 Ionic bonds form between ions of different elements. The greater the difference in electronegativity between the two elements, the greater the ionic character of the bond. Which of the following bonds would have the LEAST ionic character?

A) Na-Cl

B) K-I

C) Li-I

D) Cs-F

7 How much larger, in pm, is the mean atomic radius of the metals in the table than the mean atomic radius of the halogens in the table?

A) 26.1

B) 98.5

C) 104.75

D) 110.85

Questions 8–11 refer to the following information and figure

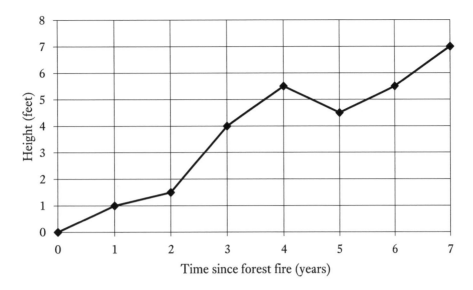

The line graph above shows the average height in feet of vegetation each year after a forest fire.

8 According to the graph, in which two years was the vegetation the closest in size?

A) Year 1 and Year 2

B) Year 2 and Year 3

C) Year 3 and Year 4

D) Year 6 and Year 7

10 Which of the following is closest to the range of vegetation height, in feet, from year 4 to year 7 after the fire?

A) 1.5

B) 2.5

C) 5.5

D) 7

9 According to the graph, what was the greatest change (in absolute value) in vegetation height between two consecutive years?

A) Year 0 and Year 1

B) Year 1 and Year 2

C) Year 2 and Year 3

D) Year 3 and Year 4

11 What is the average rate of increase, in feet per year, from one year after the forest fire to four years after the forest fire?

A) 1.375

B) 1.5

C) 4.5

D) 5.5

Questions 12–15 refer to the following information

The bar graph below shows the average monthly temperature in Celsius over a 12-month period in the town of Rupert.

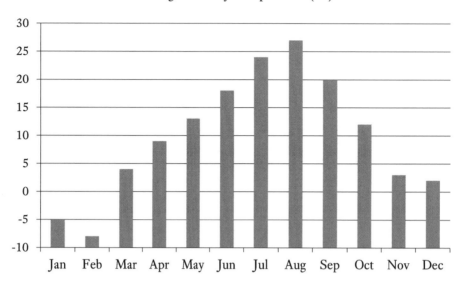

Average Monthly Temperature (°C)

12   Which of the following is the closest to the range of average monthly temperature, in degrees Celsius, in the graph?

A) 15

B) 25

C) 35

D) 45

13   If one month with an average temperature in Rupert under 15 degrees Celsius is chosen at random, what is the probability that it will begin with the letter J?

A) 0

B) $\frac{1}{12}$

C) $\frac{1}{8}$

D) $\frac{1}{4}$

14   A temperature of zero degrees Celsius is considered freezing weather. In how many of the 12 displayed months was the average monthly temperature within 10 degrees of freezing?

A) 2

B) 4

C) 6

D) 8

The formula for converting between degrees Fahrenheit (F) and degrees Celsius (C) is:

$$\frac{5}{9}(F-32)=C$$

15   In which month was the average temperature closest to 25 degrees Fahrenheit?

A) January

B) April

C) August

D) December

Probability Problem Set

[1] David has 10 baseball cards, 4 football cards and 5 hockey cards. How many more hockey cards will David need to acquire to have a one-third probability of randomly selecting a hockey card from all of his sports cards?

A) 2

B) 4

C) 7

D) 9

[2] A jar contains 20 total jelly beans. 10 of the jelly beans are blue, 7 are red, and 3 are green. Nancy withdrew one jelly bean at random, ate it, and then withdrew another jelly bean at random. What calculation gives the probability that Nancy withdrew two red jelly beans?

A) $\dfrac{7}{20} + \dfrac{6}{19}$

B) $\dfrac{7}{20} \times \dfrac{7}{20}$

C) $\dfrac{7}{20} \times \dfrac{6}{20}$

D) $\dfrac{7}{20} \times \dfrac{6}{19}$

[3] A student will be chosen at random to represent a homeroom class in student government. If the probability that a male student will be chosen is $\dfrac{3}{7}$, which of the following could NOT be the number of students in the homeroom class?

A) 21

B) 24

C) 28

D) 35

Questions 4-5 refer to the following information

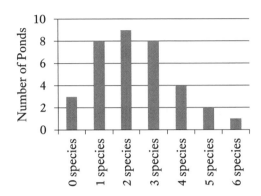

Number of Frog Species Found in 35 Ponds

[4] If you were to choose a pond at random, which of the following is the probability that the pond would have 5 frog species represented?

A) $\dfrac{2}{35}$

B) $\dfrac{2}{32}$

C) $\dfrac{5}{35}$

D) $\dfrac{5}{6}$

[5] If a pond with two or fewer frog species were selected at random, what is the probability the pond would have zero frog species in it?

A) 0

B) $\dfrac{1}{7}$

C) $\dfrac{3}{20}$

D) $\dfrac{1}{3}$

Questions 6–10 refer to the following information

The following table shows absences by class this semester at Rosalind Franklin High School:

Absences	Sophomores	Juniors	Seniors
0	10	7	3
1	12	19	14
2	17	16	22
3	30	17	34
4	25	23	28
5	20	22	19
6	25	25	12
Total:	139	129	132

6 What percentage of the senior class has at least 4 absences this semester?

A) 21.2%

B) 35.7%

C) 44.7%

D) 55.3%

7 What fraction of all students combined have no absences this semester?

A) $\dfrac{1}{100}$

B) $\dfrac{1}{44}$

C) $\dfrac{1}{20}$

D) $\dfrac{1}{10}$

8 Which class has the highest percentage of students with two or fewer absences?

A) Sophomores

B) Juniors

C) Seniors

D) Both sophomores and seniors (tied)

9 If a student from Rosalind Franklin High School with 1 absence is chosen at random, what is the probability that that person is a Junior?

A) $\dfrac{19}{400}$

B) $\dfrac{45}{400}$

C) $\dfrac{19}{129}$

D) $\dfrac{19}{45}$

10 Based on the data, if chosen at random from their respective class, how many times more likely is it for a Senior to not have 6 absences than for a Sophomore to have 6 absences (round the answer to the nearest hundredth)?

A) 0.51 times as likely

B) 1.11 times as likely

C) 4.69 times as likely

D) 5.05 times as likely

Percent Problems

Percent problems can most easily be solved, when a calculator is available, using the direct translation method, where you convert words into mathematical operators. **What** or **what percent** can be written as x, **of** as a multiplication symbol, and **is** as an equal sign. Remember to write percentages in decimal form when they appear in equations (e.g., $32\% = 0.32$). You can do this by moving the decimal point two places to the left and dropping the percent symbol. Here are a few examples:

Example 1   What is 35% of 50?

  What becomes x

  is becomes =

  35% becomes 0.35

  of becomes the multiplication symbol

  $x = 0.35 \cdot 50$

  $x = 17.5$

Example 2   63 is what percent of 72?

  $63 = x \cdot 72$

  $0.875 = x$

  Since the question asked for a percent, remember to convert 0.875 into 87.5%

Example 3   40% of what number is 80?

  $0.40 \cdot x = 80$

  $x = 200$

Sales tax   A sales tax is an additional amount you pay for goods or services based on a set tax rate (percent).

  Use this formula: **Total Price = Original Price** $\times (1 + $**Tax Rate**$)$

  Note that the tax rate should be given as a *decimal*.

Example 4   A dress is priced at \$229. The sales tax is 5%. What is the total cost of the dress, including tax?

  $\text{Cost} = 229(1 + 0.05) = 229(1.05)$

  $= 240.45$

Discount and mark-up   A discount is a decrease in price and a mark-up is an increase in price.

  These work similarly to a sales tax, and you can use the formula **New Price = Original** $\times (1 \pm $**%change**$)$.

  As with sales tax, the change should be given as a *decimal*.

Example 5   A book that was originally \$15 is marked "10% off." What is the new price?

  $\text{New Price} = 15(1 - 0.10) = 15(0.90)$

  $= 13.50$

Percent change   Positive or negative change can be found as a decimal using the formula $\dfrac{\text{new} - \text{original}}{\text{original}}$ and then converted to a percent.

Example 6   A pair of jeans is on sale for $33.75. The usual cost is $45. What is the percent discount?

$$\text{Percent Change} = \frac{33.75 - 45}{45} = \frac{-11.25}{45} = -.25.$$

The percent change is negative because it is a discount, so the jeans are 25% off.

Example 7   Erwin has been a lifeguard the past three summers. In the second summer, his salary increased 5% from the first summer. In the third summer, his salary increased 8% from the second summer. What percent greater was his salary in the third summer than his salary in the first summer?

A) 3%

B) 13%

C) 13.4%

D) 40%

If Erwin's first-summer salary is represented by x, you can calculate the second-summer salary to be $x(1 + 0.05) = 1.05x$, and, consequently, you can calculate the third-summer salary to be $1.05x(1 + 0.08) = 1.05x(1.08) = 1.134x$. Since $1.134 = 1 + \%\text{change}$, the percent change is 0.134 or 13.4%. Erwin's salary in the third summer is a 13.4% increase from his salary in the first summer. Notice, this is different than the straight 13% increase you would get if you simply added 5% and 8%, so the answer is C.

Percent Problem Set

1　What percent of 50 is 20?

A) 20%

B) 30%

C) 40%

D) 250%

2　What percent of 20 is 50?

A) 20%

B) 30%

C) 40%

D) 250%

3　35% of what number is 70?

A) 105

B) 200

C) 350

D) 2450

4　Puppy food costs $6.75. After sales tax, it costs $7.56. What is the sales tax rate?

A) 10%

B) 12%

C) 15%

D) 17.5%

5　A cake is cut into M equal pieces, and 12 of these pieces are eaten by guests at a birthday party. In terms of M, what percentage of the cake was not eaten?

A) $\left(\dfrac{M-12}{M}\right)100$

B) $\left(\dfrac{M-12}{M}\right)$

C) $\left(\dfrac{M}{12}\right)100$

D) $(M-12)100$

6　A video gaming system is selling for $150 after a 25% reduction in price. What was the original price?

A) $175

B) $187.5

C) $200

D) $225

7 50% of 24 is increased by 50%, resulting in which of the following values?

   A) 18

   B) 24

   C) 36

   D) 62

8 The price on a suit is reduced by a $\frac{1}{4}$ for a sale, and then that new price is increased by 25% after the sale. The new price is what percent of the original price?

   A) 93.75

   B) 97.5

   C) 99.5

   D) 100

9 What is 20 percent of $15x \cdot 30y$?

   A) $3xy$

   B) $18xy$

   C) $45xy$

   D) $90xy$

10 In the 2014 season, the Fairfield Cougars won exactly 36% of their games and had a total of 18 victories. How many games did they play?

   A) 36

   B) 45

   C) 50

   D) 72

11 The Merriweather Mockingbirds won 17.5% of their games and lost 33 games. How many games did they play?

   A) 35

   B) 40

   C) 42

   D) 50

12 15 students split the bill evenly for their favorite teacher's birthday present and spend $5 each. If there had been only 12 students to pay for the same present, then each student would have paid what percent more?

13 A washing machine is put on sale for 25% off the marked price. Shortly afterwards there is a going-out-of-business sale, so it is again marked down by 25% off the new price. The final sale price is what percent greater than the price of the machine if the initial discount had been 50%?

14 Jamal buys a Chemistry book for $200. After the semester is over, he sells it back to the bookstore for 60% less than his purchase price. If the store marks up the used book by p percent and sells it for $120, then what is p?

15 Sarah has 20 pens and 30 pencils. If 15% of the pens are red and 40% of the pencils are red, then what is the percentage of the writing utensils that are red?

Rate and Unit Conversion

You will often need to convert units or rates in word problems, so pay close attention to the language of a question so you can determine when two measures are linked.

Unit conversion   When a measurement of the same size and quality is related using different units.

Example 1   1 mile = 5280 feet

Rate   When a certain increase in an amount of one unit occurs for every increase of one of an otherwise unrelated unit. The word "per" will often be a signal that a rate is being used, but sometimes rates are described less formally.

Example 2   176 feet per second

Example 3   1 second of video footage costs $2

When you place equivalent measures in a fraction, you get a conversion factor. Since the numerator and denominator are equal, this factor will always be equivalent to 1, so you can always multiply by it:

$$\frac{1 \text{ mile}}{5280 \text{ feet}} \text{ or } \frac{5280 \text{ feet}}{1 \text{ mile}} \qquad \frac{176 \text{ feet}}{1 \text{ second}} \text{ or } \frac{1 \text{ second}}{176 \text{ feet}} \qquad \frac{1 \text{ second}}{2 \text{ dollars}} \text{ or } \frac{2 \text{ dollars}}{1 \text{ second}}$$

Notice the different ways you can arrange each of these conversion factors. The way you choose to arrange each will depend on what conversion you need to make. You will always be looking to eliminate units (cross out on top and bottom) until you get the unit you are looking for.

Example 4   Aunt Betty wants to film her skydive. The cameraman is an expert, so every second of footage costs $2. If a typical skydiver averages a vertical speed of 176 feet per second (free fall and chute time combined) and Aunt Betty jumps from an altitude of 3.4 miles, how much will it likely cost to record her jump?

The starting value is the quantity that is linked to the question and the only measure that doesn't have a partner. In this case it is Aunt Betty's starting height of 3.4 miles. Now that you've identified your starting point, arrange your conversion ratios and perform your calculation until you end up with a monetary unit:

$$3.4 \text{ miles} \times \frac{5280 \text{ feet}}{1 \text{ mile}} \times \frac{1 \text{ second}}{176 \text{ feet}} \times \frac{2 \text{ dollars}}{1 \text{ second}} = 204 \text{ dollars}$$

Notice that every unit that appears in a numerator can be canceled in a denominator except the unit you are looking for, dollars.

A very similar process can be used for converting between different rates.

Example 5   According to the information above, what is the average speed of a skydiver in <u>miles per hour</u>?

$$\frac{176 \ \cancel{\text{feet}}}{1 \ \cancel{\text{second}}} \times \frac{1 \text{ mile}}{5280 \ \cancel{\text{feet}}} \times \frac{60 \ \cancel{\text{seconds}}}{1 \ \cancel{\text{minute}}} \times \frac{60 \ \cancel{\text{minutes}}}{1 \text{ hour}} = \frac{120 \text{ miles}}{1 \text{ hour}}$$

It's important to examine the units and let them serve as a check to see if you did the problem correctly. Above you can see by the different strike marks that *feet*, *seconds*, and *minutes* have canceled to leave you with only *miles* and *hours*, and that the proper configuration of *miles per hour* is in the result.

Rates and Unit Conversions Problem Set

1. Which of the following correctly expresses the weight of a 150 pound person in kilograms (1kg = 2.2 lb) ?

   A) 68.2 kg

   B) 147.8 kg

   C) 152.2 kg

   D) 330 kg

2. How high is a 10 ft basketball rim when expressed in cm?
   (1 in = 2.54 cm)

   A) 47 cm

   B) 254cm

   C) 305cm

   D) 610cm

3. Khalid runs 2 miles in 16 minutes and 36 seconds. Which of the following is closest to his average speed in miles per hour?

   A) 3 mi/hr

   B) 5 mi/hr

   C) 7 mi/hr

   D) 10 mi/hr

4. A length of rope is 5ft 6in long. If it is to be cut into three equal pieces, how long will each piece be?

   A) 1ft 2in

   B) 1ft 6in

   C) 1ft 8in

   D) 1ft 10in

5. A coffee company brews coffee in 20 gallon containers. Approximately how many 12-ounce small-sized coffees can be filled from the container?
   (128 ounces = 1 gallon)

   A) 77

   B) 213

   C) 4096

   D) 30720

6. Nene rode his motorcycle for 4 hours at an average speed of 70 miles per hour. If his motorcycle gets 55 miles per gallon of gas, approximately how many gallons of gas was used during the 4-hour trip?

   A) 3

   B) 4

   C) 5

   D) 6

7 The speed of light is roughly 3.0×10^8 meters per second. What is this speed in miles per hour?
(1 mile = 1609 meters)

A) 5.1×10^1

B) 5.1×10^5

C) 1.3×10^8

D) 6.7×10^8

8 A rocket traveling at 200 meters per second is moving at what speed in kilometers per second?

A) 0.02

B) 0.2

C) 200,000

D) 200,000,000

9 Tara has a 25-meter roll of ribbon and needs to cut it into 6 inch portions to wrap around diplomas. Which calculation can be used to find how many diplomas she will be able to wrap from the roll of ribbon?
(1 inch = 2.54 cm)

A) $\dfrac{25 \times 100}{6 \times 2.54}$

B) $\dfrac{25 \times 2.54}{6 \times 100}$

C) $\dfrac{100 \times 6}{2.54 \times 25}$

D) $\dfrac{25 \times 100 \times 2.54}{6}$

10 David watches too many YouTube videos. If the average video is m minutes long, and he watches videos for an average of 5 hours each day, how many videos does David watch in a week in terms of m?

A) $300m$

B) $60\left(\dfrac{m}{35}\right)$

C) $35\left(\dfrac{60}{m}\right)$

D) $\dfrac{60}{35m}$

11 Robert ran a 40-yard dash in x seconds. What was his average speed in miles per hour?
(1 mile = 1760 yards)

A) $\dfrac{40 \times 1760}{x \times 60 \times 60}$

B) $\dfrac{40 \times x}{1760 \times 60 \times 60}$

C) $\dfrac{x \times 60 \times 60}{1760 \times 40}$

D) $\dfrac{40 \times 60 \times 60}{1760 \times x}$

12 The average gasket produced at the Sarnia MetalWorks Factory weighs 30.6 grams. The loading machinery can load gaskets by weight at a rate of 1.5 pounds per second for a maximum of 4 hours each day. What is the maximum number of gaskets that can be loaded each day (rounded to the nearest thousand)?

(1 pound = 454 grams)

A) 9,000

B) 320,000

C) 2,243,000

D) 8,335,000

13 A candle maker can make 750 candles from 332.8 liters of liquid wax. If each candle is 15 ounces when liquid, how many ounces to the nearest tenth are in 1 liter?

14 The furlong, an imperial unit of length, is approximately equal to 0.125 miles. It is also equivalent to 10 smaller units called chains. Based on these relationships, 16 chains are equivalent to how many feet?

(1 mile = 5280 feet)

The citizens of planet Tehar use the following currencies:

8 Glurfs = 11 Collywobbles

9 Zaps = 2 Dodos

5 Dodos = 7 Glurfs

15 According to the above relationships, how many Zaps are in 3 Collywobbles, to the nearest hundredth?

Statistics and Scatterplots

There are more complex statistical measurements and concepts than the ones mentioned at the beginning of this chapter. Though you will not be asked to calculate these numerically on the SAT, it is important to have a basic understanding of their meaning.

Standard deviation   a measurement of dispersion, or spread, in a set of numbers

- If the numbers in the set are bunched near the mean, the standard deviation will be small, and if they are, for the most part, far from the mean, the standard deviation will be large.

Margin of error   the maximum expected difference between an actual, usually difficult-to-measure, statistic and the estimate determined by a mathematical process

Confidence level   how likely it is that a statistic falls within a given margin of error

- SAT questions will only use 95% confidence levels. That is, a question may say that the *actual* mean, for example, of a large population has a 95% chance of falling between the lowest and highest numbers given by a particular margin of error.

Example 1   If a study shows, by using a random sample of 900 respondents, that the average amount of time adults spend driving each day is 93 minutes, and that study has a margin of error of ±4 minutes with a 95% confidence level, then there is 95% confidence that the true average amount of time adults in the entire population spend driving is between 89 and 97 minutes a day.

> **NOTE:** This does not mean that 95% of *all adults* in the population drive between 89 and 97 minutes a day. That is an example of a common error made with confidence intervals.

Bias   a flaw in the design of an experiment that hinders randomness and causes misrepresentation

Outlier   an observation or number that is very different from others in a group

Scatterplot   a graph of data points, often taken from an experiment or study, which may show trends that indicate a relationship that can be modeled closely by a function (linear, exponential…)

Association (or **correlation**)   two sets of numbers are associated (or correlated) if variation in one set can be used to predict variation in the other (though this doesn't assume one causes the other). This can be seen graphically if a scatterplot of several points appears to closely follow the path of a function graph.

- Association can be strong or weak depending on how closely the points fit onto the graph of the function.
- When association is positive and linear, the points will approximate a positive-sloped line; when it is negative and linear, the points will approximate a negative-sloped line. The points can also approximate exponential growth or decay.
- BE CAREFUL: Association between points does <u>not</u> indicate *causation*, though wrong answer choices will often try to assign a cause/effect relationship.

Statistics Problem Set

1. Dan's average score on 8 tests is 89. What is the sum of his scores on all 8 tests?

    A) 89
    B) 77
    C) 356
    D) 712

2. If set S consists of three positive integers x, y, and z such that $x < y < z$, which of the following could <u>not</u> affect the median of set S?

    A) Decreasing x
    B) Decreasing y
    C) Decreasing z
    D) Increasing x

3. Leo and Don both receive an 88 on a test. Mike receives an 89 and Rocky receives a 93. April scores a 94. Arrange the mean, median and mode of their scores in ascending order.

    A) Mode, mean, median
    B) Mode, median, mean
    C) Median, mode, mean
    D) Mean, mode, median

4. A is a set of n numbers whose average (arithmetic mean) is 9. B is another set of n numbers, created by multiplying each number in A by 3. What is the average of the numbers in set B?

    A) 3
    B) 9
    C) 12
    D) 27

35 ponds were surveyed to see how many frog species were represented in each pond. Data is presented below.

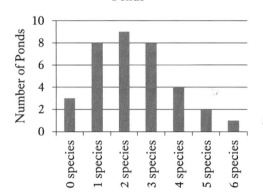

Number of Frog Species Found in 35 Ponds

5. Suppose 7 additional ponds were surveyed, and each had 5 species of frogs represented. Which of the following measurements of this data would change?

    I.   The median
    II. The mean
    III. The range

    A) I only
    B) II only
    C) I and II only
    D) II and III only

The following information and table relate to questions 6 and 7.

St. Sebastian's School held a race to raise money for a charity. The table below lists the number of contestants who completed 1, 2, 3, or 4 miles of the extremely challenging obstacle course.

Miles	Contestants
1	45
2	30
3	20
4	5

6 What is the median number of miles per contestant?

A) 1

B) 2

C) 2.5

D) 25

7 How many miles, on average, did each contestant complete?

A) 1

B) 1.85

C) 2

D) 25

8 Which of the following is most likely to cause bias in a study?

A) The size of the population

B) The ensuring of randomness in selection of a sample

C) The neglecting of randomness in selection of a sample

D) The choice of calculator the researcher uses to work out her conclusions

Heights of Students (in inches)						
38	54.5	55.5	56	56	57	57.5
57.5	58	58	58	58	58.5	58.5
59	59	59.5	59.5	60	61	85

9 The table above lists the heights of the 21 students in Mr. Murray's class. It has been determined that the outlier measurements of 38 and 85 inches are errors. If these two measurements were removed, how would the standard deviation be affected?

A) The standard deviation would increase.

B) The standard deviation would decrease.

C) The standard deviation would remain the same.

D) The standard deviation cannot be measured.

10 A clothing company wants to gather information about the habits of consumers and the effectiveness of its ad campaign by interviewing shoppers at a local mall. Over the course of two weeks, the company interviews 300 people. Why would the information gathered in these interviews not provide accurate information?

A) The population size is too small.

B) The sample size is too small.

C) Interviews are not effective methods of conducting research.

D) The sample of people will not be representative of the general population.

11 A survey was conducted to examine the number of students per class in a certain county. It was found that the mean number of students per classroom was 22, but the median number of students per classroom was 18. Which of the following situations could explain the difference between the mean and median number of students per classroom?

A) Many of the classrooms in the county have between 18 and 22 students.

B) The classrooms have numbers of students that are very close to each other.

C) There are a few classrooms that have a much higher number of students than the rest.

D) There are a few classrooms that have a much lower number of students than the rest.

Rachel	77
Monica	75
Phoebe	81
Joey	97
Chandler	79
Ross	71

14 The table above lists the test scores of 6 friends. If the outlier score is not included, what is the mean of the remaining scores?

A) 63.8

B) 76.6

C) 80.0

D) 81.8

12 If $x+1$ is the average (arithmetic mean) of $20, x, x, 12,$ and 30, what is the value of x?

A) 12

B) 19

C) 20

D) 29

13 Which number set below has the largest standard deviation?

A) $4, 5, 4, 5, 4, 5$

B) $6, 6, 6, 6, 6, 6$

C) $17, 18, 17, 18, 18$

D) $1, 4, 5, 6, 17, 18$

15 A researcher wants to know the opinions of local business owners about a town's recycling policies. The researcher obtains a list of 520 local business owners and mails a questionnaire to 60 businesses located in the downtown area. 4 of the questionnaires are completed and returned. Which of the following factors makes it least likely that a reliable conclusion can be drawn about the opinions of the local business owners regarding the town's recycling policy?

A) Population size

B) Planned sample size

C) Sample size obtained

D) Sample location

16   Rich jogged m days in May, a days in August, and s days in September, averaging x jogging days over those three months. If he jogged j days a month in both June and July, how many days a month did Rich average jogging over the five-month period?

A) $\dfrac{x+j}{2}$

B) $\dfrac{m+a+s+j}{4}$

C) $\dfrac{3x+j}{4}$

D) $\dfrac{3x+2j}{5}$

17   An inspector at a bottling plant for a soda company randomly selects 120 bottles and finds, with a 95% confidence level, that the average volume of soda that the machines are dispensing into each bottle in the plant is between 63.1 and 64.5 fluid ounces. Which of the following conclusions is most reasonable?

A)   95% of all bottles in the plant that day have between 63.1 and 64.5 fluid ounces of soda in them.

B)   95% of all bottles ever filled in that plant have between 63.1 and 64.5 fluid ounces of soda in them.

C)   95% of the capacity of each bottle in the plant is somewhere between 63.1 and 64.5 fluid ounces.

D)   It is likely that the true average volume of soda dispensed by all the machines at the plant that day is between 63.1 and 64.5 fluid ounces.

18   The margin of error of a poll conducted to determine apple preference is, with 95% confidence, ±3%. If the poll shows that 32% of people prefer gala apples to all others, what is the range of percentages within which one can be most confident that the true percentage of gala apple lovers will fall?

A)   92% – 98%

B)   32% – 38%

C)   32% – 35%

D)   29% – 35%

19   Data shows that the months in which the highest numbers of ice cream cones are eaten are the same months that have the highest incidence of shark attacks. Which of the following conclusions can be drawn from this?

A)   Ice cream causes shark attacks.

B)   Sharks are attracted to cone-shaped desserts.

C)   The threat of shark attacks causes people to eat more ice cream.

D)   No cause and effect conclusion can be made from this information alone.

20   Casey found that there is a strong positive correlation between the number of televisions at area bars and the number of bar patrons. Is he correct in concluding that many televisions in a bar will cause people to visit that bar?

A)   Yes, because televisions make bars more popular

B)   Yes, because people who like television like bars

C)   No, because correlation does not prove causation

D)   No, because there are already enough bars with many televisions in that part of town

Scatterplots Problem Set

1. Which of the following scatterplots shows a weak positive correlation between the x and y variable?

A)

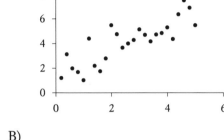

B)

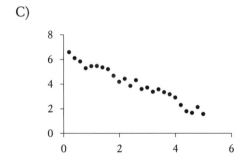

C)

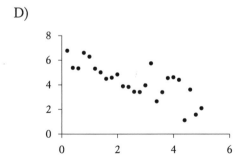

D)

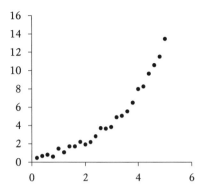

2. What type of association does the above graph have?

A) Strong, positive and linear
B) Strong, positive and non-linear
C) Weak, negative and non-linear
D) Weak, negative and linear

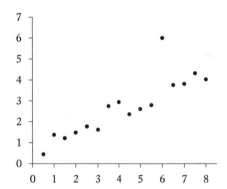

3. In the scatterplot above, which of the following is the x-coordinate of the point that is farthest from the line of best fit?

A) 1
B) 4
C) 6
D) 7

Questions 4–6 refer to the following information

Population density of damselflies was measured at varying distances from a riverbed. The data collected are presented below.

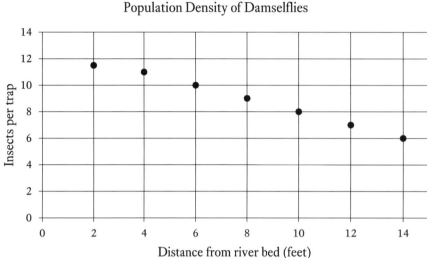

4 Which of the following descriptions best describes the data presented?

A) There is a weak positive association between population density and distance from riverbed.

B) There is a weak negative association between population density and distance from riverbed

C) There is a strong negative association between population density and distance from riverbed

D) There is a strong positive association between population density and distance from riverbed.

5 Assume that the relationship is valid for distances beyond what is shown on the graph. Based on the graph, what is the approximate population density of damselflies, in insects per trap, at 18 feet from the riverbed?

A) 4

B) 6

C) 8

D) 10

6 What is the absolute value of the approximate change in population density over distance?

A) 1 per foot

B) 3 per 2 feet

C) 1 per 2 feet

D) 1 per 4 feet

7 Researchers have discovered a strong positive correlation between body mass and fecundity of female spiders. Which of the following scatterplots could show the relationship between body mass and fecundity of female spiders?

A)

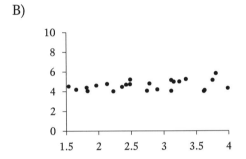

B)

C)

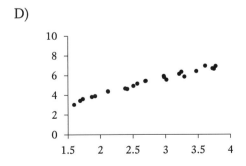

D)

Questions 8–10 refer to the following graph and information

The graph below shows the yield, in thousands of barrels, of corn and soybeans on Good Acres Farm.

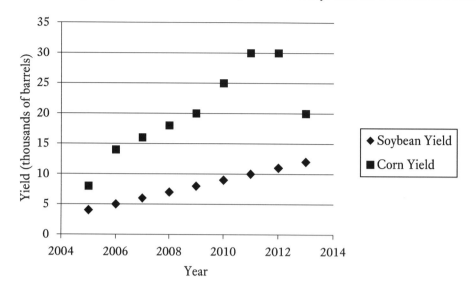

8   Which crop shows a stronger linear correlation with time?

A) Corn

B) Soybean

C) Cannot be determined

D) Neither

9   If the data points from one year were eliminated, which year's removal would best make the case that soybean and corn have similar types of correlation?

A) 2005

B) 2010

C) 2012

D) 2013

10   Which of the following is a reasonable conclusion from the data presented?

A) It is more profitable to grown corn than it is to grow soybeans.

B) The highest combined yield was in 2012.

C) The difference in yield between the two crops is due to disease factors.

D) The farm should devote more acreage to soybeans.

Additional Topics in Math

One of the ways in which the SAT differs from other standardized tests is that it emphasizes a narrower set of mathematical skills, confined mostly to algebra, functions, and data analysis. These are the areas that usually translate most directly to success in college and in the work force, but they don't encompass all of the abstract problem-solving methods that are more prevalent in other mathematical disciplines.

Still, there are six questions on every SAT that do not have a designation in Heart of Algebra, Passport to Advanced Math, or Problem Solving and Data Analysis. These are often referred to as simply "Additional Math Topics" questions, and they include explorations in:

- Basic geometry
- Trigonometry
- Characteristics and graphs of circles
- Complex numbers

Since the majority of Additional Topics questions test geometry, it is important to remember that there is a list of geometry facts and formulas in the beginning of each math section of the SAT. That reference section will look very similar to the following:

REFERENCE

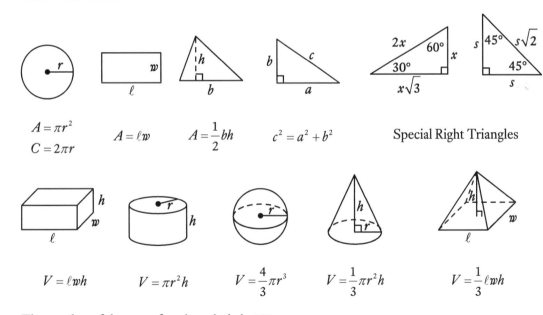

The number of degrees of arc in a circle is 360.
The number of radians of arc in a circle is 2π.
The sum of the measures in degrees of the angles in a triangle is 180.

Basic Geometry

In addition to the given reference information, it is helpful to know a few other angle relationships and geometric characteristics.

Complementary angles   a pair of angles whose sum is 90°

Supplementary angles   a pair of angles whose sum is 180°

Note that angles in a linear pair (adjacent angles which form a line) will be supplementary.

Parallel lines cut by a transversal   lines ℓ_1 and ℓ_2 on the right are parallel. The transversal line that cuts through them creates two groups of four congruent (equal in measure) angles:
$m\angle A = m\angle D = m\angle E = m\angle H$ and
$m\angle B = m\angle C = m\angle F = m\angle G$.
Also, every angle in the first group is supplementary to every angle in the second group.

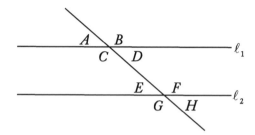
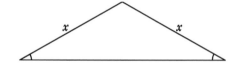

Isosceles triangle   a triangle with two congruent sides and two congruent angles opposite those two congruent sides.

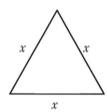

Equilateral triangle   a triangle with all three sides congruent and, thus, all three angles congruent. The angles each measure 60°.

Pythagorean triples   groups of three whole numbers that work in the Pythagorean Theorem, $a^2 + b^2 = c^2$. They include 3-4-5, 5-12-13, 8-15-17, and all of their multiples. It is not essential to memorize these, but they will save time and reduce errors, especially on the No Calculator section.

Volume

Though all pertinent volume formulas are provided in the reference area, it is helpful to know that all prisms (3D shapes with two identical base faces, like a cylinder or a rectangular solid) have volumes equal to the area of the base face multiplied by the height. Pyramidal shapes (including cones), which have only one base face and come to a point, have volumes equal to one-third of their prism counterparts.

Basic Geometry Problem Set

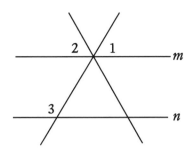

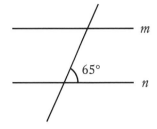

1. In the figure above, $m \parallel n$. Which of the following statements <u>must</u> be true?

   A) $\angle 1 \cong \angle 2$

   B) $\angle 2 \cong \angle 3$

   C) $m\angle 1 + m\angle 3 = 180°$

   D) $m\angle 2 + m\angle 3 = 180°$

3. What is one possibility for the difference between the measures of two of the angles in the figure above if the lines m and n are parallel to each other?

   A) $25°$

   B) $50°$

   C) $65°$

   D) $115°$

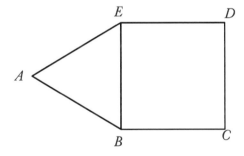

2. In the figure above, $\triangle ABE$ is equilateral and quadrilateral $BCDE$ is a square. What is the measure of $\angle AED$?

   A) $60°$

   B) $120°$

   C) $135°$

   D) $150°$

4. A swimming pool in the shape of the right circular cylinder shown above has a volume of 320π cubic feet. If the height of the pool is 5 feet, what is the area of a circular tarp, in square feet, that just covers the top of the pool?

   A) 16π

   B) 32π

   C) 64

   D) 64π

5. In $\triangle ABC$, $\angle A$ and $\angle B$ are congruent. If the measure of $\angle C$ is 98°, what is the measure of $\angle A$?

A) 41°

B) 49°

C) 82°

D) 98°

6. Gatsby leaves his dock and takes his motorboat due east for 0.5 miles to pick up Daisy. Then they motor 1.2 miles north to a private island in the middle of the sound. What is the straight-line distance, in miles, from the island to Gatsby's dock?

A) 0.7

B) 1.2

C) 1.3

D) 1.7

7. A rectangle has a length of 8 inches and an area of 48 square inches. What is the length, in inches, of its diagonal?

A) 6

B) 10

C) 12

D) 16

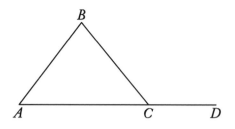

8. In the figure above, $m\angle A = 52°$, $m\angle B = x°$, and $m\angle BCD = (2x - 26)°$. What is the value of x?

A) 52

B) 76

C) 78

D) 102

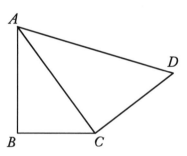

9. In the figure above, both triangles are right. If $AB = 12$, $BC = 9$, and $CD = 8$. How long is AD?

A) $\sqrt{145}$

B) $\sqrt{208}$

C) 15

D) 17

10 What is the length of a side of an equilateral triangle with a height of $4\sqrt{3}$?

A) 4

B) $4\sqrt{2}$

C) $4\sqrt{3}$

D) 8

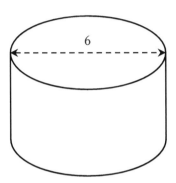

Note: Figure not drawn to scale

11 If the diameter of the right circular cylinder pictured above is half its height, what is its volume?

A) 18π

B) 27π

C) 72π

D) 108π

12 Square $ABCD$ has an area of 100. If E, F, . . and H are all midpoints of the sides of $ABCD$, what is the perimeter of square $EFGH$?

A) $5\sqrt{2}$

B) 20

C) $20\sqrt{2}$

D) $40\sqrt{2}$

13 A rectangle is divided in half, forming two squares. If each square has a perimeter of 36, what is the perimeter of the original rectangle?

A) 72

B) 60

C) 54

D) 45

14 A cone has the same volume as a sphere with radius 3. If the base radius of the cone is the same as the radius of the sphere, what is the height of the cone?

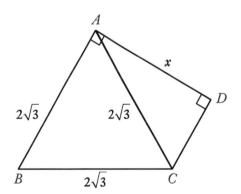

15 ABC is an equilateral triangle with each side equal to $2\sqrt{3}$. If $m\angle BAD = m\angle ADC = 90°$, what is the length of side AD ?

Similar Triangles and Trigonometry

Similar Triangles

Two non-congruent triangles that have identical angle measures are *similar* (denoted by the symbol ~), which means they have the same shape but not the same size. Though their corresponding angles are congruent, their corresponding sides are not. Instead, the corresponding sides are in proportion, so you will often have to set up an algebraic proportion to solve for a missing segment. Solve "Special Right Triangles" problems (see the reference information) using proportions in the same way.

Examples

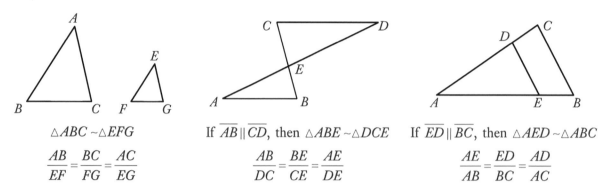

$\triangle ABC \sim \triangle EFG$

$$\frac{AB}{EF} = \frac{BC}{FG} = \frac{AC}{EG}$$

If $\overline{AB} \parallel \overline{CD}$, then $\triangle ABE \sim \triangle DCE$

$$\frac{AB}{DC} = \frac{BE}{CE} = \frac{AE}{DE}$$

If $\overline{ED} \parallel \overline{BC}$, then $\triangle AED \sim \triangle ABC$

$$\frac{AE}{AB} = \frac{ED}{BC} = \frac{AD}{AC}$$

Trigonometry

All right triangles with congruent acute angles must be similar to each other. Therefore the ratios of the sides in any right triangle with a certain acute angle are consistent and knowable. The three main trigonometric ratios are called sine, cosine and tangent (abbreviated sin, cos, and tan).

Note that the ratios of sides in right triangles that have 30°, 45°, and 60° angles are given in the reference information at the beginning of each math section. The acronym SOH-CAH-TOA can be used to remember the following:

$$\sin\theta = \frac{\text{opposite}}{\text{hypotenuse}}$$

$$\cos\theta = \frac{\text{adjacent}}{\text{hypotenuse}}$$

$$\tan\theta = \frac{\text{opposite}}{\text{adjacent}}$$

Co-functions Since switching from one acute angle in a right triangle to the other acute angle (its complement) also switches the "opposite" and "adjacent" sides, $\sin\theta° = \cos(90 - \theta)°$.

Radian Measure Often used instead of degree measure in trigonometry, a radian represents the measure of an angle necessary to intercept exactly one radius-length on the circumference of a circle. Since an entire circle is 2π radii in circumference, 2π radians = 360°.

You can covert from degrees to radians by multiplying by $\dfrac{\pi}{180}$.

Similar Triangles and Trigonometry Problem Set

1 Mann Park is in the shape of a triangle. On a map, it has borders that measure 5 inches, 7 inches, and 9 inches. If the shortest border of Mann park is 1000 meters long, how long, in meters, is its longest border?

A) 1,004

B) 1,400

C) 1,600

D) 1,800

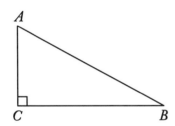

2 In the figure above, $\tan A = \dfrac{15}{8}$. If the length of $\overline{AB}$ is 51, how long is $\overline{BC}$?

A) 24

B) 34

C) 45

D) 49

3 In right triangle JKL, $\angle L$ measures 90 degrees. If $\cos J = 0.25$, what is the value of $\sin K$?

A) 0.25

B) 0.5

C) 0.75

D) 0.97

4 If $0° < x < 90°$ and $\tan x = \dfrac{4}{3}$, what is the value of $\sin x + \cos x$?

A) $\dfrac{3}{5}$

B) $\dfrac{4}{5}$

C) $\dfrac{4}{3}$

D) $\dfrac{7}{5}$

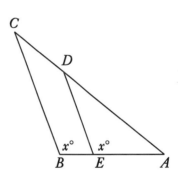

5 In the figure above, $AE = 10$, $DE = 12$, and $CB = 18$. What is BE?

A) 5

B) 6

C) 8

D) 15

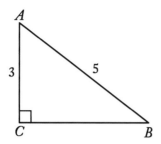

6 In the figure above, which of the following is equal to $\dfrac{3}{5}$?

A) $\sin A$

B) $\cos A$

C) $\cos B$

D) $\tan B$

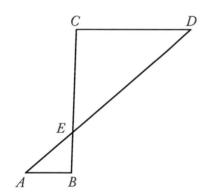

7 In the figure above, $\overline{AB} \parallel \overline{CD}$. If $AB = 12$, $CD = 30$, and $AD = 56$, what is the measure of AE?

A) 16

B) 18

C) 22.4

D) 40

8 If θ is an acute angle, then $\dfrac{\tan\theta\cos\theta}{\sin\theta}$ is equal to which of the following?

A) $\tan\theta$

B) $\sin\theta$

C) -1

D) 1

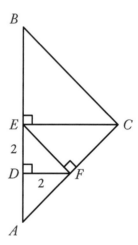

9 If all the right triangles in the figure above are similar to each other, what is the measure of BC?

A) 4

B) $4\sqrt{2}$

C) $4\sqrt{3}$

D) $6\sqrt{3}$

10 What is 210° expressed in radians?

A) $\dfrac{7\pi}{12}$

B) $\dfrac{7\pi}{6}$

C) $\dfrac{7\pi}{3}$

D) 7π

13 How many degrees are equivalent to $\dfrac{3\pi}{10}$ radians?

11 In a circle, an arc of length 12 is intercepted by a central angle of $\dfrac{2}{3}$ radians. How long is the radius of the circle?

A) $\dfrac{2}{3}$

B) 8

C) 18

D) 120

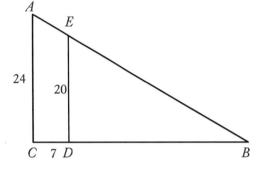

14 In the figure above, $\overline{AC} \parallel \overline{ED}$. What is the length of $\overline{DB}$?

12 If $0 < x < 90,$ which of the following statements is always true?

A) $\tan x° < 1$

B) $\sin x° + \cos x° < 1$

C) $\dfrac{\sin x°}{\cos x°} < 1$

D) $\dfrac{\sin x°}{\tan x°} < 1$

15 If $0 < x < 90$ and $\sin x° = 0.84,$ what is $\cos(90 - x)°$?

Circles

In addition to the area and circumference formulas you are given at the beginning of each math section of the SAT, there are other characteristics of circles and their graphs that should be reviewed.

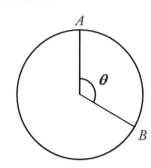

Sectors

Sectors are portions of circles created by the joining of two radii.

Arc length   the portion of the circumference of a circle that a sector carves out. The length of an arc is given by $\ell = \dfrac{\theta}{360°} \cdot 2\pi r$.

Area of a sector   The area of a sector is given by $A = \dfrac{\theta}{360°} \cdot \pi r^2$.

EQUIVALENCE OF RADII: All radii of the same circle have equal length. This property is often the key to solving a problem. Mark all radii as congruent to each other, and any angle congruence that results, and draw any relevant radii that might help flesh out a diagram.

Graphing Circles

The equation of a circle in the *xy*-coordinate plane with radius r and center (h,k) is $(x-h)^2 + (y-k)^2 = r^2$.

For example, the circle on the right has the equation $(x-2)^2 + (y-1)^2 = 4$. This circle has a radius of 2 ($r^2 = 2^2 = 4$) and its center is the point (2, 1).

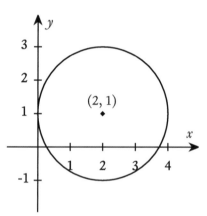

Example 1   The following equation describes a circle in the regular *xy*-plane: $x^2 - 6x + y^2 + 8y - 11 = 0$. What are the center and radius of this circle?

Here you must *complete the square* in order to get it into your desired form.

Note that $(x-3)^2 = x^2 - 6x + 9$, so $x^2 - 6x = (x-3)^2 - 9$.

Similarly, $(y+4)^2 = y^2 + 8y + 16$, so $y^2 + 8y = (y+4)^2 - 16$.

The equation can be rewritten as $(x-3)^2 - 9 + (y+4)^2 - 16 - 11 = 0$, which is equivalent to $(x-3)^2 + (y+4)^2 = 36$.

Thus the circle is centered on $(3,-4)$ and has radius 6 (since $6^2 = 36$).

Circles Problem Set

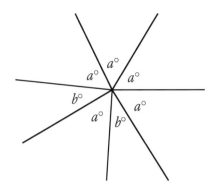

Note: Figure not drawn to scale

1 In the figure, if $a = 58$, what is b?

A) 35

B) 58

C) 64

D) 70

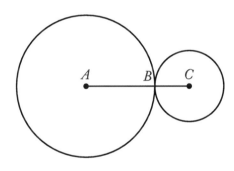

2 In the figure above, two circles are externally tangent at point B and $AC = 9$. If the radius of the larger circle is twice that of the smaller, what is the area of the smaller circle?

A) 3π

B) 4π

C) 6π

D) 9π

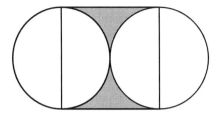

3 The radius of each of the circles above is 1. What is the area of the shaded region?

A) $2\pi - 4$

B) $8 - 2\pi$

C) $4 - \pi$

D) $4 - 2\pi$

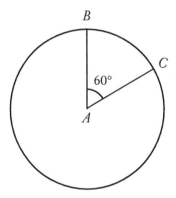

4 What is the area of sector ABC pictured in the circle above if A is the center of the circle and $AC = 3$?

A) $\dfrac{3\pi}{4}$

B) π

C) $\dfrac{3\pi}{2}$

D) 6π

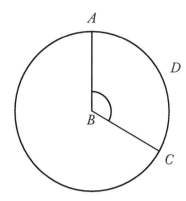

5 What is the length of arc $\overarc{ADC}$ if B is the center of the circle, $AB = 3,$ and $m\angle ABC = 120°$?

A) 9π

B) 6π

C) 3π

D) 2π

6 What is the equation of a circle in the xy-coordinate plane with a center of $(-7, 10)$ and a radius of 4 ?

A) $(x-7)^2 + (y+10)^2 = 4$

B) $(x+7)^2 + (y-10)^2 = 4$

C) $(x-7)^2 + (y+10)^2 = 16$

D) $(x+7)^2 + (y-10)^2 = 16$

7 In the xy-coordinate plane, what are the coordinates of the center of the circle whose equation is given by $(x+2)^2 + (y - \sqrt{3})^2 = 25$?

A) $(2, -\sqrt{3})$

B) $(-2, \sqrt{3})$

C) $(2, 3)$

D) $(7, 5)$

8 What is the equation of a circle with a center $(2, 3)$ and which passes through the point $(1, 1)$?

A) $(x+2)^2 + (y+3)^2 = 5$

B) $(x+2)^2 + (y+3)^2 = \sqrt{5}$

C) $(x-2)^2 + (y-3)^2 = 5$

D) $(x-2)^2 + (y-3)^2 = \sqrt{5}$

9   What is the center of the circle given by the equation $x^2 - 10x + y^2 + 6y + 2 = 0$?

A) $(5, -3)$

B) $(-5, 3)$

C) $(10, -6)$

D) $(-10, 6)$

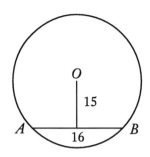

11   In the circle above, the segment extending from center O is perpendicular to chord $\overline{AB}$. What is the area of the circle?

A) 34π

B) 64π

C) 256π

D) 289π

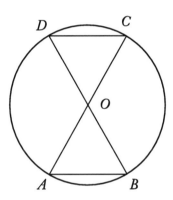

10   In the figure above, points A, B, C, and D lie on Circle O. If $m\angle DOC = 30°$, what is $m\angle OAB$?

A) $30°$

B) $60°$

C) $70°$

D) $75°$

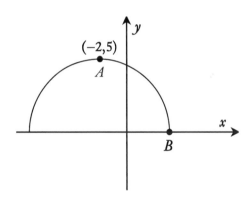

12   In the figure above, the center of the circle lies on the x-axis, directly below point A. What is the equation of the circle?

A) $(x+2)^2 + (y-5)^2 = 25$

B) $(x+2)^2 + y^2 = 25$

C) $(x-2)^2 + (y+5)^2 = 25$

D) $(x-2)^2 + y^2 = 25$

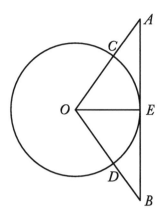

13. In the figure above, $\overline{AB}$ is tangent to circle O at E. If $AC = DB = 4$ and $OE = 6$, what is the value of AB ?

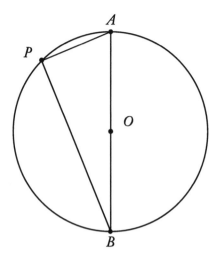

15. In the figure above, points A, B, and P are all on circle O. If $AP = 10$ and $BP = 24$, what is the measure of OB?

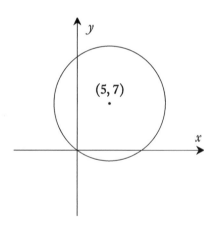

14. The figure above is the graph of a circle which goes through the origin and has a center of $(5, 7)$. If the equation of the circle can be written as $(x - 5)^2 + (y - 7)^2 = m$, what is the value of m ?

Complex Numbers

Complex numbers have the form $a + bi$, where a and b are real numbers, and i is the base of the imaginary number system equal to $\sqrt{-1}$.

Each complex number $a + bi$ has a *complex conjugate*, $a - bi$. When conjugates are multiplied, the resulting product will be a pure real number.

Complex numbers can be added and subtracted just like binomials, but when they are multiplied or divided, the property that $i^2 = -1$ complicates things. In particular, whenever anything is divided by a complex number, you should multiply both the top and bottom by the conjugate of the bottom to make the denominator real and rational. Since you are often asked to leave answers in $a + bi$ form, you may need to split up fractions like $\dfrac{5 - 3i}{7}$ into $\dfrac{5}{7} - \dfrac{3i}{7}$.

Complex Numbers Problem Set

1. What is the sum of $(3 - 5i)$ and $(-7 - 2i)$ if $i = \sqrt{-1}$?

   A) $-4 + 7i$
   B) $-4 - 3i$
   C) $-4 - 7i$
   D) $4 - 3i$

3. What is the product of $(6 - 3i)$ and $(2 + 5i)$ if $i = \sqrt{-1}$?

   A) $12 - 15i$
   B) $12 - 9i$
   C) $-3 + 24i$
   D) $27 + 24i$

2. Which of the following results from the computation $(12 - 11i) - (8 - 6i)$ if $i = \sqrt{-1}$?

   A) $-4 - 17i$
   B) $4 - 17i$
   C) $4 + 5i$
   D) $4 - 5i$

4. What is the product of $(4 - 2i)$ and $(4 + 2i)$ if $i = \sqrt{-1}$?

   A) 20
   B) 12
   C) $16 - 4i$
   D) $12 - 4i$

5. Which of the following complex numbers is equivalent to $\dfrac{12}{2+3i}$ if $i=\sqrt{-1}$?

A) $6+4i$

B) $-\dfrac{24}{5}+\dfrac{36i}{5}$

C) $\dfrac{24}{13}-\dfrac{36i}{13}$

D) $\dfrac{6}{13}-\dfrac{4i}{13}$

8. What is the value of i^6 if $i=\sqrt{-1}$?

A) -6

B) i

C) -1

D) $-6i$

6. Which of the following complex numbers is equivalent to $\dfrac{3-5i}{2+7i}$ if $i=\sqrt{-1}$?

A) $\dfrac{41}{53}-\dfrac{31i}{53}$

B) $-\dfrac{29}{53}-\dfrac{31i}{53}$

C) $-\dfrac{29}{45}+\dfrac{31i}{45}$

D) $-\dfrac{41}{45}+\dfrac{31i}{45}$

9. What is the value of i^3+i^2+i if $i=\sqrt{-1}$?

A) i

B) -1

C) $-i$

D) 1

7. What is the square of the complex number $(2-i)$ if $i=\sqrt{-1}$?

A) $3-4i$

B) $4-4i$

C) $4-5i$

D) 3

10. If $i=\sqrt{-1}$, and $2i^2-(3i)^3+4i^4=a+bi$, then what is $a+b$?

Essay Manual

The SAT essay question asks you to read a passage and then explain how the author of the passage develops his or her argument to persuade the audience. You must provide evidence from the passage to support your explanation.

Unlike a typical essay that you may write for a class, your job is *not* to agree or disagree with the author's argument. Instead, you must describe the strategies the author uses to build his or her argument.

You have 50 minutes to read the passage and write the essay. The passage will generally be between 650 and 750 words. Passages range from opinion editorials from newspapers such as *The New York Times* to speeches delivered by leaders such as Martin Luther King, Jr.

The Prompt

The prompt shown below, or a nearly identical one, is used every time the SAT is given. Part one of the prompt is provided before the passage, and part two of the prompt is provided after the passage. Read both parts of the prompt before you read the passage.

As you read the passage below, consider how [*the author*] uses:

- evidence, such as facts or examples, to support claims.
- reasoning to develop ideas and to connect claims and evidence.
- stylistic or persuasive elements, such as word choice or appeals to emotion, to add power to the ideas expressed.

Write an essay in which you explain how [the author] builds an argument to persuade [*his/her*] audience that [*author's claim*]. In your essay, analyze how [*the author*] uses one or more of the features listed above (or features of your own choice) to strengthen the logic and persuasiveness of [*his/her*] argument. Be sure that your analysis focuses on the most relevant features of the passage.

Your essay should not explain whether you agree with [*the author's*] claims, but rather explain how the author builds an argument to persuade [*his/her*] audience.

Tackling the SAT Essay

1 Read and annotate the passage

Be sure to read the passage carefully. One of the three sections of the scoring rubric (worth up to 8 points) assesses how well you comprehend the passage, so a close reading is essential. As you read, identify:

① THE AUTHOR'S ARGUMENT. Before even reading the passage, look at the second part of the prompt provided at the end of the passage. The prompt ALWAYS gives you the author's argument in the first sentence. For example, one prompt reads: "*Write an essay in which you explain how Jimmy Carter builds an argument to persuade his audience that the Arctic National Wildlife Refuge should not be developed for industry.*" The prompt will help you see why the author is writing and what he or she wants the audience to believe.

② EVIDENCE the author uses to support his/her argument. Evidence might include:

- Facts or statistics
- Quotations
- Personal experience or anecdotes

③ STYLISTIC DEVICES the author uses to build his/her argument, such as:

- Appeals to emotion
- Word choice
- Tone (See list of rhetorical devices for more examples)

④ REASONING used by the author. Examples of reasoning might be a counter-argument that the author refutes or an explanation of the evidence provided.

Mark up the passage as you read. Write the strategies you see the author using in the margin and underline or circle quotations or facts that you can cite as evidence of your claims.

Remember SOAPS as you read. Write these down as you read:

- **Speaker** Who is speaking? Consider position, time, context, gender, ethnicity, etc.
- **Occasion** What is the context/occasion of the speech? How does it affect the purpose, strategy and tone of the speech?
- **Audience** Who is the target audience? A group of high school students is very different from a group of college professors. How does the audience influence the strategies the author is using to make his argument?
- **Purpose** What does the author or speaker want?
- **Strategy** Consider the audience and the purpose—is the author using the right strategy to get his/her message across?

2 Create an Outline

After you have read the passage and before you begin writing, you MUST create an outline. Consider using a classic four or five paragraph structure. In your outline, jot down three literary strategies or techniques you are going to discuss and notes about quotes or evidence you'll use. Here's a sample outline with the information you would include:

1. Introduction
2. Word Choice and examples/quotations from text. How it contributes to argument.
3. Appeals to emotion and quotation from text. Effects on reader.
4. Statistics and how they contribute to argument.
5. Conclusion

3 Write the Essay

A. *The Introductory Paragraph*

In your introductory paragraph, you want to state the author's purpose and the strategies he or she uses to make his or her argument. You may also want to include relevant SOAPS information, such as the background of the author or speaker if you know it and why it is relevant, the occasion for the article or speech and the intended audience. Finish your introduction with a thesis statement that clearly states how the author builds his argument. Consider choosing three strategies or devices to focus on in your essay and explicitly state these three strategies in your thesis. The following is an example of an SAT essay thesis:

> "Klinenberg uses statistics, hyperbole, and reasonable alternatives to air-conditioning to build his argument that we must reduce our consumption of air conditioning."

Note in the example provided above that the student 1) states the author's argument (we must reduce our consumption of air conditioning) and 2) lists three strategies the author uses (statistics, hyperbole, and alternatives to air conditioning). These strategies will form the basis of her body paragraphs.

Sample Format for the Introduction

- State the author's argument.
  E.g. "In his article, [*author*] argues that [*author's argument*]. Remember, the SAT will always include the author's argument in the prompt.
- State your thesis, i.e. what strategies or techniques the author uses to make his/her point.
  E.g. [*Author*] uses certain strategies including [*insert your three strategies*] to urge his readers to [*repeat author's argument*]

B. Body Paragraphs

There are two ways to approach the body paragraphs:

1. Focus on one strategy in each body paragraph

   Let's say you have identified in your thesis three strategies or techniques the author uses to make his argument. In each body paragraph, you would discuss one of those strategies. For example, one body paragraph might discuss the author's word choice and the tone it creates in the passage. Perhaps the author uses words that suggest urgency. You would then analyze how the tone contributes to the author's argument. Perhaps the words connoting urgency convince the audience that immediate action is necessary. Make sure to cite specific examples of the strategy or technique you are discussing by using a short quotation from the text or by paraphrasing from the passage. For example, if you are discussing word choice, provide examples of the words used by the author and the effect they have on his argument.

   After discussing one strategy, move on to the next paragraph and discuss the next strategy stated in your thesis. Remember to start each new paragraph with a clear topic sentence that circles back to the thesis.

2. Focus on one paragraph from the passage in each body paragraph

   An alternative way of writing the essay is to choose three paragraphs in the passage and write about the rhetorical strategies used in each paragraph. For example, perhaps the author starts with a personal anecdote in the introductory paragraph of the passage, then progresses to providing statistics in a middle paragraph, and then concludes with an appeal to the audience's emotions. Your first body paragraph would discuss the author's use of the anecdote or personal experience that establishes his credibility on the subject. Your second body paragraph would discuss the evidence he provides in the form of statistics. Your third body paragraph would discuss the appeal to emotion. For each paragraph, be sure to provide concrete examples from the text.

Sample Format for Body Paragraphs

1. Topic Sentence: e.g. "[*Author*] effectively uses [*strategy*] to advance her argument that [*restate author's argument*]."
2. Provide Example: e.g. "For example, in paragraph two, she comments….[*relevant quotation*]"
3. State Effect of the strategy and why the author uses it: e.g. "The effect of [*strategy*] is …" or "By using [*strategy*], [*author*]…."
4. Explain how the strategy/technique you've identified helps the author promote his/her argument.

Transitions

As you move from one body paragraph to the next, use a transition phrase as part of your topic sentence. Sample transitions:

- In addition to…
- To further support/bolster/promote her argument, [*author*] uses …
- Another way that [*author*] promotes her argument…

Language

Vary your language. Here are some good alternatives for common words like "argue" and "show":

- Argue: contend, assert, maintain, claim, insist, reason
- Show: reveal, demonstrate, depict, illustrate, portray, express, illuminate
- Tell: convey, impart, communicate, disclose, relate

C. Concluding Paragraph

In the final paragraph, restate your thesis. Summarize the rhetorical devices used in the passage. If you have time, you could comment on whether you feel the author has used the strategies effectively. Even if you're running out of time, just add a sentence or two for the conclusion. You must have a conclusion to get 4 points on the writing portion of the score (see below).

Suggested Timing for the Essay

- CLOSE READING: 10–12 minutes
- OUTLINE: 5 minutes
- WRITING: 30 minutes
- REVIEW: 3–5 minutes

Scoring

There are three categories used to grade the SAT essay. Each category is worth 4 points, and two readers grade each essay. Each essay is therefore given three sub-scores, one for each of the three categories, and these scores range from 2–8, so the total essay score ranges from 6–24.

① READING: A successful essay shows that you understood the passage, including the interplay of central ideas and important details. It also shows an effective use of textual evidence.

② ANALYSIS: A successful essay shows your understanding of how the author builds an argument by:
- Examining the author's use of evidence, reasoning, and other stylistic and persuasive techniques
- Supporting and developing claims with well-chosen evidence from the passage

③ WRITING: A successful essay is focused, organized, and precise, with an appropriate style and tone that varies sentence structure and follows the conventions of standard written English.

Rhetorical Strategies or Techniques

The following is a partial list of common rhetorical devices and strategies authors use as they build their argument. There are many others. It's not important to pick an obscure rhetorical device to discuss in your essay. You should pick devices or strategies that help build the author's argument and that you can easily discuss.

Evidence   Could come in the form of statistics, facts, quotations, or anecdotes. Evidence is used to lend credibility to an argument. Rather than just giving an opinion, the author is backing up his argument with data.

Appeals to an audience's emotions (*Pathos*)   Does the author's text inspire feelings of pity, sympathy, anger, sorrow, joy, or another type of feeling? How does he do this? By generating an emotional connection, he may be successful in convincing you of his argument.

Logical arguments or Reasoning (*Logos*)   The author is asking the audience to think and use their intelligence to come to the same conclusion as him. Perhaps he provides data and then suggests a way for interpreting this data that supports his argument.

Credibility (*Ethos*)   Ways in which the author establishes his or her own authority to gain the trust of the audience. For example, if the author is writing about a medical issue, perhaps he uses the fact that he is a surgeon to gain credibility with the audience.

Literary Devices

Allusion   a reference to a historical or literary figure, event or subject. An author makes an allusion for a reason, so ask yourself why he or she has alluded to a particular person or event.

Anecdote   a brief story usually about a real person or event.

Analogy   a comparison of two things that are alike in some respects.

Cause–effect argumentation   reasoning that if one thing happens, a particular outcome logically follows.

Diction (word choice)   Look at individual words the author uses. Are there a lot of words that are happy words, sad words, passionate words, or angry words? What tone do these words set for the passage?

Hyperbole   exaggerated statements or words not intended to be taken literally. Again look at the word choice of the author. Are the words over the top? Why might the author be using exaggeration to make his point?

Irony   statement that is characterized by a significant difference between what is said and what is meant. What effect does irony have?

Imagery   sensory details that involve any or all of the five senses. Sensory details can make a passage more vivid or alive. It's like you're experiencing something rather than just reading about it.

Metaphor   figurative language comparing two ideas that are not related. This can help the audience better visualize the author's ideas.

Parallelism   repeating similar components or phrases in a sentence , e.g. "it was the best of times, it was the worst of times…"

Repetition   making the same point over and over.

Satire   use of humor or ridicule to expose the stupidity of an idea.

Tone   the overall mood conveyed by the author of the passage. Tone is generally created by the author's choice of words.

Sample Essay Prompt

As you read the passage below, consider how President Kennedy uses

- evidence, such as facts or examples, to support claims.
- reasoning to develop ideas and to connect claims and evidence.
- stylistic or persuasive elements, such as word choice or appeals to emotion, to add power to the ideas expressed.

Adapted from a speech delivered by President John F. Kennedy at Rice University, September 12, 1962.

1   We meet at a college noted for knowledge, in a city noted for progress, in a state noted for strength, and we stand in need of all three, for we meet in an hour of change and challenge, in a decade of hope and fear, in an age of both knowledge and ignorance.

2   No man can fully grasp how far and how fast we have come, but condense, if you will, the 50,000 years of man's recorded history in a time span of but a half-century. Stated in these terms, we know very little about the first 40 years, except at the end of them, advanced man had learned to use the skins of animals to cover himself… Only five years ago man learned to write and use a cart with wheels. The printing press came this year… Last month electric lights and telephones and automobiles and airplanes became available. Only last week did we develop penicillin and television and nuclear power, and now if America's new spacecraft succeeds in reaching Venus, we will have literally reached the stars before midnight tonight.

3   This is a breathtaking pace, and such a pace cannot help but create new ills as it dispels old, new ignorance, new problems, new dangers. Surely the opening vistas of space promise high costs and hardships, as well as high reward.

4   So it is not surprising that some would have us stay where we are a little longer to rest, to wait. But this city of Houston, this state of Texas, this country of the United States was not built by those who waited and rested and wished to look behind them. This country was conquered by those who moved forward—and so will space.

5   The exploration of space will go ahead whether we join it or not…

6   Those who came before us made certain that this country rode the first waves of the industrial revolution, the first waves of modern invention, and the first wave of nuclear power, and this generation does not intend to founder in the backwash of the coming age of space. We mean to be a part of it—we mean to lead it. For the eyes of the world now look into space, to the moon and to the planets beyond, and we have vowed that we shall not see it governed by a hostile flag of conquest, but by a banner of freedom and peace. We have vowed that we shall not see space filled with weapons of mass destruction, but with instruments of knowledge and understanding.

7   Yet the vows of this Nation can only be fulfilled if we in this Nation are first, and, therefore, we intend to be first. In short, our leadership in science and industry, our hopes for peace and security, our obligations to ourselves as well as others, all require us to make this effort, to solve these mysteries, to solve them for the good of all men, and to become the world's leading space-faring nation.

8   Within these last 19 months at least 45 satellites have circled the earth. Some 40 of them were made in

the United States of America and they were far more sophisticated and supplied far more knowledge to the people of the world than those of the Soviet Union.

9 The Mariner spacecraft now on its way to Venus is the most intricate instrument in the history of space science. The accuracy of that shot is comparable to firing a missile from Cape Canaveral and dropping it in this stadium between the 40-yard lines.

10 Transit satellites are helping our ships at sea to steer a safer course. Tiros satellites have given us unprecedented warnings of hurricanes and storms, and will do the same for forest fires and icebergs…

11 The growth of our science and education will be enriched by new knowledge of our universe and environment, by new techniques of learning and mapping and observation, by new tools and computers for industry, medicine, the home as well as the school.

12 And finally, the space effort itself, while still in its infancy, has already created a great number of new companies, and tens of thousands of new jobs. Space and related industries are generating new demands in investment and skilled personnel, and this city and this state, and this region, will share greatly in this growth. During the next 5 years the National Aeronautics and Space Administration expects to double the number of scientists and engineers in this area, to increase its outlays for salaries and expenses to $60 million a year…

13 I am delighted that this university is playing a part in putting a man on the moon.

Write an essay in which you explain how President John Kennedy builds an argument to persuade his audience that the United States should invest in space exploration. In your essay, analyze how Kennedy uses one or more of the features listed above (or features of your own choice) to strengthen the logic and persuasiveness of his argument. Be sure that your analysis focuses on the most relevant features of the passage.

Your essay should not explain whether you agree with Kennedy's claims, but rather explain how the author builds an argument to persuade his audience.

SAT Practice Test 1

IMPORTANT REMINDERS

A No. 2 pencil is required for the test.
Do not use a mechanical pencil or pen.

Sharing any questions with anyone is a violation
of the Test Security and Fairness policies and
may result in your score being canceled.

This cover is representative of what you will see on the day of the SAT.

1

1

Reading Test

65 MINUTES, 52 QUESTIONS

Turn to Section 1 of your answer sheet to answer the questions in this section.

DIRECTIONS

Each passage or pair of passages below is followed by a number of questions. After reading each passage or pair, choose the best answer to each question based on what is stated or implied in the passage or passages and in any accompanying graphics (such as a table or graph).

Questions 1–10 are based on the following passage.

This passage is adapted from Jane Austen, *Northanger Abbey*, originally published in 1817. Here, Catherine Morland, Eleanor Tilney, and her brother, Henry Tilney, discuss the merits of different kinds of reading.

"But now really, do not you think *Udolpho*[1] the nicest book in the world?" asked Miss Morland.

"The nicest—by which I suppose you mean the neatest. That must depend upon the binding,"
5 replied Henry.

"Henry," said Miss Tilney, "you are very impertinent. Miss Morland, he is treating you exactly as he does his sister. He is forever finding fault with me, for some incorrectness of language, and now he
10 is taking the same liberty with you. The word 'nicest,' as you used it, did not suit him; and you had better change it as soon as you can, or we shall be overpowered with Johnson and Blair[2] all the rest of the way."

15 "I am sure," cried Catherine, "I did not mean to say anything wrong; but it is a nice book, and why should not I call it so?"

"Very true," said Henry, "and this is a very nice day, and we are taking a very nice walk, and you are
20 two very nice young ladies. Oh! It is a very nice word indeed! It does for everything. Originally perhaps it

was applied only to express neatness, propriety, delicacy, or refinement—people were nice in their dress, in their sentiments, or their choice. But now
25 every commendation on every subject is comprised in that one word."

"While, in fact," cried his sister, "it ought only to be applied to you, without any commendation at all. You are more nice than wise. Come, Miss Morland,
30 let us leave him to meditate over our faults in the utmost propriety of diction, while we praise *Udolpho* in whatever terms we like best. It is a most interesting work. You are fond of that kind of reading?"

"To say the truth, I do not much like any other. I
35 can read poetry and plays, and things of that sort, and do not dislike travels. But history, real solemn history, I cannot be interested in. Can you?"

"Yes, I am fond of history."

"I wish I were too. I read it a little as a duty, but it
40 tells me nothing that does not either vex or weary me. The quarrels of popes and kings, with wars or pestilences, in every page; the men all so good for nothing, and hardly any women at all—it is very tiresome: and yet I often think it odd that it should be
45 so dull, for a great deal of it must be invention. The speeches that are put into the heroes' mouths, their thoughts and designs—the chief of all this must be invention, and invention is what delights me in other books."

50 "Historians, you think," said Miss Tilney, "display imagination without raising interest. I am fond of history—and am very well contented to take the false with the true. In the principal facts they have

---

[1] *The Mysteries of Udolpho*, a Gothic novel by Ann Radcliffe.

[2] Samuel Johnson wrote one of the first English dictionaries, and Hugh Blair was an influential writer and lecturer on rhetoric.

CONTINUE

sources of intelligence in former histories and
55 records, which may be as much depended on, I
conclude, as anything that does not actually pass
under one's own observation; and as for the little
embellishments you speak of, they are
embellishments, and I like them as such. If a speech
60 be well drawn up, I read it with pleasure, by
whomsoever it may be made—and probably with
much greater, if the production of Mr. Hume or Mr.
Robertson,[3] than if the genuine words of Caractacus,
Agricola, or Alfred the Great."[4]

1

Henry responds in lines 3–4 ("The nicest …
binding") to Catherine's claim about *Udolpho* by

A) expressing a deep-seated dislike of the novel.

B) inadvertently revealing his inability to
understand the meaning of her words.

C) deliberately misunderstanding her in order to
mock her word choice.

D) foolishly emphasizing the appearance of the
book instead of its content.

2

The phrase "taking the same liberty with you" in
line 10 most nearly means

A) espousing the same freedom for Catherine as a
natural right.

B) acting with similarly inappropriate romantic
license towards Catherine.

C) assuming an innate privilege common to all.

D) treating Catherine the same way without her
desiring it.

3

Miss Tilney mentions "Johnson and Blair" (line 13)
primarily to

A) make fun of her brother's tendency to be
pedantic.

B) prove that she is as well-read and knowledgeable
as her brother.

C) imply that her brother has excluded Catherine
from the conversation.

D) justify her disdain for definitions and grammar.

4

Henry repeatedly uses the word "nice" in lines 18–
20 primarily to

A) show his disapproval of the overuse and loss of
meaning of a common word.

B) mock Catherine's views, using irony to show his
disapproval of all the things he mentions.

C) endear himself to his audience, because he
knows he has upset them.

D) emphasize how pleased he is with their situation.

---

[3] David Hume and William Robertson were historians who
wrote during the 18th century.

[4] Caractacus, Agricola, and Alfred the Great were figures from
British and Roman history about whom history books were
written.

5

Which choice provides the best evidence for the answer to the previous question?

A) Lines 7–8 ("Miss Morland … sister")

B) Lines 15–17 ("I am … call it so")

C) Lines 23–24 ("people were … their choice")

D) Lines 24–26 (But now … one word")

6

Based on her opinions expressed in the passage, which of the following would Catherine most enjoy reading?

A) A treatise on the causes of the fall of the Roman empire

B) An analysis of the accuracy of the speeches in Shakespeare's history plays

C) A novel about the romantic adventures of a knight under King Arthur

D) A philosophical dialogue regarding the impact of Marco Polo's journeys

7

The word "invention" as it is used in lines 45 and 48 most nearly means

A) something the author fabricated.

B) a newly developed technology.

C) an advancement in how people understand history.

D) something that is deceptive in order to make a point.

8

According to the passage, Miss Tilney believes that speeches recorded in history books are

A) not necessarily true, but much more useful for learning than fictional novels and plays.

B) inaccurate factually, but interesting and enjoyable anyway.

C) deliberately deceptive to give a biased impression of historical events and people.

D) as trustworthy as any other information that we must accept second hand.

9

Which choice provides the best evidence for the answer to the previous question?

A) Lines 45–49 ("The speeches … books")

B) Lines 50–51 ("Historians … interest")

C) Lines 53–57 ("In the … observation")

D) Lines 57–60 ("as for the … made")

10

Miss Tilney mentions Caractacus, Agricola, and Alfred the Great primarily to

A) suggest that their speeches were probably not as good as those written by contemporary historians.

B) emphasize the importance of accurately recording the genuine words of great men throughout history.

C) make fun of her brother's overly zealous reading of the works of historical leaders.

D) compare later rhetoricians to the great speakers of the past.

1

1

Questions 11–20 are based on the following passage and supplemental material.

This passage is adapted from Mary Fisher's address to the 1992 Republican National Convention.

Tonight, I represent an AIDS community whose members have been reluctantly drafted from every segment of American society. Though I am white and a mother, I am one with a black infant struggling with
5 tubes in a Philadelphia hospital. Though I am female and contracted this disease in marriage and enjoy the warm support of my family, I am one with the lonely gay man sheltering a flickering candle from the cold wind of his family's rejection.
10 This is not a distant threat. It is a present danger. The rate of infection is increasing fastest among women and children. Largely unknown a decade ago, AIDS is the third leading killer of young adult Americans today. But it won't be third for long, because unlike other
15 diseases, this one travels. Adolescents don't give each other cancer or heart disease because they believe they are in love, but HIV is different; and we have helped it along. We have killed each other with our ignorance, our prejudice, and our silence.
20 We may take refuge in our stereotypes, but we cannot hide there long, because HIV asks only one thing of those it attacks. Are you human? And this is the right question. Are you human? Because people with HIV have not entered some alien state of being.
25 They are human. They have not earned cruelty, and they do not deserve meanness. They don't benefit from being isolated or treated as outcasts. Each of them is exactly what God made: a person; not evil, deserving of our judgment; not victims, longing for our pity—
30 people, ready for support and worthy of compassion.
My call to you, my Party, is to take a public stand, no less compassionate than that of the President and Mrs. Bush. They have embraced me and my family in memorable ways. In the place of judgment, they have
35 shown affection. In difficult moments, they have raised our spirits. In the darkest hours, I have seen them reaching not only to me, but also to my parents, armed with that stunning grief and special grace that comes only to parents who have themselves leaned too long
40 over the bedside of a dying child.
With the President's leadership, much good has been done. Much of the good has gone unheralded, and as the President has insisted, much remains to be done.

But we do the President's cause no good if we praise
45 the American family but ignore a virus that destroys it.
We must be consistent if we are to be believed. We cannot love justice and ignore prejudice, love our children and fear to teach them. Whatever our role as parent or policymaker, we must act as eloquently as we
50 speak—or we have no integrity. My call to the nation is a plea for awareness. If you believe you are safe, you are in danger. Because I was not hemophiliac, I was not at risk. Because I was not gay, I was not at risk. Because I did not inject drugs, I was not at risk.
55 My father has devoted much of his lifetime guarding against another holocaust. He is part of the generation who heard Pastor Niemoellor come out of the Nazi death camps to say:
"First they came for the Socialists, and I did not
60 speak out. Because I was not a Socialist. Then they came for the Trade Unionists, and I did not speak out. Because I was not a Trade Unionist. Then they came for the Jews, and I did not speak out. Because I was not a Jew. Then they came for me—and there was no one
65 left to speak for me."
The lesson history teaches is this: If you believe you are safe, you are at risk. If you do not see this killer stalking your children, look again. There is no family or community, no race or religion, no place left in America
70 that is safe. Until we genuinely embrace this message, we are a nation at risk.

AIDS Cases 1981-1991: Adult and Pediatric

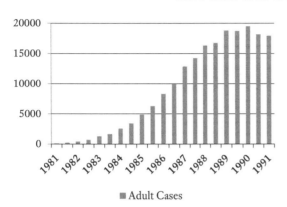

■ Adult Cases

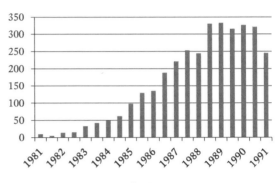

■ Pediatric Cases

Adapted from the Centers for Disease Control and Prevention website.

11

In response to the AIDS crisis, the author advocates most directly for

A) understanding and support for AIDS patients.

B) decreasing the rate of the spread of AIDS.

C) support for the President's AIDS initiatives.

D) heightened awareness of the behaviors that can lead to AIDS.

12

Which choice provides the best evidence for the answer to the previous question?

A) Lines 10–13 ("This is … today")

B) Lines 27–30 ("Each of … compassion")

C) Lines 33–36 ("They have … spirits")

D) Lines 51–54 ("If you … at risk")

13

In the first paragraph, the author most likely makes statements beginning with "though" in order to

A) separate herself from other AIDS patients.

B) highlight the role of race and sexuality in contracting AIDS.

C) draw attention to faulty stereotypes of AIDS patients.

D) emphasize her unique challenges as a white woman.

14

The author mentions an "alien state of being" in line 24 in order to

A) dehumanize AIDS patients.

B) compare physical differences between AIDS patients and healthy humans.

C) emphasize that the spread of AIDS has given people a new group identity.

D) belie the assumptions some people have made about AIDS patients.

CONTINUE

15

The author emphasizes the ways that President Bush has responded to the AIDS crisis as a

A) compassionate personal friend.

B) bold leader creating legislation to address the issue.

C) nobly intentioned but insufficiently active politician.

D) sympathetic but ineffectual figurehead.

16

Which choice provides the best evidence for the answer to the previous question?

A) Lines 27–30 ("Each of … compassion")

B) Lines 36–40 ("I have … child")

C) Lines 42–43 ("Much of … be done")

D) Lines 44–45 ("But we … destroys it")

17

As used in line 50, "integrity" most nearly means

A) completeness.

B) purity.

C) consistency.

D) righteousness.

18

The author uses the terms "we" in line 46 and "you" in line 51 to refer to

A) completely different groups of people to suggest their opposition.

B) her own party as a whole and those within her party who don't wish to show compassion.

C) the American people as a whole and those who have not yet been personally affected by AIDS.

D) those who have AIDS and those who do not.

19

The primary rhetorical purpose of citing Pastor Niemoellor (lines 59–65) is to

A) compare the devastation caused by the AIDS epidemic to that of the Holocaust.

B) quote a religious source to support the legitimacy of the author's argument.

C) indicate that the public response to the AIDS crisis is analogous to public response to the Holocaust.

D) provide historical context for the proper response to the AIDS epidemic.

20

Based on the graphs of AIDS cases provided, it can be reasonably inferred that

A) pediatric cases were a much lower percent of the total number of children than adult cases were of the adult population.

B) pediatric cases made up a small proportion of all AIDS cases.

C) all cases increased over time, but pediatric cases increased at a much lower rate.

D) pediatric AIDS cases were more severe than adult AIDS cases.

CONTINUE

Questions 21–30 are based on the following passage.

The following passage is from Dan Vergano, "Monkeys Steer Wheelchairs with Their Brains, Raising Hope for Paralyzed People." ©2014 by National Geographic.

Experimental wheelchairs and exoskeletons controlled by thought alone offer surprising insights into the brain, neuroscientists reported on Monday.

Best known for his experimental exoskeleton that
5   helped a paralyzed man kick the opening ball for
June's World Cup in Brazil, Duke University
neuroscientist Miguel Nicolelis presented the latest
"brain-machine interface" findings from his team's
"Walk Again Project" at the Society for
10 Neuroscience meeting.

"Some of our patients say they feel they are
walking on sand," says Nicolelis, describing pilot
research in which eight paralyzed patients walked
using a robotic exoskeleton that moved in response to
15 readings of the patients' brain waves. "We are
actually fooling the brain of patients to think it is not
a machine carrying them, but they feel they are
themselves walking forward."

Insights into the brains of paralyzed patients are
20 helping to drive the technology as well as leading to
new discoveries, says neuroscientist Eberhard Fetz of
the University of Washington in Seattle. Roughly
130,000 people yearly suffer spinal cord injuries
worldwide, and for more than a decade, researchers
25 have sought to help these patients using robotic
interfaces with the brain. After years of advances,
efforts such as the exoskeleton are moving into the
earliest stages of medical testing in patient
volunteers.

30 "For patients, they are probably not coming fast
enough," Fetz says. "But brain-machine interfaces
are giving us results producing a basic understanding
of neural mechanisms. That is going to happen in
parallel with developing these as tools to benefit
35 patients."

Brain-machine interfaces have become a buzzword
in recent years, triggering headlines when, for
example, Brown University's John Donoghue's
human patients drank coffee and picked up objects
40 with robotic arms controlled by brain-implanted
electrodes.

At the meeting, Nicolelis also presented research
on two rhesus monkeys that had electrodes implanted

deep in their brains that, with training, allowed the
45 animals to steer a wheelchair using thought alone.
The goal of that research is partly to help develop a
"brain pacemaker" implant that would pick up
clearer signals from thoughts to help control future
robotic prosthetics.

50 Signals from deep in the brain are much easier for
devices to read than ones picked up by electrical skin
sensors on patient's skulls. Such implants made the
monkeys relatively quick students at wheelchair
driving. "They can reliably steer the wheelchair to
55 get a grape," Nicolelis said. "They like grapes."

Fetz and colleagues have similarly shown that
brain interfaces in monkeys can "bridge" the
damaged area in a spinal cord injury, allowing
voluntary movement of muscles. "These efforts are
60 in fact coming along and offer a lot of promise," he
says.

Training paralysis patients to walk with an
experimental exoskeleton can have unexpected
benefits too. The people in Nicolelis' study showed
65 improved muscle tone, heart health, and digestion
over the last year, he says.

Most surprising has been the finding that the
faster patients walk with the exoskeleton device—a
skeletal frame equipped with 15 electrical motors
70 triggered by electroencephalogram readings—the
more natural the walking feels to them.

Paralysis also cuts off sensation from the lower
limbs, which can make standing upright feel
alarming, as if one is simply hanging in air, Nicolelis
75 says. However, the brain's ability to manufacture
"phantom" feeling, best known from amputees who
report pain from phantom limbs they no longer
possess, similarly kicks in for paralysis patients
learning to walk in an exoskeleton.

80 If they walk slow, they feel that they are walking
on sand; faster, that they are on grass, and fastest that
they are walking on hot pavement."

Despite the excitement over brain-machine
interfaces in recent years, a great deal of hard work
85 remains ahead for researchers and patients, cautions
neuroscientist Daofen Chen of the National Institute
of Neurological Disorders and Stroke, part of the
federal National Institutes of Health.

"In my personal view, brain-machine interfaces are
90 offering important tools to understand the brain,"

Chen says. "We are far from understanding the brain well enough to expect them to serve as solutions."

Fetz, however, suggests that enough progress is being made to feel good about developing robotics
95 that might help patients, both in efforts such as the exoskeleton and other advances that might bridge spinal cord injuries to restore normal functions.

21

The overall structure of this text can be best described as

A) a detailed account of an experiment's scientific procedure followed by an analysis of its results.

B) a description of an innovative technological advancement and what scientists have learned from this invention.

C) a broad overview of a serious medical diagnosis and a digression into several avenues for treatment.

D) an explanation of a bold and impractical attempt at curing a medical condition that has proven incurable.

22

What is the author's main point?

A) Current brain-machine interfaces are intrinsically flawed and require further research to resolve specific defects.

B) Brain-machine interfaces are an excellent and promising cure for various causes of paralysis.

C) People suffering from paralysis suffer from a lack of effective treatment options and future research is necessary to find alternatives to current treatments.

D) Recent advances in brain-machine interfaces have promising applications in treatment of spinal cord injury.

23

As used in line 20, "drive" most nearly means

A) maneuver.

B) transport.

C) unveil.

D) stimulate.

24

According to Fetz, the relationship between brain-machine interface research and the development of related technology is

A) one-sided, because research provides an essential basis for the development of future technologies.

B) promising, but uncertain because so much more research must be completed for the technology to provide needed solutions.

C) interdependent, because technologies provide new insights and research enables new technologies.

D) deceptive, because, despite their apparent similarity, each has its own priorities and its own timetable.

25

Which choice provides the best evidence for the answer to the previous question?

A) Lines 15–18 ("We are … forward")

B) Lines 31–35 ("But brain-machine … patients")

C) Lines 56–59 ("Fetz and … muscles")

D) Lines 89–92 ("In my personal … solutions")

259

CONTINUE

26

An advantage to using "electrodes implanted deep within" (lines 43–44) the brain is that they

A) function as a "brain pacemaker," which regulates brain activity.

B) are the best method to train monkeys to steer wheelchairs.

C) allow machines to receive clearer signals from the brain than skin sensors do.

D) are more reliable for use with wheelchairs than with exoskeletons.

27

Which choice provides the best evidence for the answer to the previous question?

A) Lines 42–45 ("At the … alone")

B) Lines 50–52 ("Signals from … skulls")

C) Lines 54–55 ("'They can … like grapes'")

D) Lines 62–66 ("Training … he says")

28

As used in line 77, "phantom" most nearly means

A) ghostly.

B) painful.

C) skeletal.

D) imagined.

29

In line 55, Nicolelis mentions that monkeys "like grapes" primarily to

A) provide an explanation for the monkeys' motivation to steer the wheelchairs.

B) indicate that the monkeys involved in the experiment were not mistreated.

C) challenge the assumption that monkeys are not able to complete tasks that benefit them.

D) offer a humorous detail that reveals his familiarity with the monkeys' habits.

30

Based on the passage as a whole, how does Fetz's attitude compare to Chen's?

A) Chen is more cautious whereas Fetz is more reckless.

B) Chen is more excited whereas Fetz is more reserved.

C) Chen and Fetz are both lukewarm.

D) Chen is more tentative whereas Fetz is more optimistic.

Questions 31–41 are based on the following passages.

The following passages are excerpted from the first Lincoln–Douglas debate on August 21, 1858 in Ottawa, Illinois. Passage 1 is adapted from Stephen Douglas's opening statement. Passage 2 is adapted from Abraham Lincoln's opening statement.

Passage 1

Mr. Lincoln, in the extract from which I have read, says that this Government cannot endure permanently in the same condition in which it was made by its framers—divided into free and slave
5 States. He says that it has existed for about seventy years thus divided, and yet he tells you that it cannot endure permanently on the same principles and in the same relative condition in which our fathers made it. Why can it not exist divided into free and slave
10 States? Washington, Jefferson, Franklin, Madison, Hamilton, Jay, and the great men of that day, made this Government divided into free States and slave States, and left each State perfectly free to do as it pleased on the subject of slavery. Why can it not exist
15 on the same principles on which our fathers made it? They knew when they framed the Constitution that in a country as wide and broad as this, with such a variety of climate, production and interest, the people necessarily required different laws and
20 institutions in different localities. They knew that the laws and regulations which would suit the granite hills of New Hampshire would be unsuited to the rice plantations of South Carolina, and they, therefore, provided that each State should retain its own
25 Legislature and its own sovereignty, with the full and complete power to do as it pleased within its own limits, in all that was local and not national. One of the reserved rights of the States, was the right to regulate the relations between Master and Servant,
30 on the slavery question. At the time the Constitution was framed, there were thirteen States in the Union, twelve of which were slaveholding States and one free State. Suppose this doctrine of uniformity preached by Mr. Lincoln, that the States should all be free or all
35 be slave had prevailed, and what would have been the result? Of course, the twelve slaveholding States would have overruled the one free State, and slavery would have been fastened by a Constitutional provision on every inch of the American Republic,
40 instead of being left as our fathers wisely left it, to

each State to decide for itself. Here I assert that uniformity in the local laws and institutions of the different States is neither possible nor desirable. If uniformity had been adopted when the Government
45 was established, it must inevitably have been the uniformity of slavery everywhere, or else the uniformity of negro citizenship and negro equality everywhere.

Passage 2

The great variety of the local institutions in the
50 States, springing from differences in the soil, differences in the face of the country, and in the climate, are bonds of Union. They do not make "a house divided against itself," but they make a house united. If they produce in one section of the country
55 what is called for by the wants of another section, and this other section can supply the wants of the first, they are not matters of discord but bonds of union, true bonds of union. But can this question of slavery be considered as among *these* varieties in the
60 institutions of the country? I leave it to you to say whether, in the history of our Government, this institution of slavery has not always failed to be a bond of union, and, on the contrary, been an apple of discord, and an element of division in the house. I ask
65 you to consider whether—so long as the moral constitution of men's minds shall continue to be the same, after this generation and assemblage shall sink into the grave, and another race shall arise, with the same moral and intellectual development we have—
70 whether, if that institution is standing in the same irritating position in which it now is, it will not continue an element of division? If so, then I have a right to say that, in regard to this question, the Union is a house divided against itself; and when the Judge
75 reminds me that I have often said to him that the institution of slavery has existed for eighty years in some States, and yet it does not exist in some others, I agree to the fact, and I account for it by looking at the position in which our fathers originally placed
80 it—restricting it from the new Territories where it had not gone, and legislating to cut off its source by the abrogation of the slave-trade thus putting the seal of legislation *against its spread*.

CONTINUE

31

Based on his argument, the author of Passage 1 sees the founding fathers as

A) anachronisms.

B) paragons.

C) conservatives.

D) heroes.

32

Which choice provides the best evidence for the answer to the previous question?

A) Lines 1–9 ("Mr. Lincoln … made it")

B) Lines 9–15 ("Why can it … made it")

C) Lines 20–27 ("They knew … national")

D) Lines 33–41 ("Suppose … decide for itself")

33

In Passage 1, the author's underlying argument is that

A) each state should determine for itself whether to allow slavery, because each state has diverse needs.

B) a majority of states are slave states, so in order to unify the country slavery should be legal everywhere.

C) mandating universal citizenship is unlawful, because citizenship should be determined by individual state governments.

D) America should be divided on the issue of slavery because that is what the founding fathers wanted.

34

The author of Passage 1 describes the terrains of South Carolina and New Hampshire in lines 21–23 in order to

A) underscore the need for political similarities despite geographic differences.

B) accentuate the extreme and potentially irreconcilable differences between states.

C) argue that differences among the states require different laws and procedures.

D) imply that the Northern states have no need for slaves based on their economies.

35

Based on the views expressed in Passage 2, the author of Passage 2 most nearly views the institution of slavery as

A) acceptable eighty years ago, but now outdated.

B) an element of diversity that enhances America's union.

C) immoral and inconsistent with American values.

D) a source of long-lasting, divisive conflict.

36

The best evidence for the previous question is found in

A) lines 49–54 ("The great … united").

B) lines 60–64 ("I leave … the house").

C) lines 74–78 ("and when … the fact").

D) lines 78–83 ("I account … *spread*").

CONTINUE

37

As used in line 66, "constitution" most nearly means

A) governing document.

B) authority.

C) composition.

D) rectitude.

38

In line 82, "abrogation" most nearly means

A) abolition.

B) increase.

C) reduction.

D) hiatus.

39

How do the authors of both passages interpret the founding fathers' approach to the legality of slavery?

A) Douglas argues that the founding fathers supported slavery federally, whereas Lincoln thinks they were opposed to slavery in all states.

B) Douglas and Lincoln both agree that the founding fathers fully supported the states' right to determine the legality of slavery.

C) Douglas claims that the founding fathers fully supported states' right to determine the status of slavery, whereas Lincoln argues that they wanted to restrict new states from legalizing slavery.

D) Douglas suggests that the founding fathers supported slave states permanently, whereas Lincoln indicates that they only supported slave states temporarily.

40

The authors of both passages most strongly agree that

A) America is comprised of diverse states.

B) slavery is a profitable institution for the South.

C) slavery is a divisive issue.

D) the founding fathers' principles must determine all laws.

41

Which choice provides the best evidence for the answer to the previous question?

A) Lines 1-9 ("Mr. Lincoln … made it") and lines 60-64 ("I leave … the house")

B) Lines 10-15 ("Washington … made it") and lines 78-83 ("I account … *spread*")

C) Lines 16-20 ("They knew … localities") and lines 49-54 ("The great … united")

D) Lines 27-30 ("One of … question") and lines 64-69 ("I ask … have")

CONTINUE

Questions 42–52 are based on the following passage and supplementary material.

This passage is adapted from Stephen Jay Gould, *The Panda's Thumb: More Reflections in Natural History.* ©1980 by W. W. Norton & Company.

The theory of plate tectonics has led us to reconstruct the history of our planet's surface. During the past 200 million years, our modern continents have fragmented and dispersed from a
5 single supercontinent, Pangaea, that coalesced from earlier continents 225 million years ago. If modern oddities are the signs of history, we should ask whether any peculiar things that animals do today might be rendered more sensible as adaptations to
10 previous continental positions. Among the greatest puzzles and wonders of natural history are the long and circuitous routes of migration followed by many animals. Some lengthy movements make sense as direct paths to favorable climates from season to
15 season; they are no more peculiar than the annual winter migration to Florida of large mammals inside metallic birds. But other animals migrate thousands of miles—from feeding to breeding grounds—with astounding precision when other appropriate spots
20 seem close at hand. Could any of these peculiar routes be rendered shorter and more sensible on a map of ancient continental positions? Archie Carr, world's expert on the migration of green turtles, has made such a proposal.
25 A population of the green turtle, *Chelonia mydas*, nests and breeds on the small and isolated central Atlantic island of Ascension. London soup chefs and victualing ships of Her Majesty's Navy found and exploited these turtles long ago. But they did not
30 suspect, as Carr discovered by tagging animals at Ascension and recovering them later at their feeding grounds, that *Chelonia* travels 2,000 miles from the coast of Brazil to feed on this "pinpoint of land hundreds of miles from other shores," this "barely
35 exposed spire in mid-ocean."
Turtles feed and breed on separate grounds for good reasons. They feed on sea grasses in protected, shallow-water pastures, but breed on exposed shores where sandy beaches develop—preferably, on islands
40 where predators are rare. But why travel 2,000 miles to the middle of an ocean when other, apparently appropriate breeding grounds are so much nearer?

(Another large population of the same species breeds on the Caribbean coast of Costa Rica.) As Carr
45 writes: "The difficulties facing such a voyage would seem insurmountable if it were not so clear that the turtles are somehow surmounting them."
Perhaps, Carr reasoned, this odyssey is a peculiar extension of something much more sensible, a
50 journey to an island in the middle of the Atlantic, when the Atlantic was little more than a puddle between two continents recently separated. South America and Africa parted company some 80 million years ago, when ancestors of the genus *Chelonia* were
55 already present in the area. Ascension is an island associated with the Mid-Atlantic Ridge, a linear belt where new sea floor wells up from the earth's interior. This upwelling material often piles itself high enough to form islands.
60 Iceland is the largest modern island formed by the Mid-Atlantic Ridge; Ascension is a smaller version of the same process. After islands form on one side of a ridge, they are pushed away by new material welling up and spreading out. Thus, islands tend to be older
65 as we move farther and farther from a ridge. But they also tend to get smaller and finally to erode away into underwater seamounts, for their supply of new material dries up once they drift away from an active ridge. Unless preserved and built up by a shield of
70 coral and other organisms, islands will eventually be eroded below sea level by waves. (They may also sink gradually from sight as they move downslope from an elevated ridge into the oceanic depths.)
Carr therefore proposed that the ancestors of
75 Ascension green turtles swam a short distance from Brazil to a "proto-Ascension" on the late Cretaceous Mid-Atlantic Ridge. As this island moved out and sank, a new one formed at the ridge and the turtles ventured a bit farther. This process continued until,
80 like the jogger who does a bit more each day and ends up a marathoner, turtles found themselves locked into a 2,000-mile journey.

CONTINUE

Figure 1

Cretaceous Period, 65 million years ago

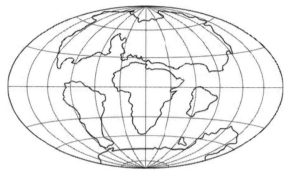

Adapted from PALEOMAP Project. © 2001 Christopher Scotese.

Figure 2

Present Day

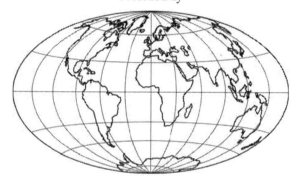

42

The author describes the turtles' journey primarily as

A) a curious phenomenon.

B) an impressive feat of memory.

C) an inexplicable outlier.

D) an unmatched instance of stamina.

43

Which choice provides the best evidence for the answer to the previous question?

A) Lines 13–18 ("Some lengthy … birds")

B) Lines 25–35 ("A population … mid-ocean'")

C) Lines 40–42 ("But why … nearer?")

D) Lines 74–82 ("Carr therefore … journey")

44

The overall structure of this text can be best described as

A) a chronological narrative of turtle migration beginning from 400 years ago until present day.

B) an argument advocating for a revolutionary theory of tectonic plate movement over time.

C) an interpretation of turtles' motives for journeying to Ascension and leaving their feeding grounds.

D) an explanation of a migratory pattern based on island formation in the Mid-Atlantic.

45

Which of the following would be most in conflict with the author's views expressed in lines 6–10 ("If modern … continental positions")?

A) Researching the evolutionary development of tadpole metamorphosis without understanding all of its effects.

B) Failing to question whether birds actually do migrate seasonally, but simply trusting observable phenomena.

C) Neglecting to consider geological history in exploring evolutionary patterns in the human genome.

D) Ignoring a computer virus that has the potential to do serious damage.

1

1

46

In line 19, "astounding" most nearly means

A) horrifying.

B) superb.

C) astonishing.

D) alarming.

47

In lines 25–59, the author's primary purpose is to

A) explain why London soup chefs did not understand the origins of the turtles they fed to the Navy.

B) argue that the turtles' long migration is unnecessary and serves only to exhaust the turtles.

C) expose the historical human interventions that have lengthened turtle migration.

D) suggest the likely relationship between a current turtle migration pattern and past continental shifts.

48

Which choice provides the best evidence for the answer to the previous question?

A) Lines 27–29 ("London … long ago")

B) Lines 36–40 ("They feed … are rare")

C) Lines 44–47 ("As Carr … surmounting them'")

D) Lines 48–52 ("Perhaps … recently separated")

49

Based on lines 48–73 it can be reasonably inferred that

A) Africa and North America will drift back together over time just as they did during the time of Pangaea.

B) new islands may be formed on the Mid-Atlantic Ridge based on the welling up and spreading out of materials.

C) Ascension will erode into a seamount soon because it does not have a shield of coral to protect it.

D) Iceland will not be affected by the natural erosion process because it is surrounded by a shield of coral.

CONTINUE

50

Carr's theory suggests that the distance of the turtles' migration has lengthened through time because

A) the island they have always swum to has moved farther and farther away as the continents have shifted.

B) the evolutionary adaptations of the turtles have made them better swimmers, able to seek better breeding grounds farther away.

C) the sea waves progressively eroded away their breeding islands, forcing them to move farther out to newly formed islands.

D) the Mid-Atlantic Ridge destroyed the island to which they originally migrated, forcing them to swim to more distant islands.

51

In lines 79–82 ("This process … journey"), the author primarily employ which rhetorical device?

A) Repetition

B) Analogy

C) Metonymy

D) Hyperbole

52

Do the maps provide support for the author's claim that the turtles' journey to their breeding ground has lengthened over time?

A) Yes, because the maps provide evidence that various islands have been formed by the mid-Atlantic Ridge.

B) Yes, because the maps show that Africa and South America have grown further apart and the Atlantic Ocean has expanded.

C) No, because the maps do not indicate the original location of their breeding ground versus their contemporary breeding ground.

D) No, because the maps do not provide sufficient evidence of tectonic plate movement.

STOP

If you finish before time is called, you may check your work on this section only.
Do not turn to any other section.

2 | | 2

Writing and Language Test

35 MINUTES, 44 QUESTIONS

Turn to Section 2 of your answer sheet to answer the questions in this section.

DIRECTIONS

Each passage below is accompanied by a number of questions. For some questions, you will consider how the passage might be revised to improve the expression of ideas. For other questions, you will consider how the passage might be edited to correct errors in sentence structure, usage, or punctuation. A passage or a question may be accompanied by one or more graphics (such as a table or graph) that you will consider as you make revising and editing decisions.

Some questions will direct you to an underlined portion of a passage. Other questions will direct you to a location in a passage or ask you to think about the passage as a whole.

After reading each passage, choose the answer to each question that most effectively improves the quality of writing in the passage or that makes the passage conform to the conventions of standard written English. Many questions include a "NO CHANGE" option. Choose that option if you think the best choice is to leave the relevant portion of the passage as it is.

Questions 1-11 are based on the following passage.

Iran's Independent Ulema

[1] From the late seventh century until around 1500 CE, Iran fulfilled this role by following a religious and economic path similar to that of the rest of the Islamic world. [2] **1** However, under the Safavids, Iran's conversion to Shi'ism moved the Iranian people in a different direction. [3] In addition to this conversion, the changing role of Iran's ulema (religious scholars) pushed the Iranians on a path even further from that followed by

1

The author is considering adding the following phrase immediately after the underlined portion:

in the early 16th century CE

Should the writer make that addition here?

A) Yes, because it provides context needed to understand the time period for the essay.

B) Yes, because it is an essential definition for understanding the paragraphs that follow.

C) No, because it diverges from the main point of the paragraph.

D) No, because it contradicts information elsewhere in the passage.

the rest of the Islamic world. [4] Since the Umayyad dynasty in 661 CE, Iran has played a role as an economic boon throughout the Islamic world. [2]

After the Safavids, the Iranian ulema divorced themselves from the secular political power, which changed the political trajectory of Iran for centuries to come. Under the Safavids, the ulema held positions in a state-controlled bureaucracy and expanded their power through acquiring soyurghal, land grants. With the fall of the central Safavid power in 1722 CE, the ulema lost their funding but successfully found new, independent sources of funding.

Now financially independent, the ulema [3] were no longer tied to a central political authority and gained autonomous power. The ulema deemed that they, as Islamic legal scholars, held utmost authority. [4] Under the Qajars, the ulema involved themselves in day to day affairs of the common people by [5] overseeing charities, marriages, funerals, and establishing justice.

2

For the sake of logic and clarity, sentence 4 should be placed

A) where it is now.

B) before sentence 1.

C) after sentence 1.

D) after sentence 2.

3

A) NO CHANGE

B) were not any longer tied to a central political authority and gained autonomous power.

C) were no longer tied to a central political authority and had gained autonomous power.

D) gained autonomous power.

4

Which choice provides the most specific chronological information?

A) NO CHANGE

B) Under the Qajars, who ruled Iran from 1785 to 1925,

C) Under the Qajars, who were also the rulers of Iran for over a century,

D) Under the Qajars, a Turkish tribe that ruled Iran through the entire 19th century,

5

A) NO CHANGE

B) overseeing charities, marriages, funerals, and justice.

C) overseeing charities, overseeing marriages, funerals, and establishing justice.

D) overseeing charities, marriages, overseeing funerals, and justice.

The ulema's independence impacted Iranian politics and distinguished Iran from its Ottoman neighbors. During the late 19th century and early 20th century both the Iranian Qajars and the Ottomans experienced constitutional [6] revolutions, however the ulema responded differently in each empire. In Iran the ulema supported a constitution because it limited the power of the state, a limitation they favored. In the Ottoman Empire, though, the ulema opposed a constitution and allied themselves with the state because the state financially supported the Ottoman ulema.

The ulema's competition for power against the state defined Iranian politics for the following centuries. Today, Iran's Ayatollah, the highest ranking of all Shi'a authorities, also [7] acts as a Supreme Leader and holds vast political control. Due to Iran's post-Safavid separation of the ulema from the state, the ulema grew more powerful and political in Iran than in anywhere else in the Middle East.

[8] Iran deviated from the rest of the Middle East beginning with the Safavid conversion in the 16th century, which resulted in its distinct religious and political demographics today. Separating from the state

---

6

A) NO CHANGE
B) revolutions, the
C) revolutions however
D) revolutions; however,

7

A) NO CHANGE
B) act as a Supreme Leader and holds
C) acts as a Supreme Leader and hold
D) act as a Supreme Leader and hold

8

A) NO CHANGE
B) However, Iran
C) Therefore, Iran
D) Finally, Iran

after the Safavid empire, [9] the ulema's power changed the political landscape of Iran and made it [10] unique of all Islamic countries. The ulema in Iran hold immense autonomous political and religious power in Iran's Islamic Republic today, whereas in the rest of the Middle East the ulema are civil servants. [11] The role of the ulema in Iran, so different from their role throughout the rest of the Ottoman world, impacted Iran's historical trajectory. It also continues to impact its contemporary politics up to today.

9

A) NO CHANGE
B) the ulemas power changed
C) the ulema used their power to change
D) the ulemas's used their power to change

10

A) NO CHANGE
B) unique among Islamic
C) unique to other Islamic
D) unique towards other Islamic

11

Which choice most effectively combines the two underlined sentences?

A) Their unique power in Iran has shaped not only Iran's historical trajectory but also its contemporary politics.

B) The role of the ulema in Iran, so different from their role throughout the rest of the Ottoman world, impacted Iran's historical trajectory, and it also continues to impact its contemporary politics up to today.

C) The role of the ulema in Iran, both impacting Iran's historical trajectory and continuing to impact its contemporary politics, is different than their role throughout the Ottoman world.

D) The role of the ulema in Iran, so different from their role throughout the rest of the Ottoman world, impacted Iran's historical trajectory; it also continues to impact its contemporary politics up to today.

2   2

Questions 12–22 are based on the following passage and supplementary material.

Are Professors an Endangered Species?

Higher education has long been a respected field as professors at universities and colleges throughout the United States have been seen [12] as essential contributors to the vast store of thought and knowledge in the sciences and humanities but also as indispensable mentors and educators to young people entering their specific fields.

[13] Therefore, the reality of higher education in the 21st century has dramatically changed the position of "professor," and both students and professors are among those who suffer from the changing economics of higher education.

[14] Though some courses at large universities may be taught by graduate students, most "professors" in lower level courses are adjunct instructors, teachers hired part-time and typically paid by the course a semester at a time.

12

A) NO CHANGE
B) as helpful
C) not only as essential
D) DELETE the underlined portion.

13

A) NO CHANGE
B) However,
C) Thus,
D) Because,

14

At this point, the writer is considering adding the following sentence.

> In their first years at college, many students will never be taught by a full-time professor.

Should the writer make this addition here?

A) Yes, because it specifies which colleges and students are affected by the change discussed in the preceding paragraph.
B) Yes, because it provides a helpful context for understanding the importance of the following sentence.
C) No, because it distracts from the main idea of the passage.
D) No, because it conflicts with information that appears later in the same paragraph.

From many local two-year community colleges to some exclusive liberal arts colleges, **15** these are often hired with little more than a perfunctory interview. Even if **16** he or she is well-qualified and excellent teachers, the lack of continuity from one semester to the next means that students will neither become connected to an academic department through their first courses nor develop relationships that might lead to a letter of recommendation or other advancement in their chosen field.

15

A) NO CHANGE

B) they

C) them

D) these instructors

16

A) NO CHANGE

B) they are well-qualified and an excellent teacher,

C) he or she is well-qualified and an excellent teacher,

D) they are well-qualified and excellent teachers,

Proportion of Instructors in Higher Education in Tenure Track Positions

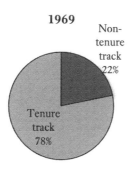

1969

Non-tenure track 22%

Tenure track 78%

2009

Tenure track 33%

Ineligible for tenure 67%

Adapted from the Association of Governing Boards of Universities and Colleges. ©2013.

CONTINUE

2

2

This lack of continuity and depth of instruction is a relatively recent [17] thing. According to the Association of Governing Boards of Universities and Colleges, in 1969, full-time, tenure-track faculty made up nearly 80% of the instructors in all institutions of higher [18] learning but [19] tenured faculty made up only one third of all instructors twenty years later.

[20] Why the change? Economic instability for higher education might account for some of the difference: tenured professors not only cost more each year, but also represent an economic obligation for many years into the future, so schools in immediate financial trouble may be unable to offer new tenure-track positions.

17

A) NO CHANGE
B) phenomenon.
C) event.
D) activity.

18

A) NO CHANGE
B) learning; whereas
C) learning, but
D) learning. Though

19

Which choice accurately reflects the information in the graph and supports the purpose of the sentence?
A) NO CHANGE
B) the group ineligible for tenure was down to below 70% by 2009.
C) tenure-track positions accounted for approximately one third of instructors by 2009.
D) the numbers of professors in all categories has risen considerably over the last 30 years.

20

Which choice best introduces this paragraph?
A) NO CHANGE
B) This is unfortunate.
C) At this rate, soon few if any full time faculty members will remain.
D) What can be done to fix this problem?

2

2

However, for most, it is more a question of priorities than of economic necessity. Since adjuncts receive minimal pay relative to the tuition and fees brought in by the students in their classes, the extensive use of adjuncts [21] are a natural choice when viewed in terms of immediate economic interest. Why pay more when the same job can be done for so much less?

A partial solution to these problems may be developing from the adjuncts themselves. Working together with groups like Adjunct Action, instructors have begun to put pressure on schools to offer better compensation and more benefits, with the goal of "creating better working conditions for themselves and better learning conditions for their students." Though the professor as a bespectacled sage in a padded jacket may be a thing of the past, such efforts may help to bring about more consistency and continuity in the classroom for both student and instructor.

Question 22 asks about the previous passage as a whole.

21

A) NO CHANGE

B) was

C) were

D) is

Think about the previous passage and included supplemental material as a whole as you answer question 22.

22

Which of the following best summarizes the data presented in the graph?

A) The number of tenure-track professors has decreased from 1969 to 2009.

B) The percentage of tenure-track professors has increased from 1969 to 2009.

C) The number of adjunct professors has increased from 1969 to 2009.

D) The percentage of non-tenure track professors has increased from 1969 to 2009.

Questions 23–33 are based on the following passage.

Shostakovich's Symphonic Statement

[23] Joseph Stalin's dictatorship in Soviet Russia during the 1930s and 1940s was founded upon Marxist theories of communism and characterized by terror. He involved himself with the music industry to ensure that all Soviet music [24] acted as propaganda and promoted his regime. Composers who did not conform to Stalin's standards were subject to public criticism, and many were exiled or persecuted. After the initial performance of his provocative Fourth Symphony, composer Dmitri Shostakovich faced harsh scrutiny from Stalin's government. As a means of survival, Shostakovich composed the final movement of his Fifth Symphony as an accurate representation of Soviet Marxist motifs.

[23]

The writer wants to craft a strong introductory sentence that moves clearly toward the main topic of the essay. Which choice best accomplishes this purpose?

A) NO CHANGE

B) Joseph Stalin's harsh dictatorship in Soviet Russia during the 1930s and 1940s was characterized by an attempt at totalitarian control of every aspect of his citizen's lives, even the music they listened to.

C) Joseph Stalin's rule of Soviet Russia in the 1930s and 1940s was so brutal that no other world leader came close to killing so many of his own people.

D) All composers have to work under difficult and pressured situations, and Dmitri Shostakovich was no exception, because of Joseph Stalin.

[24]

A) NO CHANGE

B) functioned as propaganda for his regime.

C) promoted his regime enthusiastically with nationalistic propaganda.

D) worked as propaganda to better the power of his regime.

Some musicologists argue that Shostakovich's antagonistic feelings toward Stalin undermined Shostakovich's ability to accurately portray Soviet Marxist themes. In his memoir, *Testimony*, published in 1979 by Solomon Volkov, Shostakovich wrote, "I was a formalist, a representative of an antinational direction in music." By declaring himself a formalist, Shostakovich established himself as a direct ideological enemy of Stalin and the Soviet regime. Shostakovich's abhorrence of the regime was not only ideological but also personal. [25] His sister, brother in-law and uncle had all been exiled or arrested or even died under Stalin's regime. Based on Shostakovich's intense resentment of the regime, musicologists argue that he would have had no desire to [26] neither comply with the regime nor represent the Marxist Soviet themes it embodied.

25

Which choice most clearly describes the experience of specific members of Shostakovich's family under Stalin?

A) NO CHANGE

B) Several members of Shostakovich's family suffered while Stalin was in power, and the worst suffering was that they had done nothing wrong to deserve such treatment.

C) His sister was exiled to France, his mother-in-law and brother-in-law were arrested, and his uncle, despite his communist affiliation, was arrested and held until his death.

D) His family line was decimated by the actions of the government under Stalin.

26

A) NO CHANGE

B) comply with the regime nor

C) comply with the regime or to

D) either comply with the regime or to

Shostakovich's opposition to Stalin and Soviet Marxism is undeniable; however, his opposition negates neither his desire nor his ability to portray Soviet Marxist themes **27** accurately on a basic level: Shostakovich's depiction of these themes **28** lied in his desire for survival. He understood the grave danger he faced after his Fourth Symphony was censored and realized that he had to please the government to avoid persecution. On a deeper level, Shostakovich's negative feelings towards the regime actually propelled him to create this accurate portrayal of the themes the regime epitomized.

Often, the most powerfully satirical social protest manifests as an accurate portrayal of the flaws in society. **29** For example, Mark Twain was one of the most renowned satirists in American history, and his satire was comprised of exposing truths he saw around him. In its accuracy and adherence **30** of Soviet Marxist themes, Shostakovich's Fifth Symphony Finale paints a

27

A) NO CHANGE
B) accurately, on
C) accurately, and on
D) accurately. On

28

A) NO CHANGE
B) lies
C) lie
D) lay

29

The author is considering deleting the following sentence. Should the writer make this change?

A) Yes, because it does not logically follow from the previous sentence.
B) Yes, because it introduces information that is irrelevant at this point in the passage.
C) No, because it offers a generalization to support arguments made elsewhere in the passage.
D) No, because it provides a logical introduction to the rest of the paragraph.

30

A) NO CHANGE
B) to
C) with
D) among

raw satirical portrait of Stalin's regime. `31` The legacy of his composition verifies the potency of Shostakovich's `32` moving and satirical style as today `33` listeners around the world are taken aback by the horrors of Stalin's regime revived in the performance of Shostakovich's Fifth Symphony Finale.

`31`

At this point, the writer is considering adding the following sentence.

> For example, in its abbreviated sonata-allegro form, the timpani solo introduces a brief militaristic tonality into the finale of the movement.

Should the writer make this addition here?

A) Yes, because it provides information necessary to understand the preceding sentence.

B) Yes, because supports the conclusion contained in the following sentence.

C) No, because it merely restates information contained elsewhere in the essay.

D) No, because it is overly technical and does not assist in understanding the thesis of the paragraph.

`32`

A) NO CHANGE

B) interesting and specific

C) visceral and polemical

D) challenging and weird

`33`

A) NO CHANGE

B) every listener around the world is being

C) listeners around the world is

D) listener around the world are

Questions 34–44 are based on the following passage.

Can Genes Be Patented?

—1—

In 1990, geneticist Mark Skolnick founded Myriad Genetics Inc. to use Mormon family history to study genes linked to Hereditary Breast and Ovarian Cancer (HBOC). From 1994–1996, Skolnick's team from Myriad Genetics sequenced, published, and patented the BReast CAncer 1 (BRCA1) and BReast CAncer 2 (BRCA2) genes. **34** This began a quick race to isolate more HBOC genes. After sequencing the BRCA2 gene, Myriad developed BRCAnalysis, a DNA blood test that tests for BRCA1 and BRCA2 mutations and assesses HBOC risk. The Hospital at the University of Pennsylvania ran BRCA1 and BRCA2 tests in the Genetic Diagnostic Library until Myriad **35** told them it infringed upon their patent.

34

A) NO CHANGE
B) That began a quick race to isolate more HBOC genes.
C) This discovery led to the rapid beginning of a hectic race to isolate more genes linked to HBOC.
D) DELETE the underlined portion.

35

A) NO CHANGE
B) tells the hospital it was infringing upon its patent.
C) claimed doing so infringed upon its patent.
D) claimed they infringed upon its patent by it.

—2—

Many became very frustrated with Myriad's patent due to the high cost of HBOC testing. **36** Because the probability of developing breast cancer is nearly doubled for those with BRCA1 or 2, some felt that the prohibitive cost of testing violated the rights of patients. On May 12, 2009, the American Civil Liberties Union (ACLU) filed a suit against Myriad. **37** The case, heard by Judge Robert Sweet in the Southern District of New York court, ruling that genes are not patentable. Myriad appealed this ruling and the case was heard two years later by the US Court of Appeals for the Federal Circuit.

Breast and Ovarian Cancer Risk by Age 70

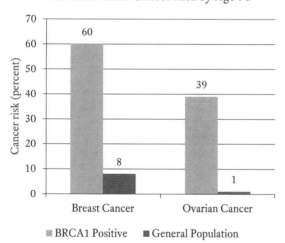

36

Which choice accurately reflects the data in the graph and best supports the point of the paragraph?

A) NO CHANGE

B) Because the likelihood of developing breast cancer is higher than that of ovarian cancer,

C) Although those with BRCA1 are somewhat more likely to develop breast cancer than members of the general population,

D) Because the lifetime risk of developing breast cancer risk is nearly eight times as great for those with BRCA1,

37

A) NO CHANGE

B) The case, heard in the Southern District of New York by Judge Robert Sweet, who ruled that genes are not patentable.

C) The case was heard in the Southern District of New York by Judge Robert Sweet, who ruled that genes are not patentable.

D) The case was heard by Judge Robert Sweet in the Southern District of New York court, he ruled that genes are not patentable.

—3—

[38] As a result, both the plaintiffs and defendants were dissatisfied with the US Court of Appeals' [39] ambiguous ruling, so they petitioned for a rehearing by the Supreme Court in August 2011. On February 17, 2012, the Supreme Court met to decide [40] whether to except the case, and on March 26, 2012, referred the decision back down to the US Court of Appeals. That August, the Court of Appeals upheld Myriad's claims to patent genes.

—4—

The plaintiffs were dissatisfied with the court's decision and realized they needed to present their case in a different light in order to get the Supreme Court to take it up after rejecting it the first time. On September 25, 2012, the ACLU and the Public Patent Foundation appealed to the Supreme Court and asked [41] them to evaluate as a larger landmark case: are genes patentable?

38

A) NO CHANGE

B) However,

C) Furthermore,

D) On the other hand,

39

The writer wants this sentence to clarify the reasons that both sides were not pleased with the finding of the court. Assuming that all of the following are true, which choice best accomplishes this?

A) NO CHANGE

B) ruling, which allowed the patenting of isolated genes but denied Myriad's right to patent the analytical process used to test for the genes, so both parties

C) unfavorable ruling that denied Myriad's right to claim copyright infringement regarding the analysis for testing the genes, so they

D) poor decision to allow patenting of isolated genes, which meant that Myriad would profit from human DNA, so the complainants and the accused

40

A) NO CHANGE

B) whether or not to except the case,

C) if they should accept the case or not,

D) whether to accept the case,

41

A) NO CHANGE

B) it

C) they

D) DELETE the underline portion

2   2

—5—

This case set a landmark precedent that genes themselves cannot be patented. [42] However, the court allowed that a lab that produces cDNA, a synthetic complement to the naturally occurring gene, can patent what it produces. Now that Myriad no longer holds patents on BRCA1 and BRCA2, other companies can use the genes to perform genetic screenings.

—6—

The Supreme Court agreed to take the case in November, heard arguments April 15, and ruled that claims on isolated DNA are invalid on June 13, 2013. Justice Clarence Thomas delivered the opinion [43] of the court: "For the reasons that follow, we hold that a naturally occurring DNA segment is a product of nature and not patent eligible merely because it has been isolated."

Question [44] asks about the previous passage as a whole.

[42]

A) NO CHANGE
B) However, cDNA, the complement of the naturally occurring template strand, can be synthetically produced in a lab and patented.
C) Unfortunately, the ruling still granted that cDNA, a complement of the naturally occurring template strand, can be produced synthetically in a lab and patented by the lab that was producing it.
D) Still, cDNA can be patented by labs.

[43]

A) NO CHANGE
B) from the court,
C) of the court,
D) of the court;

Think about the previous passage as a whole as you answer question 44.

[44]

To make the passage most logical, paragraph 5 should be placed
A) where it is now.
B) after paragraph 2.
C) after paragraph 3.
D) after paragraph 6.

STOP

If you finish before time is called, you may check your work on this section only.
Do not turn to any other section.

3 3

Math Test – No Calculator

25 MINUTES, 20 QUESTIONS

Turn to Section 3 of your answer sheet to answer the questions in this section.

DIRECTIONS

For questions 1–15, solve each problem, choose the best answer from the choices provided, and fill in the corresponding circle on your answer sheet. **For questions 16–20**, solve the problems and enter your answer in the grid on the answer sheet. Please refer to the directions before question 16 on how to enter your answers in the grid. You may use any available space in your test booklet for scratch work.

NOTES

1. The use of calculators **is not permitted**.

2. All variables and expressions used represent real numbers unless otherwise indicated.

3. Figures provided in this test are drawn to scale unless otherwise indicated.

4. All figures lie in a plane unless otherwise indicated.

5. Unless otherwise indicated, the domain of a given function f is the set of real numbers x for which $f(x)$ is a real number.

REFERENCE

$A = \pi r^2$
$C = 2\pi r$

$A = \ell w$

$A = \frac{1}{2}bh$

$c^2 = a^2 + b^2$

Special Right Triangles

$V = \ell wh$

$V = \pi r^2 h$

$V = \frac{4}{3}\pi r^3$

$V = \frac{1}{3}\pi r^2 h$

$V = \frac{1}{3}\ell wh$

The number of degrees of arc in a circle is 360.
The number of radians of arc in a circle is 2π.
The sum of the measures in degrees of the angles in a triangle is 180.

CONTINUE

3 **3**

1

If $(x-1)(x+3) = k+2$ and $x=2,$ what is the value of k?

A) 0

B) 2

C) 3

D) 4

2

$$a - b = 12$$
$$2a - 5b = 3$$

Which of the following ordered pairs (a, b) satisfies the system of equations above?

A) $(19, 7)$

B) $(7, 20)$

C) $(17, 3)$

D) $(4, 9)$

3

Which of the following is equivalent $(3a^2 + 6b^2)^2$?

A) $3a^4 + 18a^2b^2 + 36b^4$

B) $2a^2 + 36a^2b + 36b^4$

C) $9a^4 + 36a^2b^2 + 36b^4$

D) $9a^4 + 18a^2b^2 + 36b^4$

4

To rent out the back room for a party, the amount a restaurant charges, in dollars, can be represented by the expression $35 + 8hn,$ where h is the number of hours and n is the number of guests. Which of the following is the best interpretation of the number 8 in the expression?

A) There can be a maximum of 8 guests.

B) The restaurant charges $8 per hour per guest.

C) The flat rate of renting a room is $8.

D) For every additional guest, the price decreases by $8.

CONTINUE

5

$$\frac{\sqrt{x^2 - 9}}{a} = 1$$

If $x < 0$ and $a = 4$, what is the value of $x - 5$?

A) −12

B) −10

C) −9

D) −3

6

Ryan has started a tutoring company. He charges clients a monthly flat rate, as well as a rate per session. The total amount paid by a client monthly, in dollars, is $24.45x + 10.50$, where x is the number of tutoring sessions. What is Ryan's rate per session?

A) $10.50

B) $15.05

C) $24.45

D) $35.45

7

$$h(x) = 3x^3 - ax$$

For the function $h(x)$ defined above, $h(2) = 20$. What is the value of $h(-1)$?

A) −5

B) −1

C) 1

D) 5

8

If $\dfrac{a^{2x^3}}{a^4} = a^{12}$, what is the value of 2^x?

A) 2

B) 4

C) 8

D) 16

CONTINUE

Questions 9 and 10 refer to the following information.

Monthly cell phone plans A and B can be described by the two following equations, where A is the price, in dollars, under plan A, and B is the price, in dollars, under plan B after m minutes of calling in a month.

$$A = 3.85 + 0.45m$$
$$B = 7.65 + 0.25m$$

9

After how many minutes of calling will the prices under each plan be equal?

A) 14

B) 16

C) 19

D) 23

10

Miranda uses cell phone plan A and paid $8.35 last month. How many minutes worth of calls did Miranda make?

A) 10

B) 13

C) 18

D) 20

11

If $i = \sqrt{-1}$, which of the following complex numbers is equivalent to $\dfrac{4 + 2i}{2 - i}$?

A) $\dfrac{6 + 8i}{5}$

B) $\dfrac{5 - 3i}{8}$

C) $\dfrac{4 - 2i}{7}$

D) $\dfrac{1 + 9i}{3}$

CONTINUE

12

A formula used for compound interest is $A = P\left(1 + \dfrac{r}{n}\right)^{nt}$. Which of the following represents P in terms of A, n, and t?

A) $\dfrac{\left(1 + \dfrac{r}{n}\right)^{nt}}{A}$

B) $A\left(1 + \dfrac{r}{n}\right)^{nt}$

C) $\dfrac{A}{\left(1 + \dfrac{r}{n}\right)^{nt}}$

D) $\dfrac{1}{A\left(1 + \dfrac{r}{n}\right)^{nt}}$

13

The graph of line q has a slope of -2 and contains the point $(0, 8)$. Line p contains the points $(2, 7)$ and $(0, 5)$. If p and q intersect at the point (a, b), what is the value of $a - b$?

A) -5

B) 1

C) 5

D) 6

14

Which of the following is equivalent to $\dfrac{1}{x + 2} - \dfrac{1}{x - 3}$?

A) $\dfrac{2x - 1}{x^2 - x - 6}$

B) $\dfrac{2x - 5}{x^2 - x - 6}$

C) $\dfrac{2x}{x^2 - x - 6}$

D) $\dfrac{-5}{x^2 - x - 6}$

15

If, for all values of x, $(3x + a)(2x + b) = 6x^2 + cx + 6$ and $4a + 6b = 12$, what is the value of c?

A)   24

B)   18

C)   12

D)   6

CONTINUE

3 **3**

DIRECTIONS

For questions 16–20, solve the problem and enter your answer in the grid, as described below, on the answer sheet.

1. Although not required, it is suggested that you write your answer in the boxes at the top of the columns to help you fill in the circles accurately. You will receive credit only if the circles are filled in correctly.
2. Mark no more than one circle in any column.
3. No question has a negative answer.
4. Some problems may have more than one correct answer. In such cases, grid only one answer.

5. **Mixed numbers** such as $3\frac{1}{2}$ must be be gridded as 3.5 or 7/2. If $3\ 1\ /\ 2$ is entered into the grid, it will be interpreted as $\frac{31}{2}$, not $3\frac{1}{2}$.)

6. **Decimal answers:** If you obtain a decimal answer with more digits than the grid can accommodate, it may be either rounded or truncated, but it must fill the entire grid.

Answer: $\frac{7}{13}$

Write answer in boxes → 7 / 1 3 ← Fraction line

Grid in result

Answer: 2.5

2 . 5 ← Decimal Point

Acceptable ways to grid $\frac{2}{3}$ are:

2 / 3   . 6 6 6   . 6 6 7

Answer: 210 – either position is correct

2 1 0   2 1 0

NOTE: You may start your answers in any column, space permitting. Columns you don't need to use should be left blank.

CONTINUE

16

A history quiz consists of 60 points and contains questions that are either True/False or multiple-choice. If a True/False question is worth 3 points and a multiple-choice question is worth 8 points, and the quiz has at least one question of each type, what is a possible number of multiple-choice questions on the quiz?

17

If $2b^2 - 12 = 60$ and $b > 0$, what is the value of b?

18

An angle opposite a leg of a right triangle measures $w°$, and $\tan(w°) = \dfrac{3}{4}$. What is $\sin(90° - w°)$?

CONTINUE

19

$$ax + by = 16$$
$$3x + 2y = 64$$

In the system of equations above, a and b are constants. If the system has infinitely many solutions, what is the value of ab ?

20

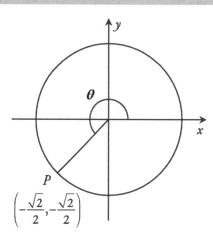

$P\left(-\dfrac{\sqrt{2}}{2}, -\dfrac{\sqrt{2}}{2}\right)$

The angle θ on the unit circle (shown above), formed when the segment that connects the origin to point $P\left(-\dfrac{\sqrt{2}}{2}, -\dfrac{\sqrt{2}}{2}\right)$ meets the positive x-axis, can be written as $\dfrac{10\pi}{a}$ radians. What is the value of a ?

STOP

If you finish before time is called, you may check your work on this section only.
Do not turn to any other section.

Math Test – Calculator

55 MINUTES, 38 QUESTIONS

Turn to Section 4 of your answer sheet to answer the questions in this section.

DIRECTIONS

For questions 1–30, solve each problem, choose the best answer from the choices provided, and fill in the corresponding circle on your answer sheet. **For questions 31–38**, solve the problems and enter your answer in the grid on the answer sheet. Please refer to the directions before question 31 on how to enter your answers in the grid. You may use any available space in your test booklet for scratch work.

NOTES

1. The use of calculators is **permitted**.

2. All variables and expressions used represent real numbers unless otherwise indicated.

3. Figures provided in this test are drawn to scale unless otherwise indicated.

4. All figures lie in a plane unless otherwise indicated.

5. Unless otherwise indicated, the domain of a given function f is the set of real numbers x for which $f(x)$ is a real number.

REFERENCE

$A = \pi r^2$
$C = 2\pi r$

$A = \ell w$

$A = \frac{1}{2}bh$

$c^2 = a^2 + b^2$

Special Right Triangles

$V = \ell w h$

$V = \pi r^2 h$

$V = \frac{4}{3}\pi r^3$

$V = \frac{1}{3}\pi r^2 h$

$V = \frac{1}{3}\ell w h$

The number of degrees of arc in a circle is 360.
The number of radians of arc in a circle is 2π.
The sum of the measures in degrees of the angles in a triangle is 180.

CONTINUE

1

A lemonade stand sells small and large cups. Small cups are sold for $2.25 and large cups are sold for $3.50. Which of the following represents the amount of money the stand makes if they sell s small cups and l large cups?

A) $2.25s - 3.50l$

B) $2.25s + 3.50l$

C) $3.50s + 2.25l$

D) $(3.50 + 2.25)(s + l)$

2

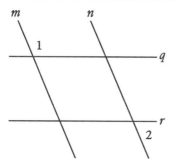

In the figure above, lines q and r and lines m and n are parallel. If the measure of angle 1 is 130 degrees, what is the measure, in degrees, of angle 2?

A) 130

B) 65

C) 50

D) 40

3

If $3a + 17$ is 6 less than 50, then what is the value of $9a$?

A) 117

B) 81

C) 27

D) 9

Questions 4 and 5 refer to the following information.

The density of a gas is inversely proportional to its volume, assuming that the mass of the gas is constant. A gas with a density of 0.50 kilograms per cubic meter has a volume of 4 cubic meters.

4

What would the density of the gas be if it filled a volume of 10 cubic meters?

A) 0.20 kg/m^3

B) 0.45 kg/m^3

C) 0.80 kg/m^3

D) 1.25 kg/m^3

5

As part of a science experiment, the volume of the gas when its density is 0.50 kg/m^3 is decreased 30 percent. What is its density after the decrease, rounded to the nearest hundredth?

A) 0.15 kg/m^3

B) 0.35 kg/m^3

C) 0.71 kg/m^3

D) 1.67 kg/m^3

6

| 1 dekaliter = 10 liters |
| 1,000 milliliters = 1 liter |

A car has a 6 dekaliter gas tank. Based on the information above, how many milliliters of gas can the car's gas tank hold?

A)   0.0006

B)   60

C)   6,000

D)   60,000

7

$$y = 2x^2 - 8x - 20$$

The equation above defines the graph of a parabola. Which of the following equations is equivalent to the equation above and shows the coordinates of the vertex of the parabola as constants?

A) $y = 2x(x - 4) - 10$

B) $y = 2(x - 2)^2 - 28$

C) $y = 2(x^2 - 4x - 5)$

D) $y = 2(x - 5)(x + 1)$

8

Number of Apartment Buildings in
4 Cities

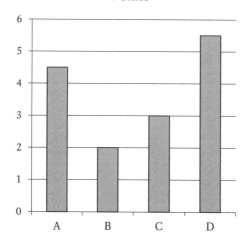

The number of apartment buildings in four different cities is shown in the graph above. If the total number of apartment buildings represented in the graph is 15,000, what are the increments of the vertical axis?

A) Tens

B) Hundreds

C) Thousands

D) Tens of thousands

9

A snack company is determining how to package a new line of chips. Bags will contain three different types of chips, identically shaped. One type has 10 calories per chip, one has 12, and one has 14. The bag can have up to 65 chips, but it must have exactly 700 calories in it. Let a represent the number of 10 calorie chips, b the number of 12 calorie chips, and c the number of 14 calorie chips. Which of the following represents this relationship?

A)
$$\frac{a}{10} + \frac{b}{12} + \frac{c}{14} = 700$$
$$a + b + c \leq 65$$

B)
$$10a + 12b + 14c \leq 700$$
$$a + b + c \leq 65$$

C)
$$a + b + c \leq 700$$
$$10a + 12b + 14c = 65$$

D)
$$10a + 12b + 14c = 700$$
$$a + b + c \leq 65$$

CONTINUE

Questions 10 and 11 refer to the following information.

$$d = 171.3 + 55t$$

The equation above models a family's distance from home during the second day of a road trip, where d represents distance in miles and t represents time, in hours, after they began driving on the second day.

10

Which of the following shows the time traveled by the family on the second day in terms of their distance from home?

A) $t = \dfrac{d - 171.3}{55}$

B) $t = \dfrac{55}{d - 171.3}$

C) $t = \dfrac{d + 171.3}{55}$

D) $t = \dfrac{d}{55} - 171.3$

11

After how many hours of driving on the second day will the family's distance from home be about 400 miles?

A)   10.39 hours

B)   5.14 hours

C)   5.08 hours

D)   4.16 hours

12

Number of printers	50
Hours the printers run per day	10
Number of days the printers are used per week	7
Number of sheets required to make the book	300
Number of sheets a printer can print per minute	50
Number of workers working the printers	4

A publishing company is printing copies of a new book. The initial print run of the book will be 10,000 copies. Based on the information above pertaining to the printers available to the company to print the book, how many days will it take for the initial print run to be run off?

A)   2

B)   20

C)   100

D)   120

Questions 13 and 14 refer to the following information.

Cost of Pizza by Toppings

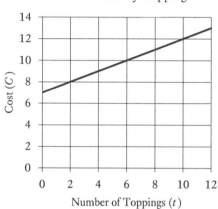

The graph above shows the cost C of a pizza as determined by the number of toppings t.

13

What does the C-intercept represent in the graph?

A) The total number of toppings on the pizza.

B) The total number of pizzas bought.

C) The cost of each additional topping.

D) The price of a pizza with no toppings.

14

Which of the following shows the relationship between C and t?

A) $C = 7t$

B) $C = t + 0.5$

C) $C = 0.5t + 7$

D) $C = t + 7$

15

A family's home pool has a capacity of 9,500 gallons. There are 3,250 gallons of water in it already. The family's hose sprays 25 gallons of water per minute. Let x represent the number of minutes that the hose is left running into the pool. Which of the following represents the set of all times that the hose is left running at which the pool will be full or overflowing?

A) $25x \geq 9,500$

B) $9,500 - 3,250 \leq x$

C) $3,250 + 25x \geq 9,500$

D) $6,250 \leq x + 3,250$

16

	Mac	PC	Total
Female	45	29	74
Male	48	30	78
Total	93	59	152

People on the street were randomly selected and asked whether they preferred to use Macs or PCs. Which of the following comprised approximately 32 percent of the total group?

A) Males who prefer Macs

B) Females who prefer Macs

C) People who prefer PCs

D) Males who prefer PCs

17

Jupiter travels a distance of approximately 4.9 billion kilometers during its orbit around the Sun. Jupiter completes an orbit in about 12 Earth years. Which of the following is closest to the number of kilometers Jupiter travels in one hour?

A)   47

B)   1,100

C)   47,000

D) 560,000

18

A survey counted the number of flowers on the bushes in a park. The average number of flowers was 34 while the median was 45. What factor most likely would account for the difference between average and median?

A) There were some bushes with extremely few flowers.

B) The mode of the data was a number greater than 34.

C) Many bushes had between 34 and 45 flowers.

D) There is little variance in the number of flowers on the bushes.

CONTINUE

19

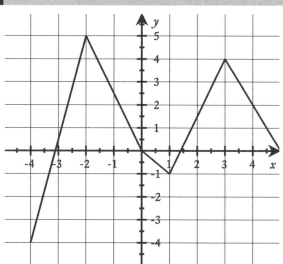

The complete graph of $f(x)$ is shown above. For which of the following values of x is $f(x)$ at its maximum?

A) −4

B) −2

C)   3

D)   5

20

A parking garage charges $11 on weekdays and $15 on weekends. If the garage brought in $53,234 in one week and a total of 4,122 people used the garage, how many people used the garage during the weekend?

A)   304

B) 1,973

C) 2,149

D) 3,549

Questions 21 and 22 refer to the following information.

A high school asked 200 underclassmen and 200 upperclassmen how many hours they spent on homework the previous night. There are 680 underclassmen and 600 upperclassmen in the school.

Hours spent on homework	Underclassmen	Upperclassmen
1	20	10
2	70	50
3	80	90
4	20	40
5	10	10

21

What is the median number of hours spent on homework by those students surveyed?

A) 2

B) 3

C) 4

D) Cannot be determined from the information given

22

Based on this data, which of the following most accurately describes the expected total numbers of students who spent 5 hours on homework last night?

A) 10 underclassmen and 10 upperclassmen spent 5 hours on homework.

B) 4 more underclassmen than upperclassmen spent 5 hours on homework.

C) 4 more upperclassmen than underclassmen spent 5 hours on homework.

D) 80 more underclassmen than upperclassmen spent 5 hours on homework.

CONTINUE

23

Harold prepared a sample of bacteria. A strain of virus killed 30 percent of the bacteria, but within a week the surviving population had grown 47 percent. Which of the following represents the value of the original population in terms of the current population p ?

A) $\dfrac{p}{1.17}$

B) $1.17p$

C) $\dfrac{p}{(0.7)(1.47)}$

D) $(0.7)(1.47)p$

24

$$x^2 + y^2 - 10y = 9$$

The equation above defines a circle in the coordinate plane. Which of the following is the length of the circle's radius?

A) 3

B) $\sqrt{10}$

C) 5

D) $\sqrt{34}$

Questions 25 and 26 refer to the following information.

$$T = 2\pi\sqrt{\frac{m}{k}}$$

The equation above describes the period T of an oscillating object attached to a spring in terms of its mass m and spring constant k .

25

Which of the following expresses the object's mass in terms of the period T and the spring constant k ?

A) $m = \dfrac{T^2 k}{2\pi}$

B) $m = \dfrac{T^2 k}{2\pi^2}$

C) $m = \dfrac{T^2 k}{4\pi^2}$

D) $m = \dfrac{T k}{2\pi}$

26

For two systems with the same spring constant, object 1 has a mass 25 times that of object 2. What fraction of the period of object 1 is that of object 2?

A) $\dfrac{1}{10}$

B) $\dfrac{1}{5}$

C) $\dfrac{1}{25}$

D) $\dfrac{1}{125}$

CONTINUE

4 **4**

27

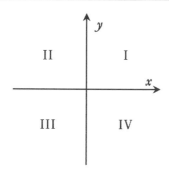

If the system of inequalities $y \le \frac{1}{3}x + 2$ and

$y > \frac{1}{2}x + 4$ were graphed on the xy-plane shown

above, which of the following quadrants would contain

at least one solution to the system?

A) Quadrant II

B) Quadrant III

C) Quadrant IV

D) None of the above

28

Clara received a score on a test that was 5 percent higher than the class average for the test. If Clara's score was 85 percent, what was the class average, rounded to the nearest whole number?

A) 78

B) 80

C) 81

D) 89

29

Emily's home library is composed of 9 identical bookshelves. Each bookshelf has 12 shelves within it, each of which contains approximately the same number of books. To find a rough estimate of the number of books in her library, Emily counted the number of books on one shelf in each bookshelf. The results are shown below.

104	92	113
93	89	101
74	97	85

Approximately how many books does Emily have in her entire collection?

A)   850

B) 7,600

C) 10,200

D) 91,600

30

For a polynomial $h(t)$, $h(3) = 7$. Which of the following must be true about $h(t)$?

A) $(t + 3)$ is a factor of $h(t)$.

B) $(t - 3)$ is a factor of $h(t)$.

C) The remainder when $h(t)$ is divided by $(t - 3)$ is 7.

D) The remainder when $h(t)$ is divided by 3 is 7.

CONTINUE

DIRECTIONS

For questions 31–38, solve the problem and enter your answer in the grid, as described below, on the answer sheet.

1. Although not required, it is suggested that you write your answer in the boxes at the top of the columns to help you fill in the circles accurately. You will receive credit only if the circles are filled in correctly.
2. Mark no more than one circle in any column.
3. No question has a negative answer.
4. Some problems may have more than one correct answer. In such cases, grid only one answer.

5. **Mixed numbers** such as $3\frac{1}{2}$ must be be gridded as 3.5 or 7/2. If $\boxed{3\,1\,/\,2}$ is entered into the grid, it will be interpreted as $\frac{31}{2}$, not $3\frac{1}{2}$.)

6. **Decimal answers:** If you obtain a decimal answer with more digits than the grid can accommodate, it may be either rounded or truncated, but it must fill the entire grid.

Answer: $\frac{7}{13}$ Answer: 2.5

Write answer → in boxes

Grid in result

← Fraction line

← Decimal Point

Acceptable ways to grid $\frac{2}{3}$ are:

Answer: 210 – either position is correct

NOTE: You may start your answers in any column, space permitting. Columns you don't need to use should be left blank.

4 **4**

31

Stan's plant grows 2.5 inches per week. It is 15 inches tall now. In how many weeks will the plant be 42.5 inches tall?

32

In the *xy*-coordinate plane, the point $(3, 8)$ lies on the graph of the function $f(x) = x^3 - bx^2 - x + 2$. What is the value of b ?

33

Joe can read at least 32 pages and as many as 40 pages per hour. Given this, what is a possible amount of time, in hours, it could take Joe to read 200 pages?

34

Number of Books Read over the
Summer by High School Students

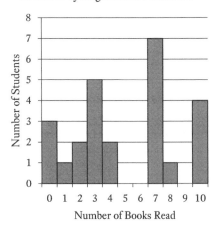

Number of Books Read

The histogram above shows the number of books read
by a class of high school students over the summer.
What is the average number of books read by each
student?

35

Herman was away from home on vacation for exactly
d days and 6 hours, for a total of 174 hours. For how
many full days was he away?

36

A store brand cereal has 40 percent fewer calories than
does the name brand cereal. The name brand has 150
calories per serving. How many calories per serving
does the store brand have?

CONTINUE

37

$$(2x+3)^2 - (4x-7) = ax^2 + bx + c$$

In the equation above, a, b, and c are constants. If the equation is true for all values of x, what is the value of ac ?

38

Darin uses an empty rubber cone to block off traffic. The cone has a volume of 810π in^3. If the cone is 30 inches high, what is its <u>diameter</u> in <u>feet</u>?

STOP

If you finish before time is called, you may check your work on this section only.
Do not turn to any other section.

This page left intentionally blank

SAT Practice Test 2

IMPORTANT REMINDERS

A No. 2 pencil is required for the test.
Do not use a mechanical pencil or pen.

Sharing any questions with anyone is a violation
of the Test Security and Fairness policies and
may result in your score being canceled.

This cover is representative of what you will see on the day of the SAT.

Reading Test

65 MINUTES, 52 QUESTIONS

Turn to Section 1 of your answer sheet to answer the questions in this section.

DIRECTIONS

Each passage or pair of passages below is followed by a number of questions. After reading each passage or pair, choose the best answer to each question based on what is stated or implied in the passage or passages and in any accompanying graphics (such as a table or graph).

Questions 1–10 are based on the following passage.

This passage is from Oscar Wilde, "The Canterville Ghost." Originally published in 1887. Here, Mr. Otis, who is the United States Minister to Britain, and his family deal with an unexpected tenant in their new lodgings.

The next morning, when the Otis family met at breakfast, they discussed the ghost at some length. The United States Minister was naturally a little annoyed to find that his present had not been
5   accepted. "I have no wish," he said, "to do the ghost any personal injury, and I must say that, considering the length of time he has been in the house, I don't think it is at all polite to throw pillows at him," — a very just remark, at which, I am sorry to say, the
10 twins burst into shouts of laughter. "Upon the other hand," he continued, "if he really declines to use the Rising Sun Lubricator, we shall have to take his chains from him. It would be quite impossible to sleep, with such a noise going on outside the
15 bedrooms."

For the rest of the week, however, they were undisturbed, the only thing that excited any attention being the continual renewal of the blood-stain on the library floor. This certainly was very strange, as the
20 door was always locked at night by Mr. Otis, and the windows kept closely barred. The chameleon-like colour, also, of the stain excited a good deal of comment. Some mornings it was a dull (almost Indian) red, then it would be vermilion, then a rich
25 purple, and once when they came down for family prayers, according to the simple rites of the Free

American Reformed Episcopalian Church, they found it a bright emerald-green. These kaleidoscopic changes naturally amused the party very much, and
30 bets on the subject were freely made every evening. The only person who did not enter into the joke was little Virginia, who, for some unexplained reason, was always a good deal distressed at the sight of the blood-stain, and very nearly cried the morning it was
35 emerald-green.

The second appearance of the ghost was on Sunday night. Shortly after they had gone to bed they were suddenly alarmed by a fearful crash in the hall. Rushing down-stairs, they found that a large suit of
40 old armour had become detached from its stand, and had fallen on the stone floor, while seated in a high-backed chair was the Canterville ghost, rubbing his knees with an expression of acute agony on his face. The twins, having brought their pea-shooters with
45 them, at once discharged two pellets on him, with that accuracy of aim which can only be attained by long and careful practice on a writing-master, while the United States Minister covered him with his revolver, and called upon him, in accordance with
50 Californian etiquette, to hold up his hands! The ghost started up with a wild shriek of rage, and swept through them like a mist, extinguishing Washington Otis's candle as he passed, and so leaving them all in total darkness. On reaching the top of the staircase he
55 recovered himself, and determined to give his celebrated peal of demoniac laughter. This he had on more than one occasion found extremely useful. It was said to have turned Lord Raker's wig grey in a

CONTINUE ▶

single night, and had certainly made three of Lady
60 Canterville's French governesses give warning before
their month was up. He accordingly laughed his most
horrible laugh, till the old vaulted roof rang and rang
again, but hardly had the fearful echo died away when
a door opened, and Mrs. Otis came out in a light blue
65 dressing-gown. "I am afraid you are far from well,"
she said, "and have brought you a bottle of Doctor
Dobell's tincture. If it is indigestion, you will find it a
most excellent remedy." The ghost glared at her in
fury, and began at once to make preparations for
70 turning himself into a large black dog, an
accomplishment for which he was justly renowned,
and to which the family doctor always attributed the
permanent idiocy of Lord Canterville's uncle, the
Hon. Thomas Horton. The sound of approaching
75 footsteps, however, made him hesitate in his fell
purpose, so he contented himself with becoming
faintly phosphorescent and vanished with a deep
churchyard groan, just as the twins had come up to
him.

1

As the passage opens, it can be inferred that the
United States Minister has just given the ghost a gift
because

A) he wants to be friendly to his host.

B) he is afraid and wants to avoid upsetting the
ghost.

C) it is expected of him as an ambassador.

D) he hopes the ghost will use the gift and be less
noisy.

2

Which choice provides the best evidence for the
answer to the previous question?

A) Lines 3-5 ("The United … accepted")

B) Lines 5-8 ("I have … at him")

C) Lines 11-15 ("if he … bedrooms")

D) Lines 19-21 ("This certainly … barred")

3

Based on lines 8-10 ("a very just … laughter") the
narrator is best described as

A) the story's protagonist.

B) an inept observer.

C) a wry commentator.

D) a circumspect apologist.

4

The tone of the narrator in lines 31-35 ("The only
… emerald-green") is best described as

A) harshly judgmental.

B) foolishly oblivious.

C) warmly compassionate.

D) subtly ironic.

CONTINUE

5

The author's purpose in referring to "Californian etiquette" in line 50 is

A) nationalistic: it emphasizes that the Minister's polite behavior is due to his American identity.

B) satirical: it characterizes the response of the United States Minister as more appropriate to the Wild West than to his own home.

C) derisive: it mocks the United States Minister's attempts to be courteous to a ghost who desires to frighten him.

D) illustrative: it contrasts American notions of acceptable domestic behavior with proper British rules for household manners.

6

As used in line 48, "covered" most nearly means

A) protected.

B) hid from.

C) aimed at.

D) put on.

7

The author mentions "Lord Raker's wig" (line 58) and "Lady Canterville's French governesses" (lines 59-60) primarily to

A) suggest that the ghost has been more successful at scaring people in the past.

B) account for the diversity of people that have visited the house.

C) provide background needed to understand the ghost's origin.

D) compare the ghost's laugh with other frightening occurrences.

8

In line 75, "fell" most nearly means

A) failed.

B) lowered.

C) evil.

D) vain.

9

As a whole, the attitude of most members of the family to their situation is

A) guileless because they have been placed in a frightening situation.

B) cruel and unusual due to their aggressive and uncharitable nature.

C) culpably ignorant, given the foreshadowing of impending disaster.

D) oddly audacious, given the apparently alarming situation they encounter.

10

Which choice provides the best evidence for the answer to the previous question?

A) Lines 16–21 ("For the … barred")

B) Lines 28–30 ("These … evening ")

C) Lines 36–43 ("The second … face")

D) Lines 68–74 ("The ghost … Horton")

310

CONTINUE

Questions 11–20 are based on the following passage and supplementary material.

The passage is adapted from Susan Daugherty, "Entrepreneur Changes Life in Uganda by Turning Waste Into Fuel." ©2014 by National Geographic.

Sanga Moses grew up barefoot in a small Ugandan village of thatched roof dwellings that lacked electricity. Yet he became his clan's first college graduate and took a bank job in Kampala.

5　Returning home for a visit from the Ugandan capital in 2009, he met his 12-year-old sister on the road. "She stood there crying, with a heavy bundle of wood on her head," Moses remembers. "She was upset because, like most rural girls, she missed days

10　of school each week searching for fuel wood."

"My sister… was losing the only opportunity she had to make her life better—education."

It wasn't the only change Moses noticed in his hometown. "When I was young, our home was

15　surrounded by national forests," he says. "Now all those trees are gone, and children must walk longer and longer distances to gather wood."

Searching for a solution to problems born of burning wood, Moses quit his job and began learning

20　everything he could about renewable resources. Eventually he came across the increasingly popular practice of turning organic waste into fuel.

"I looked out my window and saw a huge pile of sugar cane debris," he says. "Uganda is primarily

25　agricultural, but farm waste is just abandoned."

So Moses began working with engineering students to design kilns and briquetting machines.

Four years later, 2,500 farmers use his kilns to turn farm waste—coffee husks and waste from sugar cane

30　and rice—into charcoal. A company that Moses founded, called Eco-Fuel Africa, buys the char and turns it into briquettes for cooking that burn cleaner and cost less than wood.

The company takes those briquettes to market,

35　providing fuel for more than 19,000 Ugandan families. "Burning fuel wood not only destroys Uganda's trees," Moses says, but it also affects "the health and educational opportunities of our poorest people.

40　"We're giving them an alternative."

The problems that wood burning created for Moses' family and in his hometown can be seen

across sub-Saharan Africa. Eight in ten people in the region depend on wood to cook and to heat their

45　homes. As more forests are destroyed to feed that demand—in Uganda, 70 percent of protected forests are gone—families must walk more miles every day to buy increasingly scarce and costly wood.

Families in the developing world spend up to 40

50　percent of their income on cooking fuel. Besides leaving children with less time for education, it means that poor farmers are less able to afford fertilizer, causing harvests to suffer and malnutrition to rise.

55　And wood burning takes a huge toll on human health, creating smoky indoor air that leads to respiratory diseases that kill more women and children each year than HIV/AIDS.

Moses' cleaner-burning green charcoal reduces

60　indoor air pollution and has already saved more than three million dollars in energy-related expenses for Ugandans. "Families use that money to pay school fees for their children, afford three meals a day, and finance new income-generating activities," he says.

65　Indeed, farmers who work with Eco-Fuel Africa have tripled their incomes by selling char from kilns. The coarser, leftover char is used as fertilizer, which can increase harvests by more than 50 percent and create surplus crops to sell at market.

70　Moses' group also battles deforestation, investing profits into planting 12,000 new trees and partnering with local schools to make reforestation part of environmental education.

"Today young people who graduate from college

75　come to us and say, 'I don't care how much you pay me; I want to join you because I believe so strongly in what you do,' " Moses says.

Eco-Fuel Africa also looks for employees among Uganda's widows and single mothers, who often

80　struggle after husbands die of HIV/AIDS.

"They value the opportunity to become machine operators and retailers," Moses says, "bringing unbelievable commitment, dedication, and hard work to our project." "Many times when I visit villages,"

85　he continues, "a woman will grab my hand and say, 'Six months ago I could barely feed my family. Now I've been able to enroll my daughter in school and buy a solar panel and mobile phone.' "

Funding from National Geographic recently

90　helped the organization develop a briquette-making

machine that can run without electricity, so it's workable in remote rural areas.

"Now we can micro-franchise in villages far off the power grid," Moses says. "We identify
95 entrepreneurs, supply training and support, and provide technology on a credit basis so they can start sustainable businesses, create jobs, and meet local energy needs."

All while improving Ugandans' health—and
100 saving their forests.

Forest Data: Uganda from 1990–2005
(measured in hectares*)

	1990	2000	2005
Rain Forest	4,924,000	4,059,000	3,627,000
Other Wooded Areas	1,404,000	1,235,000	1,150,000
Plantations	33,000	35,000	36,000
Total Wooded Land (Forest area+ Wooded area – Plantations)	6,295,000	5,259,000	4,741,000

* 1 hectare = 10,000 square meters

Adapted from Mongabay website.

11

The second and third paragraphs (lines 5–12) mention Moses' meeting his sister primarily to

A) contrast Moses' own opportunities with those available to females from his own clan.

B) characterize Moses as compassionate in showing brotherly love.

C) illustrate one of the many negative effects of families burning wood for fuel.

D) provide a reference point to reveal the impact of Moses' education on his whole family.

12

Based on the passage as a whole, the author's attitude toward Moses' project could be best described as

A) somewhat conflicted.

B) cautious endorsement.

C) constructively critical.

D) optimistic approval.

13

Lines 26–27 serve primarily to

A) transition from a narrative about the past to a project in the present.

B) introduce the problem which the remainder of the article addresses.

C) redirect readers from the sociological impact of wood burning to its environmental impact.

D) present new ideas about how to restore the wood needed for burning.

14

One of the serious problems associated with burning wood is that

A) many people develop fatal diseases from smoke inhalation.

B) families have to spend over 40 percent of their income on wood, which inhibits overall economic success.

C) forests are protected, and so families cannot get enough wood.

D) it takes away jobs from those who most need them.

15

Which choice provides the best evidence for the answer to the previous question?

A) Lines 41–45 ("The problems … homes")

B) Lines 55–58 ("And wood … HIV/AIDS")

C) Lines 59–62 ("Moses' cleaner-burning … Ugandans")

D) Lines 70–73 ("Moses' group … education")

16

The unsold char left over from burning in the kilns has provided farmers with

A) triple their income.

B) harvests double their former yield.

C) fertilizer for their fields.

D) reforestation initiatives.

17

Which choice provides the best evidence for the answer to the previous question?

A) Lines 62–64 ("Families … says")

B) Lines 65–67 ("Indeed, farmers … kilns")

C) Lines 67–69 ("The coarser … market")

D) Lines 84–88 ("Many … phone")

18

As it is used in line 81, the word "value" most nearly means

A) appreciate.

B) enjoy.

C) determine the cost of.

D) save.

19

As it is used in line 96, the word "credit" most nearly means

A) beneficial to both parties.

B) freely given due to need.

C) belief in improvement.

D) promise of later payment.

20

The data in the included table indicate that

A) the author has exaggerated about the severity of deforestation in Uganda because some types of wooded areas are better maintained than others.

B) Moses' attempt to counteract deforestation by planting 12,000 trees has been successful because wooded areas are steadily increasing.

C) Eco-Fuel Africa's goal to reduce use of firewood is important because the amount of forested land has reduced dramatically since 1990.

D) trees are more spread out now which forces children to walk further distances to collect wood.

CONTINUE

Questions 21–31 are based on the following passage and supplementary material.

This passage is adapted from Jingwen Zhang "Twenty-first Century Genetics: Power and Responsibility." ©2013 National High School Journal of Science.

Of the relatively recent, notable advancements in the fields of medicine and biotechnology, many are connected to the study of genetics and genomics. Following Watson and Crick's discovery of the DNA
5　double helix, research on DNA and its implications in genetics and life escalated through the 1980s and 1990s to the epic, groundbreaking work of the Human Genome Project in 2003. Today, ten years later, genetic information plays a significant part in
10　public health and medicine. Along with the unveiling of genetics as an integral factor in the 21st-century world comes the realization of responsibilities and future complications that cloud its newfound role.

The expanding field of molecular biology has
15　already translated notable scientific progress from the lab bench to the clinics. For example, thorough exploration and experimentation with the ApoE and BRCA1/BRCA2 genes—associated with Alzheimer's disease and breast cancer, respectively—have allowed
20　specialists to identify high risk patients before the onset of any symptoms. Before the days of targeting the known genes, breast cancer was usually only detected by physical examinations and mammograms, and Alzheimer's went unnoticed until
25　memory loss actually began. Individuals now have the option to take a proactive, rather than reactive, stance in their medical future. Genetics is used to assess football players' (and other high-impact sports athletes') risks of getting Alzheimer's, and to
30　determine the appropriateness and effectiveness of certain medical procedures such as mastectomies. Unfortunately, the absence of the above mutations is not evidence that an individual is not at risk for breast cancer or Alzheimer's disease, since those mutations
35　are found only in a small subset of patients diagnosed clinically. Both diseases are simply too complex and can arise via multiple mechanisms.

Biotechnological advancements have also kept pace with the recently expanding role of genetics in
40　everyday life. With improvements in rapid whole-genome sequencing, companies such as 23 and Me allow the public to see some of what might come in

their future based on their unique genes. Non-invasive whole genome sequencing for fetuses, a way
45　to use maternal plasma to explore the fetal genetic information, was successfully developed in 2012 and has been seen as a large step toward improving neonatal and pediatric treatments with a genetic approach.

50　With these drastic medical advances made in part due to the advent of genetic studies, it becomes very easy to overstate the importance of genetics in changing the course of personalized medicine and in determining an individual's future. The world may
55　seem to believe that genes are all-important: information regarding genetics can be found in almost every hospital, news headlines frequently report how diseases are connected to our genes, public figures like actress Angelina Jolie—who, after
60　learning she had the breast cancer-associated version of the BRCA1 gene, had a preventive double mastectomy—advocate for preventative measures largely based on genetic tests.

These events are certainly not bad in themselves;
65　the problem arises when the public is led to believe that DNA is destiny, when the truth is that singular genetic makeup is only one of many factors contributing to disease development. In addition, although genetic information, hailed as the
70　"language" or "blueprint" of life, can seem very scientifically straightforward with little room for error or doubt, genetics itself is in fact far from an exact science. Much of the human genome has not been studied in depth yet, as it had previously been
75　thought to be "junk" DNA; it has only recently been found to be vital to the expression of exons, the coding regions. Scientists have also discovered that variants in certain genes do not result in the predicted phenotype or condition for every
80　individual, which further complicates the use of genetic information as guides to personal health forecasts. Furthermore, diseases can arise via multiple mechanisms: for example the BRCA1 and BRCA2 genes are found to be mutated only in
85　approximately 10% of patients diagnosed with breast cancer. Advancements in genetics can be extremely helpful in developing future medical treatments, but putting too much stock into it certainly can be harmful. Environmental factors—maternal smoking
90　and drinking, folic acid intake, diet and exercise,

etc.—play a significant and often deciding role as well, yet their importance is not accentuated appropriately. Using genomic information, personalized medicine may allow patients to take
95 more control of their own treatments, but if non-genetic factors are not viewed crucial as well, patients may lose some of the power they have over their health.

Lifetime Breast Cancer Risk

Group	Lifetime Breast Cancer Risk	Median Age of Breast Cancer Onset
General Population	11%	61
BRCA 1	65%	43
BRCA 2	45%	41

Adapted from K. Metcalfe and S. Narod, "Breast Cancer Prevention in Women with a BRCA1 or BRCA2 Mutation." © 2007 Bentham Open.

21

The primary purpose of the first paragraph is to

A) establish the basis for a spurious claim in order to challenge it.

B) provide the reader with the context needed for discussion which follows.

C) enumerate the limitless possibilities and the inherent risks of a scientific development.

D) argue for the significance of specific developments in genetic research.

22

As used in line 13, the word "cloud" most nearly means

A) limit.

B) darken.

C) obscure.

D) hamper.

23

According to the passage, one of the primary medical benefits to individuals which has come from genetic research is that

A) certain health risks can be identified in advance and addressed before problems develop.

B) average people now have learned enough about their own DNA to accurately predict their future health.

C) the behaviors that tend to promote the development of certain health issues can be identified and eliminated.

D) doctors now fully understand the causes of diseases and can correct genetic problems in their patients.

24

Which choice provides the best evidence for the answer to the previous question?

A) Lines 1–8 ("Of the ... in 2003")

B) Lines 14–16 ("The expanding ... clinics")

C) Lines 25–31 ("Individuals ... mastectomies")

D) Lines 86–93 ("Advancements ... appropriately")

25

The primary purpose of the fourth paragraph (lines 50–63) is to

A) discuss the problems caused by the apparent advancements in genetic research.

B) transition from a discussion of advancements in genetic research to possible concerns.

C) warn readers against accepting medical information determined through genetic advancements.

D) provide a specific, relatable example to illustrate the usefulness of genetic research.

CONTINUE

26

The author's tone regarding the idea that "DNA is destiny" (line 66) is best described as

A) disinterested.

B) optimistic.

C) cynical.

D) cautionary.

27

The author most likely uses quotation marks around the word "junk" (line 75) in order to

A) mock a widely held idea.

B) clarify which words are borrowed from another source.

C) suggest that the label is now seen as ironically inaccurate.

D) emphasize the importance of the term.

28

In order to limit an overemphasis upon genetic research as the key to solving concerns regarding certain diseases, the author

A) reminds readers that genetic research has only proven significant in dealing with Alzheimer's and breast cancer.

B) warns doctors that failure to consider non-genetic factors will lead to misdiagnosis and ineffective treatment.

C) dismisses the advancements in genetic research regarding diseases as essentially unfruitful.

D) insists upon the vital role of environmental factors in understanding and treating diseases.

29

Which choice provides the best evidence for the answer to the previous question?

A) Lines 16–21 ("For example … symptoms")

B) Lines 50–54 ("With these … future")

C) Lines 68–73 ("In addition … science")

D) Lines 89–98 (Environmental … health")

30

As used in line 88, the word "stock" most nearly means

A) inventory.

B) confidence.

C) judgment.

D) investment.

31

Based on the data in the article and the table, one can determine

A) the percentage of the total cases of breast cancer attributable to genetic causes alone.

B) the total number of cases of breast cancer linked to each genetic marker.

C) the average age of breast cancer onset for the entire population.

D) that the vast majority of cases of breast cancer develop in a population that has less than an 11 percent chance of developing the disease.

CONTINUE ➜

Questions 32–42 are based on the following passages.

In passage 1, Edmund Burke discusses Marie Antoinette in his book *Reflections on the Revolution in France*, published in 1790. Passage 2 is an excerpt from *The Rights of Man*, 1791, in which Thomas Paine responds to Burke's book.

Passage 1

It is now sixteen or seventeen years since I saw the Queen of France, then the Dauphiness,[1] at Versailles; and surely never lighted on this orb, which she hardly seemed to touch, a more delightful vision.
5 I saw her just above the horizon, decorating and cheering the elevated sphere she had just begun to move in, glittering like the morning star full of life and splendor and joy.

Oh, what a revolution! and what a heart must I
10 have, to contemplate without emotion that elevation and that fall! Little did I dream, when she added titles of veneration to those of enthusiastic, distant, respectful love, that she should ever be obliged to carry the sharp antidote against disgrace concealed in
15 that bosom; little did I dream that I should have lived to see such disasters fallen upon her, in a nation of gallant men, in a nation of men of honor, and of cavaliers! I thought ten thousand swords must have leaped from their scabbards, to avenge even a look
20 that threatened her with insult.

But the age of chivalry is gone; that of sophisters, economists, and calculators has succeeded, and the glory of Europe is extinguished forever. Never, never more, shall we behold that generous loyalty to rank
25 and sex, that proud submission, that dignified obedience, that subordination of the heart, which kept alive, even in servitude itself, the spirit of an exalted freedom! The unbought grace of life, the cheap defense of nations, the nurse of manly
30 sentiment and heroic enterprise is gone. It is gone, that sensibility of principle, that chastity of honor, which felt a stain like a wound, which inspired courage whilst it mitigated ferocity, which ennobled whatever it touched, and under which vice itself lost
35 half its evil, by losing all its grossness.

Passage 2

As to the tragic paintings by which Mr. Burke has outraged his own imagination, and seeks to work upon that of his readers, they are very well calculated for theatrical representation, where facts are
40 manufactured for the sake of show, and accommodated to produce, through the weakness of sympathy, a weeping effect. But Mr. Burke should recollect that he is writing history, and not plays, and that his readers will expect truth, and not the
45 spouting rant of high-toned exclamation…

Not one glance of compassion, not one commiserating reflection that I can find throughout his book, has he bestowed on those who lingered out the most wretched of lives, a life without hope in the
50 most miserable of prisons.[2] It is painful to behold a man employing his talents to corrupt himself. Nature has been kinder to Mr. Burke than he is to her. He is not affected by the reality of distress touching his heart, but by the showy resemblance of it striking his
55 imagination. He pities the plumage, but forgets the dying bird. Accustomed to kiss the aristocratical hand that hath purloined him from himself, he degenerates into a composition of art, and the genuine soul of nature forsakes him. His hero or his heroine must be
60 a tragedy-victim expiring in show, and not the real prisoner of misery, sliding into death in the silence of a dungeon.

32

In Passage 1, the author's initial assessment of Marie Antoinette is characterized by

A) enthusiastic admiration of her beauty and vivacious personality.

B) hesitant endorsement of her right to rule.

C) amorous infatuation with details of her physical body.

D) a desire to protect her from the coming tragedy.

---

[1] The wife of the Dauphin, who is the eldest son of the King of France.

[2] The Bastille, a prison Revolutionaries in France overthrew in order to free the prisoners held there.

33

Which choice provides the best evidence for the answer to the previous question?

A) Lines 1–2 ("It is now … Versailles")

B) Lines 4–8 ("I saw her … joy")

C) Lines 11–15 ("Little did I … bosom")

D) Lines 18–20 ("I thought … insult")

34

The author of Passage 1 repeats the phrase "little did I dream" (lines 11 and 15) in order to

A) emphasize the limits of his own ability to imagine.

B) mock the ways in which Marie Antoinette has changed because of the Revolution.

C) accentuate how unimaginable the changes which took place in France were.

D) reference the dream-like state his idolization of Marie Antoinette puts him in.

35

The author of Passage 1 characterizes "the age of chivalry" (line 21) primarily as

A) acceptable in its own time, but now superseded by a better age.

B) overly permissive of certain evils.

C) a lost ideal of honor.

D) oppressive to those of lower classes.

36

The word "grossness" as used in line 35 most nearly means

A) dirtiness of appearance.

B) disgust in reaction.

C) coarseness of manner.

D) largess of nature.

37

The most prevalent rhetorical strategy used in Passage 2 is

A) establishing an analogy between the writing of Passage 1 and drama.

B) personal attack against the character of those discussed by the author of Passage 1.

C) systematically developing a parallel point to each point in Passage 1.

D) attempting to control the emotions of the audience through theatrical effects.

38

As it is used in line 57, the word "purloined" most nearly means

A) stolen.

B) elevated.

C) hidden.

D) abstracted.

1   **1**

39

In Passage 2, the author claims "He pities the plumage, but forgets the dying bird" (lines 55–56) to suggest that the author of Passage 1 is

A) forgetting that birds are more valuable for the meaning of their death than for their outer beauty.

B) too enamored of the external appearance of honor to notice the damage it does.

C) limited in his approach, because he is unable to respond emotionally to the events he describes.

D) incomplete in his historical methods, but still trying to be honest in his emotions.

40

The two passages relate to each other primarily by

A) discussing the same events from the perspective of very different times and places.

B) sympathizing with different sides of the same conflict.

C) emphasizing different aspects of an event to reach the same conclusion.

D) struggling toward common ground from which to discuss their common values.

41

The author of Passage 2 would respond to the claim in Passage 1 regarding "the spirit of an exalted freedom" (lines 27–28) of those "in servitude" (line 27) by

A) denying their freedom existed because some of them were forced to live in terrible conditions in prison.

B) acknowledging the importance of liberty, but suggesting that it comes from nature rather than the monarch.

C) suggesting that their freedom is only outward, but not true freedom, because they merely act out a part.

D) finding their freedom to be tragic, whereas they think of it as liberating and ennobling.

42

Which choice provides the best evidence for the answer to the previous question?

A) Lines 39–42 ("where facts ... effect")

B) Lines 48–50 ("those who ... prisons")

C) Lines 51–52 ("Nature has ... to her")

D) Lines 59–60 ("His hero ... in show")

Questions 43–52 are based on the following passage.

The following passage is adapted from *An Urchin in the Storm*, published in 1987, in which Stephen Jay Gould reviews *The Evolution of Culture in Animals*, by John Tyler Bonner, and *Man, the Promising Primate*, by Peter J. Wilson.

The female mason wasp, *Monobia quadridens*, excavates a broad chamber by digging a long tube into the pith of trees and stems. She deposits a series of eggs in the tube, starting at the bottom and separating
5　each egg from the next by a curved mud partition. The partitions are shaped with their rough and convex side toward daylight and their smooth and concave side toward the cul de sac at the blind end of the chamber. The larvae feed and pupate within their
10　chambers, which the mother has provisioned with food. When the young adults emerge, they crawl toward freedom by chewing through the rough, convex sides of the partitions. If the partitions are experimentally reversed, so that the rough and
15　convex sides now point toward the cul de sac, the emerging adults cut their way into the stem, pile up at the blind end of the tube, and eventually die. Apparently, the mason wasp has evolved a rigidly programmed rule of behavior: cut through the rough
20　and convex side of the partition. In nature, obedience to this rule always leads to daylight. If a human experimenter intervenes to reverse the partitions, the wasp cannot accommodate and digs to its own death, steadfastly obeying its unbreakable rule.
25　　What the wasps lack—and what human beings possess in unparalleled abundance—is the common theme of both books: flexibility in behavior response. Bonner defines culture as "the transfer of information by behavioral means," and structures his
30　fascinating book as a survey of culture in the animal kingdom, marching up the venerable chain of being toward bigger brains, increasing behavioral complexity, and freedom from rigid genetic programs specifying "single response behaviors." Wilson
35　identifies flexibility—that is, freedom from genetic programming of specific behaviors—as the key to our evolutionary promise; he traces the origins of human culture to the structural and nongenetic (but biologically based) rules that we follow in establishing
40　systems of kinship.
　　Human flexibility has at least three complex and interrelated sources. First, we possess a brain much larger, in proper relation to the size of our bodies, than any other animal (except the bottle-nosed
45　dolphin). More circuitry increases (indeed explodes) at a far faster rate than the growth of its material substrate. A simple machine can handle tic-tac-toe; complex computers may soon be giving chess grand masters a run for it. The metaphor may be somewhat
50　mixed, but it is an arresting thought nonetheless that our brains contain more information, in an engineer's technical sense, than all the DNA in our genes.
　　Second, we have evolved our massive brains largely by the evolutionary process of neoteny: the
55　slowing down of developmental rates and the consequent retention to adulthood of traits that mark the *juvenile* stages of our ancestors. We retain the rapid fetal growth rate of neurons well beyond birth (when the brain of most mammals is nearly
60　complete), and end our growth with the bulbous cranium and relatively large brain so characteristic of juvenile primates. Neoteny also slows down our maturation and gives us a long period of flexible childhood learning. I believe that the analogy
65　between childhood wonder and adult creativity is good biology, not metaphor.
　　Third, as primates we belong to one of the few groups of mammals sufficiently unspecialized in bodily form to retain the morphological capacity for
70　exploiting a broad range of environments and modes of life. A bat has committed its forelimbs to flight, a horse to running, and a whale to balancing and paddling. Culture and intelligence at a human level have required the evolution of a free forelimb and a
75　generalized hand endowed with the capacity to manufacture and manipulate tools (both from *manus* = hand). Only the morphologically unspecialized among mammals have not made inflexible commitments to particular modes of life
80　that preclude this prerequisite to intelligence.

43

The purpose of the first paragraph (lines 1–24) in terms of the passage as a whole is to

A) offer evidence to support the passage's endorsement of biological determinism.

B) illustrate the cruelty of human experimenters in working with other forms of biological life.

C) provide a negative example to contrast with the remainder of the passage.

D) argue for genetic modification needed to allow Mason wasps to thrive.

44

Which choice provides the best evidence for the answer to the previous question?

A) Lines 18–21 ("Apparently … daylight")

B) Lines 21–24 ("If a human … rule")

C) Lines 25–27 ("What wasps … response")

D) Lines 41–42 ("Human … sources")

45

Based on the first paragraph, which of the following is NOT characteristic of a natural wasp lifecycle?

A) Larvae share chambers with siblings in order to maximize their potential success as adults.

B) Larvae develop from eggs into pupae in their chambers and only leave their chambers as young adults.

C) The *Monobia quadridens* is responsible for creating chambers in the pith of trees and providing her offspring with food.

D) As young adults in nature, wasps chew through the convex side of the partition and never through the concave side.

46

As used in line 24, "steadfastly" most nearly means

A) bravely.

B) unequivocally.

C) unfortunately.

D) assiduously.

47

Which of the following gives the best explanation of the relationship between Bonner and Wilson as expressed in the passage?

A) Wilson disagrees with Bonner by believing that flexibility is genetic whereas Wilson thinks genetics are not involved.

B) Bonner builds on Wilson's ideas by providing evidence for Wilson's novel theories of human flexibility.

C) Bonner and Wilson are in agreement in stating that genetic flexibility is key in determining brain size.

D) Wilson discusses in greater detail one of the ideas in Bonner's book by examining the biological causes of human flexibility.

CONTINUE

48

Bonner's concept of "culture" (line 28) is related to Wilson's notion of "flexibility" (line 35) in that

A) both are exclusively traits of humans.

B) both suggest aspects of animal behavior that are not genetically determined.

C) both are determined by the size of any animal's brain.

D) neither is known to have an impact on biological success.

49

According to the passage, which of the following is most analogous to the benefit of a large brain size?

A) A larger basement provides more storage space.

B) A country with more laws is more obedient and orderly.

C) A larger puppet can have more strings, which allow for more movement.

D) A more viscous substance is more fluid.

50

Which choice provides the best evidence for the answer to the previous question?

A) Line 42-45 ("First, we ... dolphin")

B) Line 45-47 ("More circuitry ... substrate")

C) Line 49-52 ("The metaphor ... genes")

D) Line 53-57 (Second, we ... ancestors")

51

Which of the following would be in most conflict with the author's description of neoteny in lines 53–66?

A) Neoteny is a biological characteristic of humans.

B) Neoteny slows down human brains.

C) Adult humans are more creative because of neoteny.

D) Children are biologically better suited to learn than adults.

52

As used in line 71, "committed" most nearly means

A) perpetrated.

B) dedicated.

C) achieved.

D) lost.

STOP

If you finish before time is called, you may check your work on this section only.
Do not turn to any other section.

CONTINUE

No Test Material On This Page

2   2

Writing and Language Test

35 MINUTES, 44 QUESTIONS

Turn to Section 2 of your answer sheet to answer the questions in this section.

DIRECTIONS

Each passage below is accompanied by a number of questions. For some questions, you will consider how the passage might be revised to improve the expression of ideas. For other questions, you will consider how the passage might be edited to correct errors in sentence structure, usage, or punctuation. A passage or a question may be accompanied by one or more graphics (such as a table or graph) that you will consider as you make revising and editing decisions.

Some questions will direct you to an underlined portion of a passage. Other questions will direct you to a location in a passage or ask you to think about the passage as a whole.

After reading each passage, choose the answer to each question that most effectively improves the quality of writing in the passage or that makes the passage conform to the conventions of standard written English. Many questions include a "NO CHANGE" option. Choose that option if you think the best choice is to leave the relevant portion of the passage as it is.

Questions 1-11 are based on the following passage.

On the Campaign Trail

[1] In my senior year of high school when I started working on campaigns as a **1** volunteer; I was immediately attracted to the energy of campaigning, thus I joined a campaign as an intern the following summer. [2] Even though doing a task like this could be exhausting and repetitive, everyone in the office was excited to contribute to the effort. [3] Upon joining the campaign, I was asked to help with **2** compiling our financial records, volunteers, and our press releases.

1

A) NO CHANGE

B) volunteer, I was immediately attracted to the energy of campaigning, so

C) volunteer I was immediately attracted to the energy of campaigning, so that

D) volunteer, I was immediately attracted to the energy of campaigning; so,

2

A) NO CHANGE

B) compiling our financial records and press releases as well as supervising volunteers.

C) compiling our financial records, coordinating our press releases, as well as supervising volunteers.

D) compiling our financial records, and press releases; and supervising volunteers.

CONTINUE

[4] Tedious tasks were not reserved for [3] volunteers; my campaign manager and I spent several hours [4] watching the World Cup and stuffing envelopes for our major mailing campaign as well. [5] Working on a campaign requires that everyone helps and that no task is "beneath" anyone. [5]

[3]

A) NO CHANGE

B) volunteers—and my

C) volunteers, my

D) volunteers: while my

[4]

The writer is considering deleting the underlined portion. Should the author make this change?

A) Yes, because this detail is irrelevant to the purpose of describing working on a campaign.

B) Yes, because this detail makes the writer's experience seem like fun.

C) No, because this detail adds necessary humor to lighten up this otherwise somber passage.

D) No, because this detail adds an example needed to understand working on a campaign.

[5]

To make the paragraph most coherent and logical, sentence 2 should be placed

A) where it is now.

B) before sentence 1.

C) after sentence 3.

D) after sentence 4.

I spent most of my weekends on the campaign canvassing, which [6] <u>involve</u> walking around a neighborhood and knocking on doors to persuade people to vote for a candidate. Although it sounds outdated, canvassing is actually one of the most effective ways to secure votes [7]. [8] <u>While canvassing, many voters got</u> the opportunity to learn more about the candidate and his policies. Some people were not receptive and slammed the door in my face, but most people were friendly and interested in hearing about the candidate.

[6]

A) NO CHANGE
B) had involved
C) involves
D) has involved

[7]

The writer is considering adding the following clause here:

> because it provides the voter with a much more personal interaction than the standard automated phone call

Assuming punctuation was adjusted, should the author make this change?

A) Yes, because this clause emphasizes the ineffectiveness of auto dialers.
B) Yes, because this clause clarifies why canvassing is still an effective mode of campaigning.
C) No, because this clause provides information that the reader can clearly infer from the context.
D) No, because this clause does not provide sufficient detail on canvassing strategies.

[8]

A) NO CHANGE
B) My canvassing provided many voters with
C) During canvassing, they all got
D) While I was canvassing the voters, got

2 **2**

[9] The week leading up to Election Day required a massive "Get Out the Vote" effort involving many volunteers, hundreds of phone calls, hours of canvassing, and many boxes of stale pizza. Each night, I made over 100 phone calls to remind voters about Election Day and to try to persuade them to vote for my candidate. In all our calls, we only successfully reached a voter 10 percent of the time because people did not pick up the phone or we had an outdated number on file. [10] Nonetheless, we were desperate to secure votes in that last week, so we did all we could and worked tirelessly around the clock. Even if we reached only a few people, we believed that our efforts would have a positive impact on both the election and the democratic process as a whole.

Nothing was more exciting than the victory party on Tuesday night after the polls closed. I rushed from my designated polling station to join my fellow workers as we watched the election results. [11] We have been running a clever, effective, and well-organized campaign, so it was exciting to see our hard work pay off. After working on this campaign, I realized the importance of being involved in our country's political process and have committed myself to continuing political engagement.

9

Which choice most vividly depicts the author's experience during the "Get Out the Vote" week?

A) NO CHANGE

B) The week leading up to Election Day required us to do a "Get Out the Vote" effort.

C) We recruited a lot of volunteers for a massive "Get Out the Vote" effort during the week leading up to Election Day.

D) "Get Out the Vote" was a big effort we led during the week leading up to Election Day with lots of volunteers working around the clock.

10

A) NO CHANGE

B) Consequently,

C) Therefore,

D) Unfortunately,

11

A) NO CHANGE

B) We have run

C) We had run

D) We are running

Questions 12–22 are based on the following passage and supplemental material.

A Waste of Nuclear Energy?

The world's rapidly growing population has demanded ever-increasing supplies of energy from a variety of sources. During the Industrial Revolution, handmade production methods gave way to mass production in coal-powered factories. In the late nineteenth century, Thomas Edison spurred the spread of electric power to run his newly invented **12** lightbulbs, and the automobile created a new and still booming market for oil. After harnessing atomic energy during the Second World War, scientists in the mid-twentieth century began applying nuclear power to civilian energy projects.

Proponents of harnessing nuclear power cite several benefits, many **13** of them seem to make it superior to other possible sources of energy. Because nuclear power reduces dependence on fossil fuels, such as oil and coal, its widespread use could lower greenhouse gas emissions caused by burning carbon-based fuels. Thus, it is an energy option that may slow devastating climate change. In addition, nuclear power plants have demonstrated the capacity to generate the large **14** numbers of power needed to meet industrial needs and the energy demands of large, urban populations. And finally, it is efficient: nuclear power yields a large energy output from a

12

A) NO CHANGE
B) lightbulbs and
C) lightbulbs; and
D) lightbulbs: and

13

A) NO CHANGE
B) of whom
C) of which
D) of these benefits

14

A) NO CHANGE
B) totals
C) aggregates
D) quantities

relatively small amount of fuel. This saves not only on direct fuel costs but also on the cost and environmental effects of transporting raw materials.

Critics of nuclear power, however, cite environmental and human health concerns about the development of nuclear power. [15] Nuclear power plants generate plenty of energy but also waste. Radioactivity levels in the waste remaining high for hundreds of thousands of years. Because radiation has been demonstrated to cause genetic mutations and cancer, it is essential to store nuclear waste safely. However, the cost both to build and to maintain secure storage of radioactive byproducts is high.

In 1986, a major disaster at a civilian nuclear plant in Chernobyl, Ukraine, highlighted for the world the potential danger of nuclear power development. [16] The long-term effects of this disaster are still being studied. The United Nations estimates the number of probable

---

15

Which choice most effectively combines the underlined sentences?

A) Radioactivity in nuclear waste remains high for hundreds of thousands of years; nevertheless, nuclear power plants generate plenty of energy.

B) Even though nuclear power plants generate plenty of energy, they have downsides that create concerns: radioactivity levels in the waste remain high for hundreds of thousands of years.

C) Though nuclear power plants produce plenty of energy, they also generate waste that remains highly radioactive for hundreds of thousands of years.

D) Generating plenty of energy, nuclear power plants also generate waste; this waste remains with high levels of radioactivity for hundreds of thousands of years.

16

At this point, the writer is considering adding the following sentence:

> This facility suffered a meltdown due to human error wherein tons of radioactive materials were released into the surrounding environment.

Should the writer make this addition here?

A) Yes, because without the knowledge that the damage was caused by human error, readers might assume that radioactive material itself is unsafe.

B) Yes, because it provides helpful information to understand the main point of the paragraph.

C) No, because the information contained in the sentence can be inferred from the rest of the paragraph.

D) No, because it distracts readers from the main topic of the paragraph.

CONTINUE

deaths associated with the disaster at around 4,000. [17] Instead, a new book by former Soviet government scientists [18] reveal that almost a million deaths, most due to cancer, may be attributable to the accident at Chernobyl.

As human beings continue to debate options for developing energy [19] sources—whether conventional, renewable, or nuclear—to meet the demands of a growing population, the importance of energy conservation should be central to the discussion. An easy way to reduce our energy consumption is to scale back our use of energy for nonessential activities. No energy source capable of [20] endowing the needs of a large population will be entirely safe and free of destructive consequences. As citizens of the world, we need to be mindful of the

17

A) NO CHANGE
B) Moreover,
C) However,
D) Regardless,

18

A) NO CHANGE
B) reveals
C) is revealing
D) would reveal

19

A) NO CHANGE
B) sources—whether conventional, renewable, or nuclear,
C) sources, whether conventional, renewable, or nuclear;
D) sources: whether conventional, renewable, or nuclear,

20

A) NO CHANGE
B) supplying
C) giving
D) donating

21 affects of our actions and strive to reduce our energy footprint. Wherever our energy comes from, we must learn to preserve our resources by using them wisely.

Question 22 asks about the previous passage as a whole.

21

A) NO CHANGE
B) affects for
C) effects of
D) effects for

Think about the previous passage and included supplemental material as a whole as you answer question 22.

22

Which statement most accurately interprets the data presented in the graph about energy consumption in the United States in 2005?

A) The amount of energy consumed from petroleum was almost twice the amount of energy consumed from coal and natural gas combined.

B) The US consumed more energy from hydro-electric power than from wood, waste, and alcohol fuels.

C) A total of 1 million Btu of geothermal, solar, and wind energy were consumed.

D) Nuclear power provided less than 10 percent of the total energy consumed.

US Energy Consumption by Source (2005)

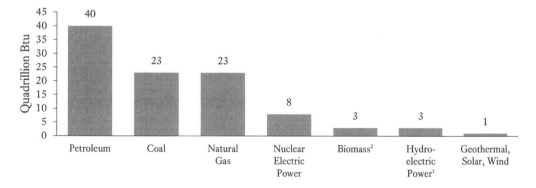

[1] Conventional Hydro-electric power. [2] Wood, waste, and alcohol fuels.

Adapted from Energy Information Administration, *Annual Energy Review 2005*. © 2006

CONTINUE

Questions 23–33 are based on the following passage.

Shakespeare's Forerunner

Christopher Marlowe may be literature's best-known second place finisher. Doomed always to stand in the shadow of Shakespeare, [23] Marlowe's work is still widely read and performed today, but his true significance as an innovator is underappreciated. Critics commonly assert that Marlowe preceded Shakespeare in writing serious tragedy for the English stage, but [24] Marlowe also kept up with Shakespeare in the development of the history play, the form most commonly associated with Shakespeare.

Shakespeare, who was then considered an undereducated upstart, wrote the three parts of *Henry VI*, [25] the second of which was originally titled *The Contention of the Noble and Illustrious Houses of York and Lancaster*, in the late 1580s, while Marlowe's *Edward II* was likely first staged in 1593. However, despite some interesting characters and powerful lines, Shakespeare's

---

[23]

A) NO CHANGE
B) Marlowe's position is assured because his plays are
C) Marlowe wrote plays that are
D) DELETE the underlined portion

[24]

Which choice most clearly emphasizes the point that Marlowe was an influence on Shakespeare's history plays?

A) NO CHANGE
B) Shakespeare was most commonly associated with history plays, though Marlowe also wrote one of the earlier history plays.
C) Marlowe also wrote a single English history play, and its effect on Shakespeare's later history plays is clear.
D) Shakespeare influenced Marlowe to write his first and only history play.

[25]

The writer is considering deleting the underlined portion, adjusting the punctuation appropriately. Should the writer make this change?

A) Yes, because the full title of Shakespeare's play is clear from the context.
B) Yes, because the phrase adds an unnecessary detail to the paragraph.
C) No, because the information is needed to make sense of the rest of the paragraph.
D) No, because the phrase provides context that readers will need to understand the main point of the essay.

---

2 **2**

Henry VI plays [26] are unstructured: they seem to exist merely to portray a loosely connected series of events but without dramatic unity. It wasn't until Marlowe, who was then regarded as the premiere playwright for the London stage, made his first foray into English history that the history [27] play became its own form of cohesive art.

　[1] In telling the story of Edward [28] II, whom was a weak and failed monarch, Marlowe [29] combined: elements of a morality play and classical tragedy. [2] In the play, history was not a collection of events but a narrative corresponding to recognizable types, a true work of art. [3] Like a character in a morality play, Marlowe's Edward is [30] shrouded by a corrupting influence, that of Gaveston, a self-indulgent flatterer who

[26]

A) NO CHANGE

B) lack structure, portraying loosely connected events without unity or purpose, dramatically speaking.

C) lack dramatic unity, presenting history only as a loosely connected series of events.

D) are less structured than his later plays, such as *Hamlet* and *King Lear*, which is also about English history.

[27]

A) NO CHANGE

B) plays become their own

C) play becomes its own

D) play, becoming a

[28]

A) NO CHANGE

B) II, who

C) II whom

D) II who

[29]

A) NO CHANGE

B) combined a morality play, with tragic aspects.

C) combined elements from both a morality play and a classical tragedy.

D) combined a morality play—together with tragic elements.

[30]

A) NO CHANGE

B) inundated

C) drowned

D) overcome

has stolen the heart of the king. [4] [31] Unlike a character in a morality play, Edward has no "good angels" to help him become a better ruler, for the king's counselors murder Gaveston only to increase their own power. [5] Then, when Edward's wife and several nobles turn against him, the audience sympathizes with the king as he loses his power and is eventually killed, turning him from a pathetic character to one who arouses the pity and fear that Aristotle claimed tragedy required. [6] Shakespeare's later history plays show evidence that he learned a great deal from Marlowe's play: aspects of classical tragedy and English morality are clear in many of Shakespeare's best historical dramas of the mid-to-late 1590s. [32]

Marlowe cannot compete with Shakespeare: he died too young, never having reached the level of subtlety and sophistication Shakespeare attained in his career. However, Marlowe should not be considered a second-place finisher to Shakespeare. It is more accurate to characterize him as the first to arrive at the finish line, whereas Shakespeare reached that line and found that he [33] had just begun to race at the point where Marlowe finished.

[31]

A) NO CHANGE
B) As opposed to
C) However, not like
D) Moreover, in the opposite way of

[32]

To make the paragraph most coherent and logical, sentence 6 should be placed

A) where it is now.
B) before sentence 1.
C) after sentence 3.
D) after sentence 4.

[33]

A) NO CHANGE
B) had only begun racing where Marlowe had stopped.
C) had enough energy to continue racing from that point on.
D) had merely begun to race.

CONTINUE

2

2

Questions 34–44 are based on the following passage.

GM Crops: Are they really safe?

Genetically modified food has become prevalent in the United States since the commercialization of genetic engineering in 1976. Over the past decade, the use of GM crops has become **34** increasingly more and more popular and now **35** accounts for roughly 94 percent of the acreage of soybeans and 93 percent of that of corn in the US. However, as GM crops have increased in **36** prevalence they have also become more controversial, and many believe that not enough long-term research has been done to ensure that they are safe for consumption.

34

A) NO CHANGE
B) more widespread
C) appallingly ubiquitous
D) the popular thing to do

35

Which of the following provides specific support for the main idea of this paragraph?

A) NO CHANGE
B) is used in many places.
C) makes growing and protecting crops much easier for farmers.
D) helps ease the burden of producing the food needed to meet the demand of the US and the world.

36

A) NO CHANGE
B) prevalence—they
C) prevalence, they
D) prevalence, and they

[37] Nonetheless, in 2012, French scientist Eric-Gilles Seralini conducted an experiment that has since become very controversial. [38] They wanted to test the toxicity of [39] Monsanto's genetically modified NK603 corn. Monsanto's NK603 corn is genetically modified to resist RoundUp, a commonly used herbicide. The experimenters tested 200 Sprague-Dawley rats in groups of 10 and fed them variations of genetically modified RoundUp-resistant corn, water with RoundUp, or unmodified corn and water. Seralini's team monitored the rats over the course of two years and observed that the rats that were fed GM corn died sooner than those fed the unmodified corn.

37

A) NO CHANGE
B) Shockingly, in 2012,
C) As a consequence, in 2012,
D) In 2012,

38

A) NO CHANGE
B) He
C) It
D) His experiment

39

Which of the following choices provides the best way to combine these two sentences?

A) Monsanto's NK603 corn, which is genetically modified to resist RoundUp, which is an herbicide commonly used.

B) Monsanto's, genetically modified to resist RoundUp, a commonly used herbicide, corn called NK603.

C) Monsanto's NK603 corn, which is genetically modified to resist the common herbicide RoundUp.

D) Monsanto's genetically modified NK603 corn: this type of corn is genetically modified to resist RoundUp, which is a commonly used herbicide.

2   2

[1] Seralini then held a press conference and published startling results with pictures of experimental rats with huge and alarming tumors. [2] Many news sources and social media sites caused an international outrage and widespread fear of genetically modified crops by reporting that GM corn caused tumors. [3] In reaction, some countries, such as Russia, banned GM corn entirely. [4] **40** On the other hand, some biology and bioethics organizations criticized the study for practicing poor science. [5] The scientists at these institutions pointed out that Seralini's sample size of 200 rats in groups of 10 **41** was far too small for an experiment lasting two years: the Organization for Economic Co-operation and Development recommends groups of at least 20 for toxicity and at least 50 for carcinogenicity tests of this length. [6] Furthermore, these rats are extremely susceptible to spontaneous tumors, making Seralini's claims about tumors particularly suspect. **42**

40

Which of the following is LEAST acceptable?

A) NO CHANGE

B) However, some

C) Though some

D) Unconvinced, other

41

A) NO CHANGE

B) were too small by far

C) is far to small

D) were far too small

42

Where is the most logical place in this paragraph to insert the following sentence?

> Another concern was that the time span was too long, because the average Sprague-Dawley rat's lifespan is less than two years.

A) After sentence 2

B) After sentence 3

C) After sentence 4

D) After sentence 5

Nonetheless, the results of [43] Seralini's experiment are undoubtedly cause for concern because GM corn is so common in our diets. However, the experimental design was flawed in many ways, and Seralini has been criticized for having an anti-GM agenda, a bias that makes his results less credible. Are GM crops safe? [44] Many scientists believe that they pose no harm, but perhaps more rigorous and accurate research could be done to make sure.

[43]

A) NO CHANGE

B) Seralini and his teams'

C) Seralinis'

D) Seralini's teams

[44]

The writer wants the last sentence to emphasize that the answer to the question "Are GM crops safe?" is both uncertain and essential to determine. Which choice best accomplishes this intention?

A) NO CHANGE

B) Though some scientists believe they are safe to consume, more rigorous long-term research must be done to ensure public health.

C) Seralini's flawed methods have not helped us to know for certain, and so we cannot really know.

D) Despite the problems with Seralini's experiment, the problems it found make it clear that GM foods are not safe to eat.

STOP

**If you finish before time is called, you may check your work on this section only.
Do not turn to any other section.**

No Test Material On This Page

Math Test – No Calculator

25 MINUTES, 20 QUESTIONS

Turn to Section 3 of your answer sheet to answer the questions in this section.

DIRECTIONS

For questions 1–15, solve each problem, choose the best answer from the choices provided, and fill in the corresponding circle on your answer sheet. **For questions 16–20**, solve the problems and enter your answer in the grid on the answer sheet. Please refer to the directions before question 16 on how to enter your answers in the grid. You may use any available space in your test booklet for scratch work.

NOTES

The use of calculators **is not permitted**.

All variables and expressions used represent real numbers unless otherwise indicated.

Figures provided in this test are drawn to scale unless otherwise indicated.

All figures lie in a plane unless otherwise indicated.

Unless otherwise indicated, the domain of a given function f is the set of real numbers x for which $f(x)$ is a real number.

REFERENCE

$A = \pi r^2$
$C = 2\pi r$

$A = \ell w$

$A = \dfrac{1}{2}bh$

$c^2 = a^2 + b^2$

Special Right Triangles

$V = \ell w h$

$V = \pi r^2 h$

$V = \dfrac{4}{3}\pi r^3$

$V = \dfrac{1}{3}\pi r^2 h$

$V = \dfrac{1}{3}\ell w h$

The number of degrees of arc in a circle is 360.
The number of radians of arc in a circle is 2π.
The sum of the measures in degrees of the angles in a triangle is 180.

CONTINUE

1

A commercial pilot flies a Cessna 182 for private passengers wishing to take trips from small airports. The total expenses for a flight can be represented by the expression $tgX + C$, where t is the number of hours travelled, g is gallons of fuel used per hour, X is a constant with units of dollars per gallon, and C is the total cost of plane inspection, parts, servicing, and hangar rental. If the price of fuel rises by 5 percent, which of the factors in the expense expression would change?

A) t

B) X

C) g

D) C

2

For $i = \sqrt{-1}$, what is the value of $3(4 - 3i) + 2i$?

A) $12 + 7i$

B) $12 - 11i$

C) $12 + 11i$

D) $12 - 7i$

3

Which of the following is equivalent to $x^{\frac{3}{4}}$ for all values of x ?

A) $\sqrt[3]{x^{\frac{1}{4}}}$

B) $\sqrt[3]{x^4}$

C) $\sqrt[4]{x^{\frac{1}{3}}}$

D) $\sqrt[4]{x^3}$

4

A group of friends is eating at a diner. Each entree costs \$5.25, and each soda costs \$1.50. If d people order an entree and p people order a soda, which of the following expressions represents the total number of dollars paid by the group?

A) $5.25p + 1.5d$

B) $6.75d$

C) $5.25d + 1.5p$

D) $5.25d - 1.5p$

CONTINUE

5

$$4x^4 + 20x^2y + 25y^2$$

Which of the following is equivalent to the expression above?

A) $(4x^2 + 5y^2)^2$

B) $(4x^2 + 10y^2)^2$

C) $(2x^2 + 5y^2)^2$

D) $(2x^2 + 5y)^2$

6

$$3a - 4b = -14$$
$$4a - 3b = -7$$

Given the system of equations above, what is the value of $a - b$?

A) -7

B) -3

C) 7

D) 10

7

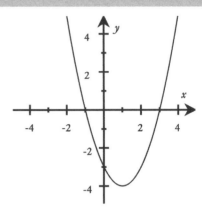

Given the function $f(x)$ shown in the graph above, which of the following must be a factor of $f(x)$?

A) $x - 1$

B) $x - 2$

C) $x - 3$

D) $x - 4$

8

If $\dfrac{p}{q} = \dfrac{4}{3}$, what is the value of $\dfrac{12q}{p}$?

A) 6

B) 8

C) 9

D) 16

9

Which of the following inequalities has a graph in the xy-plane for which y is always less than -4 ?

A) $y < (x-4)^2$

B) $y \leq (x+4)^2$

C) $y < -(x^2+4)$

D) $y \geq |x-4|$

10

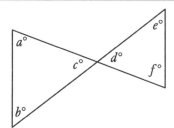

Note: Figure not drawn to scale

In the figure above, the sum of b and c is equal to the sum of f and d. Which of the following must be true?

     I. $b = f$
    II. $e = b$
   III. $a = e$

A) I only

B) III only

C) I, II, and III

D) I and III only

11

A line in the xy-plane contains the point $(3, -5)$ and has a slope of $\frac{4}{3}$. Which of the following points lies on the line?

A) $(0, -9)$

B) $(-3, 2)$

C) $(4, -5)$

D) $(3, -6)$

12

What is the sum of all values of b that satisfy $3b^2 - 2b - 4 = 0$?

A) $\dfrac{2}{3}$

B) $\dfrac{3}{2}$

C) $\dfrac{\sqrt{13}}{2}$

D) $2\sqrt{13}$

CONTINUE

13

$$\frac{16x^2 + 28x - 19}{nx - 5} = -4x - 2 - \frac{29}{nx - 5}$$

Given the equation above, in which n is a constant and $x \neq \frac{5}{n}$, what is the value of n ?

A) -8

B) -4

C) 4

D) 8

14

If $(5^b)^{3a} = 25$, what is the value of $36ab$?

A) 24

B) 12

C) 4

D) 3

15

$$J = -\frac{3}{7}(A + 78)$$

On the planet Sandor, the number of Jagons (J) and Ambloos (A) are related by the relationship given in the equation above. Based on the equation, which of the following must be true?

   I. A decrease of 1 Ambloo is equivalent to an increase of $\frac{3}{7}$ of a Jagon.

   II. An increase of 1 Ambloo is equivalent to a decrease of $\frac{3}{7}$ of a Jagon.

   III. A decrease of $\frac{7}{3}$ Ambloos is equivalent to an increase of 1 Jagon.

A) I and II only

B) I and III only

C) II and III only

D) I, II, and III

CONTINUE

DIRECTIONS

For questions 16–20, solve the problem and enter your answer in the grid, as described below, on the answer sheet.

1. Although not required, it is suggested that you write your answer in the boxes at the top of the columns to help you fill in the circles accurately. You will receive credit only if the circles are filled in correctly.
2. Mark no more than one circle in any column.
3. No question has a negative answer.
4. Some problems may have more than one correct answer. In such cases, grid only one answer.

5. **Mixed numbers** such as $3\frac{1}{2}$ must be be gridded as 3.5 or 7/2. If [3][1][/][2] is entered into the grid, it will be interpreted as $\frac{31}{2}$, not $3\frac{1}{2}$.)

6. **Decimal answers:** If you obtain a decimal answer with more digits than the grid can accommodate, it may be either rounded or truncated, but it must fill the entire grid.

Answer: $\frac{7}{13}$

Write answer in boxes → [7] [/] [1] [3] ← Fraction line

Grid in result

Answer: 2.5

[2] [.] [5] ← Decimal Point

Acceptable ways to grid $\frac{2}{3}$ are:

[2] [/] [3]   [.] [6] [6] [6]   [.] [6] [6] [7]

Answer: 210 – either position is correct

[2] [1] [0]   [2] [1] [0]

NOTE: You may start your answers in any column, space permitting. Columns you don't need to use should be left blank.

CONTINUE

16

$$x^3(x^2 - 10) = -9x$$

What is a solution to the above equation if $x > 0$?

17

$$w + x - y = 4$$
$$x - w + y = 6$$
$$3x - w = 8$$

In the system of equations above, what is the value of y?

18

$$\frac{11}{15}x - \frac{8}{15}x = \frac{1}{6} + \frac{1}{12}$$

What value of x satisfies the equation shown above?

19

At a sports memorabilia store, each football jersey costs $40 more than each hockey jersey. If 2 hockey jerseys and 4 football jerseys cost $1,000, how much does one hockey jersey cost? (Note: Disregard the $ sign when gridding your answer.)

20

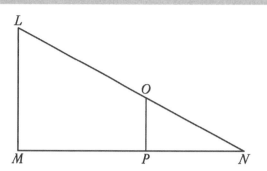

Note: Figure not drawn to scale

In the figure above, $\triangle LMN$ and $\triangle OPN$ are similar. The angles $\angle LMP$ and $\angle OPN$ are both right angles, and $LM = 9$, $OP = 6$, and $PN = 8$. What is the value of $\cos L$?

STOP

**If you finish before time is called, you may check your work on this section only.
Do not turn to any other section.**

Math Test – Calculator

55 MINUTES, 38 QUESTIONS

Turn to Section 4 of your answer sheet to answer the questions in this section.

DIRECTIONS

For questions 1–30, solve each problem, choose the best answer from the choices provided, and fill in the corresponding circle on your answer sheet. **For questions 31–38,** solve the problems and enter your answer in the grid on the answer sheet. Please refer to the directions before question 31 on how to enter your answers in the grid. You may use any available space in your test booklet for scratch work.

NOTES

1. The use of calculators **is permitted**.

2. All variables and expressions used represent real numbers unless otherwise indicated.

3. Figures provided in this test are drawn to scale unless otherwise indicated.

4. All figures lie in a plane unless otherwise indicated.

5. Unless otherwise indicated, the domain of a given function f is the set of real numbers x for which $f(x)$ is a real number.

REFERENCE

$A = \pi r^2$
$C = 2\pi r$

$A = \ell w$

$A = \dfrac{1}{2}bh$

$c^2 = a^2 + b^2$

Special Right Triangles

$V = \ell wh$

$V = \pi r^2 h$

$V = \dfrac{4}{3}\pi r^3$

$V = \dfrac{1}{3}\pi r^2 h$

$V = \dfrac{1}{3}\ell wh$

The number of degrees of arc in a circle is 360.
The number of radians of arc in a circle is 2π.
The sum of the measures in degrees of the angles in a triangle is 180.

CONTINUE

1

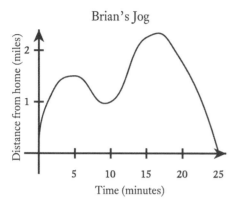

Brian's Jog

The graph above shows Brian's distance from his home during a 25-minute jog. He was feeling tired and was on his way home when he changed his mind and decided to run farther. Approximately how many minutes into his jog did Brian turn around to run farther?

A)   5 minutes

B)   9 minutes

C)   15 minutes

D)   20 minutes

2

The equation for momentum is $p = mv$, where p is momentum in kilogram meters per second, m is the mass of an object in kilograms, and v is the object's velocity in meters per second. If an object's momentum is 4 kg·m/s when its velocity is 12 m/s, what is its momentum when its velocity is 27 m/s, assuming the mass is constant?

A)   81 kg·m/s

B)   19 kg·m/s

C)   12 kg·m/s

D)   9 kg·m/s

3

Two out of every 45 people in line for a video game release are randomly chosen to receive a special prize. If there are 675 people in the line, how many will get a prize?

A) 54

B) 45

C) 30

D) 15

4

	Cream	No Cream	Total
Sugar	4	7	11
No Sugar	15	1	16
Total	19	8	27

The table above shows the distribution of coffee preferences among the members of the DC Book Club. If a club member is to be selected at random, what is the probability that the member will prefer his or her coffee with both sugar and cream or with no sugar and no cream?

A) $\dfrac{5}{27}$

B) $\dfrac{1}{4}$

C) $\dfrac{16}{27}$

D) $\dfrac{19}{27}$

CONTINUE

5

$$v_f = 6 + 2t$$

A biker has an initial velocity of 6 m/s (meters per second) before beginning to accelerate at a constant rate of 2 m/s² (meters per second squared). The equation above models the biker's final velocity v_f, in meters per second, in terms of the time t, in seconds, since the biker began accelerating. If the biker's velocity is 13 m/s, how many seconds has he been accelerating?

A) 3.5

B) 7

C) 9.5

D) 34

6

At Big Bob's Tackle shop, approximately 12 percent of shoppers are club members and 8 percent of shoppers are premium members. If there is no overlap between club and premium members and there were a total of 730 purchases made last week at Big Bob's, which of the following is most likely closest to the total number of club and premium members who made purchases last week?

A) 58

B) 88

C) 146

D) 584

7

$$R = 5x^2 - 13x + 2$$
$$S = -2x^2 + 2x + 7$$

Which of the following is equal to $R - S$?

A) $3x^2 + 15x - 5$

B) $3x^2 - 11x + 9$

C) $7x^2 - 15x - 5$

D) $7x^2 + 15x + 9$

8

The value of Carlos' car can be modeled by the equation $y = -3,046x + 24,000$, where x represents the number of years since he purchased the car, and y represents the value of the car. Which of the following best describes the meaning of the number 3,046 in the equation above?

A) The initial value of the car when Carlos purchased it

B) The estimated decrease in the value of the car per year

C) The value of the car x years after it was purchased

D) The amount that Carlos still owes on his car

9

For the function $C(x)$, $C(34) = 21$ and $C(53) = 44$.
For the function $R(x)$, $R(44) = 31$ and $R(23) = 21$.
What is $R(C(53))$?

A) 21

B) 31

C) 53

D) 94

▼

Questions 10 and 11 refer to the following information.

Car Model	Fuel Economy (miles/gallon)
Kia Soul Hybrid	105
Chevrolet Volt	93
Toyota Prius Hybrid	56
Ford Fusion	47
Honda Insight	42
Ford Mustang	26
Dodge Viper	16

The chart above shows approximations of the fuel

economy in miles per gallon for seven popular cars in

2015. The cost of gas for driving a car can be found by

using the formula $C = \dfrac{mg}{f}$, where C is the amount of

money expended on gas, m is the number of miles the

car is driven, g is the price of gas per gallon, and f is

the fuel efficiency of the car measured in miles per

gallon.

10

US Route 550 stretches 305 miles from Bernalillo, New Mexico to Montrose, Colorado. If gas costs $2.50 per gallon, how much must be spent on gas for a Kia Soul Hybrid to drive the entire length of US Route 550?

A) $0.86

B) $1.16

C) $4.49

D) $7.26

11

Gas prices fluctuate based on supply and demand. If a Ford Fusion can drive the length of Route 48 for only $12.97, how much would it cost a Ford Mustang to make the same drive at the same gas price?

A) $16.22

B) $23.45

C) $29.32

D) $46.92

▲

CONTINUE

4 **4**

12

For what value of x is $|x+2|+1=0$ true?

A) -3

B) -1

C) 0

D) For no value of x

13

$$\frac{1}{d_o} + \frac{1}{d_i} = \frac{1}{f}$$

The equation above is used to find the focal length f of a thin lens. When an object is placed at a distance d_o from a thin lens, it produces an image at a distance d_i from that lens. Which of the following gives d_i in terms of d_o and f ?

A) $f - d_o$

B) $\dfrac{1}{f - d_o}$

C) $\dfrac{f\,d_o}{d_o - f}$

D) $\dfrac{f - d_o}{f\,d_o}$

14

	Roast Beef	Turkey	Peanut Butter and Jelly	Total
Male	48	33	78	159
Female	51	40	50	141
Total	99	73	128	300

All of the students at a high school lunch were asked what their preferred sandwich was among roast beef, turkey, and peanut butter and jelly. Which of the following comprised 26 percent of those surveyed?

A) Males who prefer roast beef

B) People who prefer turkey

C) Females who prefer peanut butter and jelly

D) Males who prefer peanut butter and jelly

15

The Leghorn is a breed of chicken originating in Italy. It is a good layer of white eggs, laying an average of 280 eggs per year. Which of the following equations represents n, the average number of <u>dozens</u> of eggs produced by a Leghorn chicken in m <u>months</u>?

A) $n = \dfrac{280m}{(12)(12)}$

B) $n = \dfrac{280m}{12}$

C) $n = 12m + 280$

D) $n = 280m$

CONTINUE

Questions 16 and 17 refer to the following information.

	Education	Environment & Recreation	Health Care	Human Services	Infrastructure, Housing & Economic Development	Law & Public Safety
FY16	7,718,943	211,233	18,608,181	4,103,619	2,284,184	2,620,984
FY15	7,478,954	197,421	17,616,167	3,956,955	2,201,409	2,644,481
FY14	7,284,482	188,161	16,284,388	3,696,711	2,114,165	2,566,129
FY13	6,933,564	176,208	14,956,428	3,502,458	1,765,973	2,451,851

Adapted from Massachusetts Budget and Policy Center website.

The table above lists the Massachusetts budgets (in thousands of dollars) for some government programs during several fiscal years.

16

Which of the following best approximates the average rate of change in the yearly budget for education during the fiscal years shown?

A) $200 million

B) $260 million

C) $350 million

D) $790 million

17

Which ratio is closest to that of the budget for Human Services in FY15 to that of FY14?

A) Law & Public Safety FY15 to FY14

B) Environment & Recreation FY16 to FY15

C) Health Care FY15 to FY14

D) Infrastructure, Housing & Economic Development FY14 to FY13

CONTINUE

18

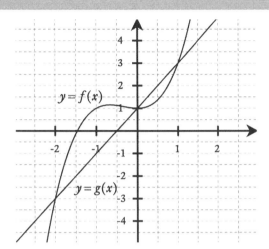

Graphs of the functions f and g are shown in the xy-plane above. For how many of the values of x in the domain pictured above does $f(x) + g(x) = 2f(x)$?

A) 0

B) 1

C) 2

D) 3

19

	Spent under $100	Spent $100 or more
Shopped online	19	56
Shopped at the mall	36	39

A survey was done of people who spent an hour shopping in a mall and online, recording whether they spent more or less than $100. The results are shown above. If one of those who spent under $100 were randomly selected for further questioning, what is the probability that they shopped at the mall?

A) $\frac{39}{95}$

B) $\frac{36}{75}$

C) $\frac{36}{55}$

D) $\frac{19}{75}$

CONTINUE

Questions 20 and 21 refer to the following information.

Perry is selling lemonade at the county fair, and his profit $P(n)$, in dollars, can be modeled by the equation $P(n) = \frac{5}{2}n - 12$, where n equals the number of cups he sells. His sister Jasmine is selling orange juice at the same fair, and her profit $J(n)$, in dollars, can be modeled by the equation $J(n) = 4n - 30$, where n equals the number of cups she sells.

20

By how many dollars does each cup of orange juice sold affect the profit that Jasmine makes?

A)   4

B) $\frac{5}{2}$

C) -12

D) -30

21

In the morning, Perry and Jasmine each manage to sell 32 cups of juice. Which of the following describes their relative profits as n increases?

A) Initially Perry had a greater profit, but after they had each sold 12 cups of juice Jasmine had the greater profit.

B) Initially Jasmine had a greater profit, but after they had each sold 12 cups of juice Perry had the greater profit.

C) Initially Perry had a greater profit, but after they had each sold 18 cups of juice Jasmine had a greater profit.

D) Initially Jasmine had a greater profit, but after they had each sold 18 cups of juice Perry had a greater profit.

22

Which of the following is the equation for a circle with a diameter whose endpoints are at $(-2, 6)$ and $(6, 0)$?

A) $(x-4)^2 + (y-3)^2 = 13$

B) $(x-2)^2 + (y-3)^2 = 25$

C) $(x-2)^2 + (y-3)^2 = 100$

D) $(x-6)^2 + y^2 = 100$

CONTINUE

23

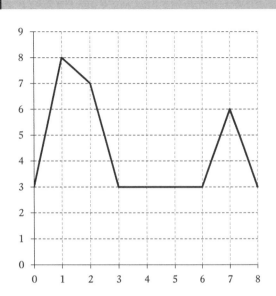

The graph above is that of the function $g(x)$. Which of the following is equal to 3?

     I. $g(0)$
     I. $g(3)$
     II. $g\left(\dfrac{11}{2}\right)$

A) I and II
B) II only
C) I, II, and III
D) None of the above

24

$$h = -4.9t^2 + 14t + 2$$

David found a stone on the beach. He threw the stone upward with an initial velocity of 14 meters per second from 2 meters in the air. The stone is caught by David's friend at the same height at which David released it. The equation above models the height h, in meters, of the stone in terms of the time t, in seconds. After approximately how many seconds does David's friend catch the stone?

A) 0.4
B) 2.9
C) 3.0
D) 4.9

CONTINUE

Jane thinks her homework will take x hours, where x is greater than 3. She tells her friend that the amount of time her homework actually takes will be within 15 minutes of her estimate. If what Jane tells her friend is true, and it takes her y hours to finish her homework, then which of the following accurately describes the relationship between Jane's estimate and the actual result?

A) $|y - x| = 15$

B) $|y - x| < 15$

C) $-0.25 < y - x < 0.25$

D) $y - x < 2.75$

26

In order to determine if generic cold medicine is as effective in remedying the symptoms of a cold as name-brand cold medicine, a research study was conducted. From a large population of people, 200 people with colds were randomly selected. Half of the participants chose to receive the name-brand medicine, and half chose to receive the generic medicine. The resulting data showed that participants who received name-brand cold medicine had significantly improved cold symptoms as compared to those who received the generic medicine. Based on the design and results of the study, which of the following is the best conclusion?

A) The results prove that name-brand medicine can improve cold symptoms better than generic medicine.

B) The results prove that generic medicine is not effective in treating cold symptoms.

C) The results are questionable because of how participants were assigned to their groups.

D) The results are questionable because the experiment needs to be repeated with more participants.

	Regular Sales	3D Sales	Total Sales
Space Battles			$3,040
Servitors			$1,272

The table above shows the sales for a Monday matinee at Bob's Movie Barn. Regular tickets cost $10 and 3D tickets cost $14. If *Space Battles* sold twice as many 3D tickets as regular, and if *Servitors* sold 25 percent more regular tickets than 3D tickets, which of the following is closest to the percent of the revenue from ticket sales that were from 3D shows?

A) 52%

B) 53%

C) 68%

D) 74%

CONTINUE

28

During a road trip, George drove 35 percent more miles today than he did yesterday. If he drove 428 miles today, how many miles did he drive yesterday (rounded to the nearest whole mile)?

A) 317

B) 349

C) 393

D) 578

29

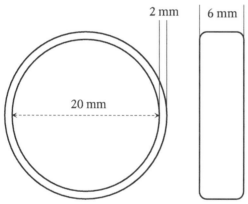

The above diagram shows the design for a simple gold wedding band. Which of the following is closest to the volume of gold necessary to make this wedding band?

A)   830 mm^3

B)   1440 mm^3

C)   1580 mm^3

D)   3320 mm^3

30

A line given by the equation $y = mx$ passes through the points $(27, k)$ and $(k, 48)$. What is the value of m?

A) $\dfrac{3}{4}$

B) $\dfrac{9}{16}$

C) $\dfrac{4}{3}$

D) $\dfrac{16}{9}$

CONTINUE

DIRECTIONS

For questions 31–38, solve the problem and enter your answer in the grid, as described below, on the answer sheet.

1. Although not required, it is suggested that you write your answer in the boxes at the top of the columns to help you fill in the circles accurately. You will receive credit only if the circles are filled in correctly.
2. Mark no more than one circle in any column.
3. No question has a negative answer.
4. Some problems may have more than one correct answer. In such cases, grid only one answer.
5. **Mixed numbers** such as $3\frac{1}{2}$ must be be gridded as 3.5 or 7/2. If $3\,1\,/\,2$ is entered into the grid, it will be interpreted as $\frac{31}{2}$, not $3\frac{1}{2}$.)
6. **Decimal answers:** If you obtain a decimal answer with more digits than the grid can accommodate, it may be either rounded or truncated, but it must fill the entire grid.

Answer: $\frac{7}{13}$

Write answer in boxes →

← Fraction line

Grid in result

Answer: 2.5

← Decimal Point

Acceptable ways to grid $\frac{2}{3}$ are:

Answer: 210 – either position is correct

NOTE: You may start your answers in any column, space permitting. Columns you don't need to use should be left blank.

31

Year	Number of Gold Medals
1984	83
1988	36
1992	37
1996	44
2000	40
2004	35
2008	36
2012	46

The table above shows the number of Gold Medals won by the United States during each Summer Olympics since 1984. What is the difference between the median and the mode of the number of gold medals won?

32

In a board game, each player starts with a certain number of points. The goal is to get rid of all of the chips one has. For every chip a player has at the end of the game, the player loses 3 points. At the end of the game, one of the players had 50 points and had 50 chips. How many points did the player start with?

33

$$-x(2x+1)+x(7+x)$$

If the expression above is rewritten in the form $ax^2 + bx + c$, where a, b, and c are constants, what is the value of $a + b$?

4 **4**

34

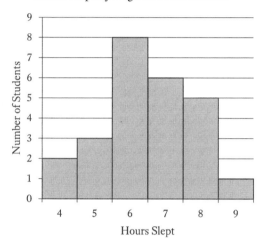

Hours Slept by High School Students

The histogram above shows the number of hours slept the previous night by a group of teenagers. Based on the histogram, what was the average number of hours slept, rounded to the nearest hundredth?

35

Brian has a square-shaped patio. He decides to extend the length so that it will be 5 feet shorter than 5 times the width. If the final area of the patio will be 1,050 square feet, what is the length, in feet, of one side of the patio before the extension?

36

Ignacio sells refurbished guitars. In order to maintain his profit margin, Ignacio must sell his guitars for an average price of $500. This month he's already sold 11 guitars for $425 each and 3 guitars for $475 each. If Ignacio has 6 more guitars to sell, what must be the average price of these last guitars in order to maintain his profit margin? (Note: Disregard the $ sign when gridding your answer.)

CONTINUE

4 4

Questions 37 and 38 refer to the following information.

Supercomputer *LEP*, at a military base, can do 2 million calculations in one second. Moore's Law says that computer chip performance doubles every 2 years. The military base always uses the most current technology to upgrade its supercomputers, so in 4 years, supercomputer *LEP* will do 8 million calculations in one second according to Moore's Law.

37

A military spy camera with a 3.2 gigapixel lens requires a computer that can do 1.92 billion calculations per <u>minute</u>. In how many years will supercomputer *LEP* be able to power the spy camera?

38

How many times more powerful, in calculations per second, is supercomputer *LEP* now than it was 20 years ago?

STOP

If you finish before time is called, you may check your work on this section only.
Do not turn to any other section.

SAT Practice Test 3

IMPORTANT REMINDERS

A No. 2 pencil is required for the test.
Do not use a mechanical pencil or pen.

Sharing any questions with anyone is a violation
of the Test Security and Fairness policies and
may result in your score being canceled.

This cover is representative of what you will see on the day of the SAT.

Reading Test

65 MINUTES, 52 QUESTIONS

Turn to Section 1 of your answer sheet to answer the questions in this section.

DIRECTIONS

Each passage or pair of passages below is followed by a number of questions. After reading each passage or pair, choose the best answer to each question based on what is stated or implied in the passage or passages and in any accompanying graphics (such as a table or graph).

Questions 1–10 are based on the following passage.

This passage is adapted from Charles Dickens, *Hard Times*, originally published in 1854.

Thomas Gradgrind, sir. A man of realities. A man of facts and calculations. A man who proceeds upon the principle that two and two are four, and nothing over, and who is not to be talked into allowing for

5 anything over. Thomas Gradgrind, sir—peremptorily Thomas—Thomas Gradgrind. With a rule and a pair of scales, and the multiplication table always in his pocket, sir, ready to weigh and measure any parcel of human nature, and tell you exactly what it comes to.

10 It is a mere question of figures, a case of simple arithmetic. You might hope to get some other nonsensical belief into the head of George Gradgrind, or Augustus Gradgrind, or John Gradgrind, or Joseph Gradgrind (all supposititious, non-existent persons),

15 but into the head of Thomas Gradgrind—no, sir!

In such terms Mr. Gradgrind always mentally introduced himself, whether to his private circle of acquaintance, or to the public in general. In such terms, no doubt, substituting the words "boys and

20 girls," for "sir," Thomas Gradgrind now presented Thomas Gradgrind to the little pitchers before him, who were to be filled so full of facts.

Indeed, as he eagerly sparkled at them from the cellarage before mentioned, he seemed a kind of

25 cannon loaded to the muzzle with facts, and prepared to blow them clean out of the regions of childhood at one discharge. He seemed a galvanizing apparatus, too, charged with a grim mechanical substitute for the tender young imaginations that were to be

30 stormed away.

"Girl number twenty," said Mr. Gradgrind, squarely pointing with his square forefinger, "I don't know that girl. Who is that girl?"

"Sissy Jupe, sir," explained number twenty,

35 blushing, standing up, and curtseying.

"Sissy is not a name," said Mr. Gradgrind. "Don't call yourself Sissy. Call yourself Cecilia."

"It's father as calls me Sissy, sir," returned the young girl in a trembling voice, and with another

40 curtsey.

"Then he has no business to do it," said Mr. Gradgrind. "Tell him he mustn't. Cecilia Jupe. Let me see. What is your father?"

"He belongs to the horse-riding, if you please,

45 sir."

Mr. Gradgrind frowned, and waved off the objectionable calling with his hand.

"We don't want to know anything about that, here. You mustn't tell us about that, here. Your father

50 breaks horses, don't he?"

"If you please, sir, when they can get any to break, they do break horses in the ring, sir."

"You mustn't tell us about the ring, here. Very well, then. Describe your father as a horsebreaker. He

55 doctors sick horses, I dare say?"

"Oh yes, sir."

"Very well, then. He is a veterinary surgeon, a farrier, and horsebreaker. Give me your definition of a horse."

CONTINUE

60   (Sissy Jupe thrown into the greatest alarm by this
     demand.)
        "Girl number twenty unable to define a horse!"
     said Mr. Gradgrind, for the general behoof of all the
     little pitchers. "Girl number twenty possessed of no
65   facts, in reference to one of the commonest of
     animals! Some boy's definition of a horse. Bitzer,
     yours."
        The square finger, moving here and there, lighted
     suddenly on Bitzer, perhaps because he chanced to sit
70   in the same ray of sunlight which, darting in at one of
     the bare windows of the intensely white-washed
     room, irradiated Sissy. His cold eyes would hardly
     have been eyes, but for the short ends of lashes
     which, by bringing them into immediate contrast with
75   something paler than themselves, expressed their
     form. His short-cropped hair might have been a mere
     continuation of the sandy freckles on his forehead
     and face. His skin was so unwholesomely deficient in
     the natural tinge, that he looked as though, if he were
80   cut, he would bleed white.
        "Bitzer," said Thomas Gradgrind. "Your
     definition of a horse."
        "Quadruped. Graminivorous. Forty teeth, namely
     twenty-four grinders, four eye-teeth, and twelve
85   incisive. Sheds coat in the spring; in marshy
     countries, sheds hoofs, too. Hoofs hard, but requiring
     to be shod with iron. Age known by marks in mouth."
     Thus (and much more) Bitzer.
        "Now girl number twenty," said Mr. Gradgrind.
90   "You know what a horse is."

1

The first paragraph (lines 1–15) primarily serves to

A) describe a character's habitual activities,
    personal interests, and passionately held beliefs.

B) characterize the seriousness of one man's
    approach to life.

C) introduce the ways in which a certain teacher is
    different from his students.

D) clarify to readers that they should not suppose
    Gradgrind will be like his relatives.

2

The author refers to the students as "little pitchers"
(lines 21 and 63) in order to

A) hint at their tendency to misbehave and cause
    disruptions.

B) reveal how insignificant their ideas are relative to
    those of their teacher.

C) use a metaphor to indicate their desire for
    greater knowledge.

D) show that Gradgrind views them as merely
    vessels to be filled with facts.

3

Based on the descriptions in the passage, Thomas
Gradgrind views his task with his pupils primarily as

A) solving a problem using the methods and tools of
    modern science.

B) sternly reprimanding students so that they will
    be more obedient to him.

C) violently replacing ignorance and imagination
    with accurate information.

D) personally mentoring them as they move from
    childhood to maturity.

4

Which choice provides the best evidence for the
answer to the previous question?

A) Lines 2–11 ("A man … arithmetic")

B) Lines 24–30 ("he seemed … away")

C) Lines 67–75 ("The square … form")

D) Lines 82–87 ("Quadruped … Bitzer")

CONTINUE

5

In line 27, the word "discharge" most nearly means

A) emancipation.

B) shot.

C) excrescence.

D) lesson.

6

In line 62, the word "behoof" most nearly means

A) putting on of horseshoes.

B) taking away of difficulties.

C) mockery.

D) benefit.

7

The narrator suggests that Mr. Gradgrind may have called upon Bitzer because of

A) Bitzer's physical location relative to Sissy.

B) Gradgrind's confidence in Bitzer's superior knowledge of horses.

C) Bitzer's clipped way of providing accurate, factual information in response to questions.

D) Gradgrind's own lack of certainty about the answer.

8

Which choice provides the best evidence for the answer to the previous question?

A) Lines 61–66 ("Girl … yours")

B) Lines 67–71 ("The square … Sissy")

C) Lines 71–77 ("His cold … face")

D) Lines 82–87 ("Quadruped … Bitzer")

9

Bitzer's definition of a horse is

A) personal, being based on his own experiences with his father.

B) impertinent, for he has shown himself to be too pedantic in his explanation.

C) incorrect in context but accurate based on his own limited understanding.

D) accurate insofar as it relays many factual details about the animal.

10

The tone of Mr. Gradgrind's words to Sissy (lines 88–89) after hearing Bitzer's definition is

A) ironic: Sissy already knew what a horse was, and thus did not need the definition.

B) mocking: Bitzer's definition was foolish, and now he must provide a better definition for both of them.

C) gloating: Bitzer's answer evinced the success of his method in its thorough-going attention to specific detail.

D) relieved: he no longer has to explain things to Sissy, whose ignorance annoys him.

Questions 11-20 are based on the following passage.

This passage is adapted from President Ronald Reagan's speech to a joint session of Congress on the Program for Economic Recovery, April 28, 1981.

It's been half a year since the election that charged all of us in this government with the task of restoring our economy. And where have we come in these six months? Inflation, as measured by the Consumer

5 Price Index, has continued at a double-digit rate. Mortgage interest rates have averaged almost 15 percent for these six months, preventing families across America from buying homes. There are still almost eight million unemployed. The average

10 worker's hourly earnings after adjusting for inflation are lower today than they were six months ago, and there have been over 6,000 business failures.

Six months is long enough. The American people now want us to act and not in half-measures. They

15 demand and they've earned a full and comprehensive effort to clean up our economic mess. Because of the extent of our economy's sickness, we know that the cure will not come quickly and that even with our package, progress will come in inches and feet, not in

20 miles. But to fail to act will delay even longer and more painfully the cure which must come. And that cure begins with the federal budget. And the budgetary actions taken by the Congress over the next few days will determine how we respond to the

25 message of last November 4th. That message was very simple. Our government is too big, and it spends too much.

For the last few months, you and I have enjoyed a relationship based on extraordinary cooperation.

30 Because of this cooperation we've come a long distance in less than three months. I want to thank the leadership of the Congress for helping in setting a fair timetable for consideration of our recommendations. And committee chairmen on both

35 sides of the aisle have called prompt and thorough hearings. We have also communicated in a spirit of candor, openness, and mutual respect. Tonight, as our decision day nears and as the House of Representatives weighs its alternatives, I wish to

40 address you in that same spirit.

The Senate Budget Committee, under the leadership of Pete Domenici, has just today voted out a budget resolution supported by Democrats and

Republicans alike that is in all major respects

45 consistent with the program that we have proposed. Now we look forward to favorable action on the Senate floor, but an equally crucial test involves the House of Representatives. The House will soon be choosing between two different versions or measures

50 to deal with the economy. One is the measure offered by the House Budget Committee. The other is a bipartisan measure, a substitute introduced by Congressmen Phil Gramm of Texas and Del Latta of Ohio.

55   On behalf of the Administration, let me say that we embrace and fully support that bipartisan substitute. It will achieve all the essential aims of controlling government spending, reducing the tax burden, building a national defense second to none,

60 and stimulating economic growth and creating millions of new jobs. At the same time, however, I must state our opposition to the measure offered by the House Budget Committee. It may appear that we have two alternatives. In reality, however, there are

65 no more alternatives left.

The committee measure quite simply falls far too short of the essential actions that we must take. For example, in the next three years, the committee measure projects spending $141 billion more than

70 does the bipartisan substitute. It regrettably cuts over $14 billion in essential defense spending, funding required to restore America's national security. It adheres to the failed policy of trying to balance the budget on the taxpayer's back. It would increase tax

75 payments over a third, adding up to a staggering quarter of a trillion dollars. Federal taxes would increase 12 percent each year. Taxpayers would be paying a larger share of their income to the government in 1984 than they do at present. In short,

80 that measure reflects an echo of the past rather than a benchmark for the future. High taxes and excess spending growth created our present economic mess; more of the same will not cure the hardship, anxiety, and discouragement it has imposed on the American

85 people.

Let us cut through the fog for a moment. The answer to a government that's too big is to stop feeding its growth. Government spending has been growing faster than the economy itself. The massive

90 national debt which we accumulated is the result of

CONTINUE

the government's high spending diet. Well, it's time to change the diet and to change it in the right way.

Inflation Rates in America 1975–1985
as of January 1

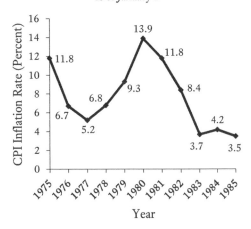

Adapted from the US Bureau of Labor and Statistics website.

11

From this passage it can be inferred that Reagan's primary goal is to

A) reduce inflation and mortgage interest rates expediently because they are damaging the economy.

B) work with Congress to create more job opportunities with higher wages to help those who are unemployed.

C) introduce a stimulus package in Congress because increasing government spending will fuel economic recovery.

D) encourage Congress to pass a bipartisan measure that will control government spending.

12

The primary purpose of the first paragraph (lines 1–12) is to

A) portray the American economy in a state of irreparable disaster.

B) highlight the failures of Congress in the past six months.

C) provide significant context for the need to restore the economy.

D) show several conflicting metrics for measuring the state of the economy.

Which of the following suggestions conflicts most with Reagan's views in lines 13–27?

A) Congress must increase government spending on infrastructure to help the economy improve gradually.

B) Congress must implement comprehensive measures because the economy is in a state of disrepair and needs drastic change.

C) Congress must act swiftly and decisively because the American people are frustrated and demand action.

D) Congress must shrink the size of the federal budget because the government is recklessly spending too much money.

In line 37, "candor" most nearly means

A) sincere obfuscation.

B) careful reverence.

C) impartial honesty.

D) cloaked partisanship.

15

Which of the following is a specific reason Reagan recommends rejecting the House Budget Committee's measure?

A) It was not introduced by the Senate Budget Committee and thus is not bipartisan in its origins.

B) It cuts spending on the development of necessary weapons for national defense.

C) It does not go far enough to reduce government spending.

D) It would raise taxes on too many Americans for the benefit of too few.

16

Which choice provides the best evidence for the answer to the previous question?

A) Lines 61–63 ("At the same … Committee")

B) Lines 66–70 ("The committee … substitute")

C) Lines 79–81 ("In short … future")

D) Lines 83–85 ("more of … people")

17

In line 86, "cut through the fog" most nearly means

A) deeply contemplate the issue.

B) clarify what has been obscured.

C) attack the problem.

D) identify what is clouding the issue.

18

An economist claims that inflation rates had already begun to fall prior to the implementation of the proposals discussed in this passage. Does evidence from the passage or the graph support this claim?

A) No; lines 3–5 ("And where … rate") prove that the rate was still rising.

B) No; the graph shows that inflation rates reached their height during 1981.

C) Yes; lines 57–61 ("It will … jobs") suggest what has already been accomplished.

D) Yes; the graph shows that inflation rates were lower by the start of 1981.

19

The graph shows that, prior to "the election that charged all of us in this government with the task of restoring our economy" (lines 1–3), inflation rates had

A) consistently increased for over a decade.

B) more than doubled since 1977.

C) not directly impacted overall economic growth.

D) outpaced mortgage interest rates.

20

Based on the graph one can infer that 1977–1983 was a period of

A) economic stability.

B) economic expansion.

C) economic recession.

D) economic change.

CONTINUE

Questions 21–31 are based on the following passages.

The following passages discuss explanations for the variety and similarity among biological species. Passage 1 is adapted from Robert Chambers, *Vestiges of the Natural History of Creation*, first published in 1844. Passage 2 is adapted from Charles Darwin, *On the Origin of Species*, first published in 1859.

Passage 1

Confining our attention, in the meantime, to the animal kingdom—it does not appear that this gradation passes along one line, on which every form of animal life can be, as it were, strung; there may be
5   branching or double lines at some places; or the whole may be in a circle composed of minor circles, as has been recently suggested. But still it is incontestable that there are general appearances of a scale beginning with the simple and advancing to the
10 complicated. The animal kingdom was divided by Cuvier into four sub-kingdoms, or divisions, and these exhibit an unequivocal gradation in the order in which they are here enumerated: Radiata (polypes), mollusca (pulpy animals), articulate (jointed
15 animals), vertebrate (animals with internal skeleton). The gradation can, in like manner, be clearly traced in the classes into which the sub-kingdoms are Subdivided, as, for instance, when we take those of the vertebrate in this order—reptiles, fishes, birds,
20 mammals.

While the external forms of all these various animals are so different, it is very remarkable that the whole are, after all, variations of a fundamental plan, which can be traced as a basis throughout the whole,
25 the variations being merely modifications of that plan to suit the particular conditions in which each particular animal has been designed to live. Starting from the primeval germ, which, as we have seen, is the *representative* of a particular order of full-grown
30 animals, we find all others to be merely advances from that type, with the extension of endowments and modification of forms which are required in each particular case; each form, also, retaining a strong affinity to that which precedes it, and tending to
35 impress its own features on that which succeeds.

Passage 2

In considering the Origin of Species, it is quite conceivable that a naturalist, reflecting on the mutual affinities of organic beings, on their embryological relations, their geographical distribution, geological
40 succession, and other such facts, might come to the conclusion that each species had not been independently created, but had descended, like varieties, from other species. Nevertheless, such a conclusion, even if well founded, would be
45 unsatisfactory, until it could be shown how the innumerable species inhabiting this world have been modified so as to acquire that perfection of structure and co-adaptation which most justly excites our admiration. Naturalists continually refer to external
50 conditions, such as climate, food, etc., as the only possible cause of variation. In one very limited sense, as we shall hereafter see, this may be true; but it is preposterous to attribute to mere external conditions, the structure, for instance, of the woodpecker, with
55 its feet, tail, beak, and tongue, so admirably adapted to catch insects under the bark of trees. In the case of the mistletoe, which draws its nourishment from certain trees, which has seeds that must be transported by certain birds, and which has flowers
60 with separate sexes absolutely requiring the agency of certain insects to bring pollen from one flower to the other, it is equally preposterous to account for the structure of this parasite, with its relations to several distinct organic beings, by the effects of external
65 conditions, or of habit, or of the volition of the plant itself.

The author of the "Vestiges of Creation" would, I presume, say that, after a certain unknown number of generations, some bird had given birth to a
70 woodpecker, and some plant to the mistletoe, and that these had been produced perfect as we now see them; but this assumption seems to me to be no explanation, for it leaves the cause of the coadaptations of organic beings to each other and to
75 their physical conditions of life, untouched and unexplained.

It is, therefore, of the highest importance to gain a clear insight into the means of modification and coadaptation. As many more individuals of each
80 species are born than can possibly survive; and as, consequently, there is a frequently recurring struggle

for existence, it follows that any being, if it vary however slightly in any manner profitable to itself, under the complex and sometimes varying conditions
85 of life, will have a better chance of surviving, and thus be naturally selected. From the strong principle of inheritance, any selected variety will tend to propagate its new and modified form.

21

In listing the sub-kingdoms of animals in lines 13–15, the author intends to arrange them from

A) most complicated to least sophisticated.

B) least similar to humans to most similar to humans.

C) smallest to largest.

D) simplest to most complex.

22

In contrasting the analogy of "gradation … along one line" (line 3) with that of "a circle composed of minor circles" (line 6), the author shows

A) that biological life varies in complexity based on simple, predictable steps.

B) that the variations among biological life-forms are more complex than a single line can illustrate.

C) how the varied shapes of life-forms indicate their position in the gradation of kingdoms.

D) the inaccuracy of Cuvier's model of kingdoms and sub-kingdoms of life.

23

In line 35, the word "impress" most nearly means

A) influence.

B) amaze.

C) infer.

D) imprint.

24

In passage 1, the author's use of the words "fundamental plan" (line 23) and "designed" (line 27) suggest

A) that variations in animal species are present according to a deliberate intention.

B) the relationship of specific instances of biological diversity to the overall pattern.

C) the method by which specific variations of life that exist in nature came to be.

D) an ironic mockery of the ideas to which the author is fundamentally opposed.

25

In lines 37–38, the phrase "mutual affinities" most nearly means

A) shared values.

B) united affections.

C) shared similarities.

D) visible attributes.

26

The author of passage 2 suggests that the specific variations evident in living things are best accounted for by

A) a new form of life being brought forth from an existing form spontaneously.

B) existing forms of life choosing to alter specific attributes as an act of their own will.

C) attributes that increase the likelihood of survival naturally predominating in the inheritance of characteristics.

D) each form of life being designed specifically to suit its climate, geography, and purpose.

CONTINUE

27

Which choice provides the best evidence for the answer to the previous question?

A) lines 36–43 ("it … species")

B) lines 56–66 ("In … itself")

C) lines 68–76 ("after … unexplained")

D) lines 79–88 ("As … form")

28

The repeated use of the word "preposterous" (lines 53 and 62) in passage 2 serves primarily to

A) reveal the significance and novelty of the author's findings.

B) mock the unscientific methods that others have used to draw their conclusions.

C) remind the audience that theories are not untrue simply because they are improbable.

D) emphasize the absurdity of a particular explanation when carried to its logical conclusion.

29

The second passage responds to the first by

A) making use of its most important data and its biological perspective but disagreeing with its fundamental conclusions.

B) agreeing with its central observations but offering an explanation for the mechanism behind the phenomena discussed.

C) describing as foolish and misguided methodologies employed by the author of passage 1.

D) concurring with its author's final conclusions but quibbling with the logical structure of the argument.

30

The author of passage 2 would respond to the explanation given in lines 27–35 ("Starting … succeeds") by

A) criticizing the author for failing to explain how these advancements took place.

B) denying the possible existence of a primeval germ, making the conclusion specious.

C) agreeing with the specific observation but limiting the scope of the conclusions that can be drawn from it.

D) pointing out the lack of verifiable evidence to support the specific conclusion drawn.

31

Which choice provides the best evidence for the answer to the previous question?

A) lines 67–70 ("The author … mistletoe")

B) lines 72–76 ("but … unexplained")

C) lines 77–79 ("It is … coadaptation")

D) lines 86–88 ("From … form")

CONTINUE

Questions 32–42 are based on the following passage.

The following passage is adapted from Nelson Mandela, "I Am Prepared to Die," originally delivered on April 20, 1964. Mandela gave this speech as the opening statement of his defense case in the Rivonia Trial in Pretoria, South Africa.

The lack of human dignity experienced by Africans is the direct result of the policy of white supremacy. White supremacy implies black inferiority. Legislation designed to preserve white
5 supremacy entrenches this notion. Menial tasks in South Africa are invariably performed by Africans. When anything has to be carried or cleaned the white man will look around for an African to do it for him, whether the African is employed by him or not.
10 Because of this sort of attitude, whites tend to regard Africans as a separate breed. They do not look upon them as people with families of their own; they do not realize that they have emotions—that they fall in love like white people do; that they want to be with
15 their wives and children like white people want to be with theirs; that they want to earn enough money to support their families properly, to feed and clothe them and send them to school. And what "house-boy" or "garden-boy" or laborer can ever hope to do
20 this?

Pass laws, which to the Africans are among the most hated bits of legislation in South Africa, render any African liable to police surveillance at any time. I doubt whether there is a single African male in South
25 Africa who has not at some stage had a brush with the police over his pass. Hundreds and thousands of Africans are thrown into jail each year under pass laws. Even worse than this is the fact that pass laws keep husband and wife apart and lead to the
30 breakdown of family life.

Poverty and the breakdown of family life have secondary effects. Children wander about the streets of the townships because they have no schools to go to, or no money to enable them to go to school, or no
35 parents at home to see that they go to school, because both parents (if there be two) have to work to keep the family alive. This leads to a breakdown in moral standards, to an alarming rise in illegitimacy, and to growing violence which erupts everywhere. Life in
40 the townships is dangerous. There is not a day that goes by without somebody being stabbed or assaulted. And violence is carried out of the townships into the white living areas. People are afraid to walk alone in the streets after dark.
45 Housebreakings and robberies are increasing, despite the fact that the death sentence can now be imposed for such offences. Death sentences cannot cure the festering sore.

The only cure is to alter the conditions under
50 which Africans are forced to live and to meet their legitimate grievances. Africans want to be paid a living wage. Africans want to perform work which they are capable of doing, and not work which the Government declares them to be capable of. Africans
55 want to be allowed to live where they obtain work, and not be endorsed out of an area because they were not born there. Africans want to be allowed to own land in places where they work, and not to be obliged to live in rented houses which they can never call
60 their own. Africans want to be part of the general population, and not confined to living in their own ghettoes. African men want to have their wives and children live with them where they work, and not be forced into an unnatural existence in men's hostels.
65 African women want to be with their menfolk and not be left permanently widowed in the Reserves. Africans want to be allowed out after eleven o'clock at night and not to be confined to their rooms like little children. Africans want to be allowed to travel in
70 their own country and to seek work where they want to and not where the Labor Bureau tells them to. Africans want a just share in the whole of South Africa; they want security and a stake in society.

Above all, we want equal political rights, because
75 without them our disabilities will be permanent. I know this sounds revolutionary to the whites in this country, because the majority of voters will be Africans. This makes the white man fear democracy.

But this fear cannot be allowed to stand in the way
80 of the only solution which will guarantee racial harmony and freedom for all. It is not true that the enfranchisement of all will result in racial domination. Political division, based on color, is entirely artificial and, when it disappears, so will the
85 domination of one color group by another.

CONTINUE

During my lifetime, I have cherished the ideal of a democratic and free society in which all persons live together in harmony and with equal opportunities. It is an ideal which I hope to live for and to achieve. But
90 if needs be, it is an ideal for which I am prepared to die.

32

Based on the passage as a whole, what is the author's main point?

A) Africans need political power so that they will be able to control the government since they are the majority.

B) White people in South Africa are racist in both their official policies and personal attitudes towards Africans.

C) Africans need equal rights, in part because of the social problems created by inequality.

D) The standard of living for Africans is appalling, and policies have to be put in place to provide assistance to them.

33

In line 5, "menial" most nearly means

A) lowly.

B) manual.

C) easy.

D) sycophantic.

34

Which of the following best reflects how the author suggests whites view Africans?

A) Africans cannot be trusted to work in areas where whites are the dominant race.

B) Africans exist to serve whites by doing things that they consider beneath them.

C) Africans deserve basic human rights, but should be kept separate, maintaining Apartheid.

D) Africans are inherently inferior to whites morally, physically, and mentally.

35

Which choice provides the best evidence for the answer to the previous question?

A) Lines 1–5 ("The lack … notion")

B) Lines 5–9 ("Menial … not")

C) Lines 37–40 ("This … dangerous")

D) Lines 45–48 ("Housebreakings … sore")

36

In terms of the argument as a whole, the primary function of the third paragraph (lines 31–48) is to

A) enumerate unintended consequences of a discriminatory policy referenced in the previous paragraph.

B) contrast the list of the benefits of a law explained earlier in the passage by examining its societal costs.

C) explain ways in which Africans have changed in order to show that they haven't always been dangerous.

D) provide an example of a rule that is based on the assumption of white supremacy mentioned at the beginning of the passage.

37

As it is used in line 50, the word "meet" most nearly means

A) come together with.

B) deal with.

C) match up with.

D) coincide with.

CONTINUE

1

1

38

The author uses a repetitive sentence structure in the fourth paragraph (lines 49–73) in order to

A) criticize the government for its failure to enforce regulations, which has allowed poor conditions to become so widespread.

B) stress the importance of the restrictions on Africans but show that they do not go far enough to address the real problem.

C) emphasize the distance between what Africans want and what their government allows them to do.

D) reveal the value of reasonable aspirations and contrast them with the poor outcomes of those desires.

39

Based on the author's views, what is the main reason white South Africans resist granting equal rights to Africans?

A) They worry that they will no longer have social inferiors to do tasks they prefer not to themselves.

B) They believe that equality will enable Africans to continue their criminal behavior and make society less safe as a whole.

C) They fear it would result in the overturning of pass laws, which protect white people from African crime.

D) They are concerned that African political power will be too great if they represent a majority of voters.

40

Which choice provides the best evidence for the answer to the previous question?

A) Lines 21–23 ("Pass ... time")

B) Lines 45–48 ("Housebreakings ... sore")

C) Lines 75–78 ("I know ... democracy")

D) Lines 81–85 ("It is ... another")

41

The author repeats the word "ideal" several times in the final paragraph (lines 86–91) primarily to

A) highlight the impracticality of his dream.

B) juxtapose his goals with the reality of his situation.

C) emphasize his longing for something better.

D) set a clear, achievable goal for himself and his society.

42

Based on the passage as a whole, the author believes that "pass laws" (line 21) are

A) salutary in their immediate impact on individuals but deleterious in their effect on families.

B) designed for the maintenance of a stable society but harmful in some of their unintended effects.

C) responsible for many Africans being illegally arrested and for the breakdown of familial relationships.

D) unfair in subjecting Africans to police harassment and detrimental to the unity of African families.

CONTINUE

Questions 43–52 are based on the following passage.

This passage is adapted from S. Galinez et al., "Stroke: Historical Review and Innovative Treatments." ©2014 by the National High School Journal of Science.

The medical knowledge of strokes has progressed significantly from ancient understandings of the brain and nervous system to modern technological advances in both treatment and prevention. The first
5 historical reference to the nervous system was found in ancient Egyptian records dating back to 3500 BCE, when Papyrus described the brain and the fluids that covered the brain.

Hippocrates, in 400 BCE, first described paralysis
10 and convulsion or seizures that resulted after brain injuries, along with the observation that paralysis to the opposite side of the body resulted when a section from one half of the brain was injured. In the 17th century, Thomas Willis conducted a detailed study of
15 the brain and nervous system at Oxford University. Willis did experiments on cadavers and discovered that dye injected into one carotid artery would be expelled from the opposing carotid artery. He classified the nerves of the brain and described the
20 communication of the arteries at the base of the brain that we now call the Circle of Willis. He also recognized that lesions in a specific part of the brain led to weakness in an associated part of the body.

In the 1800s carotid surgery became a more
25 prevalent procedure and reports of successful closures of injuries to the carotid arteries were documented. The first documented case of successful carotid artery surgery in the United States was performed by Dr. Amos Twitchell in New
30 Hampshire on October 18, 1807. Another milestone came in 1927 when Egas Moniz of Portugal successfully performed cerebral arteriograms for the study of cerebral tumors.

Despite these advances, there were actually very
35 few effective treatments for an acute stroke. In the early 1900s most of the treatments for stroke patients were limited to rehabilitation after an acute stroke, and most patients were usually left with permanent and severe deficits. In the 1950s it was recognized
40 that disease in the carotid arteries could also cause transient ischemic attacks resulting in temporary weakness or blindness that resolved within a few hours, and that these attacks could be warning signs

for future strokes. Doppler ultrasound studies were
45 first used to identify plaque and disease in the carotid arteries, and aggressive treatment of high blood pressure also was found to be very important.

In the 1960s carotid endarterectomy was greatly improved but this procedure was used mostly for
50 stroke prevention and there was still no effective treatment after an acute stroke. The invention of the computed tomography scan (CT scan) greatly assisted in the diagnosis of stroke, and it became widely used in the United States to help distinguish
55 between the different types of stroke. In the 1970s aspirin was found to be very effective in stroke prevention. In the 1980s another breakthrough was the discovery that cigarette smoking was a definite risk factor for stroke; after this, smoking cessation
60 programs became very important. A major breakthrough came in 1996 when the FDA approved stroke treatment using tissue plasminogen activator, a protein that is now widely used to break down blood clots. Soon rapid diagnosis became crucial for
65 immediate treatment, whereas in the past rehabilitation was the most common response and doctors often waited 12–24 hours before giving a diagnosis of acute stroke.

As advances continue in the future, strokes may
70 become a temporary illness for which rapid and minimally invasive treatments allow for maximum recovery. Such treatments would be coupled with an emphasis on healthy lifestyles and prevention. For immediate improvement in blood flow to the area of
75 the stroke, we suggest an ultrasound device that allows delivery of Vascular Endothelial Growth Factor (VEGF) directly into the affected tissue with minimal risk to the patient. A specialized minute pellet provides a dual mechanism of releasing
80 medication into the affected tissue: Fifty percent is processed onto a porous scaffold and immediately released, and the remaining fifty percent is processed into specialized glycolide spheres with semipermeable membranes to provide additional
85 sustained release of the medication into the affected tissue. The pellet thus provides both immediate and sustained gradual delivery of VEGF to provide immediate and sustained neovascularization. We propose that VEGF administered directly into acute
90 ischemic tissue will lead to dramatic advances in the treatment of stroke.

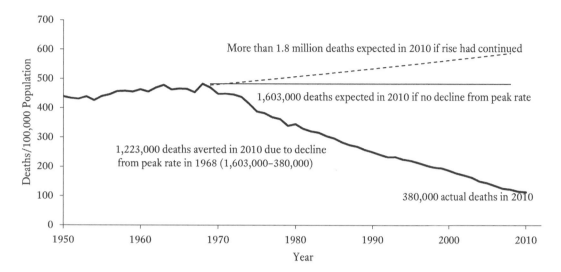

Adapted from the National Heart, Lung, and Blood Institute, National Institutes of Health website.

43

The authors' primary intention in the passage is to

A) debunk Hippocrates' observations on the brain because they are outdated and modern research has provided better answers.

B) argue that a stroke is now easily curable with a simple rehabilitation effort if it is caught in the preliminary phases.

C) convey the severity of acute stroke and the long term effects it has on a person's longevity, memory, and quality of life.

D) provide a brief history of stroke research and delineate contemporary technological advancements.

44

The tone of the passage is best described as

A) critical but constructive.

B) rhetorical and pedantic.

C) measured and inquisitive.

D) informative and optimistic.

CONTINUE

45

Based on the passage, in relation to the work of Hippocrates, Willis' research

A) repudiates some of the findings of Hippocrates by discovering alternate causes of paralysis and brain injury.

B) confirms all of Hippocrates' claims by using dye stain experiments to reaffirm Hippocrates' hypotheses on paralysis.

C) builds on Hippocrates' earlier findings by studying certain arteries in the brain and describing communication between them.

D) is unrelated to that of Hippocrates, because Willis studied arteries which do not pertain to brain injuries.

46

According to the passage, why is the study of the carotid artery important for an understanding of strokes?

A) A faulty carotid artery causes cerebral arteriograms.

B) Diseased carotid arteries can lead to stroke.

C) A stroke causes damage to the carotid artery.

D) Willis discovered the carotid artery.

47

Which choice provides the best evidence for the answer to the previous question?

A) Line 16–20 ("Willis … brain")

B) Line 24–30 ("In the 1800s … 1807")

C) Line 30–35 ("Another … stroke")

D) Line 39–44 ("In the 1950s … strokes")

48

In line 78, "minute" most nearly means

A) condensed.

B) very small.

C) very brief.

D) insignificant.

49

In line 90, "dramatic" most nearly means

A) unbelievable.

B) theatrical.

C) impressive.

D) drastic.

50

According to the authors, which of the following actions would minimize the likelihood of permanent damage from a stroke for some individuals?

A) Making a specific lifestyle change in order to reduce the complications that result from stroke

B) Using aspirin before and immediately after a stroke to prevent the escalation of symptoms

C) Using Doppler ultrasounds to detect high blood pressure and treating high blood pressure prior to suffering a stroke

D) Diagnosing an acute stroke quickly and beginning treatment immediately

51

Which choice provides the best evidence for the answer to the previous question?

A) Lines 44–47 ("Doppler … important")

B) Lines 55–57 ("In the … prevention")

C) Lines 57–60 ("In the … important")

D) Lines 64–68 ("Soon … stroke")

52

Based on the graph, if the number of deaths from strokes had continued to rise at the rate it rose from 1950 to 1970, roughly how many deaths per 100,000 would have been expected for 2010?

A) 1,800,000

B) 1,223,000

C)   590

D)   475

STOP

If you finish before time is called, you may check your work on this section only.
Do not turn to any other section.

2   2

Writing and Language Test

35 MINUTES, 44 QUESTIONS

Turn to Section 2 of your answer sheet to answer the questions in this section.

DIRECTIONS

Each passage below is accompanied by a number of questions. For some questions, you will consider how the passage might be revised to improve the expression of ideas. For other questions, you will consider how the passage might be edited to correct errors in sentence structure, usage, or punctuation. A passage or a question may be accompanied by one or more graphics (such as a table or graph) that you will consider as you make revising and editing decisions.

Some questions will direct you to an underlined portion of a passage. Other questions will direct you to a location in a passage or ask you to think about the passage as a whole.

After reading each passage, choose the answer to each question that most effectively improves the quality of writing in the passage or that makes the passage conform to the conventions of standard written English. Many questions include a "NO CHANGE" option. Choose that option if you think the best choice is to leave the relevant portion of the passage as it is.

Questions 1-11 are based on the following passage and supplementary material.

Immunizations and Global Health

[1] Immunization the process of inoculation and vaccination through the artificial introduction of infectious material, has been a tremendous boon for world

1

A) NO CHANGE

B) Immunization, the process of inoculation and vaccination through the artificial introduction of infectious material has

C) Immunization, the process of inoculation and vaccination through the artificial introduction of infectious material, has

D) Immunization: the process of inoculation and vaccination through the artificial introduction of infectious material, has

CONTINUE ▶

2

2

health. However, in recent years **2** it has unfairly come under attack. **3** It is necessary that we must understand immunization properly because it is essential for public health. With population density increasing, the prevention of the spread of infectious diseases is growing in importance.

A clear example of the importance of immunization is the successful vaccination effort against paralytic poliomyelitis, commonly known as **4** polio, a helpful disease to study to learn more about immunization. Until the mid-twentieth century, polio was a serious public health concern in the United States. In the twenty states that kept track of the spread of polio, nearly 58,000 cases were reported in 1952, with over 3,000 people dying and nearly 22,000 left with mild to disabling paralysis.

5 Therefore, Jonas Salk began testing the first vaccine for polio in 1952. By 1955, it was determined that the vaccine was **6** safe and affective. In the years since, polio has effectively been eradicated in the industrialized world.

2
A) NO CHANGE
B) they have attacked immunization unfairly.
C) its unfairly come under attack.
D) immunization has unfairly come under attack.

3
A) NO CHANGE
B) It is absolutely requisite for us that immunization must be understood properly
C) It is very important for us that we must understand immunization properly
D) Immunization must be understood properly

4
A) NO CHANGE
B) polio, a virus through which one can become more knowledgeable of immunization.
C) polio, through which one can better comprehend immunization.
D) polio.

5
A) NO CHANGE
B) Also in 1952,
C) In response to these outbreaks,
D) However, in another development,

6
A) NO CHANGE
B) safe, and effective.
C) safe and effective.
D) safe, and affective.

CONTINUE

However, for much of the world, particularly developing countries, polio is still a serious concern; with the high level of interaction between members of nearly all societies, it could certainly **7** reemerge in the industrial world. In 2014, the World Health Organization said the international spread of polio "constitutes an extraordinary event and a public health risk to other countries for which a coordinated international response is essential." In some war-torn countries, children have not had the opportunity to be vaccinated. Afghanistan, Cameroon, Equatorial Guinea, Ethiopia, Iraq, Nigeria, Pakistan, and Syria **8** are all currently experiencing polio patients and also have relatively low rates of vaccination.

Unfortunately, vaccination is also becoming a concern in some industrialized nations for entirely different reasons. **9** Its' use have been opposed by some concerned parents in America, the UK, and Ireland in recent years. Most of these parents' concerns stem from a 1998 article **10** made specious claims establishing a link between MMR (measles, mumps, and rubella) vaccines and autism. Though the lead author of that paper was discredited and the article itself retracted, a number of celebrity supporters have promulgated these faulty findings, creating an irrational fear of vaccines in some people and decreasing vaccination rates in some areas.

7
A) NO CHANGE
B) happen again
C) bounce back
D) exist more

8
Assuming that each is true, which of the following best suggests a link between low rates of vaccination and higher rates of infection?

A) NO CHANGE
B) are all currently suffering from serious outbreaks of polio and have some of the lowest vaccination rates in the world.
C) are countries that have low vaccination rates right now and have some problems with polio as well.
D) currently have problems with vaccinating for polio.

9
A) NO CHANGE
B) It's use has
C) Its use having
D) Its use has

10
A) NO CHANGE
B) that made specious claims establishing a link
C) had made specious claims establishing a link
D) which was making specious claims establishing a link

This decrease has allowed a resurgence of previously controlled diseases even in places where levels of infection were at or near zero for some time.

So, what is to be done? Perhaps an educational campaign to inform people about what vaccines are, how they work, how safe they are, and why they are so important to public health is the best place to start.

Question **11** asks about the previous passage as a whole.

Think about the previous passage and included supplemental material as a whole as you answer question 11.

11

Which choice best reflects the information presented in the graph and the passage?

A) Since the introduction of the polio vaccine in 1955, the average yearly number of reported polio infections in the United States has dramatically decreased until it reached zero.

B) Since 1955, the average yearly number of reported polio infections in the United States has only decreased after fluctuating in previous years.

C) Since 1955, the average yearly number of reported polio infections in the United States has fluctuated, sometimes reaching levels close to pre-1955, but the overall trend is a decrease.

D) Since the introduction of the polio vaccine in 1955, the average yearly number of reported polio infections in the United States has fluctuated, but a small decrease may be attributable to vaccination.

Paralytic Poliomyelitis: Number of cases reported in United States, 1950–2010

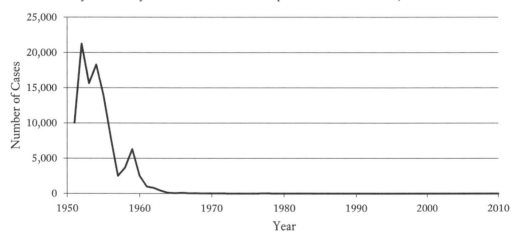

Adapted from the Centers for Disease Control and Prevention website.

CONTINUE

2   2

Questions 12–22 are based on the following passage.

An Artist's Home

—1—

When I was growing up in China during the Cultural
Revolution, artistic creativity was stifled. Art exhibits
were shut down by the police, and [12] various artistic
techniques were forbidden. [13] The only art that was
endorsed by the government was political propaganda. It
represented the ideas of the ruling political party. Many
artists were sentenced to years in labor camps and
prisons. My philosophy differed from that of the
government. I believed that art should be a personal
expression of inner thoughts and beliefs rather than a tool
of external control.

—2—

In my free time I used to visit my local library.
[14] There I explored a world that I was eager to learn
about, that of traditional Chinese art. The library became
a place of comfort for me, whereas in school I was never
the kind of student that teachers liked and did not fit in
with my classmates. The pursuit of a formal education
seemed unnecessary to me because the material I was told
to study in school did not seem relevant to my life.
However, I never gave up expressing myself artistically.

[12]

Which choice most clearly specifies some of the
artistic techniques that were banned?

A) NO CHANGE

B) some techniques employed by artists

C) artistic techniques such as woodcuts and splashing
   ink

D) many different kinds of artistic techniques

[13]

Which choice most effectively combines the
underlined sentences?

A) The only art that was endorsed by the government
   was political propaganda; this propaganda
   represented the ideas of the ruling political party.

B) The government endorsed only art that was
   essentially propaganda for the ruling political
   party.

C) The political propaganda that the government
   endorsed was the only art that represented the
   ideas of the ruling political party.

D) The art that represented the ideas of the ruling
   political party was the only political propaganda
   endorsed by the government.

[14]

A) NO CHANGE

B) When I was there, visiting the library,

C) While visiting the library,

D) Meanwhile,

—3—

When the government threatened to arrest me for my artistic views, I moved to the United **15** States and studied fine art at a college in New York. There I learned in an unfamiliar setting the history and techniques of the great painters of many traditions. **16** My education changed the way in which I viewed myself as a person and, as a result, the way in which I viewed art.

—4—

Many years after the Cultural Revolution, I returned to my home town to display my artworks in an **17** exhibit titled: "Words and Scenes: Modern Chinese Paintings." My artwork, including some works that formerly would have been prohibited, **18** was displayed with that of other contemporary painters.

15

A) NO CHANGE
B) States, and studied
C) States; and studied
D) States and studied,

16

The author is considering adding the following sentence at this point:

> I also learned a lot about American culture, from movies to fast food.

Should the author make this addition?

A) Yes, because it provides a broader view of the author's American experience.
B) Yes, because the following sentence is unclear without this context.
C) No, because it is irrelevant to the main idea of the paragraph.
D) No, because the information is easily assumed by readers.

17

A) NO CHANGE
B) exhibit, titled, "Words
C) exhibit titled "Words
D) exhibit titled, "Words

18

A) NO CHANGE
B) were displayed
C) displayed
D) displaying

CONTINUE

2 **2**

—5—

After completing university and obtaining my PhD in Fine Arts and Art History, I began working as a professor of Chinese art, specializing in calligraphy. My friends and I formed [19] a cluster of Chinese artistic intellectualism and were able to explore new avenues of cultural expression without the constraints we had felt in our home country. However, my distance from the epicenter of my native culture created within me a nostalgia for my childhood home, an urge to see the rolling hills of the Chinese countryside, [20] and a desire to further my understanding of Chinese culture.

—6—

For three weeks, I met with [21] locals, old friends, idealistic art students, and reporters from around the world. My visit was short, but it was meaningful to me to return to the land of my first home and to no longer feel constrained artistically.

Question [22] asks about the previous passage as a whole.

19

A) NO CHANGE
B) an enclave
C) a bunch
D) an arrangement

20

A) NO CHANGE
B) and desired
C) and desiring
D) desiring

21

A) NO CHANGE
B) locals—old friends, idealistic art students, and reporters from around the world.
C) local's, old friends; idealistic, art students; and reporters from around the world.
D) local's friends, idealistic students and reporters from around the world.

Think about the previous passage as a whole as you answer question 22.

22

To make this passage most logical, paragraph 4 should be placed

A) where it is now.
B) after paragraph 1.
C) after paragraph 3.
D) after paragraph 5.

CONTINUE

2

2

Questions 23-33 are based on the following passage.

Designing Board Games

Designing board games for a living is an interesting—though not a particularly lucrative—job. I have to [23] craft a theme, develop rules, supervise artists, coordinate test groups, organize marketing, supply chain management, and often finance the entire project while still making enough money so that I can eat every day and live indoors.

The first step in my process is to come up with an idea: it may be a theme, like intergalactic trading among alien races, or a mechanism, like rolling a unique kind of die. Often, even when I feel like I have a great idea, I find out that someone else has already done something similar, and I have to go back to the drawing board.

After I decide on a concept for my game, the next step is determining a design. This is the most intellectually challenging part of the enterprise. I have to make sure that every mechanism, rule, and accompanying piece of text makes sense in the context of the whole game, a task that [24] is like brain surgery and rocket science combined.

23

A) NO CHANGE

B) craft a theme, develop rules, supervise artists, coordinate test groups, organize marketing, and supply chain management,

C) craft a theme, develop rules, supervise artists, marketing, supply chain management,

D) craft a theme, develop rules, supervise artists, coordinate test groups, organize marketing, manage the supply chain,

24

Which choice provides a conclusion for the sentence that is most consistent with writer's tone and the main idea of this paragraph?

A) NO CHANGE

B) is really super confusing and hard to do.

C) requires both attention to detail and systematic thinking.

D) requires impossible to obtain skills that no one has.

CONTINUE

2

2

During the design process, I refine the rules with help from others who playtest my prototype. Playtesting helps [25] ensure that my ideas make sense to someone other than just me. I usually will play the game I'm working on hundreds of times before I can finalize the rules.

While I am designing rules, I also work with a contract artist to produce relevant and affordable illustrations to go along with the game. Usually, most of this work goes into the game [26] itself; but some of it gets saved for publicity materials.

Once a game is nearly ready, I can begin exploring publishing options. One possibility is to contract with a known publisher to manage the printing, marketing, and distribution of my game. This is the lowest-risk option but also the least financially rewarding. [27] Another possibility, which comes with a higher risk of failure but also sometimes leads to the biggest profits, [28] are to self-publish.

[25]
A) NO CHANGE
B) insure that
C) unsure that
D) DELETE the underlined portion

[26]
A) NO CHANGE
B) themselves, but
C) themselves; but
D) itself, but

[27]
Which choice most logically follows the previous sentence?
A) Professional board game publishers retain most of the profits of the games that they sell.
B) Professional board game publishers often have in-house art staff.
C) Professional board game publishers rarely market games until development is nearly completed.
D) Professional board game publishers can be organized as partnerships or corporations.

[28]
A) NO CHANGE
B) will be
C) is
D) that is

CONTINUE →

I have many more funding options now than I did a decade ago thanks to crowd funding websites. [29] Previously, I would pay for not only the development but [30] also for the manufacture and distribution of a game. Now that I can use the internet to gather support to cover these costs prior to incurring them, the potential for losing money beyond my initial investment is greatly reduced.

[29]

The writer is considering adding the following sentence here.

These websites allow potential buyers to pool their money so that designers know they will sell enough units to make manufacturing a game profitable.

Should the writer make this change?

A) Yes, because it clarifies a potentially unfamiliar term.

B) Yes, because it provides a specific example that supports the preceding sentence.

C) No, because it is unrelated to the subject matter of the paragraph.

D) No, because it was previously explained in the passage.

[30]

A) NO CHANGE

B) also, the manufacturing and distribution.

C) the manufacture and distribution as well, of a game.

D) also the manufacture and distribution of a game.

CONTINUE

[1] Although there are fewer financial risks than in the past, it remains difficult to make large profits by selling board games. [2] Thus, success is a relative term: a game is considered successful if 10,000 copies are sold in a year. [3] Further, my new games face a lot of competition because there are many other games on the market, and older, established games tend to sell the most copies. **31**

32 To wrap things up, the profit margin for board games is also extremely thin. On average, a game that I design costs between four and ten dollars per unit to manufacture. Then it costs about that much again in shipping to get each unit to the United States. If I sell the copies myself, I have to keep thousands of them in my garage for years as they **33** slowly trickle away. If, on the other hand, I sell a game through a distribution company, that company will take half the profits from each sale. After paying the artist, manufacturing company, and distributor, I'm lucky if I make much more than minimum wage on the time I spend on the entire endeavor.

31

To improve the cohesion and flow of this paragraph, the writer wants to add the following sentence.

> The primary reason for this difficulty is that most board games don't sell many copies.

The sentence would most logically be placed

A) before sentence 1.

B) after sentence 1.

C) after sentence 2.

D) after sentence 3.

32

What choice provides the best introduction to the paragraph?

A) NO CHANGE

B) Conclusively,

C) To summarize,

D) DELETE the underlined portion (and adjust capitalization appropriately).

33

A) NO CHANGE

B) eventually fall to the wayside.

C) are gradually purchased.

D) gently fade into nothingness.

Questions 34–44 are based on the following passage.

Charles Dickens—Medical Expert?

When celebrated author Charles Dickens died, his life was commemorated in many newspapers of his day. An obituary for the author also appeared, perhaps [34] surprisingly in another publication—the *British Medical Journal*. This probably seems curious to many modern readers. [35] Why, one might ask, would an author noted for his fictional writings be honored by an obituary in a leading medical journal?

The field of medicine has long paid tribute to [36] Dickens' keen eye about subtle detail and his description of the physiology and presentation of illnesses. Indeed, it has been hypothesized that his descriptions of the physical attributes and behaviors of his characters are so specific that one can diagnose from them a variety of diseases such as tuberculosis, Tourette's syndrome, and supranuclear palsy. For his time, Dickens had a remarkably [37] modern, medical approach, to describing illness. He had the eye of a clinician and recorded symptoms like a trained physician.

34

A) NO CHANGE
B) surprisingly, in another publication the
C) surprisingly—in another publication—the
D) surprisingly, in another publication: the

35

The author wants to revise this sentence so that, instead of asking a question, it clearly expresses the main idea of the passage as a whole. Which of the following choices best accomplishes this?

A) Although he is best known today as a novelist, Charles Dickens deserves to be recognized for his scientific acumen and contributions to the medical field as well.
B) Charles Dickens was one of the foremost men of his day, and so he deserved to be remembered by all people in all fields.
C) Charles Dickens wrote many novels, and his ideas in those novels made a deep impact in many fields of study.
D) Despite having made several contributions to medical science, Charles Dickens is much more important as a novelist than a scientist.

36

A) NO CHANGE
B) Dicken's keen eye for
C) Dickens keen eye about
D) Dickens' keen eye for

37

A) NO CHANGE
B) modern, medical approach
C) modern medical approach
D) modern—medical approach—

2   2

[1] One medical field that Dickens has played a notable part in is that of sleep disorders. [2] One hundred twenty years after the *Pickwick Papers* was written, one of the work's characters, Joe the Fat Boy, **38** inspired the research of Sydney Burwell and his colleagues. [3] Although their claims were later shown to be inaccurate, their conclusions laid the groundwork for further study of the causes of Pickwickian Syndrome. [4] Joe is described by Dickens as an obese boy with a ruddy face and gluttonous tendencies **39** that are consistently either sleeping or extremely drowsy. [5] The researchers used the name Pickwickian Syndrome to describe a condition presented by one of their patients, who bore a resemblance, in appearance and behavior, to the character Joe. [6] The researchers concluded that their patient's somnolence was due to an excess of carbon dioxide caused by heavy breathing during sleep. **40**

In addition to his contributions through his careful description of the symptoms of his characters, Dickens also inspired interest in developing fields of medical study further. In his famous novel *A Christmas Carol*, for example, Dickens arouses sympathy for the crippled Tiny Tim, and this portrayal, together with those of other Dickensian characters, **41** have led to developments in

38

A) NO CHANGE
B) challenged
C) started
D) fired up

39

A) NO CHANGE
B) whom is
C) which are
D) who is

40

To make this paragraph most logical, sentence 3 should be placed

A) where it is now.
B) after sentence 1.
C) after sentence 4.
D) after sentence 6.

41

A) NO CHANGE
B) have lead
C) has led
D) had lead

CONTINUE

the fields of orthopedics and pediatrics and contributed to the emerging cultural understanding of the importance of compassionate care for those with various kinds of disabilities. Dickens also exposed the unsanitary conditions of urban life in many of his novels, creating an awareness of a developing health crisis caused by the rapid industrialization of his time. **42** He showed that his dedication to this cause in London went beyond fiction. He was also a leader in making public demands for the establishment of a London Department of Health. **43** Dickens wrote his novels with an observant eye and a compassionate heart.

42

The writer wants to combine the following two underlined sentences to show the relationship between them. Which choice best accomplishes this?

A) Because he was leading public demands for the establishment of a London Department of Health, Dickens was clearly showing his dedication to this cause in London.

B) He showed that his dedication to this cause in London went beyond fiction, and he was also a leader demanding the establishment of a London Department of Health.

C) By leading public demands for the establishment of a London Department of Health, Dickens showed that his dedication to this cause went beyond fiction.

D) Dickens, as the leader of public demands for the establishment of a London Department of Health, showed that his dedication to this cause in London went beyond fiction.

43

The author is considering deleting the underlined sentence. Should the author make this change?

A) Yes, because it contradicts the rest of the passage as a whole.

B) Yes, because it does not support the main point of the paragraph.

C) No, because it is needed to understand the following paragraph.

D) No, because it provides a new example to support the main idea.

CONTINUE

Although Charles Dickens was a prolific author—he wrote fifteen novels and many short stories—his works hold an importance beyond their literary value. Although his influence on the world of literature is certainly what he is best remembered for, Charles Dickens made significant contributions to the field of medicine as well. [44] He also made contributions to many other fields unrelated to literature.

44

Which choice concludes the essay with a final, vivid example to illustrate the point of the essay as a whole?

A) NO CHANGE

B) By carefully describing characters like Old Bill Barley the gout sufferer in *Great Expectations*, Dickens has helped the world better understand many maladies and their symptoms.

C) He will always be remembered as both a great writer and a humanitarian who showed philanthropy whenever possible, which is a legacy that any novelist should envy.

D) Many of Dickens' contemporaries wrote more novels than Charles Dickens, and their works should be explored to consider how they might contribute to our understanding of medical practice and research.

STOP

**If you finish before time is called, you may check your work on this section only.
Do not turn to any other section.**

No Test Material On This Page

Math Test – No Calculator

25 MINUTES, 20 QUESTIONS

Turn to Section 3 of your answer sheet to answer the questions in this section.

DIRECTIONS

For questions 1-15, solve each problem, choose the best answer from the choices provided, and fill in the corresponding circle on your answer sheet. **For questions 16-20,** solve the problems and enter your answer in the grid on the answer sheet. Please refer to the directions before question 16 on how to enter your answers in the grid. You may use any available space in your test booklet for scratch work.

NOTES

The use of calculators **is not permitted**.

All variables and expressions used represent real numbers unless otherwise indicated.

Figures provided in this test are drawn to scale unless otherwise indicated.

All figures lie in a plane unless otherwise indicated.

Unless otherwise indicated, the domain of a given function f is the set of real numbers x for which $f(x)$ is a real number.

REFERENCE

$A = \pi r^2$ $A = \ell w$ $A = \dfrac{1}{2}bh$ $c^2 = a^2 + b^2$ Special Right Triangles

$C = 2\pi r$

$V = \ell w h$ $V = \pi r^2 h$ $V = \dfrac{4}{3}\pi r^3$ $V = \dfrac{1}{3}\pi r^2 h$ $V = \dfrac{1}{3}\ell w h$

The number of degrees of arc in a circle is 360.
The number of radians of arc in a circle is 2π.
The sum of the measures in degrees of the angles in a triangle is 180.

CONTINUE

1

If $3x + 12 = 21$, what is the value of $2x + 8$?

A) 16

B) 14

C) 7

D) 3

3

$$f(x) = \frac{c}{3}x + 2$$

In the function given above, c is a constant. If $f(6) = -6$, what is the value of $f(-9)$?

A) −10

B) −4

C) −2

D) 14

2

Which of the following expressions can equal −1 for some value of a?

A) $|a-3| + 2$

B) $|a-2| + 1$

C) $|a-1|$

D) $|a-2| - 2$

4

The number of auto workers that joined a particular union between 1960 and 1985 is three times the number of auto workers that joined between 1986 and 2010. If 9,600 workers joined the union between 1960 and 1985 and n workers joined between 1986 and 2010, which of the following equations is true?

A) $9600n = 3$

B) $9600 = 3n$

C) $\frac{n}{3} = 9600$

D) $n + 3 = 9600$

CONTINUE

5

Which of the following expressions is equivalent to $2(3x-1)(-x+4)$?

A) $-3x^2 + 13x - 4$

B) $-6x^2 - 8$

C) $-6x^2 + 26x - 8$

D) $-12x^2 + 52x - 16$

6

$$2x - 3y = 9$$
$$ax - 5y = 3$$

What value of a will result in the above system of equations having no solutions?

A) $\dfrac{10}{3}$

B) $\dfrac{2}{3}$

C) $-\dfrac{2}{3}$

D) $-\dfrac{10}{3}$

7

In a project for business class, Bobby launched a website with humor and pop culture content and aimed to get as many visitors to the website as possible. On day 6 there were 20 visitors to the website, and on day 18 there were 320 visitors. Which of the following best describes the average change in visitors to the website over the given period?

A) The number of visitors to the website increased by an average of 18.25 visitors per day.

B) The number of visitors to the website increased by an average of 25 visitors per day.

C) The number of visitors to the website increased by an average of 69 visitors per day.

D) The number of visitors to the website increased by an average of 71 visitors per day.

8

$$6x - 4y = 14$$
$$2x - 3y = 3$$

According to the system of equations above, what is $x + y$?

A) -3

B) 1

C) 4

D) 8

9

The graph of $y = (x+7)^2$ intersects the line $y = 16$ at the two points M and N. What is the length of $\overline{MN}$?

A)   6

B)   8

C)   10

D)   12

10

$$nA = 360$$

The above equation shows the relationship between the measure A, in degrees, of an exterior angle of a regular polygon and n, the number of sides of the polygon. If a regular polygon's exterior angle is greater than 80 degrees, what is the greatest number of sides it can have?

A) 4

B) 5

C) 6

D) 8

11

Amanda, Jesse, and Liana buy three gifts for a baby shower and split the cost evenly. Two of the gifts cost d dollars each, the third gift costs $6 less than each of the other two, and there is 10 percent tax on the total purchase. What is the amount paid by each of the gift givers, in dollars?

A) $d - 2$

B) $2d - 6$

C) $1.1d - 2.2$

D) $3.3d - 6.6$

12

$$x = 6 - 5i$$
$$y = 2 + i$$

If $i = \sqrt{-1}$, what is the value of b in the quotient $\dfrac{x}{y}$ when written in the form $a + bi$ (where a and b are real numbers)?

A) $-\dfrac{16}{3}$

B) $-\dfrac{16}{5}$

C) $\dfrac{7}{5}$

D) $\dfrac{16}{5}$

CONTINUE

13

$$y = a(x+3)(x-5)$$

The equation above represents a quadratic function with a as a non-zero constant and vertex of (m, n). Which of the following is equal to n?

A) -8

B) $-4a$

C) $-12a$

D) $-16a$

14

In 2015, it was estimated that a town of 43,560 had an annual population increase of 15.5%. At this rate of growth, which of the following functions models how many people live in the town t years after 2015?

A) $P(t) = 43,560(15.5)^t$

B) $P(t) = 43,560(1.155)^t$

C) $P(t) = 15.5(43,560)^t$

D) $P(t) = 43,560(0.155)^t$

15

Which of the following is equivalent to $\dfrac{8x+2}{3x-1}$?

A) $2 + \dfrac{2x+4}{3x-1}$

B) $6x - 2$

C) $3x + \dfrac{1}{2x+4}$

D) $2 - \dfrac{3x+5}{3x-1}$

CONTINUE

DIRECTIONS

For questions 16–20, solve the problem and enter your answer in the grid, as described below, on the answer sheet.

1. Although not required, it is suggested that you write your answer in the boxes at the top of the columns to help you fill in the circles accurately. You will receive credit only if the circles are filled in correctly.
2. Mark no more than one circle in any column.
3. No question has a negative answer.
4. Some problems may have more than one correct answer. In such cases, grid only one answer.
5. **Mixed numbers** such as $3\frac{1}{2}$ must be be gridded as 3.5 or 7/2. If $3\ 1\ /\ 2$ is entered into the grid, it will be interpreted as $\frac{31}{2}$, not $3\frac{1}{2}$.)
6. **Decimal answers:** If you obtain a decimal answer with more digits than the grid can accommodate, it may be either rounded or truncated, but it must fill the entire grid.

Answer: $\frac{7}{13}$ Answer: 2.5

Write answer in boxes → | 7 | / | 1 | 3 | | 2 | . | 5 |

← Fraction line

Grid in result

← Decimal Point

Acceptable ways to grid $\frac{2}{3}$ are:

| 2 | / | 3 | | . | 6 | 6 | 6 | | . | 6 | 6 | 7 |

Answer: 210 – either position is correct

| 2 | 1 | 0 | | 2 | 1 | 0 |

NOTE: You may start your answers in any column, space permitting. Columns you don't need to use should be left blank.

CONTINUE

16

$$2a + 4b = 12$$
$$5a - 2b = 30$$

Given the system of equations above, if (a, b) is a solution, what is the value of b?

17

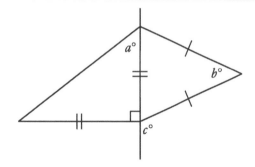

Note: Figure not drawn to scale

Two isosceles triangles are shown in the figure above.

If $b = \frac{2}{3}a$, what is the value of c?

18

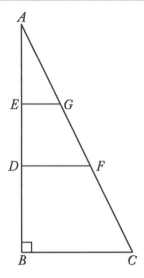

Note: Figure not drawn to scale

In the figure above, $AB = 8$ and $BC = 6$. If D is the midpoint of $\overline{AB}$, E is the midpoint of $\overline{AD}$, $\overline{AB} \perp \overline{BC}$, and $\overline{EG} \parallel \overline{DF} \parallel \overline{BC}$, what is the length of $\overline{FG}$?

CONTINUE

19

If $w = 12\sqrt{2}$ and $\frac{1}{4}w = \sqrt{2x}$, what is the value of x?

20

If $x^3 - 7x^2 + 3x - 21 = 0$, what is a real number solution for x?

STOP

If you finish before time is called, you may check your work on this section only.
Do not turn to any other section.

Math Test – Calculator

55 MINUTES, 38 QUESTIONS

Turn to Section 4 of your answer sheet to answer the questions in this section.

DIRECTIONS

For questions 1–30, solve each problem, choose the best answer from the choices provided, and fill in the corresponding circle on your answer sheet. **For questions 31–38**, solve the problems and enter your answer in the grid on the answer sheet. Please refer to the directions before question 31 on how to enter your answers in the grid. You may use any available space in your test booklet for scratch work.

NOTES

1. The use of calculators **is permitted**.

All variables and expressions used represent real numbers unless otherwise indicated.

Figures provided in this test are drawn to scale unless otherwise indicated.

All figures lie in a plane unless otherwise indicated.

Unless otherwise indicated, the domain of a given function f is the set of real numbers x for which $f(x)$ is a real number.

REFERENCE

$A = \pi r^2$
$C = 2\pi r$

$A = \ell w$

$A = \dfrac{1}{2}bh$

$c^2 = a^2 + b^2$

Special Right Triangles

$V = \ell w h$

$V = \pi r^2 h$

$V = \dfrac{4}{3}\pi r^3$

$V = \dfrac{1}{3}\pi r^2 h$

$V = \dfrac{1}{3}\ell w h$

The number of degrees of arc in a circle is 360.
The number of radians of arc in a circle is 2π.
The sum of the measures in degrees of the angles in a triangle is 180.

CONTINUE

4 **4**

1

Flannery is a cab driver. She will start tomorrow's shift with $300 and will make an average of $45 an hour throughout the day. In order to rent, fuel, and insure her cab, Flannery must pay a cab fee of $150 when she returns her cab at the end of each day. If Flannery's goal is to leave work with $420 tomorrow, which of the following expressions could be used to find the number of hours Flannery must work to reach her goal?

A) $45n - 150 = 120$

B) $45n - 150 = 420$

C) $45n + 150 = 120$

D) $45n - 150 = 270$

2

a	3	6	9	12
$f(a)$	−2	−1	0	1

The table above shows some values of the linear function f. Which of the following defines f?

A) $f(a) = \frac{1}{3}a - 3$

B) $f(a) = -\frac{1}{3}a - 1$

C) $f(a) = a - 5$

D) $f(a) = 2a - 8$

3

Tweets per Day

The graph above shows the number of Tweets produced by a pop star in the two weeks from December 17th through January 1st. Based on the graph, which of the following best describes the general trend in her tweets from December 17th to January 1st?

A) Tweets generally increased each day after December 17th.

B) Tweets generally decreased each day after December 17th.

C) Tweets reached a maximum on December 31st.

D) Tweets generally increased until December 25th and then generally decreased.

4

Tires are tested by sampling 24 tires from each batch of 600. If 87.5 percent of the tires in a sample pass inspection, how many tires in the batch would most likely pass inspection?

A) 525

B) 550

C) 575

A) 579

4 **4**

5

When 4 times some integer z is subtracted from 12, the result is 32. What is the result when 3 times z is added to 7?

A) 22

B) −5

C) −8

D) −48

6

Population of Five Countries

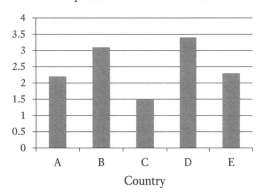

The populations of five different countries are shown in the graph above. If the total population of the countries is 1.25 million people, which of the following is an appropriate title for the vertical axis?

A) Population (in thousands)

B) Population (in hundreds of thousands)

C) Population (in millions)

D) Population (in hundreds of millions)

7

The graph of the function $g(x)$ is a line that contains points in quadrants I, II, and III. The graph of the function $g(x) - 2$ is a line that contains points in quadrants I, III, and IV. Which of the following statements about the function $g(x)$ is true?

A) It has a y-intercept between $(0, 2)$ and the origin.

B) It has a y-intercept between $(0, -2)$ and the origin.

C) It has a negative slope.

D) It has a slope of zero.

8

Laura can read 2 pages of her favorite book in 75 seconds. If she reads at this same rate, which of the following is closest to the number of pages she can read in 1 hour?

A) 24

B) 48

C) 96

D) 192

4

4

Smoking Status (Determined number of cigarettes per day)	Weight Status			
	Normal	Overweight	Underweight	Total
Non-smoker	543	1,903	53	2,499
Light (1–5)	171	375	32	578
Moderate (6–15)	234	306	35	575
Heavy (16–25)	381	618	47	1046
Very Heavy (> 25)	133	325	11	469
Total	1,462	3,527	178	5,167

The table above shows the results of a study that examined the relationship between cigarette smoking and weight. Based on the table, if a participant who smoked between 6 and 25 cigarettes per day were selected at random, which of the following is closest to the probability that the participant was underweight?

A) 0.016

B) 0.045

C) 0.051

D) 0.061

Questions 10 and 11 refer to the following information.

The graph below shows both the height and reach (measured from the left middle fingertip to the right middle fingertip when arms are spread) of the 10 gold medalists for boxing in the 2012 Summer Olympic Games.

Height and Reach of 2012 Olympic Boxing Gold Medalists

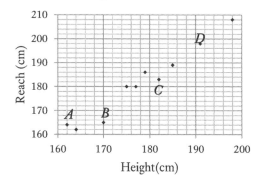

10

What is the height of the shortest boxer with a reach of at least 184 cm?

A) 162 cm

B) 164 cm

C) 179 cm

D) 185 cm

Of the labeled boxers, who has the smallest ratio of height to reach?

A) *A*

B) *B*

C) *C*

D) *D*

CONTINUE

12

Which of the following is <u>not</u> a solution to the inequality $4x - 3 \geq 2x + 7$?

A) 3

B) 5

C) 7

D) 9

13

Age of Sample (Years)	Number of Carbon-14 atoms
0	3.2×10^{12}
5,730	1.6×10^{12}
11,460	8.0×10^{11}
17,190	4.0×10^{11}
22,920	2.0×10^{11}
28,650	1.0×10^{11}

The table above shows the estimated number of Carbon-14 atoms in a sample over the course of five half lives. Which of the following describes the relationship between the age of the sample and the estimated number of Carbon-14 atoms?

A) Decreasing linear

B) Increasing linear

C) Exponential growth

D) Exponential decay

Questions 14 and 15 refer to the following information.

The graph below models the total monthly cost C, in dollars, of using a gym u times.

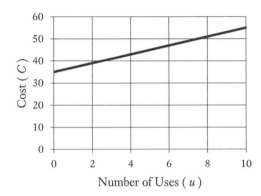

14

What does the C-intercept represent in the graph?

A) The minimum number of monthly uses

B) The base cost of a gym membership each month

C) The cost of the first use of the gym

D) The total cost of using the gym per month

15

Which of the following represents the relationship between number of uses and cost?

A) $C = 2u$

B) $C = \frac{1}{2}u + 35$

C) $C = 2u + 35$

D) $C = \frac{1}{2}u$

4 **4**

16

Stories					
5	5	5	6	6	6
6	7	7	7	9	9
10	11	12	14	15	25

The table above shows the number of stories in each of the apartment buildings on Elm Street. The 25 story building is an outlier. If that building is removed from the set, which of the following will change the most?

A) Mean

B) Median

C) Range

D) All change by the same amount

17

A professional football team practices 6 days a week. A water boy for the team knows that the players drink about 200 gallons of water during each day of practice. If the water filter in the utility room pours water at a rate of 9 gallons per minute, how many hours a week does the water boy spend filling water containers?

A) $\dfrac{20}{9}$

B) 3

C) 5

D) 6

18

If $14p - 22 \geq -10$, what is the maximum possible value of $11 - 7p$?

A) -5

B) 0.86

C) 2.29

D) 5

19

	Pizza	Chinese	Burgers	Total
Lunch	71	32	47	150
Dinner	52	45	53	150
Total	123	77	100	300

A mall food court has three options: pizza, Chinese food, and burgers. People were surveyed on their choices at lunchtime and at dinnertime to see if there were noticeable differences in preferences for each meal. The results are shown above. Based on the data, what is the probability that someone who had dinner at the food court did <u>not</u> eat Chinese food?

A) $\dfrac{45}{150}$

B) $\dfrac{77}{150}$

C) $\dfrac{105}{150}$

D) $\dfrac{118}{150}$

Questions 20 and 21 refer to the following information.

Company	Rental Insurance I (in dollars)	Reservation Fee R (in dollars)	Truck Rental T (in dollars per mile)	Gas Expenses G (in dollars per mile)
A	35	20	0.60	0.10
B	25	40	0.75	0.12
C	0	50	0.75	0.15

The total cost, $c(x)$, for renting a truck for a day in terms of the number of miles driven, x, is given by $c(x) = (T+G)x + I + R$.

20

For what range of miles will the total cost of renting a truck from company A be greater than or equal to the total cost of renting a truck from company C?

A) $x \leq 25$

B) $x \geq 0$

C) $x \geq 500$

D) Company C's trucks are never less expensive than company A's

21

If the relationship between the total cost, $c(x)$, of renting a truck from any of the companies for x miles were graphed in the xy-plane, what would the slope of the line represent?

A) The total cost of gas

B) The cost of reservation

C) The total cost of renting the truck

D) The cost of per-mile expenses

22

Jerry opens a savings account with $200. If the bank account is supposed to grow at an exponential rate, which of the following could represent Jerry's bank account balance at the end of each year for four consecutive years?

A) $210, $220, $230, $240

B) $310.10, $420.20, $530.30, $640.40

C) $210, $220.50, $231.53, $243.10

D) $300, $400, $500, $600

23

A linear function has distinct intercepts at $(h, 0)$ and $(0, k)$. If $h - k = 0$, which of the following can be concluded about the slope of the line?

A) It is zero.

B) It is positive.

C) It is negative.

D) Nothing can be determined about the slope from this information.

24

If $g(b) = 20b^3 - 15b^2 + 25b$ and $f(b) = 4b^2 - 3b + 5$, then what is the value of $\dfrac{f(b) - g(b)}{5b - 1}$?

A) $f(b)$

B) $-f(b)$

C) $g(b)$

D) $-b \cdot g(b)$

25

The Florida Aquarium is going to increase the volume of its cylindrical tank by 50 percent. If the radius is increased by 18 percent, the height of the tank would have to be increased by what percent (rounded to the nearest tenth of a percent)?

A) 27.1%

B) 12.0%

C) 7.7%

D) 2.0%

CONTINUE

26

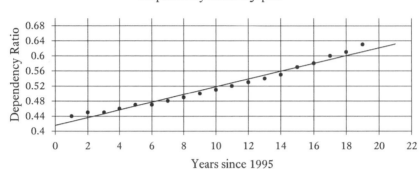

Dependency Ratio in Japan

In economics, the dependency ratio is an age-population ratio of those typically not in the labor force to those typically in the labor force. More specifically, the dependency ratio is defined as

$$\text{Dependency Ratio} = \frac{\text{Number of people under age 15 or over age 65}}{\text{Number of people aged 16–65}}.$$

The scatterplot above shows the dependency ratio for Japan for each year since 1995. The line of best fit is also shown and has the equation $y = 0.103x + 0.416$. Which of the following statements about the above data is true?

A) In 1995, the dependency ratio for Japan was between 0.42 and 0.41.

B) In 2005, the number of people of working age in Japan was 51 percent of those whose ages were below 15 or above 65.

C) The dependency ratio for Japan increases by a value of 0.103 each year.

D) In 2002, Japan had 48 people that were not of working age for every 100 working-age people.

27

A line segment in the coordinate plane has endpoints $A(1, 3)$ and $B(5, 1)$. Which of the following is the equation of a line perpendicular to segment $\overline{AB}$ intersecting $\overline{AB}$ at its midpoint?

A) $y = \frac{1}{2}x + \frac{1}{2}$

B) $y = \frac{1}{2}x + \frac{5}{2}$

C) $y = 2x - 1$

D) $y = 2x - 4$

28

The population of mosquitos in a biology laboratory can increase by 50 percent every 2 weeks. If a population started with 200 mosquitos, which expression gives the number of mosquitos after d days?

A) $200(0.5)^{\frac{d}{14}}$

B) $200(1.5)^{\frac{d}{14}}$

C) $200(0.5)^{14d}$

D) $200(1.5)^{14d}$

CONTINUE

4 **4**

29

The function $f(x)$ is a quadratic function such that $f(x)+5=0$ yields exactly one real solution. Which of the following could be $f(x)$?

A) $f(x)=x^2+10x+20$

B) $f(x)=(x-5)^2$

C) $f(x)=(x+5)^2+5$

D) $f(x)=x^2+10x-5$

30

$$R=16(2)^A$$
$$P=4(2)^B-5$$

In the equations above, A and B are constants. If B is two less than A, then what is the value of P in terms of R?

A) $P=\dfrac{R}{16}+5$

B) $P=\dfrac{R}{16}-5$

C) $P=\dfrac{R}{4}$

D) $P=4R-5$

CONTINUE

DIRECTIONS

For questions 31–38, solve the problem and enter your answer in the grid, as described below, on the answer sheet.

1. Although not required, it is suggested that you write your answer in the boxes at the top of the columns to help you fill in the circles accurately. You will receive credit only if the circles are filled in correctly.
2. Mark no more than one circle in any column.
3. No question has a negative answer.
4. Some problems may have more than one correct answer. In such cases, grid only one answer.
5. **Mixed numbers** such as $3\frac{1}{2}$ must be be gridded as 3.5 or 7/2. If $3\;1\;/\;2$ is entered into the grid, it will be interpreted as $\frac{31}{2}$, not $3\frac{1}{2}$.)
6. **Decimal answers:** If you obtain a decimal answer with more digits than the grid can accommodate, it may be either rounded or truncated, but it must fill the entire grid.

Answer: $\frac{7}{13}$

Answer: 2.5

Write answer in boxes →

←— Fraction line

Grid in result

←— Decimal Point

Acceptable ways to grid $\frac{2}{3}$ are:

Answer: 210 – either position is correct

NOTE: You may start your answers in any column, space permitting. Columns you don't need to use should be left blank.

CONTINUE

4 **4**

31

Allie can type between 30 and 45 words per minute. Given this, what is a possible number of <u>hours</u> it might take Allie to type 5,400 words?

32

Last month Genie and Sarah sold a total of 299 sunglasses. If Genie sold 67 fewer sunglasses than Sarah, how many sunglasses did Sarah sell?

33

The acre is a unit of area that can be calculated by multiplying one chain (a unit of length) by one furlong (another unit of length). One chain is 66 feet and one furlong is 660 feet. How many acres are there in a plot of land that has an area of 87,120 square feet?

34

If a circle has a radius of 12 units, what is the measure, in degrees, of the central angle that subtends an arc with a length of 8π ?

CONTINUE

4 📱 **4**

35

240 boys and 100 girls have been accepted to Buzz Cut Military College. If the college wants to cap male acceptances to 60 percent of the total acceptances, and is prepared to not accept any more boys, then how many additional girls should it admit?

36

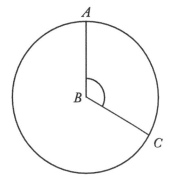

In the figure above, the circle centered at B has a diameter of 10 units. If the area of the smaller sector ABC is between 24 and 25 square units, then what is one possible value of the measure, in degrees (rounded to the nearest degree), of $\angle ABC$?

Questions 37 and 38 refer to the following information.

A study shows that after the average man turns 40, he begins to lose height at the rate of approximately 0.1% each year. Mr. Celio is exactly 40 years old and 76 inches tall, and he uses the equation $H = 76v^t$ to measure his height at any age t years in the future.

37

What value should Mr. Celio use for v ?

38

To the nearest tenth of an inch, what does Mr. Celio expect his height to be when he turns 70?

STOP

If you finish before time is called, you may check your work on this section only.
Do not turn to any other section.

SAT Practice Test 4

IMPORTANT REMINDERS

1
A No. 2 pencil is required for the test.
Do not use a mechanical pencil or pen.

2
Sharing any questions with anyone is a violation
of the Test Security and Fairness policies and
may result in your score being canceled.

This cover is representative of what you will see on the day of the SAT.

Reading Test

65 MINUTES, 52 QUESTIONS

Turn to Section 1 of your answer sheet to answer the questions in this section.

DIRECTIONS

Each passage or pair of passages below is followed by a number of questions. After reading each passage or pair, choose the best answer to each question based on what is stated or implied in the passage or passages and in any accompanying graphics (such as a table or graph).

Questions 1–10 are based on the following passage.

This passage is adapted from Stephen Crane, *Maggie, A Girl of the Streets*. Originally published in 1893.

A very little boy stood upon a heap of gravel for the honor of Rum Alley. He was throwing stones at howling urchins from Devil's Row who were circling madly about the heap and pelting at him.

5 His infantile countenance was livid with fury. His small body was writhing in the delivery of great, crimson oaths.

"Run, Jimmie, run! Dey'll get yehs," screamed a retreating Rum Alley child.

10 "Naw," responded Jimmie with a valiant roar, "dese fellas can't make me run."

Howls of renewed wrath went up from Devil's Row throats. Tattered gamins on the right made a furious assault on the gravel heap. On their small,

15 convulsed faces there shone the grins of true assassins. As they charged, they threw stones and cursed in shrill chorus.

The little champion of Rum Alley stumbled precipitately down the other side. His coat had been

20 torn to shreds in a scuffle, and his hat was gone. He had bruises on twenty parts of his body, and blood was dripping from a cut in his head. His wan features wore a look of a tiny, insane demon.

On the ground, children from Devil's Row closed

25 in on their antagonist. He crooked his left arm defensively about his head and fought with cursing fury. The little boys ran to and fro, dodging, hurling stones and swearing in barbaric trebles.

From a window of an apartment house that

30 upreared its form from amid squat, ignorant stables, there leaned a curious woman. Some laborers, unloading a scow at a dock at the river, paused for a moment and regarded the fight. The engineer of a passive tugboat hung lazily to a railing and watched.

35 Over on the Island, a worm of yellow convicts came from the shadow of a building and crawled slowly along the river's bank.

A stone had smashed into Jimmie's mouth. Blood was bubbling over his chin and down upon his ragged

40 shirt. Tears made furrows on his dirt-stained cheeks. His thin legs had begun to tremble and turn weak, causing his small body to reel. His roaring curses of the first part of the fight had changed to a blasphemous chatter.

45 In the yells of the whirling mob of Devil's Row children there were notes of joy like songs of triumphant savagery. The little boys seemed to leer gloatingly at the blood upon the other child's face.

Down the avenue came boastfully sauntering a lad

50 of sixteen years, although the chronic sneer of an ideal manhood already sat upon his lips. His hat was tipped with an air of challenge over his eye. Between his teeth, a cigar stump was tilted at the angle of defiance. He walked with a certain swing of the

55 shoulders which appalled the timid. He glanced over into the vacant lot in which the little raving boys from Devil's Row seethed about the shrieking and tearful child from Rum Alley.

"Gee!" he murmured with interest. "A scrap.

60 Gee!"

CONTINUE

He strode over to the cursing circle, swinging his shoulders in a manner which denoted that he held victory in his fists. He approached at the back of one of the most deeply engaged of the Devil's Row
65　children.

"Ah, what deh heck," he said, and smote the deeply-engaged one on the back of the head. The little boy fell to the ground and gave a hoarse, tremendous howl. He scrambled to his feet, and
70　perceiving, evidently, the size of his assailant, ran quickly off, shouting alarms. The entire Devil's Row party followed him. They came to a stand a short distance away and yelled taunting oaths at the boy with the chronic sneer. The latter, momentarily, paid
75　no attention to them.

"What deh heck, Jimmie?" he asked of the small champion.

Jimmie wiped his blood-wet features with his sleeve.
80　"Well, it was dis way, Pete, see! I was goin' teh lick dat Riley kid and dey all pitched on me."

Some Rum Alley children now came forward. The party stood for a moment exchanging vainglorious remarks with Devil's Row. A few stones were thrown
85　at long distances, and words of challenge passed between small warriors. Then the Rum Alley contingent turned slowly in the direction of their home street. They began to give, each to each, distorted versions of the fight. Causes of retreat in
90　particular cases were magnified. Blows dealt in the fight were enlarged to catapultian power, and stones thrown were alleged to have hurtled with infinite accuracy.

1

Throughout the passage, the author is primarily concerned with

A) clearly assigning guilt to the parties responsible for the instigation of a deplorably violent incident.

B) carefully reporting an incident of violence as clearly as possible.

C) overtly mocking the ignorance and brutality of the people involved in a conflict.

D) subtly providing readers with a reason to take action against the unjust actions he portrays.

2

According to Jimmie, the incident began because

A) he was defending his home neighborhood in Devil's Row when the local boys ganged up on him.

B) he would not leave when the local boys found him in Devil's Row and tried to chase him away.

C) he first threw stones at the boys from Devil's Row and they then threw stones back at him.

D) he was fighting one of the boys from Devil's Row and the rest of the boys joined the fight.

3

Which choice provides the best evidence for the answer to the previous question?

A) Lines 1–4 ("A very ... him")

B) Lines 8–13 ("Run ... throats")

C) Lines 76–81 ("What ... me")

D) Lines 89–93 ("Causes ... accuracy")

4

The description of Jimmie in lines 18–23 ("The little … demon") most strongly characterizes him as

A) poor but noble.

B) foolish and ignorant.

C) pitiable though fierce.

D) aggressive and arrogant.

5

The primary purpose of lines 29–34 ("From a … watched") is to

A) provide a broader spectrum of the social issues that underlie the conflict presented.

B) reveal the indifference of those who observe the violence occurring.

C) suggest that the conflict is insignificant and uninteresting to any outside observers.

D) create a contrast between the problems of the boys and the purposeful labor of those around them.

6

The boys from Devil's Row retreat from the conflict primarily because of

A) the irenic presence of an adult who has become aware of the situation.

B) their inability to match the anger and vehemence of Jimmie.

C) their sense of fairness and sympathy in response to Jimmie's helplessness.

D) the involvement of a large defender of the Rum Alley boy.

7

Which choice provides the best evidence for the answer to the previous question?

A) Lines 29–31 ("From … woman")

B) Lines 38–44 ("A stone … chatter")

C) Lines 66–72 ("Ah … him")

D) Lines 82–88 ("The party … street")

8

As it is used in lines 18 and 77, the word "champion" most nearly means one who

A) defends someone or something.

B) has won a competition.

C) is superior to others in the same field.

D) is to be congratulated.

9

As it is used in line 87, the word "contingent" most nearly means

A) depending upon.

B) group.

C) unforeseen element.

D) challenger.

10

In lines 89–93 ("Causes … accuracy"), the author indicates

A) the kinds of distortions that the boys create in retelling the story of the fight.

B) the scale and significance of the scuffle between the two parties as well as its likely outcomes.

C) the kinds of misunderstandings that have arisen regarding the conflict since its resolution.

D) that the reality of the past is never as good as it seems to be in the recollections of those who experienced it.

Questions 11–20 are based on the following passage and supplementary material.

This passage is adapted from Ralph Calel, "The Founding Fathers v. The Climate Change Skeptics." ©2014 by The Public Domain Review.

The United States has in recent years become a stronghold for climate change skepticism, especially since the country's declaration in 2001 that it would not participate in the Kyoto Protocol. Far from the
5 ambivalence of the American response to modern theories, the country's founders were vocal proponents of early theories of man-made climate change. The country's founders were keen observers of climatic trends and might even be counted among
10 the first climate change advocates. They wrote extensively in favor of the idea that settlement was improving the continent's climate, and their efforts helped to lay the foundation of modern meteorology.
From the start, the project to colonize North
15 America had proceeded on the understanding that climate followed latitude; so dependent was climate on the angle of the sun to the earth's surface, it was believed, that the word 'climate' was defined in terms of parallels of latitude. New England was expected to
20 be as mild as England, and Virginia as hot as Italy and Spain. Surprised by harsh conditions in the New World, however, a great number of the early settlers did not outlast their first winter in the colonies.
A view formed in Europe that the New World was
25 inferior to the Old. In particular, medical lore still held that climate lay behind the characteristic balance of the Hippocratic humors—it explained why Spaniards were temperamental and Englishmen reserved—and it was believed that the climate of the
30 colonies caused physical and mental degeneration. The respected French naturalist Georges-Louis Leclerc explained in his encyclopedia of natural history that "all animals of the New World were much smaller than those of the Old. This great
35 diminution in size, whatever may be the cause, is a primary kind of degeneration." He speculated that the difference in climate might be the cause. Swedish explorer Pehr Kalm observed in his travel diary that the climate of the New World caused life—plants and
40 animals, including humans—to possess less stamina, stature, and longevity than in Europe.

In the New World, refuting such theories became a matter of patriotism. The colonists set about arguing that their settlement was causing a gradual
45 increase in temperatures and improvement of the flora and fauna of North America. Benjamin Rush, physician and signatory of the Declaration of Independence, speculated that, if cultivation kept pace with clearing of new lands, climate change
50 might even reduce the incidence of fevers and disease. Thomas Jefferson was especially eager to rebut the proponents of the theory of climatic degeneracy. He expended substantial efforts to this effect with page after page of animal measurements
55 showing that the American animals were not inferior to their European counterparts. He also had help from James Madison, who shared his own measurements and urged Jefferson to use them in his arguments.
60   The Founders did not settle for mere advocacy: they wanted more and better evidence. On the question of whether the winters were getting milder, Ben Franklin encouraged the president of Yale University to make steady wintertime observations in
65 different parts of the country. Madison made regular observations at his estate, which he assiduously entered into his meteorological journals. Jefferson, too, kept meticulous records, and encouraged his friends and colleagues to submit their measurements
70 to the American Philosophical Society to show the effect of clearing and culture towards the changes of climate. Jefferson himself made significant contributions to the development of modern meteorology, promoting methodological
75 standardization and expansion of geographical coverage and calling for the establishment a national meteorological service.
Modern reconstructions show that although there was a brief warming period in New England during
80 the late 1700s, Jefferson's measurements predate any actual man-made climate change. The theories of Jefferson and his contemporaries could not consider the modern understanding of the greenhouse effect. Their theories led to a belief that a changing climate
85 would necessarily be beneficial, whereas today there is an awareness of the dangers of climate change.
Yet one should not belittle the efforts of these early climate change advocates. Their search for evidence resulted in substantial contributions to

CONTINUE ➡

90 zoology and was instrumental to the foundation of
modern meteorology and climatology. Far from a
stronghold of climate change skepticism, as the
United States is sometimes seen today, the country's
founders were vocal proponents of early theories of
95 man-made climate change, writing extensively in
favor of the theory that settlement was improving the
continent's climate. Today's climate change

advocates may recognize in themselves some of the
overzealousness of the Founding Fathers and
100 therefore better guard against potential fallacies.
Skeptics may recognize in themselves the often anti-
scientific spirit of the degeneracy-theorists and thus
make greater efforts to engage constructively in the
scientific enterprise today.

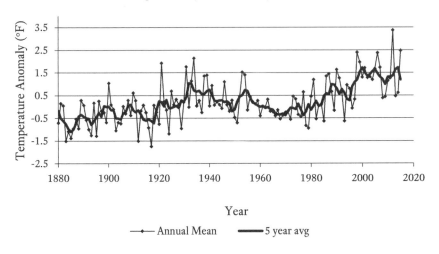

US Temperature (Annual Mean) 1880–2015

Year

—— Annual Mean   —— 5 year avg

Adapted from NASA Goddard Institute for Space Studies website. © 2016

11

The main point of the passage is that

A) the founding fathers believed in global warming,
so Americans today should follow their lead and
take action on climate change.

B) understanding the history, science, and politics
of climate change in the time of the founding
fathers may help people approach these issues
today.

C) climate change skepticism and advocacy both
have a long history in the United States.

D) man-made climate change was not achieved
during the time of the founding fathers and thus
is not likely to be possible today.

12

As it is used in line 5, "ambivalence" most nearly
means

A) apathy.

B) uncertainty.

C) neutrality.

D) negativity.

CONTINUE

13

Based on the passage, at least some of the founding fathers believed that man-made climate change was

A) a myth since all climate change is based on world-wide weather patterns and changes.

B) possible to achieve through the actions of colonizing and likely to bring about positive effects.

C) desirable as a means of creating conditions for humans to have a greater biological advantage over other species.

D) a falsehood spread by the prejudices of those who viewed Europe as superior to the Americas.

14

Which choice provides the best evidence for the answer to the previous question?

A) Lines 36–37 ("He … cause")

B) Lines 42–43 ("In the New … patriotism")

C) Lines 43–46 ("The colonists … America")

D) Lines 51–56 ("Thomas … counterparts")

15

The author of the passage mentions Georges-Louis Leclerc's and Pehr Kalm's ideas primarily to

A) suggest that modern notions regarding climate change have their origins in the thought of respected European thinkers.

B) offer examples of scientists whose ideas support the beliefs of the founding fathers.

C) mock them as foolish compared to current views and the notions of early colonists.

D) explain the founding fathers' interest in studying and even trying to impact the climate of the United States.

16

As it is used in line 51, the word "eager" most nearly means

A) restless.

B) nervous.

C) keen.

D) prepared.

17

The passage suggests that the historical example discussed is applicable to modern climate concerns in that

A) the mistakes of the founders can help people today to be more careful about inaccurate assumptions in their own thinking.

B) the arguments the founders made are directly applicable to the central questions regarding climate change today.

C) the past beliefs illuminate the foolishness of the still-prevalent belief that man-made climate change is a positive force.

D) the anti-scientific thinking that spurred Jefferson and others is the basis of the views of those who deny man-made climate change.

18

Which choice provides the best evidence for the answer to the previous question?

A) Lines 4–8 ("Far … change")

B) Lines 60–61 ("The Founders … evidence")

C) Lines 97–100 ("Today's … fallacies")

D) Lines 101–104 ("Skeptics … today")

1   **1**

19

Which of the following gives the best summary of the information provided in the graph?

A) Average temperatures in the United States have steadily increased since the time of the founding fathers.

B) Average temperatures in the United States have fluctuated over the past 130 years, but never more than ±1 °F.

C) After a century of fluctuation above and below long-term averages, the past thirty years show a trend of increasing average temperatures.

D) The temperature fluctuations that Jefferson measured were more significant than the changes measured over the past 130 years.

20

The information provided in the graph suggests that the variation in average temperatures from year to year

A) is greater than the mean variation over a five-year period.

B) is insufficient to indicate a measurable difference over greater periods of time.

C) is decreasing while overall temperatures are increasing.

D) never changes more than 0.1 °F.

CONTINUE

Questions 21–30 are based on the following passage.

This passage is adapted from Lydia Pyne, "Neanderthals in 3D: L'Homme de La Chapelle." ©2015 by The Public Domain Review. Here, Pyne considers the significance of a landmark publication in paleoanthropology.

On August 3, 1908, French prehistorian Jean Bouyssonie, his brother, Amédée Bouyssonie, and their colleague Louis Bardon found a Neanderthal skeleton in a system of caves near La Chapelle-aux-
5 Saints in south-central France. The discovery was exciting for the newly-emerging field of paleoanthropology because the Neanderthal was found in its original, undisturbed archaeological context—in situ—and excavations of the skeleton
10 revealed that it was more complete than anything else in the fossil record. La Chapelle quickly became an iconic fossil within scientific and popular circles and went on to inspire everything from dioramas at the Field Museum of Natural History to science fiction's
15 *A Guerre du Feu* (Quest for Fire.)
After the skeleton was excavated, the Bouyssonies sent the remains to the eminent Marcellin Boule, the Director of the Laboratory of Palaeontology at the prestigious Musée d'Histoire Naturelle in Paris.
20 Boule conducted a two-year detailed anatomical study of the fossil that culminated in a hefty monograph, *L'Homme Fossile de La Chapelle-aux-Saints*, published in 1911. *L'Homme* was the first and most comprehensive publication of Neanderthal
25 skeletal anatomy in scientific literature, establishing the La Chapelle skeleton as the most complete fossil reference for early paleo-studies. Boule's detailed anatomical description of the skeleton provided a framework for any new Neanderthal fossils
30 discovered, and the 1911 reconstructions of La Chapelle became the basis for all subsequent Neanderthal research. The book is filled with chapters of anatomical descriptions, careful measurements, photographs of the skeleton in the
35 ground, prior to excavation, as well as sketches of geomorphic cross-sections from the cave. In addition to the tables of metrics and photographs of the La Chapelle fossil, Boule included another type of medium that gave readers of *L'Homme* a way to
40 interact with the fossil for themselves. At the back of the book, Boule included six stereoscopic plates of the Neanderthal skull.

By the time *L'Homme* was published, the stereoscope would have been a familiar object, one of
45 the many optical toys—along with kaleidoscopes, zoetropes and cameras—through which the nineteenth-century eye had peered in wonder. The stereoscope's particular trick was to give a two-dimensional image an illusion of depth. Gazing
50 through its viewfinder, the two slightly offset images of the stereoscopic plate, or stereogram, positioned in front would combine to create an illusion of three dimensions.
The device, however, was much more than just a
55 toy or illustrative distraction—it developed into an important tool for laboratory and scientific work in the late nineteenth and early twentieth centuries. Just as telescopes and microscopes expanded what is visible, the stereoscope expanded how researchers
60 were able to see different specimens.
As fossils were themselves too rare and important to send between researchers, proxies—casts, measurements, sketches, photographs, and highly detailed descriptions—were needed to provide
65 accurate and sufficient information. Drawing from a tradition of stereoscopic anatomical atlases, the La Chapelle-aux-Saints Neanderthal plates gave the reader a first-person experience of interacting with the fossil in three dimensions.
70 The stereo cards of the Neanderthal skull gave readers of the *L'Homme Fossile de La Chapelle-aux-Saints* the opportunity to see for themselves the complexity of the Neanderthal cranium. This added dimensionality of the stereo cards helped bring the
75 La Chapelle skeleton to the forefront of paleoanthropological research in the early twentieth century—the stereo plates deepened viewers' connections to the fossil. (*L'Homme's* beautifully detailed stereoscopic prints of each bone from the
80 skeleton were the 1911 version of data sharing.) While it is easy to think of 3D rendering of fossils as a recent technological phenomenon, stereograms offer a glimpse at the explanatory power of stereoscopic images and highlight the connections three-
85 dimensional viewing made between viewer and object. Boule's inclusion of stereoscopic images of the La Chapelle Neanderthal helped solidify the fossil's iconic status in the early-twentieth-century paleoanthropology.

21

Based on the passage, what can be reasonably inferred about the La Chapelle skeleton?

A) The La Chapelle skeleton is the only Neanderthal that has ever been discovered.

B) The fossil remains that were found were unusually complete.

C) Scientists were initially ignorant of the scientific value of the La Chapelle skeleton.

D) The skull of the La Chapelle skeleton was never found.

22

As it is used in line 9, "in situ" most nearly means

A) in a seated position.

B) into an underground location.

C) in its original setting.

D) in a place set aside for a purpose.

23

It can be inferred from the passage that the Bouyssonnie brothers sent the La Chapelle skeletal remains to Marcellin Boule in order to

A) encourage him to make stereoscopic plates of the Neanderthal skull.

B) allow him to distribute the fossils to other researchers.

C) enable him to conduct a complete anatomical study.

D) prove to Boule that the skeleton they found was iconic.

24

As it is used in line 17, "eminent" most nearly means

A) distinguished.

B) conspicuous.

C) grandiose.

D) noble.

25

The primary purpose of the second paragraph (lines 16-42) is to shift the focus of the passage from the discovery of the fossil to

A) an explanation of the fossil's achievement of iconic status and its impact on modern science.

B) an analysis of the influence of a scientist's contributions to a particular field of study.

C) biographical information of an important scientist and a summary of his anatomical study.

D) a detailed description of a scientific publication about the fossil which included an example of an important optical technology.

26

Which choice provides the best evidence for the answer to the previous question?

A) Lines 16–19 ("After…Paris")

B) Lines 23–27 ("L'Homme … studies")

C) Lines 27–32 ("Boule's…research")

D) Lines 36–42 ("In addition…skull")

27

According to the passage, one difference between a stereoscope and a kaleidoscope is

A) the stereoscope created an illusion of three dimensions.

B) the stereoscope was a familiar object to people in the nineteenth century.

C) the kaleidoscope was an optical toy and the stereoscope was not.

D) the kaleidoscope was more similar to zoetropes and cameras than the stereoscope was.

28

In lines 78-80 ("L'Homme's...sharing") the author includes a comparison between stereoscopic prints and modern data sharing in order to

A) provide the reader with a metaphor for envisioning what stereoscopic prints look like.

B) give the reader a better understanding of the purpose and impact of Boule's inclusion of stereoscopic images in his book.

C) describe in modern terms how Boule made the stereoscopic images that he included in his book.

D) emphasize the significant differences between a method of data sharing in 1911 and the modern technology used today.

29

It can be reasonably inferred that the reaction of Boule's colleagues to the stereograms in his book would most likely have been

A) bewildered confusion: the stereoscope was an unusual object and viewed as a distraction at the turn of the century.

B) sincere appreciation: they provided a first-person experience of an important discovery.

C) grudging acceptance: in 1911 stereograms weren't as useful for presenting images as photographs.

D) surprised delight: stereoscopic images had never been used in a scientific publication before.

30

Which choice provides the best evidence to the previous question?

A) Lines 54-57 ("The device ... centuries")

B) Lines 61-65 ("As ... information")

C) Lines 73-78 ("This ... fossil")

D) Lines 86-89 ("Boule's ... paleoanthropology")

Questions 31–41 are based on the following passage and supplementary material.

This passage is Susan B. Anthony's speech "Women's Rights to Suffrage." She delivered the speech in 1873 after she was fined for illegally attempting to vote.

Friends and Fellow Citizens: I stand before you tonight under indictment for the alleged crime of having voted at the last presidential election, without having a lawful right to vote. It shall be my work this
5 evening to prove to you that in thus voting, I not only committed no crime, but, instead, simply exercised my citizen's rights, guaranteed to me and all United States citizens by the National Constitution, beyond the power of any State to deny.
10 The preamble of the Federal Constitution says: "We, the people of the United States, in order to form a more perfect union, establish justice, insure domestic tranquility, provide for the common defense, promote the general welfare, and secure the
15 blessings of liberty to ourselves and our posterity, do ordain and establish this Constitution for the United States of America."

It was we, the people; not we, the white male citizens; nor yet we, the male citizens; but we, the
20 whole people, who formed the Union. And we formed it, not to give the blessings of liberty, but to secure them; not to the half of ourselves and the half of our posterity, but to the whole people—women as well as men. And it is a downright mockery to talk to
25 women of their enjoyment of the blessings of liberty while they are denied the use of the only means of securing them provided by this democratic-republican government—the ballot.

For any State to make sex a qualification that must
30 ever result in the disfranchisement of one entire half of the people is to pass a bill of attainder, or an ex post facto law, and is therefore a violation of the supreme law of the land. By it the blessings of liberty are forever withheld from women and their female
35 posterity. To them this government has no just powers derived from the consent of the governed.

To them this government is not a democracy. It is not a republic. It is an odious aristocracy; a hateful oligarchy of sex; the most hateful aristocracy ever
40 established on the face of the globe; an oligarchy of wealth, where the rich govern the poor, an oligarchy of learning, where the educated govern the ignorant, or even an oligarchy of race, where the Saxon rules the African, might be endured; but this oligarchy of
45 sex, which makes father, brothers, husband, sons, the oligarchs over the mother and sisters, the wife and daughters of every household—which ordains all men sovereigns, all women subjects, carries dissension, discord and rebellion into every home of
50 the nation.

Webster, Worcester and Bouvier all define a citizen to be a person in the United States, entitled to vote and hold office.

The only question left to be settled now is: Are
55 women persons? And I hardly believe any of our opponents will have the hardihood to say they are not. Being persons, then, women are citizens; and no State has a right to make any law, or to enforce any old law, that shall abridge their privileges or
60 immunities. Hence, every discrimination against women in the constitutions and laws of the several States is today null and void, precisely as is every one against Negroes.

Impact of Women's Suffrage on Voter Turnout
(averaged across all states)

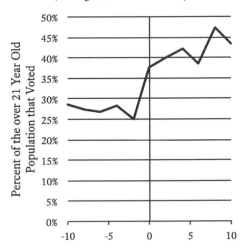

The horizontal axis shows the years before and after women were given the right to vote in different states: Year zero is the first year in which women were allowed to vote in different states.

Adapted from John R. Lott Jr. and Lawrence W. Kenny, "Did Women's Suffrage Change the Size and Scope of Government?" ©1999 by The University of Chicago.

1   1

31

The author constructs an argument in favor of women's suffrage by

A) claiming that women in America worked to earn the right to vote.

B) comparing it to Negro emancipation.

C) quoting established laws that explicitly support women's suffrage.

D) showing that disenfranchisement of women is unconstitutional.

32

Which choice provides the best evidence for the answer to the previous question?

A) Lines 11–17 ("We the people … America")

B) Lines 18–24 ("It was we … men")

C) Lines 29–33 ("For any … the land")

D) Lines 54–57 ("The only … not")

33

Throughout the passage, the speaker's tone is best described as

A) forceful.

B) pedantic.

C) irate.

D) despondent.

34

The author quotes the preamble of the Constitution lines 11–17 ("We the people…America") in order to

A) mimic its rhetorical strategies to enhance the legitimacy of her argument.

B) analyze it to further advance her primary argument.

C) suggest, by way of inference and direct argument, that it is outmoded.

D) suggest an alteration by way of amendment to the US Constitution.

35

In line 33, "supreme" most nearly means

A) unquestionable.

B) perfect.

C) highest.

D) rare.

36

Based on lines 33–38 ("By it … aristocracy"), which of the following can be inferred as a larger consequence of female disenfranchisement?

A) It undermines true democracy.

B) Women's voices and those of their posterity will forever be silenced.

C) Women's issues will be neglected.

D) Only white males have the blessing of liberty.

1   **1**

37

How does the author distinguish between the oligarchies mentioned in lines 40–44 ("an oligarchy … might be endured") and the oligarchy of sex mentioned in lines 44–50 ("but this oligarchy … home of the nation")?

A) Other oligarchies are more short term.

B) The oligarchy of sex pertains to everyone.

C) The oligarchy of sex is more damaging to those it harms.

D) Other oligarchies are more politically charged.

38

In line 60, "immunities" most nearly means

A) pardons.

B) exceptions.

C) protections.

D) inoculations.

39

The author draws a link between women and Negroes to suggest that

A) both need to be enfranchised because of the ways they have been mistreated by oppressive rulers.

B) the two groups need to collaborate for civil rights activism because their goals are the same.

C) women should be sympathetic to Negroes, and vice versa, because both have struggled through the same challenges.

D) the same reasoning that makes discrimination against Negroes unconstitutional also makes discrimination against women unconstitutional.

40

Which choice provides the best evidence for the answer to the previous question?

A) Lines 18–20 ("It was we…the Union")

B) Lines 37–41 ("To them…the poor")

C) Lines 43–47 ("even an oligarchy… household")

D) Lines 60–63 ("Hence…against Negroes")

41

The graph most strongly suggests that women's suffrage resulted in

A) no discernible impact upon on the outcomes of specific elections or the participation of specific individuals.

B) no change in the trend for voter participation prior to suffrage.

C) an immediate increase in voter participation and a maintaining of at least a 10 percent total increase for ten years.

D) a doubling of total voter participation due to both genders being allowed to vote followed by a slow return to previous percentages.

CONTINUE

Questions 42–52 are based on the following passages.

Passage 1 is adapted from a 1913 translation of J.H. Fabre's *The Life of the Fly.* Passage 2 is adapted from Stephen Jay Gould's 1982 essay "Nonmoral Nature."

Passage 1

The considerations which I have set forth seem to me strictly logical: the Anthrax,[1] owing to the very fact that he is free to take his nourishment where he pleases on the body of the fostering larva, must, for
5 his own protection, be made incapable of opening his victim's body. I am so utterly convinced of this harmonious relation between the eater and the eaten that I do not hesitate to set it up as a principle. I will therefore say this: whenever the egg of any kind of
10 insect is not fastened to the larva destined for its food, the young grub, free to select the attacking point and to change it at will, is as it were muzzled and consumes its provisions by a sort of suction, without inflicting any appreciable wound. This
15 restriction is essential to the maintenance of the victuals in good condition. My principle is already supported by examples many and various, whose depositions are all to the same effect. All insects— flies, ichneumon flies and beetles—scrupulously
20 spare their foster mother; they are careful not to tear her skin, so that the vessel may keep its liquid good to the last.

The wholesomeness of the victuals is not the only condition imposed: I find a second, which is no less
25 essential. The substance of the fostering larva must be sufficiently fluid to ooze through the unbroken skin under the action of the sucker. The necessary fluidity is realized as the time of the metamorphosis draws near. When they wished Medea to restore
30 Pelias to the vigor of youth, his daughters cut the old king's body to pieces and boiled it in a cauldron, for there can be no new existence without a prior dissolution. We must pull down before we can rebuild; the analysis of death is the first step towards
35 the synthesis of life. The substance of the grub that is to be transformed into a bee begins, therefore, by disintegrating and dissolving into a fluid broth. The materials of the future insect are obtained by a general recasting. Even as the founder puts his old
40 bronzes into the melting pot in order afterwards to

cast them in a mold whence the metal will issue in a different shape, so life liquefies the grub, a mere digesting machine, now thrown aside, and out of its running matter produces the perfect insect, bee,
45 butterfly or beetle, the final manifestation of the living creature.

Passage 2

As I read through the nineteenth- and twentieth-century literature on ichneumons, nothing amused me more than the tension between an intellectual
50 knowledge that wasps should not be described in human terms and a literary or emotional inability to avoid the familiar categories of epic and narrative, pain and destruction, victim and vanquisher. We seem to be caught in the mythic structures of our
55 own cultural sagas, quite unable, even in our basic descriptions, to use any other language than the metaphors of battle and conquest. We cannot render this corner of natural history as anything but story, combining the themes of grim horror and fascination
60 and usually ending not so much with pity for the caterpillar as with admiration for the efficiency of the ichneumon.

I detect two basic themes in most epic descriptions: the struggles of prey and the ruthless
65 efficiency of parasites. Although we acknowledge that we may be witnessing little more than automatic instinct or physiological reaction, still we describe the defenses of hosts as though they represented conscious struggles. Thus, aphids kick and
70 caterpillars may wriggle violently as wasps attempt to insert their ovipositors. The pupa of the tortoiseshell butterfly (usually considered an inert creature silently awaiting its conversion from duckling to swan) may contort its abdominal region so sharply that attacking
75 wasps are thrown into the air. The caterpillars of *Hapalia,* when attacked by the wasp *Apanteles machaeralis,* drop suddenly from their leaves and suspend themselves in air by a silken thread. But the wasp may run down the thread and insert its eggs
80 nonetheless. Some hosts can encapsulate the injected egg with blood cells that aggregate and harden, thus suffocating the parasite.

[1] The Anthrax is a type of bee fly.

42

The author of Passage 1 refers to a "harmonious relation between the eater and the eaten" in line 7 to suggest that

A) insects are as comfortable in the role of predator as of prey.

B) the particular characteristics of each are best suited to enact their roles.

C) the symbiotic relationship between the two is mutually beneficial.

D) the euphonious sound produced by the two is compelling to the author.

43

In the first paragraph of Passage 1 (lines 1–22), the terms "victuals," "foster mother," and "vessel" refer to

A) the larva being devoured.

B) the maternal care given to insects.

C) nature's providential arrangements.

D) the Anthrax as it nourishes itself.

44

The author of Passage 1 mentions the "founder" and the "melting pot" (lines 39–40) primarily to

A) provide support for his claims regarding the nature of insect hierarchy.

B) suggest the infinite variety of actions within every area of insect life.

C) show one application of insect life to human affairs.

D) compare the insect transformation to a more familiar image.

45

As it is used in line 15, "restriction" most nearly means

A) conscious restraint.

B) necessary limitation.

C) surprising constriction.

D) unavoidable choice.

46

The best evidence for the validity of the claim in lines 48–53 ("nothing … vanquisher") is found in

A) Lines 1–2 ("The considerations … logical")

B) Lines 8–11 ("I will … food")

C) Lines 25–29 ("The substance … near")

D) Lines 29–33 ("When … dissolution")

47

The primary point of the first paragraph of Passage 2 (lines 47–62) is to

A) point out a problem many scientists have in writing about nature.

B) introduce a common misconception about the nature of insect life and suggest a method to correct it.

C) deride the writings of naturalists of the past in order to assert the superiority of collecting data to offering explanations.

D) insist upon the impossibility of true objectivity in scientific studies by exploring past examples.

CONTINUE ➤

1

1

48

The author of Passage 2 would most likely respond to the statement made in lines 33–35 ("We ... life") of Passage 1 by

A) accepting the evidence behind the claim but offering a contradictory interpretation of that evidence.

B) agreeing that life and death are undeniably and irrevocably linked and suggesting further proofs of the linkage.

C) denying that such themes about the nature of human life and death can be drawn from the world of insects.

D) quibbling over the specific words but valuing the effort to convey the truths of life through the study of insects.

49

Which choice provides the best evidence for the answer to the previous question?

A) Lines 49–55 ("the tension ...sagas")

B) Lines 59–62 ("combining ... ichneumon")

C) Lines 63–65 ("I detect ... parasites")

D) Lines 75–82 ("The caterpillars ... parasite")

50

The author of Passage 2 presents the relationship between "automatic instinct" and "conscious struggles" as contrasting

A) basic needs and loftier goals.

B) lower and higher forms of life.

C) scientific fact and human interpretation.

D) nonmoral and immoral actions.

51

The two passages relate to each other in that

A) Passage 2 criticizes aspects of Passage 1's research methodology.

B) Passage 1 is an example of the trend Passage 2 examines.

C) Passage 1 raises a concern that Passage 2 resolves.

D) Passage 2 concurs with the conclusions drawn in Passage 1 using new data.

52

The author provides the references in lines 69–82 ("Thus ... parasite") primarily to

A) provide more accurate descriptions of insect behavior than those he criticizes.

B) reveal the inefficient nature of actual relations in the natural world.

C) mock the methods of observation most common in earlier naturalists.

D) suggest the faulty kinds of descriptions given in previous works on insect behavior.

STOP

If you finish before time is called, you may check your work on this section only.
Do not turn to any other section.

2   2

Writing and Language Test

35 MINUTES, 44 QUESTIONS

Turn to Section 2 of your answer sheet to answer the questions in this section.

DIRECTIONS

Each passage below is accompanied by a number of questions. For some questions, you will consider how the passage might be revised to improve the expression of ideas. For other questions, you will consider how the passage might be edited to correct errors in sentence structure, usage, or punctuation. A passage or a question may be accompanied by one or more graphics (such as a table or graph) that you will consider as you make revising and editing decisions.

Some questions will direct you to an underlined portion of a passage. Other questions will direct you to a location in a passage or ask you to think about the passage as a whole.

After reading each passage, choose the answer to each question that most effectively improves the quality of writing in the passage or that makes the passage conform to the conventions of standard written English. Many questions include a "NO CHANGE" option. Choose that option if you think the best choice is to leave the relevant portion of the passage as it is.

Questions 1-11 are based on the following passage.

Dylan Goes Electric

—1—

In the summer of 1965, folk music was flourishing, both gaining a wider audience and spreading political messages through the medium of song. Perhaps the best known figure to emerge from this movement in the early 1960s was Bob **1** Dylan, whose songs were often political protests disguised as simple folk ballads. [A] His **2** songs, "Masters of War" and "Blowin' in the Wind" railed against war profiteers and the purposeless destruction of war, and songs like "The Times They Are A-Changin'" and "A Hard Rain's A-Gonna Fall" were

1

A) NO CHANGE
B) Dylan's
C) Dylan, who's
D) Dylan, his

2

A) NO CHANGE
B) songs "Masters of War," and "Blowin' in the Wind,"
C) songs "Masters of War" and "Blowin' in the Wind"
D) songs, "Masters of War," and "Blowin' in the Wind,"

CONTINUE

seen as prophecies of a coming revolution of peace, freedom, and equality.

—2—

Thus, when Dylan came to play the Newport Folk **3** Festival for the third year in a row in July 1965, promoters and fans were ready for another set of his familiar acoustic guitar and harmonica arrangements and excited to hear the "voice of a generation" continue to lead the call for political change in the form of folk music. What Dylan did instead **4** lead to immediate controversy, even **5** bitter anger. Apparently irritated by criticism that the Paul Butterfield Blues Band had received for playing electric blues, Dylan shocked his audience by performing with a full electric rock **6** band, and played new songs without political themes, such as

3

The author would like to revise this sentence to clarify the context of the performance in terms of the main idea of this paragraph. Which choice best accomplishes this?

A) Festival, a yearly folk festival held at Newport, RI,

B) Festival, the premier traditional folk music event at the time,

C) Festival, a precursor to later concerts like Bonnaroo, Coachella, and Lollapalooza,

D) Festival, a great opportunity for any new artist to make a mark on the world of folk music,

4

A) NO CHANGE

B) leads

C) led

D) has lead

5

A) NO CHANGE

B) sardonic vitriol.

C) depressed dejection.

D) unhappiness in some folks.

6

A) NO CHANGE

B) band and playing

C) band playing

D) band, they played

CONTINUE

his now-classic "Like a Rolling Stone," 7 a song which would later be named the greatest rock song of all time by *Rolling Stone* magazine. [B]

—3—

But many people did not approve of this development. The response of the Newport audience was mixed, with both boos and cheers audible between songs in the recording; however many key figures in the folk movement were incredibly upset by his decision. [C] Listening to Dylan's performance at Newport, folk singer Pete Seeger allegedly threatened to cut the power cables with an ax, though he later claimed he did so because he was concerned that the audience could not understand Dylan's lyrics rather than offended at his electrically amplified sound. [D] Soon after, Joan Baez, who had often performed with Dylan, penned a song "To Bobby," imploring him to write folk songs of political protest again. 8 Universally, both Dylan's new sound and new themes were seen by some as failures to live up to his artistic duty.

7

The writer is considering deleting the underlined portion and changing the preceding comma to a period. Should the writer make this change?

A) Yes, because it adds information that is not relevant to the point of the sentence.

B) Yes, because it contradicts the rest of the sentence.

C) No, because it is needed to understand the main idea of the sentence.

D) No, because it provides a connection necessary to understand the next paragraph.

8

A) NO CHANGE

B) Furthermore, both

C) Conversely, both

D) Thus, both

CONTINUE

—4—

Dylan's 1965 Newport performance has been re-examined to determine just how negative the initial [9] reaction was, Dylan saw the performance as an opportunity to take a new direction as an artist. In his view, the audience that made him popular had no more right to restrict his themes or control his choices as an artist than the government they wanted him to agitate against. [10]

Question [11] asks about the previous passage as a whole.

9

A) NO CHANGE
B) reactions were, Dylan
C) reaction was, but Dylan
D) reactions were, though Dylan

10

The author wants to add a sentence that effectively concludes the story by reiterating its main ideas and considering its relevance today. Which choice best accomplishes this?

A) Dylan has remained a popular and idiosyncratic artist, one of America's treasures as a songwriter, performer, and icon.
B) Dylan has continued to defy expectations in his long and successful career, changing his sound and themes freely to express his artistic independence.
C) Interestingly, Dylan later went on to record multiple acoustic folk records and wrote many more songs of political protest, so his change was short-lived.
D) Surprisingly, many of his fans from back in 1965 have since changed their minds about Dylan's decision, and they now can download the whole concert!

Think about the previous passage as a whole as you answer question 11.

11

The author wants to add the following sentence to the essay:

> Dylan claims he didn't necessarily mean to offend: he saw changing his sound and themes as a natural part of his development as an artist.

Where should this addition be made?

A) Point A in Paragraph 1.
B) Point B in Paragraph 2.
C) Point C in Paragraph 3.
D) Point D in Paragraph 3.

CONTINUE

Questions 12–22 are based on the following passage and supplementary material.

Exercise: It Does a Brain Good

—1—

For many years, there has been an overwhelming amount of research supporting the health and fitness benefits of regular exercise. However, recent research suggests that exercise may promote positive outcomes not only for the body but also for the mind. Studies indicate that aerobic exercise may have surprising effects on mental well-being, including **12** unexpected short-term psychological benefits and long-term cognitive benefits.

—2—

13 In addition to these immediate psychological benefits of exercise, consistent exercise has been shown to have more long-term mental benefits, as well. A recent study suggests that regular aerobic exercise can improve long-term cognitive functioning. The University of Minnesota study conducted in 2014 by Dr. David R. Jacobs and his **14** colleagues' testing the cardiorespiratory fitness (CRF) of healthy young people

12

A) NO CHANGE
B) unforeseen
C) inexplicable
D) DELETE the underlined portion.

13

Which of the following best combines the two underlined sentences?

A) A recent study suggests that regular aerobic exercise not only provides immediate psychological benefits but also improves long-term cognitive functioning.

B) A recent study suggests that regular aerobic exercise can improve long-term cognitive functioning in addition to its providing immediate psychological benefits from regular aerobic exercise.

C) On top of these immediate psychological benefits of exercise, consistent exercise has been shown to have more long-term mental benefits, as well; for example, a recent study suggests that regular aerobic exercise can improve long-term cognitive functioning.

D) In addition to these immediate psychological benefits of exercise, more long-term mental benefits of consistent exercise have been shown, and a study has suggested that regular aerobic exercise can improve long-term cognitive functioning.

14

A) NO CHANGE
B) colleague's tested
C) colleagues tests
D) colleagues tested

with an average age of 25. Jacobs and his team then re-tested as many of the same individuals as possible 25 years later. [15] Its results serve as a reminder of the importance of not only exercising while young, but also maintaining a consistent exercise program into middle age. First, those who showed greater CRF when first tested showed higher cognitive abilities across the [16] board, particularly for verbal memory. Second, those whose CRF decreased less between the initial test and the follow-up over two decades later showed better executive functioning—one of the key elements of effective mental activity—than those whose CRF had deteriorated more over the time between tests, indicating a less active lifestyle in the intervening years.

—3—

First, many studies in recent years have suggested that aerobic exercise [17] —even just ten minutes of brisk walking—can reduce symptoms for those who suffer from [18] anxiety or depression symptoms. Further, many psychologists and doctors recommend regular exercise [19] as apart of a program, together with medication and

15

A) NO CHANGE
B) Their results serve
C) Its result serves
D) Their results has served

16

A) NO CHANGE
B) board; particularly
C) board—particular
D) board: in particularly

17

The writer is considering deleting the underlined portion. Should the writer make this change?
A) Yes, because it contradicts the paragraph's emphasis on exercising more.
B) Yes, because it is already implied by the beginning of the sentence.
C) No, because it gives a detail that may help readers understand the point.
D) No, because it defines the unfamiliar term "aerobic exercise."

18

A) NO CHANGE
B) symptoms of anxiety or depression.
C) anxiety or depression.
D) anxiety symptoms or depression symptoms.

19

A) NO CHANGE
B) as apart in
C) as a part about
D) as a part of

therapy, to treat symptoms of these disorders. 20 <u>Even those</u> without a diagnosed anxiety or depression disorder, regular exercise has been shown to increase mental functioning and reduce stress.

—4—

These studies are just two recent pieces of evidence that add to our understanding of the many ways in which exercise benefits us—ways that go beyond physical fitness. 21 <u>Most people, when asked about the benefits of exercise, don't think of mental and psychological aspects.</u> Perhaps as these kinds of benefits become more widely proven and known, more people will be willing to take the time to reap the many benefits of exercise.

Responses to the Request to "State a Benefit of Exercise"

Benefit of Exercise	Number of Respondents	Percent of Respondents
Increased physical fitness	206	45.9
Control of chronic diseases	99	22
Prevention of chronic diseases	91	20.3
Mental well being	44	9.8
Other	9	2

Adapted from TJR Babwah and P. Nunes, "Exercise Habits in Trinidad: motivating forces and barriers." ©2010 by The University of the West Indies.

Question 22 **asks about the previous passage as a whole.**

20

A) NO CHANGE
B) Even for those
C) Even they
D) Even for them

21

The writer would like to revise this sentence to add specific data from the table to support the main point of the paragraph. Which choice best accomplishes this intention?

A) According to a recent survey, most people see the benefits of exercise as related primarily to long-term physical health, with very few citing cognitive or psychological benefits.

B) According to a recent survey, less than 10 percent of respondents cited mental well-being as a benefit of exercise.

C) Surprisingly, over 45 percent of people in a recent survey claimed that physical fitness was a benefit of exercise.

D) Physical fitness is still the main benefit of exercise that the majority of people think of, according to a recent survey, though other kinds of benefits are also cited.

Think about the previous passage as a whole as you answer question 22.

22

In order for the passage to be most logical, paragraph 3 should be placed

A) where it is now.
B) before paragraph 1.
C) after paragraph 1.
D) after paragraph 4.

CONTINUE ▶

2   2

Questions 23–33 are based on the following passage and supplementary material.

Napping on the Job

The Centers for Disease Control and Prevention (CDC) consider lack of sleep to be a public health concern. According to a recent poll, [23] almost 30 percent of American adults reported sleeping six hours or less per night, which is not enough sleep. [24] It has become common knowledge—lack of sleep is associated with serious health [25] problems, such as, heart disease, high blood pressure, diabetes, and stroke. Adults who sleep poorly at night often report having trouble performing daily tasks. Even small sleep deficits have

Sleep Duration of U.S. Adults Aged 20+
(according to CDC survey)

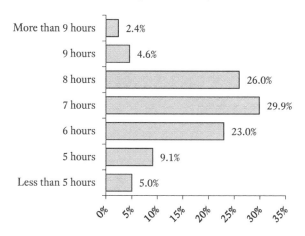

Adapted from CDC. ©2011 by the Centers for Disease Control and Prevention.

23

The writer wants to use the specific data in the graph to show how widespread the problem of insufficient sleep is. Which choice best accomplishes this?

A) NO CHANGE

B) many American adults sleep less than 5 hours per night, which is dangerously less than the recommended 7–9 hours per night.

C) only 3 percent of American adults get more than 10 hours of sleep each night, and only 7–9 hours are recommended.

D) over 35 percent of American adults reported sleeping 6 hours or less per night, well below the 7–9 hours recommended for adults.

24

The writer would like to change the beginning of this sentence to indicate that the majority of Americans are unaware of the health risks associated with a lack of sleep. Which choice best accomplishes this goal?

A) Some consequences of insufficient sleep may be temporary, but others are chronic and life threatening;

B) Both epidemiological and sleep deprivation studies support an alarming conclusion:

C) The CDC has partnered with other organizations in a widespread campaign to alert the public to a growing concern among health professionals:

D) A popular magazine recently published several articles discussing illnesses stemming from sleep deprivation—

25

A) NO CHANGE

B) problems such as:

C) problems; such as

D) problems, such as

CONTINUE

noticeable impacts on coordination, alertness, and concentration. [26]

In the workplace, these deficits add up to decreased productivity, accidents, and lost revenue. An overtired [27] workforce many researchers have found, is less active and therefore less productive. By some estimates, the loss of productivity due to sleepiness among workers costs US businesses $63 billion dollars annually, and preventable workplace accidents cost businesses $31 billion dollars. The health of both workers and businesses depends on finding a way for employees to meet their sleep requirements.

One solution to daytime sleepiness comes from the National Aeronautics and Space Administration (NASA). In the eighties and nineties, NASA conducted field experiments in an effort to improve alertness and responsiveness among pilots. Reviewing the results, [28] pilot error was reduced significantly and performance was boosted by as much as 100 percent by taking short naps while on duty.

---

[26]

The writer is considering adding the following sentence:

> Sleep deprivation also affects teenagers: 70 percent of high-school students report sleeping fewer than the recommended number of hours a night.

Should the writer make this addition here?

A) Yes, because it introduces the central topic of the following paragraph.

B) Yes, because it allows the reader to compare the reported sleep statistics of workers to those of students.

C) No, because it contradicts evidence provided earlier in the paragraph.

D) No, because it focuses on data that is not directly related to the main point of the passage.

[27]

A) NO CHANGE

B) workforce: many

C) workforce, many

D) workforce—many

[28]

A) NO CHANGE

B) short naps were discovered while on duty by researchers to reduce pilot error significantly and boost performance by as much as 100 percent.

C) researchers discovered that short naps while on duty reduced pilot error significantly and boosted performance by as much as 100 percent.

D) a discovery was made that short naps while on duty reduced pilot error and boosted performance by as much as 100 percent.

2   2

Inspired by such studies, a growing number of employers have implemented nap-friendly policies in the workplace. Businesses from Ben and Jerry's to the New York Times have installed nap stations where tired workers can lie down to [29] reserve mentally and physically.

Experts recommend including several features in the development of a napping-friendly workplace environment. Employers should clearly designate the area in which employees can rest. It is important for workers to have a separate, dedicated space for napping because it reminds them that napping is a break from the regular work routine. In order to maximize rest time, napping should occur in a cool, dark, and quiet place.

[30] Ideally, the formulation of napping policies should be part of a discussion about how to create a workplace culture that is safe, healthy, and productive. Additionally, overtired workers should be evaluated for potential health problems contributing to [31] there fatigue. Proponents of workplace naps point out that employees are allowed to eat and exercise on breaks. Sleep, they argue, is a biological necessity and needs to be

29

A) NO CHANGE
B) recharge
C) resurrect
D) enliven

30

A) NO CHANGE
B) Nevertheless, the
C) Consequently, the
D) Alternatively, the

31

A) NO CHANGE
B) their
C) one's
D) his or her

CONTINUE ▶

accommodated by employers as well. That an increasing number of employers are supportive of napping practices [32] which is encouraging to sleep activists. [33] Soon, predicts author and sleep activist Arianna Huffington, nap rooms will be "as common as conference rooms."

[32]

A) NO CHANGE
B) that
C) and
D) DELETE the underlined portion.

[33]

The writer would like to conclude the paragraph with a sentence indicating that accommodating workplace napping is a trend among employers that will continue to increase in popularity. Which choice best accomplishes this goal?

A) NO CHANGE

B) Increasingly, their message is spreading to colleges and universities, and nap centers are springing up in campus libraries across the country to provide hard-working students a reprieve during study sessions.

C) Napping at work has proven beneficial, and in the future, more employees might sleep during work hours.

D) Employers continue to cite improved employee health, increased productivity, and reduced turnover rates as incentives for implementing napping policies.

Questions 34–44 are based on the following passage.

Public Transportation

Ever since Henry Ford popularized the automobile in the early 20th century, the United States **34** had been a nation of cars. In 1956, President Eisenhower signed the Federal-Aid Highway **35** Act, which funded a 41,000 mile national system of interstate highways. The new highway system unified the country, **36** making it possible to travel by car throughout almost every state. Nonetheless, in the past decade more Americans have depended less on their cars, and the use of public transportation has increased by more than 20 percent in response to economic, health, and environmental concerns related to automobile use. In 2014, Americans took 10.8 billion trips on public transportation, the greatest number of trips in a single year in nearly 60 years. Responding to increased demand, many communities are investing in infrastructure for public transport.

Public transit is a key component of the economy in many regions. For those workers who use it, public transit provides an efficient and reliable method of travel. In fact, the majority of trips on public transportation are to and from the workplace. **37** However, public transit can also financially benefit individuals. For some, using public transportation is a logical response to high gas prices, and public transportation may even eliminate the need to have a car altogether.

34

A) NO CHANGE
B) has been
C) is
D) was

35

A) NO CHANGE
B) Act; and it funded
C) Act: funding
D) Act, which was funding

36

The author would like to conclude the sentence by indicating that the car became symbolic of American values. Which choice best accomplishes this goal?

A) NO CHANGE
B) allowing Americans to commute to work and encouraging the expansion of suburbs.
C) and the car became synonymous in the public imagination with American independence and individuality.
D) and within a decade, the number of car sales increased by more than 50 percent.

37

A) NO CHANGE
B) Moreover,
C) Even so,
D) Regardless,

2

2

Driving is not only an economic burden but also a public health concern. Vehicle crashes are a significant cause of death in the United States: **38** in 2014, over 35,000 deaths resulted from almost 30,000 fatal crashes. The act of operating a vehicle itself creates stress, which adversely affects the health of drivers. Consistently, drivers who experience the longest commutes to work report the lowest sense of well-being and mood. Additionally, vehicle emissions contribute to the poor air quality that is linked to a variety of **39** ailments: including asthma, chronic bronchitis, and heart disease.

Using public transportation reduces the emissions **40** engaged in poor air quality, ozone depletion, and global climate change by as many as 37 million metric tons of carbon dioxide annually. Public transit also uses **41** as much energy per passenger as private vehicles, which saves the US more than 11 million gallons of

38

Which statement best supports the claim made previously in the sentence?

A) NO CHANGE

B) the number of licensed drivers increased from 163 million in 1988 to 210 million in 2010.

C) according to a recent survey, American drivers were ranked as the seventh worst in the world.

D) in 2010, the rate of alcohol impairment among drivers involved in fatal crashes was four times higher at night than during the day.

39

A) NO CHANGE

B) ailments—including

C) ailments, including

D) ailments; including

40

A) NO CHANGE

B) available

C) developed

D) implicated

41

Which choice results in a logical introduction to the second part of the sentence?

A) NO CHANGE

B) less energy per passenger than private vehicles,

C) more energy per passenger than private vehicles,

D) an unmeasurable amount of energy per passenger,

CONTINUE

gasoline each day. Environmental advocates cite these and other reasons [42] for use of and investment in public transit infrastructure.

[43] The development and expansion of public transit systems positively impacts local communities. The construction of infrastructure projects creates green jobs and extends subway lines and bus routes to new areas. Since 45 percent of Americans have no access to any mode of public transportation, expanding the country's transit systems would benefit millions of Americans, allowing [44] these to benefit from the modes of transportation vital to healthy communities. Although cars continue to remain the transportation mode of choice for most Americans, transportation researchers expect that growing energy and car ownership costs, an awareness of public and personal health risks, environmental concerns, and improved access will continue to increase the use of public transportation throughout the country.

42

A) NO CHANGE
B) for use of and investing in
C) for using and to invest in
D) for use and investing in

43

The writer is considering deleting this sentence. Should the writer make this change?

A) Yes, because it contradicts the paragraph's claim that some communities currently are not served by any form of public transportation.

B) Yes, because it doesn't include any statistics to support its assertion that expanding public transit provides benefits to local communities.

C) No, because it provides a logical introduction to the paragraph and sets up the information that follows.

D) No, because it provides an example of the impact of public transportation.

44

A) NO CHANGE
B) whom
C) those
D) them

STOP

**If you finish before time is called, you may check your work on this section only.
Do not turn to any other section.**

Math Test – No Calculator

25 MINUTES, 20 QUESTIONS

Turn to Section 3 of your answer sheet to answer the questions in this section.

DIRECTIONS

For questions 1–15, solve each problem, choose the best answer from the choices provided, and fill in the corresponding circle on your answer sheet. **For questions 16–20**, solve the problems and enter your answer in the grid on the answer sheet. Please refer to the directions before question 16 on how to enter your answers in the grid. You may use any available space in your test booklet for scratch work.

NOTES

1. The use of calculators **is not permitted**.

2. All variables and expressions used represent real numbers unless otherwise indicated.

3. Figures provided in this test are drawn to scale unless otherwise indicated.

4. All figures lie in a plane unless otherwise indicated.

5. Unless otherwise indicated, the domain of a given function f is the set of real numbers x for which $f(x)$ is a real number.

REFERENCE

$A = \pi r^2$
$C = 2\pi r$

$A = \ell w$

$A = \dfrac{1}{2}bh$

$c^2 = a^2 + b^2$

Special Right Triangles

$V = \ell w h$

$V = \pi r^2 h$

$V = \dfrac{4}{3}\pi r^3$

$V = \dfrac{1}{3}\pi r^2 h$

$V = \dfrac{1}{3}\ell w h$

The number of degrees of arc in a circle is 360.
The number of radians of arc in a circle is 2π.
The sum of the measures in degrees of the angles in a triangle is 180.

CONTINUE

3 **3**

1

What is the value of $8a + 5$ if $4a = 24$?

A) 6

B) 29

C) 48

D) 53

2

Given the function $f(x) = 3x^2 - 4x$, which of the following is equal to $f(2x)$?

A) $6x^2 - 4x$

B) $12x^2 - 8x$

C) $18x^3 - 6x^2$

D) $36x^2 - 8x$

3

What is the value of $5x$ if $\dfrac{3}{x} = \dfrac{21}{x+12}$?

A) 15

B) 10

C) 5

D) 2

4

$$\frac{m}{n} = 3$$
$$6(n-4) = m$$

Given the system of equations above, what is the value of n?

A) 4

B) 8

C) 16

D) 24

CONTINUE

5

If $\dfrac{y+2x}{x}=\dfrac{10}{3}$, which of the following must also be true?

A) $\dfrac{x}{y}=\dfrac{3}{16}$

B) $\dfrac{x}{y}=\dfrac{3}{4}$

C) $\dfrac{y+x}{y}=\dfrac{3}{4}$

D) $\dfrac{y-2x}{y}=-\dfrac{3}{8}$

6

The point (p,q), where p and q are positive integers, lies on the line given by the equation $y=mx+3$, where m is a constant. What is the slope of the line in terms of p and q?

A) $\dfrac{q-3}{p}$

B) $\dfrac{p-3}{q}$

C) $\dfrac{3-q}{p}$

D) $\dfrac{3-p}{q}$

7

If $x-3=\sqrt{p(x-3)}$, where $p=2$, what are the possible values of x?

A) 3 and 5

B) 3 only

C) 5 only

D) 1 and 5

8

Which of the following equations represents a line that is perpendicular to the line with the equation $6x+2y=9$?

A) $y=-3x+4$

B) $y=-\dfrac{1}{3}x-5$

C) $y=\dfrac{1}{3}x+2$

D) $y=3x-3$

9

Katie is an English tutor. The amount of money, p, Katie profits in dollars can be modeled by the equation $44.50h = p + 2.20h$, where h represents the number of hours spent tutoring and \$2.20 is an average per-student travel expense. What does 44.50 represent in this equation?

A) The total amount of money charged by Katie after working h hours

B) The amount of money Katie charges per hour

C) The number of students whom Katie has tutored

D) The total amount of money paid by a student after h hours

10

In a table tennis tournament that begins with a draw of 64 people, half of the players are eliminated each round. Which of the following functions represents the number of people left in the tournament after r rounds?

A) $f(r) = 64(2)^r$

B) $f(r) = \frac{1}{2}(64)^r$

C) $f(r) = 64\left(\frac{1}{2}\right)^r$

D) $f(r) = 2\left(\frac{1}{2}\right)^{-r}$

11

Which of the following complex numbers is equivalent to $\frac{6 + 3i}{2 - 5i}$? (Note: $i = \sqrt{-1}$)

A) $\frac{-3 - 15i}{25}$

B) $\frac{12 + 5i}{16}$

C) $\frac{-3 + 36i}{29}$

D) $\frac{-5 - 5i}{21}$

12

$$A = 14.6 + 2.35d$$
$$B = 6.9 + 3.45d$$

In the equations above, A and B represent the heights, in centimeters, of two plants d days after a starting date. For what value of d will the plants have equal heights?

A) 11

B) 9

C) 7

D) 6

3 **3**

13

If for all x, $(ax+4)(3x+b)=18x^2+cx+12$, what is the value of c?

A) 30

B) 24

C) 18

D) 15

14

Given the equations $3x+4y=20$ and $y=x(-x-4)$, how many solutions (x, y) exist for the system?

A) 0

B) 1

C) 2

D) Cannot be determined

15

If $4a-2b=10$, what is the value of $\dfrac{9^a}{3^b}$?

A) 9^2

B) 3^{10}

C) 3^5

D) 3^2

CONTINUE

DIRECTIONS

For questions 16–20, solve the problem and enter your answer in the grid, as described below, on the answer sheet.

1. Although not required, it is suggested that you write your answer in the boxes at the top of the columns to help you fill in the circles accurately. You will receive credit only if the circles are filled in correctly.
2. Mark no more than one circle in any column.
3. No question has a negative answer.
4. Some problems may have more than one correct answer. In such cases, grid only one answer.
5. **Mixed numbers** such as $3\frac{1}{2}$ must be be gridded as 3.5 or 7/2. If $3\,1\,/\,2$ is entered into the grid, it will be interpreted as $\frac{31}{2}$, not $3\frac{1}{2}$.)
6. **Decimal answers:** If you obtain a decimal answer with more digits than the grid can accommodate, it may be either rounded or truncated, but it must fill the entire grid.

Answer: $\frac{7}{13}$ Answer: 2.5

Write answer in boxes → ← Fraction line

Grid in result

← Decimal Point

Acceptable ways to grid $\frac{2}{3}$ are:

Answer: 210 – either position is correct

NOTE: You may start your answers in any column, space permitting. Columns you don't need to use should be left blank.

CONTINUE

16

If $k > 0$ and $k^4 + 5 = 21$, what is the value of k ?

17

$$3j - k = -4$$
$$2j + 5k = 3$$

According to the system of equations above, what is the value of $j + k$?

18

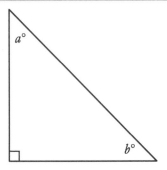

Note: Figure not drawn to scale

In the triangle above, the cosine of $b°$ is equal to 0.8. What is the value of the sine of $a°$?

CONTINUE

3 **3**

19

As a probe descends to the Kuril Trench in the Pacific Ocean, it records the amount of dissolved oxygen in the water in units of parts per million (ppm). At depths below 2,000 meters, the dissolved oxygen drops at a constant rate of d ppm for every change in depth of 100 meters, until it reaches zero. At a depth of 2,530 meters, the dissolved oxygen is measured to be 205 ppm. At a depth of 3,030 meters, the dissolved oxygen is measured to be 65 ppm. What is the value of d ?

20

If $b = 3\sqrt{5}$ and $4b = \sqrt{5x}$, what is the value of x ?

STOP

If you finish before time is called, you may check your work on this section only.
Do not turn to any other section.

Math Test – Calculator

55 MINUTES, 38 QUESTIONS

Turn to Section 4 of your answer sheet to answer the questions in this section.

For questions 1–30, solve each problem, choose the best answer from the choices provided, and fill in the corresponding circle on your answer sheet. **For questions 31–38**, solve the problems and enter your answer in the grid on the answer sheet. Please refer to the directions before question 31 on how to enter your answers in the grid. You may use any available space in your test booklet for scratch work.

NOTES

1. The use of calculators is **permitted**.

2. All variables and expressions used represent real numbers unless otherwise indicated.

3. Figures provided in this test are drawn to scale unless otherwise indicated.

4. All figures lie in a plane unless otherwise indicated.

5. Unless otherwise indicated, the domain of a given function f is the set of real numbers x for which $f(x)$ is a real number.

REFERENCE

$A = \pi r^2$
$C = 2\pi r$

$A = \ell w$

$A = \dfrac{1}{2}bh$

$c^2 = a^2 + b^2$

Special Right Triangles

$V = \ell w h$

$V = \pi r^2 h$

$V = \dfrac{4}{3}\pi r^3$

$V = \dfrac{1}{3}\pi r^2 h$

$V = \dfrac{1}{3}\ell w h$

The number of degrees of arc in a circle is 360.
The number of radians of arc in a circle is 2π.
The sum of the measures in degrees of the angles in a triangle is 180.

4 **4**

1

Luis is having carpeting installed in his living room. Each square yard of carpeting costs $50, and the labor for the installation costs $160. If Luis spends $710 to carpet his living room, what is the area of Luis' living room in square yards?

A) 11

B) 13

C) 14

D) 15

2

Given that 1 lb of coffee beans can make 40 cups of coffee, how many cups of coffee can be made from 20 oz of coffee beans (1 lb = 16 oz)?

A)   8

B)   44

C)   50

D)   86

3

A museum sells three types of tickets: child, adult, and senior. Child tickets cost $10, adult tickets cost $15, and senior tickets cost $12. Which of the following represents the amount of money the museum makes if they sell c child tickets, a adult tickets, and s senior tickets?

A) $10a + 12s + 15c$

B) $10c + 12s - 15a$

C) $10c + 12s + 15a$

D) $(10 + 12 + 15)(c + s + a)$

4

$$v = 27 + 6t$$

A car drives at an initial velocity of 27 miles per hour before accelerating at a constant rate of 6 miles per hour per second in order to get on the highway. The equation above models the car's velocity v, in miles per hour, in terms of the time t, in seconds, that the car has been accelerating. If the car's velocity is 66 miles per hour, how many seconds has it been accelerating?

A)   6.5

B)   11

C)   15.5

D)   33

CONTINUE

4   **4**

5

If $\frac{28}{9}z = \frac{35}{3}$, what is the value of z ?

A) $\frac{15}{4}$

B) $\frac{5}{4}$

C) $\frac{4}{5}$

D) $\frac{4}{15}$

6

| 1 dekaliter = 10 liters |
| 1,000 milliliters = 1 liter |

A juice company ships its product in boxes each containing 3 dekaliters of juice. Based on the information above, how many milliliters are there in each box?

A)   0.0003

B)   30

C)   300

D) 30,000

7

Electronics City Computer Sales				
	April	May	June	Total
Vishal	10	11	7	28
Josh	4	8	6	18
Sonny	12	14	14	40
Gigi	9	8	6	23
Total	35	41	33	109

The table above shows the number of computers sold over a three-month period by each member of the sales staff at Electronics City. Sonny's May and June computer sales together make up what fraction of all computers sold in the three-month period?

A) $\frac{28}{40}$

B) $\frac{14}{40}$

C) $\frac{40}{109}$

D) $\frac{28}{109}$

CONTINUE

4 **4**

Questions 8 and 9 refer to the following information.

Assuming its mass is constant, an object's momentum is directly proportional to its velocity. A bowling ball rolling with a velocity of 2 meters per second has a momentum of 12 kilogram-meters per second.

8

What will be the ball's momentum if it has a velocity of 10 meters per second?

A)   2.4 kg·m/s

B)   20 kg·m/s

C)   60 kg·m/s

D)   240 kg·m/s

9

The bowling ball starts out with a velocity of 4 meters per second but by the time it hits the pins its speed has decreased 27 percent. What is its momentum when it hits the pins?

A)   6.48 kg·m/s

B)   17.52 kg·m/s

C)   27.00 kg·m/s

D)   70.08 kg·m/s

10

The function $f(x)$ has zeros (roots) at $x = 5$, $x = 2$, and $x = -3$. Which of the following could be the function $f(x)$?

A) $(x^2 - 2x - 15)(x - 2)$

B) $(x^2 - 2x - 15)(x + 2)$

C) $(x^2 - 2x + 15)(x - 2)$

D) $(x^2 + 2x + 15)(x - 2)$

CONTINUE

11

Eddy surveyed 50 students who were waiting in line to buy lunch in his school's cafeteria. Since 45 of the 50 students surveyed said they preferred the school lunch to the local fast food restaurant, Eddy concluded that exactly 90 percent of the entire school's 330 students would prefer the school lunch to the fast food restaurant. His friends had the following criticisms of Eddy's conclusion:

Kate said one cannot make conclusions about an exact percentage of a population based on a sample of it.

Elizabeth said that Eddy's conclusions are unreliable because of a bias in his chosen sample.

Ian said that there is no whole number, and thus no appropriate number of people, that is exactly 90 percent of 330.

Which of Eddy's friends is/are correct?

A) Kate only

B) Kate and Elizabeth only

C) Elizabeth and Ian only

D) All three are correct

12

Scores							
35	71	72	75	77	85	87	87
87	87	87	88	88	88	90	91
92	93	93	93	95	96	100	100

The table above shows the scores that students in a biology class received on their final exam. The score of 35 is an outlier. If that score were removed from the set, which of the following would change by the greatest amount?

A) Mean

B) Median

C) Range

D) Mode

13

$$h(t) = 80,000\left(1 - \frac{12}{100}\right)^t$$

Leonardo just bought a new boat whose value depreciates at a rate of 12 percent per year. The expression above gives the value of his boat, in dollars, after t years has passed. Which of the following expressions could be used to determine the number of years it would take for the value of his boat to decrease by 25 percent?

A) $20,000 = 80,000\left(1 - \frac{12}{100}\right)^t$

B) $20,000 = 80,000\left(1 - \frac{25}{100}\right)^t$

C) $60,000 = 80,000\left(1 - \frac{12}{100}\right)^t$

D) $60,000 = 80,000\left(1 - \frac{12}{100}\right)^{4t}$

14

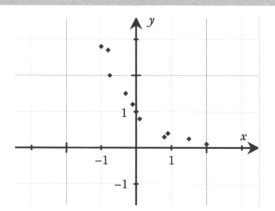

The above scatterplot shows a relationship that can be approximately modeled by which of the following equations if $0 < m < 1$?

A) $y = m^x$

B) $y = x^m$

C) $y = -mx$

D) $y = \dfrac{x}{m}$

15

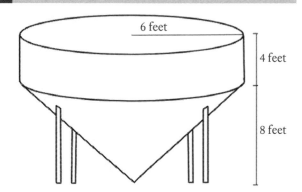

Vladimir owns a food company that sells blueberry jam in 18 in³ jars. He makes his jam in large vats as shown above, composed of a cone base and a shorter cylindrical body. If a batch of jam fills the vat to the very top, approximately how many jars can he fill from one vat of blueberry jam (12 in = 1 ft)?

A) 14,000

B) 25,000

C) 42,000

D) 72,000

CONTINUE

4 **4**

16

A large group of students took a test. The median score was 75 while the average score was 81. Which factor would, if true, best account for the difference between the average and median scores?

A) Most of the students scored in the C range (71–80).

B) No students failed the test (scored below 65).

C) No students scored higher than 90.

D) A few students scored much higher than the rest of the class.

17

Mario is cutting a pipe that is 66 inches long into three pieces. The second piece is 50 percent longer than the first, and the third piece is twice as long as the second. How long, in inches, is the longest piece?

A) 12

B) 18

C) 24

D) 36

18

Sheila had a bag of small candies, of which she gave away 70 percent. Her friend returned to Sheila a quantity of candy that equaled 20 percent of the amount Sheila had remaining after giving away the 70 percent. What is the original amount of candy in the bag in terms of the amount, x, that Sheila has now?

A) $(0.3)(1.2)x$

B) $\dfrac{x}{(0.3)(1.2)}$

C) $0.5x$

D) $2x$

19

Mrs. Brennan wants to buy x computers for her company and has a budget of B dollars. If she buys x computers today, they will cost $1,000 each, and she will need to raise an additional $2,000, but if she waits two months, the computers will cost $900 each and she will have $400 left over. What is the value of B?

A) $24,000

B) $22,000

C) $21,600

D) $20,000

CONTINUE

Questions 20–22 refer to the following information.

The table below shows the number of international tourists visiting 10 countries over a three-year period.

International Tourism: Number of Arrivals per Year			
Country Name	2011	2012	2013
France	81,550,000	83,051,000	84,726,000
United States	62,821,000	66,657,000	69,768,000
Spain	56,177,000	57,464,000	60,661,000
China	57,581,000	57,725,000	55,686,000
Italy	46,119,000	46,360,000	47,704,000
Turkey	34,654,000	35,698,000	37,795,000
Germany	28,374,000	30,411,000	31,545,000
United Kingdom	29,306,000	29,282,000	31,169,000
Russian Federation	24,932,000	28,177,000	30,792,000
Thailand	19,230,000	22,354,000	26,547,000
Total	440,744,000	457,179,000	476,393,000

20

If the figures for the international tourists in 2012 were represented in a pie chart, what would be the best approximation for the measurement of the central angle for the portion of the pie chart representing the number of international tourists visiting the United States?

A) 37°

B) 46°

C) 52°

D) 74°

21

Which of the following best approximates the percent increase from 2012 to 2013 in the number of international tourists visiting Thailand?

A) 16%

B) 19%

C) 28%

D) 38%

22

The average increase, per year, for international tourists going to Germany between 2011 and 2013 is closest to that of which other country?

A) United Kingdom

B) China

C) France

D) Spain

CONTINUE

23

Vocabulary Quiz Scores	
Test Score	Number of Students
100	1
90	5
80	10
70	8
60	2

The table above shows the distribution of test scores in Mrs. Keaton's English class. Which of the following sets of test scores, if added, would change the standard deviation of the distribution the least?

A) 90, 90, 90

B) 70, 80, 85

C) 100, 100, 60

D) 60, 60, 60

Questions 24 and 25 refer to the following information.

$$F = \frac{Gm_1 m_2}{r^2}$$

The equation above defines the force, in newtons, of gravity between two objects in terms of the masses of the two objects m_1 and m_2 and the distance between the two objects r. G is the universal gravitational constant, equaling approximately 6.674×10^{-11}.

24

Which of the following expresses the square of the distance between two objects as defined by the masses of the two objects and the force of gravity between them?

A) $r^2 = \dfrac{m_1 m_2}{GF}$

B) $r^2 = \dfrac{Gm_1 m_2}{F}$

C) $r^2 = \dfrac{F}{Gm_1 m_2}$

D) $r^2 = FGm_1 m_2$

25

The Planet Quenya's elliptical orbit around its star is shaped such that the farthest distance away from the star (at the aphelion) is three times the nearest distance (at the perihelion). If the gravitational attraction between the planet and its star is called g, then what is the ratio of g at the aphelion to g at the perihelion?

A) $\dfrac{1}{3}$

B) $\dfrac{1}{9}$

C) $\dfrac{1}{27}$

D) $\dfrac{1}{81}$

CONTINUE

4 **4**

26

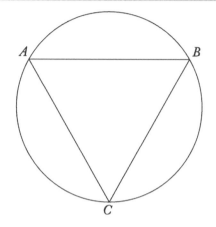

If $\triangle ABC$ is equilateral and the length of $\overparen{ABC}$ is 18π, what is the radius of the circle?

A)   6

B)   9

C)   13.5

D)   18

27

In order to ride the Kiddie Coaster at the local amusement park, a child must be at least 34 inches tall and no taller than 56 inches. Which of the following expressions can be used to determine whether a child h inches tall can ride the coaster?

I. $34 \geq h \geq 56$

II. $|h - 45| \leq 11$

III. $56 - h > 22$

A) I only

B) II only

C) I and III only

D) I, II, and III

The population of an ant colony is expected to increase by 34 percent from one month to the next over the course of a year. What type of relationship should be expected between the age of the colony, in months, and its population over that year?

A) A linear relationship whose graph has a positive slope

B) A linear relationship whose graph has a negative slope

C) An exponential relationship in which higher populations correspond to higher ages of the colony

D) A quadratic relationship in which higher populations correspond to higher ages of the colony

29

For a polynomial $f(x)$, $f(4)=5$. Which of the following must therefore be true about $f(x)$?

A) The leading coefficient of $f(x)$ is 4.

B) The remainder when $f(x)$ is divided by $(x-4)$ is 5.

C) $(x-4)$ is a factor of $f(x)$.

D) $(x-5)$ is a factor of $f(x)$.

	Less than 3 hours	3 to 6 hours	More than 6 hours	Total
Class 1	6	19	5	30
Class 2	8	15	7	30
Total	14	34	12	60

A teacher asked the students in two of his classes how many hours they had spent studying for their recent midterm. The results are shown in the table above. If a student is chosen from those that studied at most 6 hours, what is the probability the student is from Class 1?

A) $\dfrac{5}{30}$

B) $\dfrac{5}{12}$

C) $\dfrac{25}{48}$

D) $\dfrac{25}{30}$

CONTINUE

4 4

DIRECTIONS

For questions 31–38, solve the problem and enter your answer in the grid, as described below, on the answer sheet.

1. Although not required, it is suggested that you write your answer in the boxes at the top of the columns to help you fill in the circles accurately. You will receive credit only if the circles are filled in correctly.
2. Mark no more than one circle in any column.
3. No question has a negative answer.
4. Some problems may have more than one correct answer. In such cases, grid only one answer.

5. **Mixed numbers** such as $3\frac{1}{2}$ must be be gridded as 3.5 or 7/2. If $3|1|/|2|$ is entered into the grid, it will be interpreted as $\frac{31}{2}$, not $3\frac{1}{2}$.)

6. **Decimal answers:** If you obtain a decimal answer with more digits than the grid can accommodate, it may be either rounded or truncated, but it must fill the entire grid.

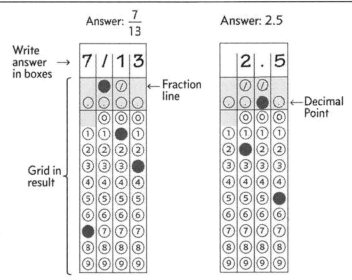

Answer: $\frac{7}{13}$

Answer: 2.5

Write answer in boxes

← Fraction line

Grid in result

← Decimal Point

Acceptable ways to grid $\frac{2}{3}$ are:

Answer: 210 – either position is correct

NOTE: You may start your answers in any column, space permitting. Columns you don't need to use should be left blank.

CONTINUE

4 🖩 **4**

31

A tree with an initial height of 1 meter grows at an average rate of 1.2 meters per year. At that rate, how many years will it take for the tree to reach a height of 19 meters?

32

A partially filled gas tank contains 2 gallons of gasoline. If a fuel pump can pump at 0.5 gallons per second and the maximum capacity of the tank is 14 gallons, after how much time (in seconds) will the tank be full?

33

The graph of the function $g(x) = 2x^2 - 6x + c$ contains the point $(2, 5)$ in the standard xy-coordinate plane. What is the value of c?

CONTINUE

4 **4**

34

Andy and Jen plan to save a combined $420 each month, and Jen will contribute $80 more than Andy each month. How much (in dollars) will Andy have contributed after six months?

35

$$x^2 + y^2 - 6x - 8y = -16$$

The equation above defines a circle in the *xy*-coordinate plane. What is the length of the circle's radius?

36

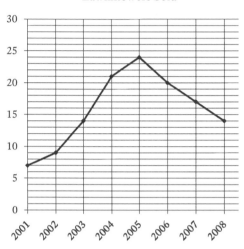

Lawnmowers Sold

The line graph above shows the number of lawnmowers sold at a local hardware store between the years 2001 and 2008. According to the graph, the number of lawnmowers sold in 2001 is what fraction of the number sold in 2004?

CONTINUE

4 **4**

37

$$h(x) = \frac{1}{(x+3)^2 + (x+3) - 42}$$

For what value of $x > 0$ is the function $h(x)$ above undefined?

38

Anthony deposited $1,200 into a bank account that pays interest at an annual rate of 1.5 percent. Anthony's friend Shaun found an account that earns 3 percent interest compounded annually and made an initial deposit of $1,000 into this account at the same time Anthony made his. After ten years if neither Anthony nor Shaun deposit or withdraw any additional money into their accounts, how much more money will Anthony have in his account than Shaun will have in his? (Round your answer to the nearest dollar and disregard the $ sign when gridding your response.)

STOP

If you finish before time is called, you may check your work on this section only.
Do not turn to any other section.

Manual Answer Keys

Reading Test Manual Answer Key

Special SAT Reading Strategies

Command of Evidence Questions

Practice Passage

1	C	5	A	
2	D	6	B	
3	B	7	D	
4	C			

Words in Context Questions

Practice Passage

1	C	8	D	15	D
2	A	9	A	16	D
3	C	10	C	17	B
4	B	11	D	18	A
5	A	12	D	19	C
6	C	13	A		
7	A	14	B		

Figure-Based Questions

Try It!

1	B

Practice Set

1	C
2	A
3	C

Practice Passages

Social Science

1	A	5	B	9	C
2	C	6	A	10	A
3	D	7	D	11	C
4	C	8	C		

Science

12	B	16	A	20	C
13	D	17	C	21	A
14	C	18	D	22	A
15	C	19	C		

Literature

23	D	27	A	31	C
24	B	28	B	32	D
25	B	29	A		
26	D	30	A		

Challenge

33	C	37	D	41	B
34	A	38	D	42	D
35	A	39	C	43	B
36	B	40	A	44	C

Writing and Language Test Manual Answer Key

Expression of Ideas

Questions without Questions

Try It!
1. A   3. A
2. C   4. D

Practice Set
1. D   6. A   11. A
2. D   7. C   12. B
3. A   8. A   13. D
4. C   9. B   14. C
5. B   10. D   15. B

Writer's Intention Questions

Try It!
1. B

Practice Set
1. A   6. B   11. B
2. C   7. B   12. C
3. D   8. A   13. A
4. B   9. A   14. A
5. A   10. D

Add/Delete Questions

Try It!
1. C
2. B

Practice Set
1. D   5. A
2. A   6. A
3. B   7. D
4. C

Ordering Questions

Try It!
1. C

Practice Set
1. C
2. C
3. C
4. A
5. D

Sentence Combining

Try It!
1. B

Practice Set
1. B   6. B
2. A   7. D
3. C   8. B
4. C   9. B
5. A

Figure-Based Questions

Try It!
1. B

Practice Set
1. A
2. D
3. C
4. D

Standard English Conventions

Sentence Structure

Try It! (other correct answers are possible for many questions)

1. speaker, Jonathan
2. and then
3. However out   /   be, Crighton
4. Math; however, he
5. making
6. match; hence,   /   trophy: it
7. I grew
8. game did   /   play: I
9. NO CHANGE   /   traumatized because   /   unexpectedly and
10. of which

Practice Set

1	B	8	A	15	B
2	D	9	C	16	C
3	D	10	C	17	D
4	C	11	A	18	B
5	D	12	B	19	A
6	B	13	D	20	C
7	D	14	B		

Punctuation: Essential and Nonessential Elements

Try It! (other correct answers are possible for many questions)

1. dog that bit my child should never
2. kind woman, gave
3. Humanity, which receives
4. was musically gifted, composed
5. her socks, she walked
6. presidency, who must be at least 35, campaign
7. Teasing that turns into bullying has
8. musician Michael
9. Children interested in helping others are
10. packages, the mailman tripped
11. My sister Lily coaches   /   players who are injured.
12. sharpener, which I bought online, broke

Practice Set

1	B	5	A	9	C
2	B	6	D	10	B
3	A	7	B	11	D
4	C	8	D	12	C

Punctuation: Other Uses

Commas—Try It! (other correct answers are possible for many questions)
1. fascinating Spanish town, but
2. Intense(,) daily aerobic / blood circulation, heart-health, and
3. way to the friendly neighborhood
4. dark blue Corvette and / new black leather
5. well, but / unique, appetizing dishes / us and

Semicolons, Colons, and Dashes—Try It! (other correct answers are possible for many questions)
1. guitar as if
2. steps, opened the creaky old door,
3. the city: the beach, the architecture,
4. soda: / peer pressure,
5. monuments; however, / architecture, especially / cities like / Vienna, and

End Marks and Quotation Marks—Try It! (other correct answers are possible for many questions)
1. that nobody / known?
2. declared, "The / with respect."

Practice Set

1	B	6	C	11	D
2	D	7	C	12	B
3	C	8	D	13	A
4	C	9	A	14	B
5	A	10	C	15	C

Verb Usage

Try It! (other correct answers are possible for many questions)
1. writes
2. NO CHANGE / must choose
3. rake / tell
4. have / starting
5. are / live
6. should have corrected / was
7. could not have had any / would be
8. had found / would have appealed

Practice Set

1	A	6	C	11	C
2	C	7	B	12	B
3	D	8	B	13	C
4	A	9	D	14	D
5	C	10	C	15	A

Pronouns

Try It! (other correct answers are possible for many questions)
1. of its problems
2. who the robbers / they
3. the police / he or she is.
4. I really need sleep
5. Whom
6. which is / NO CHANGE

Practice Set

1	C	6	D
2	D	7	D
3	C	8	B
4	A	9	C
5	A	10	D

Parallelism and Comparisons

Try It! (other correct answers are possible for many questions)
1. NO CHANGE / skating.
2. fool or playing
3. time management.
4. nor / best sport.
5. to those of working from an office.
6. or in Central America / the US.
7. write, proofread, and e-mail the essay
8. They are paying not only

Practice Set

1	D	5	D	9	D
2	B	6	D	10	C
3	D	7	B	11	B
4	C	8	C	12	A

Apostrophes

Try It!
1. NO CHANGE / amphibian's tail
2. Smiths' friend's dog
3. grassroots bring-out-the vote / its
4. It's / you're
5. You're / her eyes.
6. books' covers were / their
7. NO CHANGE / shops
8. Stephen and Seth's / its / their audience's thinking.
9. NO CHANGE
10. dog's collar / Joan's dogs' collars / their collars.

Practice Set

1	A	4	C
2	C	5	D
3	A	6	D

Modifiers

Try It! (other correct answers are possible for many questions)
1. with no hard wood floors to a family.
2. children brownies
3. John missed the flight.
4. the seven dwarves found the job more manageable.
5. the research center amazed the scientists by still having
6. Steve gave a disgusting and hilarious description of the projectile vomit striking his eyeball.

Practice Set

1	C	5	B
2	C	6	B
3	A	7	C
4	C		

Idioms and Usage

Try It! (other correct answers are possible for many questions)
1. personal computer / necessary for learning
2. fewer advantages at / than students
3. inconsistent with your performance in / direct effect of
4. between two / effect relationships effectively.
5. different from / of Baltimore.
6. from leaving / eluded / many more years.

Practice Set

1	C	5	A	9	D
2	D	6	B	10	A
3	C	7	C		
4	D	8	C		

Mathematics Test Manual Answer Key

Strategies

Backsolving

1	C	6	D	11	B
2	D	7	D	12	A
3	B	8	B	13	D
4	B	9	B	14	D
5	D	10	D	15	D

Plugging in Numbers

Problem Set 1

1	D	6	B	11	A
2	D	7	D	12	C
3	D	8	D	13	B
4	C	9	D	14	B
5	C	10	B	15	A

Problem Set 2

1	C	6	B	11	B
2	A	7	D	12	B
3	A	8	B	13	B
4	D	9	C	14	B
5	A	10	B	15	B

Calculator

1	C	5	A	9	B
2	B	6	B	10	A
3	D	7	C		
4	B	8	C		

Arithmetic Skills

1	57	11	4	21	13.5
2	41	12	20	22	18
3	5	13	1	23	100
4	5	14	4	24	7
5	18	15	190	25	80
6	$\frac{11}{9}$	16	7	26	88
		17	9	27	60
7	16	18	20	28	50%
8	$\frac{1}{14}$	19	12	29	20%
		20	12	30	125%
9	$\frac{25}{9}$				
10	$\frac{3}{5}$				

No-Calculator

1	C	6	C	11	D
2	B	7	C	12	C
3	C	8	C	13	D
4	A	9	C	14	B
5	B	10	A	15	D

Heart of Algebra

Algebraic Translation

1	B	8	A	15	C
2	D	9	D	16	A
3	C	10	A	17	A
4	B	11	C	18	B
5	B	12	A	19	D
6	D	13	C	20	D
7	B	14	A		

Solving Linear Equations and Inequalities

1	B	6	A	11	D
2	B	7	C	12	C
3	D	8	C	13	D
4	C	9	B	14	$3/5 < x < 1$
5	C	10	D	15	3001

Functions

Try It!

1	18	5	2.4	9	13
2	16	6	$a^2 + 2$	10	2
3	5	7	$4a^2 + 2$		
4	8	8	$4b^2 + 8b + 6$		

Problem Set

1	C	5	B	9	4
2	B	6	B	10	3
3	A	7	C		
4	C	8	C		

Linear Functions

Try It!

1	B	2	C

Problem Set

1	B	8	A	15	C
2	C	9	D	16	C
3	C	10	D	17	A
4	D	11	A	18	D
5	B	12	D	19	18
6	C	13	A	20	3
7	D	14	B		

Systems of Equations and Inequalities

1	D	8	C	15	D
2	C	9	D	16	A
3	A	10	C	17	2.5
4	B	11	A	18	9
5	C	12	A	19	18
6	D	13	A	20	2
7	C	14	A		

Passport to Advanced Math

Exponents

Try It!

1. 9
2. 2
3. $\dfrac{1}{2^4} = \dfrac{1}{16}$
4. 8
5. 12
6. 2

Try It!

1. 36
2. 9

Problem Set

1. B
2. B
3. D
4. D
5. C
6. C
7. D
8. C
9. B
10. C
11. D
12. B
13. 9
14. 0
15. 8

Distributing

1. C
2. B
3. C
4. D
5. C
6. D
7. B
8. B
9. 36
10. 13

Factoring

1. A
2. B
3. C
4. A
5. D
6. D
7. B
8. D
9. C
10. C
11. C
12. C
13. 9
14. 2
15. 7

Radicals and Fractional Exponents

1. A
2. C
3. A
4. C
5. A
6. D
7. D
8. C
9. C
10. 8

Fractional Operations and Equations

1. D
2. D
3. D
4. B
5. B
6. C
7. C
8. 60
9. $\dfrac{1}{4}$
10. 2

Literal Equations

1. D
2. A
3. C
4. A
5. A
6. B
7. D
8. D
9. C
10. D
11. D
12. D
13. C
14. A
15. A

Quadratic Functions

1. C
2. A
3. A
4. C
5. B
6. D
7. A
8. C
9. C
10. B
11. C
12. B
13. B
14. A
15. A
16. C
17. B
18. D
19. 0
20. 12

Polynomial Functions

1. C
2. C
3. A
4. C
5. B
6. C
7. B
8. B
9. B
10. C
11. B
12. 2 or 3
13. $\dfrac{4}{5}$
14. 3
15. $\dfrac{3}{2}$

Exponential Functions

1. C
2. B
3. D
4. D
5. D
6. D
7. B
8. D
9. D
10. C
11. A
12. C
13. C
14. 1.06
15. 504

Additional Functions and Transformations

1. B
2. A
3. A
4. A
5. B
6. C
7. C
8. B
9. D
10. D
11. D
12. D
13. D
14. A
15. D
16. D
17. B
18. D
19. B
20. C

Data Analysis and Problem Solving

Data Analysis

1	A	6	C	11	B
2	B	7	D	12	C
3	C	8	A	13	C
4	A	9	C	14	C
5	C	10	B	15	A

Probability

1	A	5	C	9	D
2	D	6	C	10	D
3	B	7	C		
4	A	8	B		

Percent

1	C	6	C	11	B
2	D	7	A	12	25
3	B	8	A	13	12.5
4	B	9	D	14	50
5	A	10	C	15	30

Rate and Unit Conversion

1	A	6	C	11	D
2	C	7	D	12	B
3	C	8	B	13	33.8
4	D	9	A	14	1056
5	B	10	C	15	7.01

Statistics

1	D	8	C	15	C
2	A	9	B	16	D
3	B	10	D	17	D
4	D	11	C	18	D
5	C	12	B	19	D
6	B	13	D	20	C
7	B	14	B		

Scatterplots

1	A	5	A	9	D
2	B	6	C	10	B
3	C	7	D		
4	C	8	B		

Additional Topics in Math

Basic Geometry

1	C	6	C	11	D
2	D	7	B	12	C
3	B	8	C	13	C
4	D	9	D	14	12
5	A	10	D	15	3

Similar Triangles and Trigonometry

1	D	6	B	11	C
2	C	7	A	12	D
3	A	8	D	13	54
4	D	9	B	14	35
5	A	10	B	15	0.84

Circles

1	A	6	D	11	D
2	D	7	B	12	B
3	C	8	C	13	16
4	C	9	A	14	74
5	D	10	D	15	13

Complex Numbers

1	C	6	B
2	D	7	A
3	D	8	C
4	A	9	B
5	C	10	29

Practice Test Answer Keys

Question Types

Reading Question Types

WIC   **Words in Context:** These questions ask about the meaning or use of specific words or phrases as they are used in the passage.

COE   **Command of Evidence:** These questions are usually in two parts, with the first being a challenging reading comprehension question and the second question providing line numbers to choose from for the best evidence for the correct answer. When these questions are paired, **both** questions are coded as **COE** in the answer keys.

IG   **Informational Graphic:** These questions are based on what the test calls "supplemental materials," such as graphs, tables or maps.

RC   **Reading Comprehension:** These questions make up the remainder of the test questions, asking about such things as tone, main ideas, or inferences.

Writing Question Types

SEC   **Standard English Conventions:** These questions are based on rules for grammar and correct usage, covering topics such as punctuations, pronoun reference, sentence structure and more.

EOI   **Expression of Ideas:** These questions are based on the context of the passage, so there are no rules to learn to answer them. They often ask students to do certain compositional tasks, including ordering of sentences or paragraphs, transitioning between ideas, adding or deleting text, and much more.

Math Question Types

HOA   **Heart of Algebra:** These questions involve the kind of basic algebraic translation, equation solving, and linear expression found in a first-year Algebra class.

PAM   **Passport to Advanced Math:** These questions involve the kind of algebraic form changes and higher level functions found both in a first-year and a second-year Algebra class.

PSD   **Problem Solving and Data Analysis:** These questions include manipulating data from graphs and tables, as well as data representation topics such as percent, probability, and statistics.

ATM   **Additional Topics in Math:** These questions include geometry and trigonometry topics, plus a few lesser-taught topics such as complex numbers.

How to Score your SAT Practice Test

Math

1. Count the number of correct answers on Sections 3 and 4 and add them up to find your raw score.

2. Use the Raw Score Conversion Table on the following page to convert your raw score to a scaled score on the 200–800 point scale.

Evidence-Based Reading and Writing

1. First count the number of correct answers on Section 1 (the Reading Test). That is your Reading raw score. Use the Raw Score Conversion Table to convert your Reading raw score to a scaled score.

2. Next, count the number of correct answers on Section 2 (the Writing and Language Test). That is your Writing and Language raw score. Use the Raw Score Conversion Table to convert your Writing and Language raw score to a scaled score.

3. Add your Reading scaled score to your Writing and Language scaled score, and multiple the sum by 10. This is your Evidence-Based Reading and Writing Test score.

Example

> Tarika took SAT Practice Test 1 and answered 35 of the 52 questions correctly on the SAT Reading Test and 24 of the 44 questions correctly on the SAT Writing and Language Test. Using the Raw Score Conversion Table for Test 1, she calculates that she received an SAT Reading Test score of 29 and an SAT Writing and Language Test score of 26. She adds 29 to 26 (giving a total of 55) and then multiplies 55 by 10 to determine her SAT Evidence-Based Reading and Writing Section score of 550.

Total Score out of 1600

Add your Evidence-Based Reading and Writing Section score to your Math Section score. The result is your total score on the SAT Practice Test on a scale of 400–1600.

Test 1: Answer Key

Reading Test

Q	A	TYPE	Q	A	TYPE	Q	A	TYPE	Q	A	TYPE	Q	A	TYPE
1.	C	RC	11.	A	COE	21.	B	RC	31.	B	COE	42.	A	COE
2.	D	WIC	12.	B	COE	22.	D	RC	32.	B	COE	43.	C	COE
3.	A	RC	13.	C	RC	23.	D	WIC	33.	A	RC	44.	D	RC
4.	A	COE	14.	D	RC	24.	C	COE	34.	C	RC	45.	C	RC
5.	D	COE	15.	A	COE	25.	B	COE	35.	D	COE	46.	C	WIC
6.	C	RC	16.	B	COE	26.	C	COE	36.	B	COE	47.	D	COE
7.	A	WIC	17.	C	WIC	27.	B	COE	37.	C	WIC	48.	D	COE
8.	B	COE	18.	C	WIC	28.	D	WIC	38.	A	WIC	49.	B	RC
9.	D	COE	19.	C	RC	29.	A	RC	39.	C	RC	50.	C	RC
10.	A	RC	20.	B	IG	30.	D	RC	40.	A	COE	51.	B	RC
									41.	C	COE	52.	B	IG

Writing and Language Test

Q	A	TYPE	Q	A	TYPE	Q	A	TYPE	Q	A	TYPE
1.	A	EOI	12.	C	SEC	23.	B	EOI	34.	D	EOI
2.	B	EOI	13.	B	EOI	24.	B	EOI	35.	C	EOI
3.	D	EOI	14.	B	EOI	25.	C	EOI	36.	D	EOI
4.	B	EOI	15.	D	SEC	26.	C	SEC	37.	C	SEC
5.	B	SEC	16.	D	SEC	27.	A	SEC	38.	B	EOI
6.	D	SEC	17.	B	EOI	28.	D	SEC	39.	B	EOI
7.	A	SEC	18.	C	SEC	29.	B	EOI	40.	D	EOI
8.	A	EOI	19.	C	EOI	30.	B	SEC	41.	B	SEC
9.	C	SEC	20.	A	EOI	31.	D	EOI	42.	B	EOI
10.	B	SEC	21.	D	SEC	32.	A	EOI	43.	A	SEC
11.	A	EOI	22.	D	EOI	33.	A	SEC	44.	D	EOI

Math Test – No Calculator

Q	A	TYPE	Q	A	TYPE	Q	A	TYPE
1.	C	HOA	11.	A	ATM	16.	3 or 6	HOA
2.	A	HOA	12.	C	PAM	17.	6	PAM
3.	C	PAM	13.	A	HOA	18.	4/5 or 0.8	ATM
4.	B	HOA	14.	D	PAM	19.	3/8 or 0.375	HOA
5.	B	PAM	15.	D	PAM	20.	8	ATM
6.	C	HOA						
7.	B	PAM						
8.	B	PAM						
9.	C	HOA						
10.	A	HOA						

Math Test – Calculator

Q	A	TYPE	Q	A	TYPE	Q	A	TYPE	Q	A	TYPE
1.	B	HOA	11.	D	HOA	21.	B	PSD	31.	11	HOA
2.	C	ATM	12.	A	PSD	22.	B	PSD	32.	2	PAM
3.	B	HOA	13.	D	PSD	23.	C	PSD	33.	$5 \leq x \leq 6.25$ or $5 \leq x \leq 25/4$	HOA
4.	A	PSD	14.	C	PAM	24.	D	ATM	34.	5	PSD
5.	C	PSD	15.	C	HOA	25.	C	PAM	35.	7	HOA
6.	D	PSD	16.	A	PSD	26.	B	PAM	36.	90	PSD
7.	B	PAM	17.	C	PSD	27.	B	HOA	37.	64	PAM
8.	C	PSD	18.	A	PSD	28.	C	PSD	38.	3/2 or 1.5	ATM
9.	D	HOA	19.	B	PAM	29.	C	PSD			
10.	A	PAM	20.	B	HOA	30.	C	PAM			

Test 1: Raw Score Conversion Table

Raw Score	Reading Test	Writing and Language Test	Mathematics Test
0	10	10	200
1	10	11	200
2	10	12	210
3	11	12	230
4	12	13	250
5	13	14	270
6	14	15	280
7	15	16	300
8	16	17	320
9	16	18	340
10	17	18	350
11	18	19	360
12	18	20	370
13	19	21	390
14	20	21	410
15	20	22	420
16	21	23	430
17	21	24	450
18	22	25	460
19	22	25	470
20	23	26	480
21	23	26	490
22	23	27	500
23	24	28	510
24	24	28	520
25	25	29	530
26	25	29	540
27	26	30	550
28	26	31	560
29	27	31	570
30	27	32	580
31	28	33	590
32	28	33	600
33	28	33	600
34	29	34	610
35	29	35	620
36	30	35	630
37	30	36	640
38	31	37	650
39	31	38	660
40	32	38	670
41	32	39	680
42	33	39	690
43	33	40	700
44	34	40	710
45	35		710
46	35		720
47	36		730
48	37		730
49	38		740
50	39		750
51	39		750
52	40		760

Raw Score	Reading Test	Writing and Language Test	Mathematics Test
53			770
54			780
55			790
56			790
57			800
58			800

Test 2: Answer Key

Reading Test

Q	A	TYPE	Q	A	TYPE	Q	A	TYPE	Q	A	TYPE	Q	A	TYPE
1.	D	COE	11.	C	RC	21.	B	RC	32.	A	COE	43.	C	COE
2.	C	COE	12.	D	RC	22.	C	WIC	33.	B	COE	44.	C	COE
3.	C	RC	13.	A	RC	23.	A	COE	34.	C	RC	45.	A	RC
4.	D	RC	14.	A	COE	24.	C	COE	35.	C	RC	46.	D	WIC
5.	B	RC	15.	B	COE	25.	B	RC	36.	C	WIC	47.	D	RC
6.	C	WIC	16.	C	COE	26.	D	RC	37.	A	RC	48.	B	RC
7.	A	RC	17.	C	COE	27.	C	RC	38.	A	WIC	49.	C	COE
8.	C	WIC	18.	A	WIC	28.	D	COE	39.	B	RC	50.	B	COE
9.	D	COE	19.	D	WIC	29.	D	COE	40.	B	RC	51.	B	RC
10.	B	COE	20.	C	IG	30.	B	WIC	41.	A	COE	52.	B	WIC
						31.	D	IG	42.	B	COE			

Writing and Language Test

Q	A	TYPE	Q	A	TYPE	Q	A	TYPE	Q	A	TYPE
1.	B	SEC	12.	A	SEC	23.	C	SEC	34.	B	EOI
2.	B	SEC	13.	C	SEC	24.	C	EOI	35.	A	EOI
3.	A	SEC	14.	D	EOI	25.	B	EOI	36.	C	SEC
4.	A	EOI	15.	C	EOI	26.	C	EOI	37.	D	EOI
5.	D	EOI	16.	B	EOI	27.	A	SEC	38.	B	SEC
6.	C	SEC	17.	C	EOI	28.	B	SEC	39.	C	EOI
7.	B	EOI	18.	B	SEC	29.	C	SEC	40.	C	SEC
8.	B	SEC	19.	A	SEC	30.	D	EOI	41.	A	SEC
9.	A	EOI	20.	B	EOI	31.	A	SEC	42.	D	EOI
10.	A	EOI	21.	C	SEC	32.	A	EOI	43.	A	SEC
11.	C	SEC	22.	D	EOI	33.	D	EOI	44.	B	EOI

Math Test – No Calculator

Q	A	TYPE	Q	A	TYPE	Q	A	TYPE
1.	B	HOA	11.	A	HOA	16.	1 or 3	PAM
2.	D	ATM	12.	A	PAM	17.	8	HOA
3.	D	PAM	13.	B	PAM	18.	1.25 or 5/4	HOA
4.	C	HOA	14.	A	PAM	19.	140	HOA
5.	D	PAM	15.	D	HOA	20.	3/5 or .6	ATM
6.	B	HOA						
7.	C	PAM						
8.	C	HOA						
9.	C	PAM						
10.	D	ATM						

Math Test – Calculator

Q	A	TYPE	Q	A	TYPE	Q	A	TYPE	Q	A	TYPE
1.	B	PSD	11.	B	PSD	21.	A	HOA	31.	2.5 or 5/2	PSD
2.	D	HOA	12.	D	HOA	22.	B	ATM	32.	200	HOA
3.	C	HOA	13.	C	PAM	23.	C	PAM	33.	5	PAM
4.	A	PSD	14.	D	PSD	24.	B	PAM	34.	6.48	PSD
5.	A	HOA	15.	A	PSD	25.	C	HOA	35.	15	ATM
6.	C	PSD	16.	B	PSD	26.	C	PSD	36.	650	PSD
7.	C	PAM	17.	B	PSD	27.	C	PSD	37.	8	PAM
8.	B	HOA	18.	D	PAM	28.	A	PSD	38.	1024	PAM
9.	B	PAM	19.	C	PSD	29.	A	ATM			
10.	D	PSD	20.	A	HOA	30.	C	HOA			

Test 2: Raw Score Conversion Table

Raw Score	Reading Test	Writing and Language Test	Mathematics Test
0	10	10	200
1	10	10	200
2	11	11	210
3	12	11	230
4	13	12	250
5	14	13	270
6	15	14	280
7	16	15	300
8	17	16	320
9	17	17	340
10	18	17	350
11	19	18	360
12	19	19	370
13	20	20	390
14	21	20	410
15	21	21	420
16	22	22	430
17	22	23	450
18	23	24	460
19	23	24	470
20	24	25	480
21	24	25	490
22	25	26	500
23	25	27	510
24	26	27	520
25	26	28	530
26	26	28	540
27	27	29	550
28	27	30	560
29	28	30	570
30	28	31	580
31	29	32	590
32	29	32	600
33	29	33	600
34	30	33	610
35	30	34	620
36	31	34	630
37	31	35	640
38	32	36	650
39	32	37	660
40	33	38	670
41	33	38	680
42	34	39	690
43	34	39	700
44	35	40	710
45	36		710
46	36		720
47	37		730
48	38		730
49	39		740
50	40		750
51	40		750
52	40		760

Raw Score	Reading Test	Writing and Language Test	Mathematics Test
53			770
54			780
55			790
56			790
57			800
58			800

Test 3: Answer Key

Reading Test

Q	A	TYPE	Q	A	TYPE	Q	A	TYPE	Q	A	TYPE	Q	A	TYPE
1.	B	RC	11.	D	RC	21.	D	RC	32.	C	RC	43.	D	RC
2.	D	RC	12.	C	RC	22.	B	RC	33.	A	WIC	44.	D	RC
3.	C	COE	13.	A	RC	23.	D	WIC	34.	B	COE	45.	C	RC
4.	B	COE	14.	C	WIC	24.	A	RC	35.	B	COE	46.	B	COE
5.	B	WIC	15.	C	COE	25.	C	WIC	36.	A	RC	47.	D	COE
6.	D	WIC	16.	B	COE	26.	C	COE	37.	B	WIC	48.	B	WIC
7.	A	COE	17.	B	WIC	27.	D	COE	38.	C	RC	49.	C	WIC
8.	B	COE	18.	D	IG	28.	D	RC	39.	D	COE	50.	D	COE
9.	D	RC	19.	B	IG	29.	B	RC	40.	C	COE	51.	D	COE
10.	C	RC	20.	D	IG	30.	A	COE	41.	C	RC	52.	C	IG
						31.	B	COE	42.	D	RC			

Writing and Language Test

Q	A	TYPE	Q	A	TYPE	Q	A	TYPE	Q	A	TYPE
1.	C	SEC	12.	C	EOI	23.	D	SEC	34.	D	SEC
2.	D	SEC	13.	B	EOI	24.	C	EOI	35.	A	EOI
3.	D	EOI	14.	A	EOI	25.	A	EOI	36.	D	SEC
4.	D	EOI	15.	A	SEC	26.	D	SEC	37.	C	SEC
5.	C	EOI	16.	C	EOI	27.	A	EOI	38.	A	EOI
6.	C	SEC	17.	C	SEC	28.	C	SEC	39.	D	SEC
7.	A	EOI	18.	A	SEC	29.	A	EOI	40.	D	EOI
8.	B	EOI	19.	B	EOI	30.	D	SEC	41.	C	SEC
9.	D	SEC	20.	A	SEC	31.	B	EOI	42.	C	EOI
10.	B	SEC	21.	A	SEC	32.	D	EOI	43.	B	EOI
11.	A	EOI	22.	D	EOI	33.	C	EOI	44.	B	EOI

Math Test – No Calculator

Q	A	TYPE	Q	A	TYPE	Q	A	TYPE
1.	B	HOA	11.	C	HOA	16.	0	HOA
2.	D	HOA	12.	B	ATM	17.	105	ATM
3.	D	PAM	13.	D	PAM	18.	2.5 or 5/2	ATM
4.	B	HOA	14.	B	PAM	19.	9	PAM
5.	C	PAM	15.	A	PAM	20.	7	PAM
6.	A	HOA						
7.	B	PAM						
8.	C	HOA						
9.	B	PAM						
10.	A	HOA						

Math Test – Calculator

Q	A	TYPE	Q	A	TYPE	Q	A	TYPE	Q	A	TYPE
1.	A	HOA	11.	D	PSD	21.	D	HOA	31.	$2 \leq x \leq 3$	HOA
2.	A	PAM	12.	A	HOA	22.	C	PAM	32.	183	HOA
3.	D	PSD	13.	D	PAM	23.	C	HOA	33.	2	PSD
4.	A	PSD	14.	B	HOA	24.	B	PAM	34.	120	ATM
5.	C	HOA	15.	C	HOA	25.	C	PSD	35.	60	PSD
6.	B	PSD	16.	C	PSD	26.	D	PSD	36.	110, 111, 112, 113, 114, or 115	ATM
7.	A	PAM	17.	A	PSD	27.	D	ATM	37.	.999	PAM
8.	C	PSD	18.	D	HOA	28.	B	PAM	38.	73.8	PAM
9.	C	PSD	19.	C	PSD	29.	A	PAM			
10.	C	PSD	20.	A	PSD	30.	B	PAM			

Test 3: Raw Score Conversion Table

Raw Score	Reading Test	Writing and Language Test	Mathematics Test
0	10	10	200
1	10	10	200
2	10	10	220
3	11	10	240
4	12	11	270
5	13	12	280
6	14	13	290
7	15	14	310
8	16	15	330
9	16	16	350
10	17	16	360
11	18	17	370
12	18	18	380
13	19	19	400
14	20	19	420
15	20	20	430
16	21	21	440
17	21	21	460
18	22	22	470
19	22	22	480
20	23	23	490
21	23	23	500
22	23	24	510
23	24	25	520
24	24	26	530
25	25	26	540
26	25	26	550
27	26	27	560
28	26	28	570
29	27	28	580
30	27	29	590
31	28	30	600
32	28	30	610
33	28	31	610
34	29	31	620
35	29	32	630
36	30	32	640
37	30	33	650
38	31	34	660
39	31	35	670
40	32	36	680
41	32	37	690
42	33	38	700
43	33	39	710
44	34	40	720
45	35		720
46	35		730
47	36		740
48	37		740
49	38		750
50	39		760
51	39		760
52	40		770

Raw Score	Reading Test	Writing and Language Test	Mathematics Test
53			780
54			780
55			790
56			790
57			800
58			800

Test 4: Answer Key

Reading Test

Q	A	TYPE	Q	A	TYPE	Q	A	TYPE	Q	A	TYPE	Q	A	TYPE
1.	B	RC	11.	B	RC	21.	B	RC	31.	D	COE	42.	B	RC
2.	D	COE	12.	B	WIC	22.	C	WIC	32.	C	COE	43.	A	WIC
3.	C	COE	13.	B	COE	23.	C	RC	33.	A	RC	44.	D	RC
4.	C	RC	14.	C	COE	24.	A	WIC	34.	B	RC	45.	B	WIC
5.	B	RC	15.	D	RC	25.	D	COE	35.	C	WIC	46.	D	COE
6.	D	COE	16.	C	WIC	26.	D	COE	36.	A	RC	47.	A	RC
7.	C	COE	17.	A	COE	27.	A	RC	37.	B	RC	48.	C	COE
8.	A	WIC	18.	C	COE	28.	B	RC	38.	C	WIC	49.	A	COE
9.	B	WIC	19.	C	IG	29.	B	COE	39.	D	COE	50.	C	WIC
10.	A	RC	20.	A	IG	30.	C	COE	40.	D	COE	51.	B	RC
									41.	C	IG	52.	D	RC

Writing and Language Test

Q	A	TYPE	Q	A	TYPE	Q	A	TYPE	Q	A	TYPE
1.	A	SEC	12.	D	EOI	23.	D	EOI	34.	B	SEC
2.	C	SEC	13.	A	EOI	24.	C	EOI	35.	A	SEC
3.	B	EOI	14.	D	SEC	25.	D	SEC	36.	C	EOI
4.	C	SEC	15.	B	SEC	26.	D	EOI	37.	B	EOI
5.	A	EOI	16.	A	SEC	27.	C	SEC	38.	A	EOI
6.	B	SEC	17.	C	EOI	28.	C	SEC	39.	C	SEC
7.	A	EOI	18.	C	EOI	29.	B	EOI	40.	D	EOI
8.	D	EOI	19.	D	SEC	30.	A	EOI	41.	B	EOI
9.	C	SEC	20.	B	SEC	31.	B	SEC	42.	A	SEC
10.	B	EOI	21.	B	EOI	32.	D	SEC	43.	C	EOI
11.	B	EOI	22.	C	EOI	33.	A	EOI	44.	D	SEC

Math Test – No Calculator

Q	A	TYPE	Q	A	TYPE	Q	A	TYPE
1.	D	HOA	11.	C	ATM	16.	2	PAM
2.	B	PAM	12.	C	HOA	17.	0	HOA
3.	B	HOA	13.	A	PAM	18.	0.8 or 4/5	ATM
4.	B	HOA	14.	A	PAM	19.	28	HOA
5.	B	HOA	15.	C	PAM	20.	144	PAM
6.	A	HOA						
7.	A	PAM						
8.	C	ATM						
9.	B	HOA						
10.	C	PAM						

Math Test – Calculator

Q	A	TYPE	Q	A	TYPE	Q	A	TYPE	Q	A	TYPE
1.	A	HOA	11.	B	PSD	21.	B	PSD	31.	15	HOA
2.	C	PSD	12.	C	PSD	22.	C	PSD	32.	24	HOA
3.	C	HOA	13.	C	PAM	23.	B	PSD	33.	9	PAM
4.	A	HOA	14.	A	PSD	24.	B	PAM	34.	1020	HOA
5.	A	HOA	15.	D	ATM	25.	B	PAM	35.	3	ATM
6.	D	PSD	16.	D	PSD	26.	C	ATM	36.	1/3 or .333	PSD
7.	D	PSD	17.	D	HOA	27.	B	HOA	37.	3	PAM
8.	C	PAM	18.	B	PSD	28.	C	PSD	38.	49	PAM
9.	B	PSD	19.	B	HOA	29.	B	PAM			
10.	A	PAM	20.	C	PSD	30.	C	PSD			

Test 4: Raw Score Conversion Table

Raw Score	Reading Test	Writing and Language Test	Mathematics Test
0	10	10	200
1	10	10	200
2	10	10	210
3	11	10	230
4	12	11	250
5	13	12	270
6	14	13	280
7	15	14	300
8	16	15	320
9	16	16	340
10	17	16	350
11	18	17	360
12	18	18	370
13	19	19	390
14	20	19	410
15	20	20	420
16	21	21	430
17	21	22	450
18	22	23	460
19	22	23	470
20	23	24	480
21	23	24	490
22	23	25	500
23	24	26	510
24	24	26	520
25	25	27	530
26	25	27	540
27	26	28	550
28	26	29	560
29	27	29	570
30	27	30	580
31	28	31	590
32	28	31	600
33	28	32	600
34	29	32	610
35	29	33	620
36	30	33	630
37	30	34	640
38	31	35	650
39	31	36	660
40	32	37	670
41	32	37	680
42	33	38	690
43	33	39	700
44	34	40	710
45	35		710
46	35		720
47	36		730
48	37		730
49	38		740
50	39		750
51	39		750
52	40		760

Raw Score	Reading Test	Writing and Language Test	Mathematics Test
53			770
54			780
55			790
56			790
57			800
58			800

Tips for Peak Performance

The Week Before the Test

- **Get eight hours of sleep each night.** Remember, sleep makes you smart. Studies have shown strong links between inadequate sleep and many aspects of test taking including attention span, emotional intelligence, attention to detail and oral recall.
- **Eat lots of complex carbohydrates and healthy protein.** Breads, pastas and other complex carbs give you energy you will need for the five-hour marathon ahead of you.
- **Visualize carefully the test you are about to take.** Top performers (including athletes, actors and dancers) often use visualization to create a mental image of success. In your mind, create a detailed picture of the test—from section to section. Visualize yourself achieving your targets in each part of the test. As you do this, try to anticipate potential distractions (stress, a loud classmate, an overly watchful proctor, etc.) and then visualize yourself proceeding calmly and confidently through all such distractions.

The Night Before the Test

- **No studying past 9:00 PM.** Last-minute cramming leads to last-minute jitters, and it can keep your brain whirring long past the time you stop studying—which will keep you from falling asleep. Read a book for school, go for a run, or watch a movie. Do something fun that doesn't keep you up late. The idea is to be completely relaxed on test day.
- **Lay out your pencils, appropriate calculator, ID, Admission ticket, watch (with no beeps!), and a snack.** Check the batteries on your calculator. Granola bars are a good snack. So are PB&J sandwiches. Starbucks bottled beverages can help give some people a nice mid-test boost.
- **Go to bed!** If you can't fall asleep, don't worry. Just lying in bed can be very restful. Read a boring book, if you like. That might help put you to sleep.

Test Day

- **Wake up early!** Studies show that it takes the average person about three hours (after waking up) to function at peak capacity. The SAT begin around 8:00 in the morning. Try to wake up at least 2 or 2.5 hours before the test.
- **Get some aerobic exercise.** Because of the length of the test (including filling out forms and breaks, the SAT can last up to 4.5–5 hours), you can end up feeling quite brain-dead toward the end. Aerobic exercise oxygenates your blood and can help you to focus for longer amounts of time.
- **Get a big, healthy breakfast with some protein.** Try not to eat heavy foods that can be difficult to digest. Eggs and toast, cereal, bagels with cheese, and such foods generally work well. Remember, standardized testing is a stressful, draining process.
- **Dress in Layers.** Test centers can be very warm (A/C not working) or very cool (A/C cranked up!). If you wear several layers, you can adjust your clothing according to the temperature of the room.
- **Breathe.** Deep breathing is a great relaxation technique. It also helps in blood circulation. During the test, remember to stretch and breathe deeply often.
- **Fifteen minutes of Reading or Math in the morning.** Often students find that they are not completely awake for the first section of the test. Doing a reading passage on the morning of the test can help wake you up.
- **Test-day checklist**: Snack, Pencils, Photo ID, Watch (no beeps), Admission ticket, Appropriate Calculator (e.g. a TI–84).
- Go CRUSH the test!

Notes Regarding Score Improvements Reported on the Back Cover

1. SAT score improvements are calculated by subtracting the baseline score from the super-scored SAT score. Most tutoring students come to us in the summer before 11th grade. We thus use either an actual baseline SAT or the 10th grade PSAT as the baseline test. Students who came to us after taking the 11th grade PSAT improved almost as much, and their improvements are available on our website, marksprep.com.

2. In 2016, the SAT changed from a 2400-point scale to a 1600-point scale. Improvements on both tests are included on the graph.

3. In the class of 2017, because of the changes to the SAT, very few of our students took the SAT. Most of our students took the ACT, so we have not shown SAT data for that class.

4. Full score improvements are available on marksprep.com. Calculations include data from students who saw us for six or more tutoring sessions and include approximately 99 percent of students who have worked with us. The data have been verified by parents of the students seen.

5. On average, students see us for 10–11 tutoring sessions before a first administration of an SAT or ACT and 5–6 tutoring sessions before a second administration, for a total of 15–17 50-minute tutoring sessions.

6. The years in the graph refer to the graduating class year of the students, not the year in which we tutored them.

Made in the USA
Middletown, DE
25 May 2019